Platforms of Innovation

Dynamics of New Industrial Knowledge Flows

Edited by

Philip Cooke

Centre for Advanced Studies, Cardiff University, Wales, UK

Carla De Laurentis

Centre for Advanced Studies, Cardiff University, Wales, UK

Stewart MacNeill

Birmingham University Business School, England, UK

Chris Collinge

Birmingham University Business School, England, UK

Edward Elgar

Cheltenham, UK • Northampton, MA, USA

Published by
Edward Elgar Publishing Limited
The Lypiatts
15 Lansdown Road
Cheltenham
Glos GL50 2JA
UK

Edward Elgar Publishing, Inc.
William Pratt House
9 Dewey Court
Northampton
Massachusetts 01060
USA

A catalogue record for this book
is available from the British Library

Library of Congress Control Number: 2010922134

MIX
Paper from
responsible sources
FSC® C018575

ISBN 978 1 84844 029 6

Typeset by Servis Filmsetting Ltd, Stockport, Cheshire
Printed and bound by MPG Books Group, UK

Contents

Contributors

Antje Blöcker, WZB, Tiergarten, Berlin, Germany.

Olivier Brossard, LEREPS, Political Studies Institute, University of Toulouse, France.

Chris Collinge, Business School, University of Birmingham, England.

Philip Cooke, Centre for Advanced Studies & Centre for Economic & Social Analysis of Genomics (CESAGen), Cardiff University, Wales.

Carla De Laurentis, Centre for Advanced Studies, Cardiff University.

Henrik Halkier, SPIRIT, University of Aalborg, Denmark.

Ulrich Jürgens, WZB Social Science Research Centre, Berlin, Germany.

Robert Kaiser, Technical University of Munich, Germany.

Michael Liecke, Ludwig Maximilans-University of Munich.

Stewart MacNeill, Business School, University of Birmingham, England.

Jesper Manniche, Centre for Regional and Tourism Research, Bornholm, Denmark.

Adreene Staines, Business School, University of Birmingham, England.

Simone Strambach, Philipps-University Marburg, Germany.

Jérôme Vicente, LEREPS, Political Studies Institute, University of Toulouse, France.

Preface

Today, the world is in rather a turmoil. There is an overarching environmental crisis, the solution to which seems, for once, to be evident from the analysis and advice proferred by the leading global climate change experts and their research communities. However, the world's political leaders could not agree a new protocol for the moderation of climate change emissions at their United Nations summit in Copenhagen in December 2009 because many of the most important were mentally locked-in to vertical thinking, primarily of their own national 'silo', rather than giving equivalence to the horizontal perspective that would have encompassed the world and its needs. A second global crisis simultaneously enveloping the world economy at the decade's end was the global financial crisis. In the book, at various points, key things are said about what this crisis represents; it is a far deeper version of the telecoms or dot.com crisis at the beginning of the twenty-first century, that presaged the demise of many business leaders and, for a few, led to incarceration and even death. This recession shared the previous one's neoliberal business and governmental dogma that the way to become unbelievably wealthy is by stoking up the stock valuation of companies.

This dogma is argued in the book to be a function of yet another crisis, albeit in some ways a less dramatic one than that concerning global warming. This is the transition from an Industrial Age to a knowledge economy paradigm. In the former, valuation of publicly quoted firms was measured largely in terms of tangible assets. In the knowledge economy such valuation is performed largely in terms of intangible assets. The main one, and the subject of this book, is knowledge in its various economic forms, from intellectual property, as represented in copyrights and patents, to that of a collaterized debt obligation (CDO) squared and other financial derivatives. It was shown that trading in such intangibles at what subsequently proved to be fictitious valuations was the proximate cause of the global financial crisis of 2008–9. Just as occurred nearly a decade earlier, the core problem, whether of trading in oil and telecom futures then or CDOs squared more lately, is that value has been conflated with price, and risk conflated with uncertainty. Both result in spurious measurements whose vulnerability is hidden in the upswing by 'irrational exuberance' but exposed in the downswing as expressions of myopia, followed by panic and, more often than not, folly on the part of those responsible. 'It's only when the tide goes out that you learn who was swimming naked', as Warren Buffett,[1] who is widely respected for understanding the importance of these things in the financial sphere, has put it. Or, more appropriate in a knowledge flows context, 'in the kingdom of the blind, the one-eyed man is king/woman is queen/person is monarch', as Desiderius Erasmus did not quite put it some years earlier.

These kinds of thoughts stimulated a response, in the form of a winning proposal to the European Union's Sixth Framework Programme for Research and Technological Development from two of this book's co-authors, S. MacNeill and C. Collinge, to perform a pioneering analysis of contemporary knowledge flow processes and products among European firms and their global interlocutors, the sectors in which such firms had traditionally been thought – at least by governments – to reside, and the multilevel governance agencies that nowadays habitually interact with firms with a view to assisting, in particular, their innovation efforts. Innovation is thus seen as a major trigger of contemporary knowledge flow patterns, because in global terms it is seen as the key to increased productivity, competitiveness and growth. This book reports only on part of the whole Eurodite project, as it came to be called. It is mainly concerned with the extent to which firms and economic governance entities incorporate lateral thinking in their decision-making about ways to exploit knowledge to become more innovative. In the Industrial Age, after 100 years of regulators allowing innovations to be sold with relatively little testing and trialling, most products were not allowed onto the market without having been examined for unexpected side-effects or hidden weaknesses. Accordingly, quality standards rose exponentially in the final quarter of the twentieth century. However, financial services are not even yet in the Industrial Age but something more akin to the Dark Ages with respect to the public examination of their products prior to release on the market. One aspect of the research reported in the book concerns the extent to which such 'examination knowledge' is deployed today. An interim conclusion is that it contributes to the emergence of 'platforms of innovation' where firms leave more and more of their business to suppliers with expertise in processes that may be closely linked to client requirements but far away from client expertise. But other forces reinforce this tendency towards innovative platforms, as the book shows, and these include environmental concerns, energy issues, trading regimes, market structures and policy or regulatory interventions.

In putting this book together we the authors are grateful to the small army, including its many foot soldiers as well as the numerous academic generals on display, involved in the Eurodite project. They are too many to mention by name but all their affiliations are listed in Chapter 2. The coordination of the book was managed by the first two co-authors and they wish to thank their Centre for Advanced Studies colleagues for their advice and occasional scepticism about what we thought Eurodite was finding in relation to what their, sometimes neighbouring, projects were finding. As mere lieutenants in the Eurodite army the 'Cardiff lot' had few of the complex organizational challenges faced by 'General Command' in Birmingham. Accordingly, the book benefited from occasional Eurodite sideshows organized by Stewart, Chris and their capable support staff in partner locations of culinary accomplishment like Toulouse, Turin and, we dare say, Cardiff, where much of the conceptual advancement arising from the research design and findings were discussed and agreed. We are ineffably thankful to the European Union for making such an interesting call, finding our modest proposals worthy of support and we hope that the results provide them, other policy-makers and our academic peers with plenty of food for thought.

Philip Cooke,
Carla De Laurentis,
Stewart MacNeill and
Chris Collinge
Cardiff and Birmingham, January 2010

NOTE

1. Quoted by Lowe (1997), pp. 165–6.

1. Trends and drivers of the knowledge economy

Philip Cooke and Carla De Laurentis

1.1 INTRODUCTION

This introductory chapter sets the scene for the research subsequently reported. These findings arose from a comparative European Union (EU) funded 6th Framework Programme for Research and Technological Development Integrated Project entitled Regional Trajectories to the Knowledge Economy: a Dynamic Model, the acronym for which was Eurodite. For simplicity, the acronym is used throughout the book to refer to the research project. Being an Integrated Project of five years' duration meant that the project was large in scope and scale. It had a larger than normal number of partners – some 28, based in different regions throughout the EU and beyond – and was, accordingly, intellectually and organizationally complex. The intellectual complexity arose from the key focus of Eurodite, which was to understand knowledge flows of key actors in the economies being studied. While there existed some literature on the subject, there was no coherent and comprehensive methodology for studying 'knowledge in practice' readily available. Hence, much effort was expended on evolving such a methodology as a prerequisite for conducting the proposed research.

In the chapters that follow, it will be seen how the finally adopted methodology evolved. This was assisted but also, on occasions, rendered more difficult by the triple focus of the research. This involved, first, understanding knowledge flows among firms and between firms and other institutional actors of consequence, such as governments, universities, public research laboratories and intermediaries.

Second, an element which became one of the most original dimensions of the research findings, knowledge flow at the level of the industry or sector was to be studied. This was of particular interest because of a widespread but unconfirmed suspicion among numerous research team members that not only was the idea of a sector something of an anachronistic statistical construct – even, accordingly, a variety of fiction – but that if it had ever had any purchase of significance for firms, that was diminishing almost daily. To foreshadow a conclusion of the book, what we found was a matrix of knowledge flows; some, possibly a declining portion of the whole, remained what we came to refer to as 'cumulative' knowledge flows. These were thought of as vertical – even somewhat linear – although linearity was seldom of the command-and-control kind but rather subject to intricate negotiation and refinement. This was because they were relatively confined to the sector, although the value chains through which such flows occurred could range quite widely. So much was not novel knowledge by any means, but nevertheless was a useful corrective to the larger claims of knowledge transdisciplinarity (Gibbons et al., 1994) or even open innovation (Chesbrough, 2003). Complementing these, however, were a bewildering array of horizontal knowledge flows, many of which not only crossed putative sectoral boundaries but also brought together, sometimes in new industrial specialities like 'film tourism', 'security gaming' or 'bio-oenology', or new business practices such as 'cross-branding', 'agro-automotive research' and 'green creativity', industries that are sectorally very far apart.

Knowledge flows were thus to be seen as distributed unexpectedly widely in the horizontal dimension as well as operating more conventionally in the vertical dimension. To distinguish these knowledge flow types, the terms 'cumulative' (sectoral) and 'combinative' or sometimes 'composite' (distributed) were introduced by a process of iteration between conceptualization and empirical research and concept testing. These make up one very important matrix finding about knowledge flows in the contemporary economy. Of course, as soon as a scientific frame is placed around an aspect of complex reality – in this case a two-dimensional box – that step invites the question of whether there might be a third dimension in the diagonal. This has occasionally been discussed in the past in the literature on industry organization in reference to the binary notions of vertical and horizontal integration or disintegration (Gold, 1986; Coles and Hall, 2008), but the relative paucity of information on the subject suggests that the idea adds relatively little value. Similarly, one suspects diagonal knowledge flows may not yield as much of value as conceivable; in any case we neither looked for nor found them, although we do not rule out their possible existence.

The third dimension of the research asked questions of the extent to which interfirm and firm-institutional as well as intra- and intersectoral knowledge flows might be changing in ways that inscribed territories differently in economic – or, more accurately, economic geographical – terms. The logic of this research question is the manner in which economic geographers and regional scientists (for example Massey, 1984; Scott,

1988, Krugman, 1991; 1995) had hitherto shown that industry organization depended intimately on territorial, especially regional, characteristics. What is the difference between territorial and regional structure? This turns out to be extremely important to the findings of the book in relation to policy inasmuch as economic processes occur territorially without apparent concern for national or regional boundaries – yet national and, it seems increasingly, regional governance makes a difference in the ways in which such economic processes operate.

Key here, and discussed at length in Chapter 12, are the governance styles of different administrations. In particular, it can be hypothezised, where a regional governance body, charged as most are with economic development, entrepreneurship and regional innovation systems promotion and support (Cooke et al., 2004; Potter, 2009), is forewarned of paradigmatic change in the knowledge flows requirements of contemporary global competition, it is in a relatively strong position *ceteris paribus* to discharge its responsibilities to its clients. In the research reported in Chapter 12 we show that we discovered precisely that. In other words, accomplished regional governance bodies were not only in a position to inform firms and sectors of the value of cross-pollination to enhance regional innovation, but some are even acting as catalytic actors, overcoming market-based intersectoral communication failures by putting in place matrix methods for platform building among firms across sectors. In this manner, an accomplished regional governance mechanism can help make its economy an innovation node rather than merely a network member or worse. This we also consider an original finding of value from the Eurodite research project.

1.2 SOME THEORETICAL STEPPING STONES

Mention has now been made of the three-dimensional research approach taken in seeking to understand the extent of change in the ways knowledge circulates to facilitate innovation and competitiveness in the contemporary economy. Now, it is important to record in outline at least, given that fuller explanations follow in the text of other chapters, how we constructed frameworks from new or existing theories and concepts as instruments to enable us to move together towards the conduct of the comparative research, in over 20 regions with coverage of at least seven sectors and their subsequently discovered variants.

First, some work had to be done to frame useful categories for analysis of knowledge. This is detailed in section 1.4.1 of this chapter and it involved elaborating a conceptual model, first outlined before the project

began, and then exploring its value in a general and a specifically conceptual way, meaning identifying elements of the model of particular promise
for the research (Cooke, 2007a, 2009). This was called a knowledge
capabilities model and it sought to capture key features of knowledge as
an active force in shaping regional foregrounding and backgrounding of
certain important features of knowledge. To note a few for illustrative
purposes: firstly, the term 'asymmetric knowledge' was introduced, based
on George Akerlof's insights into asymmetric information that led to so
many important debates in mainstream economics like principal–agent
relations, market failure and adverse selection problems. Whereas Akerlof
spoke of information we had a more active usage better captured in the
concept of knowledge, and where he wrote about individual-level, often
contractual relations, we were interested in problems of collective action.
Nevertheless, it was fruitful to apply these ideas in an original way as a lens
through which to analyse regional economic development disparities. We
confirmed that, in a knowledge economy, unlike a traditional Industrial
Age resource-based economy, the role of knowledge institutions enables
the construction of regional advantage as never before (Cooke et al.,
2006). Moreover, there is less fixity and more flexibility regarding the
manner in which knowledge resources are mobilized.

A second useful concept was that associated with knowledge asymmetries and this concerned knowledge domains. That is, it is not unknown,
but nevertheless we reconfirmed it, that certain regions are privileged by
being sole or scarce repositories of knowledge which is valuable in terms
of economic development. Clearly it helps that Silicon Valley – which in
our terms is a territory rather than a regional governance entity – is the
world's leading repository of both research and commercial knowledge of
information and communication technology (ICT). Similarly, Cambridge,
Massachusetts and the Greater Boston area have this asset in relation to
medical biotechnology. One of our study cases centred on Wageningen
in the east Netherlands has, at a scale of magnitude smaller than the US
exemplars, global knowledge capabilities in agro-food biotechnological
research (or exploration) and commercialization (or exploitation) knowledge. North Jutland in Denmark, another Eurodite case-study region,
has world-leading exploitation knowledge in renewable energy, evolved
from its success in the contest with California in the 1970s to produce the
best wind turbine design for renewable energy production. In both cases
wide platforms of knowledge form: in the first case, agro-food, nutrition
science, food engineering, biotechnology, chemistry and so on; and in
the second, of key importance for renewable energy expertise and associated combinations of expertise are knowledge of wind, wave, tidal, solar,
biomass and biogas technologies, power station and other construction,

design consultancy, pipework, boilers and so on. In this manner customized orders rather than standardized orders can be met by a constellation of interacting firms joined, as appropriate, by large firms but not dominated by them.

Mention has been made of the two other types of theoretical framing device utilized to give coherence to the complex research task indicated. The first of these, building on the regional knowledge capabilities model (section 1.4.1, Figure 1.1) was formation of a number of conceptual grids, described below, of which one was crucial to the sector studies that revealed a certain unravelling of sectoral stereotypes, and the other assisted understanding of why and how corporate and sectoral development trajectories were unravelling. The first took previous work on knowledge phases in the transformation of laboratory bench knowledge that might contain elements of tacit, potentially hard-to-explain scientific knowledge, through an often lengthy and iterative process of testing and trialling, culminating in commercialization of an innovative product or process (Cooke, 2005a). In shorthand these knowledge phases became: (1) exploration; (2) examination; (3) exploitation. This extended a famous article of James March (1991) who differentiated corporate exploration from exploitation activities but, like many of his successors, left the all-important testing and trialling process unexamined.

Juxtaposed to this (Table 1.2 in section 1.4.2 below) is another perspective on knowledge, the origins of which go back at least to Kant and later to the logical positivist philosophers at the Café Central in pre-war Vienna. Later still, Laestedius (1998) linked 'symbolic knowledge' to the Kantian dualism to capture the importance of non-technological knowledge to contemporary advanced industrial economies. This line of thinking has been utilized and reviewed by Asheim and Gertler (2005). Juxtapositions such as that shown in Tables 1.2 and 1.3 (in section 1.4.2 below) illuminate the taxonomy of functional knowledge categories – an abstract topic to be sure – most usefully. Many of the succeeding chapters find utility in the frameworks even to the final stages of the empirical research, as may be seen.

Finally, attention is drawn to a different kind of framework that provided a valuable service in making coherent the difficult task of conducting comparative analysis of seven widely different industry sectors. We refer here to the work of Storper and Salais (1997). The value of this perspective peaked at this first empirical stage of the research where the interrogation of sectoral characteristics was conducted by experts in those fields drawing upon their own empirical studies and those of others. It was striking that almost by osmosis a sizeable minority of early draft presentations drew attention to a process of diminution of standardized in favour of more dedicated or

customized production in their sector. Others pointed to the same phenomenon more according to the nature of the industry under inspection.
Thus in biopharmaceuticals 'designer drugs' were a new and fast-growing
niche whereas conventional biochemical treatments were not. In tourism,
customized packages and individualized travel were displacing the conventional holiday package tour to Spain and such destinations. Accordingly, a
consensus emerged that a framework that captured such divergences would
be desirable in which to situate each account and highlight emergent trends.
This Storper and Salais (1997) successfully did, and it was used in all the
sectoral analyses, as can be seen from Chapters 3 to 9.

1.3   MARKETS, STATES AND NETWORKS IN THE KNOWLEDGE ECONOMY

What is the knowledge economy? The general argument about the salience
of the knowledge economy in sectoral, skills and spatial terms embraces
the position of Castells (1996), widely known for the observation that productivity and competitiveness are, by and large, a function of knowledge
generation and information processing, and that this has involved a type of
economic metamorphosis entailing a different way of thinking about economies. Thus the balance between knowledge and resources has shifted so
far towards the former that knowledge has become much the most important factor determining standards of living – more than land, capital or
labour. Today's most advanced economies are fundamentally knowledge-
based (Dunning, 2000). Even neoclassicists like Paul Romer recognize that
technology (and the knowledge on which it is based) has to be viewed as an
equivalent third factor to capital and land in leading economies (Romer,
1990). Inevitably this leads on to issues of the generation and exploitation
of knowledge. The knowledge economy approach is perfectly capable of
recognizing that there is already a yawning gap between rich and poor
nations which is accelerating under 'knowledge capitalism' (Burton-Jones,
1999). There is also a growing gap within societies. The superiority here,
compared to more radical macro-perspectives extolling the power of scale,
is that policy inferences are more accessible. Popular commentators like
Charles Leadbeater have argued for the need to 'innovate and include' and
that 'spread' effects of successful knowledge economies have be stimulated
democratically: 'We must breed an open, inquisitive, challenging and
ambitious society' (Leadbeater, 1999). However in recent years the corporate sector has increasingly patented intellectual property rights (IPR)
for broad innovations, for example in relation to genetic research, seeking
superprofits from outlicensing such knowledge on the market.

Thus what, if anything, distinguishes 'knowledge markets' from more normal ones? Going back to Arrow (1962), the main difference is that knowledge is not appropriable in the way that natural resources or even labour-time can be owned and not transgressed by others. Knowledge thus has the character to some extent of 'public goods'. Public goods, in comparison with private goods, are those for which their consumption is repeatable. That is, their consumption by one person does not deny consumption of the same good by another person. Such consumption does not result in depletion of the goods or dissatisfaction by previous consumers. As Best (2001) puts it: 'The value of a cooking recipe to the original user does not diminish with its diffusion to new users'. The concept of public goods is also important to markets in modern or 'new growth theory'. This is because new growth theory has productivity increases as endogenous to production. Unlike old growth theory that rested on an assumption of diminishing returns to scale, new growth theory assumes increasing returns to scale in features such as productivity. Productivity in turn may be 'made' in production processes by, for example, internal (endogenous) innovation or skills upgrading. Or it may be 'bought' as, for instance, knowledge such as research and development (R&D) purchased from a university or in the market. The same supplier of research may simultaneously also produce, external to the firm, other upgraded human capital. This may have more scientific, technological, managerial or creative content and value than its preceding cohorts. Knowledge may also be 'imported' as a public good, otherwise known as 'localized knowledge spillovers'. These ideas about the importance of innovation and 'talent' to productivity are also central to new growth theory. They are also the 'central dogma' of the Washington Consensus after Capra (2003) and Kay (2003). This argues for the policy connection whereby innovation positively affects productivity, which in turn creates growth and ultimately competitiveness. This dogma underpins the economic policies of virtually all governments and multilateral agencies from the International Monetary Fund (IMF) to the United Nations Industrial Development Organization (UNIDO).

In general, therefore, 'knowledge' of the kind under discussion increases the complexity of transactions in markets; raising, in particular, issues of intellectual property (IP) as represented in patents, trademarks, brand names, copyright and their licensing. Section 1.3.1 refers to the important role of the state as financier of crucial processes regarding exploration knowledge through public investments. Section 1.3 then turns to the study of markets in structuring knowledge value chains in the knowledge economy, pointing out their asymmetric efficiencies and inefficiencies, which also have spatial dimensions. Finally, attention is devoted to the enhanced role of networks and new network forms of thinking in relation to securing competitiveness in the knowledge value chain in the knowledge economy.

1.3.1 The State in the Knowledge Economy

We may outline three historic phases during the industrial era with regard to the state's involvement in knowledge production. The first is the period of competitive and consolidating capitalism up to approximately the end of the nineteenth century. For some economies this involved a laissez-faire model of state intervention generally, and particularly with regard to knowledge production. Firms were lightly regulated, knowledge generation was private or under Church control, and even universities in the most laissez-faire countries like the UK were private and philanthropically provided, if not beneficiaries of ancient royal prerogative. For more mercantilist economies where the state intervened for protectionist reasons, knowledge exploration was initially tacit and only towards the end of the era embedded in large corporations, classically as with Bayer, whose laboratory discoveries gave rise to the first, modern industrial knowledge generation centres, the forerunner of the industrial R&D lab. In the US, Cold Spring Harbor Laboratory, established more than a century ago, remains a private, non-profit basic research and educational institution. Nowadays, some 330 scientists conduct groundbreaking research in cancer, neurobiology, plant genetics and bioinformatics. Cold Spring Harbor Laboratory is one of eight National Cancer Institute-designated basic research centres in the US. In 1907, Theodore Vail combined the AT&T (formerly American Bell) and Western Electric engineering departments into a single organization that, in 1925, would become Bell Telephone Laboratories. Bell Labs made several significant innovations such as the first commercially viable system for adding sound to motion pictures. Combined with studio and theatre equipment manufactured by Western Electric, this system moved Hollywood quickly from silence to sound. The first demonstration of television in the United States in April 1927 was another notable first for Bell Labs.

It was not until the second phase of industrialization and, especially, the industrialization of warfare that direct state funding of research began. Some early forms of intervention prior to this included the Netherlands state suspension of current international patenting norms, faced with that country's perceived economic backwardness at the outset of the last century in respect of new electrical technologies. The Philips company was simply allowed to copy the Edison light bulb and other foreign innovations and to escape prosecution by dint of national re-regulation in this sphere

(Zegveld, 2005). But with the onset of global warfare and the arrival of and growth in demand for aeronautics, modern naval capabilities like submarines, and high-power ordinance, special institutes for researching and advancing designs of equipment were established by governments, sometimes taking over historically royal prerogatives – particularly concerning arsenals and even shipyards.

Thereafter, up to and including the Second World War, states took responsibility for advanced research in many countries. Mussolini established research institutes for aeronautics in Naples and Varese that remain Italy's main research centres for aeronautics. Even in the US, where, for example, in 1946, representatives from nine major eastern universities – Columbia, Cornell, Harvard, Johns Hopkins, Massachusetts Institute of Technology, Princeton, the University of Pennsylvania, the University of Rochester and Yale – formed a non-profit corporation to establish a new nuclear-science facility, Brookhaven National Laboratory, so strategic was it in terms of warfare that it was 'nationalized'. On 21 March 1947, the US War Department transferred the site on Long Island to the US Atomic Energy Commission (AEC), which was the federal agency that oversaw the founding of Brookhaven National Laboratory and was a predecessor to the present US Department of Energy (DOE). The AEC also provided the initial funding for Brookhaven's research into the peaceful uses of the atom. Today, Brookhaven Lab is one of ten national laboratories under DOE's Office of Science, which provides the majority of the Laboratory's research funding and direction. Founded in 1977 as the 12th cabinet-level department, DOE oversees much of the science research in the US through its Office of Science (Chesbrough and Socolof, 2000).

The third phase of state involvement in public research has been the massive increase in research funding that occurs in US and some European universities. From being principally institutions responsible for the transmission of established scientific knowledge, universities have become major recipients of government and private (including foundation) research funding. The US has led this charge, although it has not had a programme especially to shut down national public laboratories. Nevertheless they have become far more involved in the examination knowledge aspect of research more generally, with responsibilities in relation to standards, testing, trialling and such like, whereas the cutting edge of much exploration knowledge is increasingly found in university laboratories. By now, for example, it is instructive to observe how dependent the US National Institutes of Health have become upon a few leading US universities for knowledge exploration and examination in recent years (Cooke, 2007b).

It is from this and other base funding supplied by the National Science

Foundation and the Departments of Energy and Defense that much US healthcare research is funded. It thus stimulates entrepreneurship on the part of academic entrepreneurs who set up firms or license new knowledge that they have discovered or invented to other firms, such as the large US pharmaceuticals firms that dominate the global drugs market. Much the same was true of the origins of ICT which, through detailed designs developed and funded by the US Department of Defense, was enabled to grow through contracts paid to Bell Labs Nobel laureate engineer William Shockley and the eight PhD students he took from New Jersey to Santa Clara county who set up firms like Intel, AMD and National Semiconductor that spawned Silicon Valley. Thereafter, localized knowledge spillovers, and the involvement of Stanford University in providing the world's first science park and appropriate engineering talent grew to nurture the industry through generations that involved Netscape, Silicon Graphics, Sun Microsystems, Oracle, Yahoo, Google and many others, some of which became behemoths . In sum, this is how, in the US, public research budgets and contracts fuel the knowledge economy in key areas of societal concern from healthcare to security and defence. Simultaneously, many corporations that pioneered R&D in corporate laboratories have closed or otherwise attenuated them, for instance Bell Labs itself, Dupont, Procter & Gamble and General Electric now rely far more on sourcing knowledge from 'open innovation' (Chesbrough, 2003) than they did hitherto.

Comparable processes have occurred in Europe. The aforementioned Philips of the Netherlands is now committed to an 'open innovation' strategy which includes close partnership with small university spin-out businesses and university research institutes, as in 'DSP Valley' a network linking KU Leuven, Philips and Aachen University across the borders of the Netherlands, Belgium and Germany. It specializes in digital signals processing (DSP) (data compression) technology. From the above, this is more a relatively compact economic territory than a region, but in light of later policy models discussed in Chapter 12, it is also a case, accordingly, of pronounced private governance. Thus although the mother research institute IMEC was publicly funded at its inception, a model of academic entrepreneurship has now definitely taken root on the Leuven campus. The latter is now a paradigm case of development of a platform policy of related variety clusters in e-security, mechatronics, telephony, life sciences and agro-food to which global firms like Philips and others are attracted. Moreover, the world-renowned engineering capabilities at Aachen Technical University allow an international megacentre to flourish based on clusters, academic entrepreneurship, and large firm outsourcing in electronics in general and DSP in particular. Elsewhere in

Europe, firms like Ericsson, Siemens, Glaxo, AstraZeneca and Novartis already outsource substantial knowledge acquisition to smart entrepreneurial firms and university research institutes within and beyond Europe, including Asian 'tigers' like Singapore and 'giants' like China and India. The struggle now is for Europe to generate swiftly sufficient 'knowledge entrepreneurs' to take a significant share of the burgeoning global market for knowledge capture, processing and transfer, something universities remain globally competitive at doing but in which the EU 'knowledge industry' has not yet begun to challenge the US.

1.3.2 Markets in the Knowledge Economy

One of the weaknesses of innovation systems theory is that it pays insufficient attention to markets, particularly financial markets in the study of the transformation of exploration knowledge through examination knowledge to exploitation knowledge in the knowledge value chain (KVC) of innovative industries or 'platforms' in which it is interested. This is something that should be corrected in 'knowledge system' studies. Admittedly, this can look like a tall order, given the relative absence of definitive analyses of the ways markets function in the knowledge economy, and in particular, how they are different from markets in the 'Industrial Age'. Accordingly, much of what follows is newly written and little informed by a not very rich 'knowledge markets' literature.

The first task is to elaborate the notion of capturing the externalization and outsourcing of knowledge as discussed in relation to the role of the state in the knowledge economy. For purposes of compatibility, this must capture the elements of 'the three exes' of exploration, examination and exploitation knowledge. This is conducted illustratively for the healthcare and medical bioscience 'platform' in Cooke (2005a, 2007b). There we see that there is a mix of public and private economic activity even during the exploration knowledge stage. This involves the knowledge services including screening, sequencing, imaging, bioinformatics and biosoftware (ICT) applications required to enable exploration work to be conducted. Thereafter, and – as with exploration stage work – interactively, there is demand for proof-of-concept, preclinical, trialling, testing and diagnostic services from the market, mostly supplied by clinical research organizations (CROs) themselves, however, dependent on public healthcare patient databases (let alone animal houses for mammalian testing) for the trialling of treatments. Firm incubation, patent law and venture capital then become more involved alongside large pharmaceuticals and bioengineering and 'biologics' firms that synthesize the materials that realize the drug-based treatment or diagnostic platforms necessary for commercialization

*Table 1.1   High- and low-ranking UK university–industry co-publishing
            sectors, 1995–2000*

High-ranking sectors	Annual average U–I co-publications	Low-ranking sectors	Annual average U–I co-publications
1. Pharmaceuticals	659	15. Metals	29
2. Chemicals	128	16. Materials	25
3. Utilities	107	17. Machinery	18
4. Biotechnology	92	17. Software	18
5. Electronics	88	19. Automotive	15
6. Food	82	20. Electrical	11

Source: Adapted from Calvert and Patel (2002).

at the exploitation stage. Here private transactions outweigh public until, ironically for this 'platform', final sales are made to the normally public or quasi-public healthcare system. Moreover other public bodies, notably those focused on regulatory issues dealing with bioethics, clinical excellence and drug approval, make even the commercialization of knowledge in the form of innovations – remarkably and with notable complexity – a matter of public involvement in fundamentally private production but public consumer markets.

In the knowledge economy, other industries and platforms are probably less complex than the healthcare sector, not least because healthcare is often a public oligopsonistic quasi-market or even, as in the UK, a public, overwhelmingly monopsonistic one. For example, ICT is less science-driven (analytical knowledge) and more engineering-driven (synthetic knowledge), so the dependence on universities is less (Table 1.1). The dominance of non-ICT (except electronics) in the co-publication data between firms and universities in Table 1.1 is remarkable, as is the overwhelming predominance of pharmaceuticals co-publishing. Software, automotive and electrical industry–university co-publications are almost non-existent by comparison.

Hence, most interactions occur in the private sector and often in the examination phase of the KVC. This is even truer in the automotive sector, where R&D is frequently purchased along with design expertise in the KVC rather than done in-house. Thereafter, as with ICT, much iteration occurs at the examination knowledge stage while exploitation or commercialization is less and less the main function of the assemblers and more and more in the hands of third-party supply chain management firms, and engineering consultancies. Hence ICT and automotives show a significant 'outsourcing of logistics' characteristic that is not evident yet in medical bioscience markets. Marketization now runs very deep in synthetic knowledge markets where competition is very strong, global and with rising competitors coming up from hitherto small, low-volume producer markets like India and China. Reverse takeovers from the latter to the traditional producer markets could easily be anticipated, with weaker but still valuable brands like the UK MG Rover Company but latterly also former parts of Ford and General Motors being among those picked off relatively early.

A distinctive feature of markets in the knowledge economy concerns financial markets. These have been transformed by deregulation, the rise of derivatives and the switch in value accounting from dominance by tangible values to dominance by intangibles. This switch now places value on 'talent' and 'goodwill' far more than it did, and more than it used to upon tangibles like inventory and equipment. Dunning (2000) estimates this switch as one which favoured tangible assets in company accounts by 80:20 in the 1950s to a situation where it was 30:70 in the late 1990s and now can conservatively be estimated at an average of 20:80 in the 2000s – a complete reversal in 50 years. This causes tremendous asymmetries in boom times as the histories of AOL vis-à-vis Time Warner and more recently Google testify, where in the former case an extremely high stock market valuation enabled a fast-growth Internet enterprise to take over a sluggishly performing stock market corporation such as Time Warner. By 2003 the asymmetry was corrected and what suddenly became AOL Time Warner reverted to traditional Time Warner with AOL transformed into an online and e-mail subsidiary, its name scratched off the company's brass plates. Yet in 2006, with the huge rise in broadband markets, Internet trading and e-commerce more generally, AOL had yet to be sold off – despite Carl Icahn and other disaffected shareholders' efforts to get their way. By 2010 AOL was for sale, but in recessionary conditions that made the dot.com bust of 2001 pale into insignificance, AOL still had no takers. Equally Google, despite its Chinese misadventures, had been valued greater than General Electric until 2009 when it engaged in expensive knowledge-based shopping sprees, like eBay and buying what experts considered an overpriced Internet telephony firm like Skype (Klein, 2003).

But more important in terms of commercialization of financial knowledge is the rise of hedge funds, which hedge against rises and declines in market values by the sophisticated use of futures and derivatives markets, spotting underperforming Industrial Age dinosaurs (like Time Warner) or swathes of the German, French and Italian economies that retain bloated administrative staffs and underperforming share prices. These 'locusts', as they were termed in Germany, were the vanguard for introducing a liberal market ethos into coordinated markets cushioned for decades by state subsidies and state protectionism policies.

A second source of such intervention by new market actors has been that of 'private equity' firms. These arose from the success in the US and the UK of venture capitalists who accumulated vast wealth from 1990s technology investments that they later – until the credit crunch paralysed them – preferred to invest safely in utilities and retailing rather than the risky science and engineering markets from which they originated. In terms of their effects upon less knowledge-based sectors in the knowledge economies of the advanced world, these are fairly indistinguishable from hedge funds. Both have the inefficiencies and poor shareholder return of firms in coordinated (and liberal) markets in their sights.

Finally, stock markets themselves became more volatile in the knowledge economy, partly for the accounting difficulties that saw the managers of firms like Enron, WorldCom and Tyco in court (some in jail) alongside complicit accountancy companies like Arthur Andersen, and partly due to the hype and corrupt 'talking-up' of firm prospects by firms that had an interest through investing in such firms in their share value being taken up. This all seems rather quaint when set against the depradations wrought by many of the world's leading banks and investment houses on the global economy in the aforementioned credit crunch of 2008–09, of which more later (Chapter 11). Notice also, for example, how firms that boosted their asset value in the dot.com boom by valuing symbolic knowledge like 'goodwill' extremely high in the good times had, when the good times were over, to downgrade such valuations; one of the largest being the UK firm Vodafone which in early 2006 reduced the £81.5 billion of goodwill value on its balance sheet by between £23 billion and £25 billion as it lowered its expectations and those of the sector's growth prospects. Hence the huge stock market valuations that arose also for small and medium-sized enterprises (SMEs) with promising and sometimes impossible market claims were reined back as market realities re-exerted themselves.

1.3.3 Networks in the Knowledge Economy

There are three main kinds of networks focused upon the knowledge value chain in the knowledge economy. First are intellectual, research networks involving global knowledge creation, exchange and transfer arising from joint research, co-publication and patenting; second are research and co-publication activities between industry and research institutes or university centres of excellence; and third are knowledge alliances between firms, large and small. Increasingly, as knowledge outsourcing becomes the norm in some industries (90 per cent in oil and gas; 60 per cent in ICT; 52

per cent in pharmaceuticals) partnerships between large firms and smaller firms have risen above those 'strategic alliances' that were common for knowledge generation among multinationals in the 1980s and 1990s. This is mainly because large firms, generally speaking, had as we have seen 'lost the plot' in R&D compared to the specialist firms closer to the heart of new technologies, products and processes.

This means that 'knowledge entrepreneurship' is a litmus test of an economy's innovativeness. That is, economies – especially regional economies – may be measured for growth in terms of their knowledge entrepreneurship asymmetries. Regions may show that they have globally competitive 'knowledge domains' in research as have, for example, Wageningen-Nijmegen in the eastern Netherlands (fruit and vegetables) or Saskatchewan (rape seed oil), Missouri (cotton, soya) and South Australia (wine and plant science) in agro-food, each with between 25 per cent and 50 per cent of firms in their agro-food industry being research-led biotechnology businesses. Other regions like Connecticut, Southern California–San Diego and Scotland are less powerful as agro-food knowledge domains because only 1–3 per cent of incumbents among each region's more than 90 member agro-food firms is in biotechnology. As a case in point, San Diego is a global leader knowledge domain for healthcare biotechnology since well over 60 per cent of its healthcare businesses are based upon biotechnology research, a statistic that applies even more strongly in Scotland (74 per cent) in the healthcare sector. Others in this position for healthcare include Massachusetts (Cambridge–Boston), Northern California (San Francisco–Silicon Valley), Eastern England (Cambridge), Medicon Valley (Copenhagen–Lund; see Chapter 12) and Stockholm–Uppsala. These all have at least 60 per cent of their healthcare firms involved in biotechnology research as well as having the presence of world-class research institutes such as Whitehead in Cambridge (MA, USA), Sanger in Cambridge (UK), Salk and Scripps in San Diego and Karolinska in Stockholm.

As noted in the preceding theoretical discussion on knowledge capabilities, intellectual powerhouse regions and their institutions with 'star' scientists network together globally to advance research knowledge but also to create business opportunities for themselves and others as academic and non-academic 'knowledge entrepreneurs'. Data in Cooke (2007b, 2009) detail global bioscientific knowledge networks involving elite institute, 'star' scientist research co-publication for the period 1998–2004. Here we see dense international publishing networks in which the following four aspects are of theoretical and empirical pertinence to this book. First, an international collaborative biosciences publication core of 'star' scientists and leading research institutes clearly exists. In the US it is centred upon Boston, Cambridge, MA, San Francisco, San Diego and New York City

– the last-named being strong in research but less so in commercialization. Second, there is a penumbra of various lesser global research nodes
centred upon Stockholm, Cambridge and Oxford (UK), Singapore, Paris,
Toronto and Tokyo. These often have a few or one strong network partner
in one of the US platforms. Despite their geographic non-proximity, the
two Cambridges are relationally proximate, as are Pasteur Institute in
Paris and New York University or Karolinska Institute in Stockholm
with Harvard Medical School. Beyond that for publication in top US
journals is a 'third circle' of the lesser co-publishing locales including the
likes of Hebrew University, Jerusalem, Uppsala University, University of
Montreal, Oxford and London universities and the National University
of Singapore. Third, among the 'penumbras' there are also co-publication
links but far weaker than those through the network hierarchy to the US
centres. Finally, by contrast there remains a strong intranodality of linkages among co-publishers in geographical proximity, optimizing localized
'global capabilities', especially in the aforementioned US platforms but
also elsewhere to a lesser extent, as in London, Cambridge, Oxford and
Toronto.

Much the same – albeit attenuated – pattern applies for co-patenting
among a similar network of global research institutes and their high-impact
bioscientists. Three features are apparent. First, the network is tighter and
even more focused regarding multiple interactions on patenting among
the strongest centres in the co-publishing hierarchy noted above. Thus the
East and West Coast US platforms predominate, often partnering single
institutes in locations outside the US. Second, the outlier co-patenting and
co-publishing centres are even less interactive in co-patenting than in co-
publishing even though these often represent so-called 'global cities' like
Paris and Tokyo. Rather, lesser cities with globally leading-edge 'knowledge domains' like Jerusalem and Geneva show up as at least as important
as more celebrated locations. Finally, it is clear that new actors enter the
networks since some are biotechnology firms, unlike the evidence on co-
publishing which is dominated by research institutes, medical schools and
university centres of excellence.

Finally, attention must be paid to the interactions of large firms as well
as large and smaller firms. Clearly knowledge flows among these, especially as we move further from the exploration towards the exploitation
phase of the KVC. We can draw some useful inferences regarding this in
respect of the ICT industry compared to biotechnology. This was subject
of a study conducted by Cooke et al. (2007) based on original questionnaire and interview studies from a UK and Austria survey of knowledge
flows among ICT firms, defined as those engaged in software, and telecoms and computer hardware – compared with biotechnology firms. A

first relevant finding comparing the two – somewhat asymmetrically scaled – sectors related to what factors encouraged them to locate in proximity to other firms in their sector or platform. There were important distinctions in the answers, which here refer only to the UK findings. The data showed that for ICT firms, universities were ranked lower as 'proximity partners' than they were for biotechnology firms. Unsurprisingly, for this is one of the most common findings from regional innovation system studies (for example Cooke et al., 2004) 'customers' tend to loom large or at least larger for ICT than for biotechnology firms. Strikingly, in regard to propinquity, 'customers' ranked lowest in biotechnology but highest for ICT. Other public research, such as that conducted in non-university laboratories, is ranked very low by ICT but of medium influence in terms of proximity drivers by biotechnology firms.

Thus a picture is relatively easily and correctly formed of ICT and biotechnology as having polar opposite rationales for proximate interaction in research and innovation. Whereas biotechnology firms cluster around universities and, to a lesser extent, other public laboratories for research knowledge and related interactions, meanwhile interacting distantly with customers, many of which are pharmaceuticals multinationals, ICT firms prefer to cluster close to customer firms, keeping research at a distance. This was an original finding on networks, different kinds of knowledge flow (research knowledge compared to innovation knowledge, which is near market and thus less spatially constrained) and sectoral variety for both industries that told us much about the nature of and differences between them. First, both collaborate intensively but ICT more nationally than either locally or globally as in the case of biotechnology. Second, ICT is more market-than science-focused in its proximity practices, a sign that innovation is more important and swifter than in biotechnology. Third, and of policy relevance, a region is well advised to have localized ICT multinational customers to help promote its nascent ICT cluster; while for biotechnology this is relatively unimportant and proximity to an accomplished medical or other biosciences research capability is of greater importance for cluster-building.

Further findings on ICT alone showed that most UK ICT collaboration in R&D occurs nationally, with the host region some way behind, but much more engaged except for customer–collaboration interaction) for most variables than at the non-national level. A partial exception to this is that 'suppliers' are relatively important to R&D collaboration in both the EU and North America, as indeed are customers. Thus a picture forms of UK ICT firms much engaged in transatlantic supply chains bolstered by UK and regional R&D collaborations with a wide range of support actors, especially universities. Hence, while R&D is less a factor in proximate location for UK ICT firms, especially compared to the proximity force of innovation and market partners, UK and regional R&D is more important for R&D collaboration than that from abroad, including North America, which is a nexus of R&D collaboration of minor significance. Thus, in terms of the thesis advanced above about the difficulty of comparing, in this instance, even high-tech sectors, it is clear that firms gather for different reasons. However, given that ICT and bio-technology clustering in the UK is driven by different knowledge dynamic imperatives – research for biotechnology, innovation for ICT – both collaborate rather than only compete. Thus both are intimately involved in interacting collaboratively with customer firms with which they engage for purposes of conducting 'open innovation' and or 'R&D outsourcing' according to the study findings. Further, these firms value proximity in this regard; to repeat: with national and regional consultants, customers and universities for ICT firms; and with national and regional universities, but more transatlantic customers and suppliers, for biotechnology firms. Hence, a further elaboration is a greater valuation by the latter of func-tional or relational proximity than geographical for innovation through distant networks.

1.4   THE GENERALIZED THEORETICAL FRAMEWORK: REGIONS, SECTORS AND FIRMS IN THE KNOWLEDGE ECONOMY

Before highlighting the findings of the sectoral reports, it is necessary to evolve a theoretical framework for understanding the importance of regional knowledge capabilities, how they influence organizational prac-tices of industries, and what these knowledge implications are for firms in various kinds of knowledge value chains. This is evolutionary in origin, interested in the economics of search and selection practices of firms in contexts where variety acts as 'evolutionary fuel' in Hodgson's vivid phra-seology (Hodgson, 1993). By evolutionary fuel is meant iterative, trial-and-error interactive feedback from experimentation by actors in order to survive and prosper economically. The greater the variety, the greater the opportunity for innovation arising from interactions with other actors. It has been shown empirically that opportunities for the swiftest innovation occur in conditions of proximate and related variety (Boschma, 2005). Cities are one variant of this, but because their variety is often fragmented as well as partly related, they are less fruitful than settings with only related variety of the kind typically found in regional innovation systems. This perspective settles at the apex of a conceptual triangle between Jacobs

(1969) who advocated sectoral diversification, and Glaeser et al. (1992) who advocated specialization as key wellsprings of innovative growth.

The approach is thus post-sectoral, recognizing innovative growth to be facilitated through knowledge or technology platforms characterized by openness of knowledge flows and knowledge spillovers; nevertheless it contains sectoral categories for practical purposes. The reason for this platform emphasis is observable, for example, where a location specializing in leading-edge research in, say, sensors may find numerous applications of such technology in many related yet extensive fields where lateral absorptive capacity is high. Of course, not every single industry can be exactly like this, but more and more, knowledge-utilizing industries and firms see themselves as targeting general-purpose, flexible applications in a form of pervasive innovation (Cooke, 2006c). This is especially pronounced in science-based industry but increasingly common as more industries and firms become science users if not producers. As we shall further see, even the food industry, which the Organisaton for Economic Co-operation and Development (OECD) and EU see as 'low-tech', actually used historically (since the 1950s) agro-chemicals and pesticides straight from science and technology (S&T), which it continues so to do, and produces advanced scientific and technological knowledge. Firms habitually cooperate closely in research with, for example, university bioscientists, nutritionists and food technologists. Much of this is now the acutest 'worlds of production' conflict because of health scares and obesity associated with 'industrial agriculture', giving the swiftest market rise of all 'alternative foods' to the retro-innovation of organic or 'eco' farming. Now, what were only yesterday often thought of as regions in decline because of 'low-tech' agricultural specialization have become arenas for some of the most exciting innovation related to the bioenergy, bioremediation, 'cleantech' and healthy food production platform. Hence, there are grounds for advancing a knowledge-theoretical framework that links together these new elements and highlights the role of varieties of knowledge in contributing a testable explanation of regional developmental asymmetries.

1.4.1 A Regional Knowledge Capabilities Model

The key elements are presented in Figure 1.1 and discussed subsequently (Cooke, 2009). We start from the centre of the diagram, denoting a region in which a mix or bundle of widely in-demand knowledge capabilities evolves. Connecting to north-west in the diagram, and compared to other regions, this expresses its privileged asymmetric knowledge endowment from a variety of knowledge organizations and institutions. Exploration knowledge organizations, such as research institutes, knowledge networks

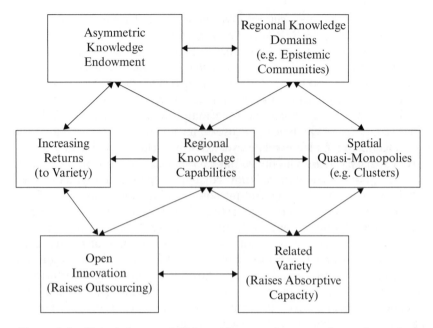

*Figure 1.1   Knowledge capabilities and economic geography: a theoretical
                framework*

among individuals (for example 'lunar societies'; Uglow, 2003) and knowledge leadership figures (for example possible future Nobel – or Oscar –
laureates) coexist with examination knowledge equivalents for standard
setting, trialling, testing and patenting, and exploitation knowledge bodies
such as entrepreneurs, investors and related professional talent. Deprived
regions lack many or all of these knowledge asset 'bundles'.

Regions should not be expected to contain all knowledge interaction
possibilities, even if they are strong. However, many external-to-the-region
interactions will likely occur, with expertise in appropriate other regional
knowledge domains concentrating in 'global talent pools'. The evolutionary fuel is supplied (linking westward in Figure 1.1) by the attraction of a
variety of imitative and innovative talent to the region, a Schumpeterian
'swarming' realizing increasing returns to related variety (south-eastward
diagrammatic connection) where innovation may move swiftly through
various parts of the business 'platform'. Related variety, where it exists,
nourishes lateral absorptive capacity (intersectoral or platform) because
cognitive distance between platform subfields is low (think of 'general-
purpose innovations', after Helpman, 1998).

Moving north-east in Figure 1.1, these processes result in the presence of regional 'knowledge domains'. The dictionary definition of 'knowledge domain' is a region or realm with a distinctive knowledge base, common principles, rules and procedures, and a specific semantic discourse. This naturally fits well with the concept of the epistemic community (similar to, but more focused than 'communities of practice') with its own professional discourse and interests. Such monopolistic features are frequently characteristic of, for example, clusters that in regional terms may display related variety; for example varieties of engineering expertise in the industrial districts of Emilia-Romagna in Italy in a spectrum exemplified by Ferrari cars and Ducati motor cycles (both Modena) to Sasib in packaging machinery (Bologna) and drgSystems machine tools (Piacenza) (Harrison, 1994). We could say exactly the same about Baden-Württemberg.

These and other clusters have spatial quasi-monopolistic or 'club' characteristics, exerting exclusion and inclusion mechanisms to aspirant 'members' consequent upon their knowledge value to the club. If such industries operated as markets rather than knowledge quasi-monopolies it is difficult to see why spatial 'swarming' would occur. But many firms are willing to pay super-rents of 100–300 per cent to locate in high-technology clusters, even when they are professed non-collaborators, to access anticipated localized knowledge spillovers (Cooke, 2005b). These are, of course, 'diseconomies of agglomeration' which they are willing to put up with. Finally, to the south-west of Figure 1.1, it is precisely such localized knowledge spillovers that induce what Chesbrough (2003) calls 'open innovation' whereby large firms outsource their R&D to purchase advanced 'pipeline' knowledge, and access regional knowledge spillovers via 'channels' (Owen-Smith and Powell, 2004). These processes interact in complex, non-linear ways displayed graphically in Figure 1.1, to explain regional knowledge asymmetries. Variations in the market value of regional knowledge combinations also contribute significantly to associated regional income disparities (Boschma and Frenken, 2003). Being an evolutionary growth process, successive increasing returns may be triggered from any point within or beyond the confines of Figure 1.1.

1.4.2 Sectors and Firms: Knowledge Generation and Knowledge Domains

As noted, there is a large question over the validity, reliability and even meaning of the notion of 'sector', but for now three criticisms can be made. First, the sector notion is merely a statistician's artefact that is an increasingly misleading representation of reality. Second, sector classifications are little changed since their nineteenth-century origins to enable identification of such activities as biotechnology, nanotechnology, clean technology or new media. Third, modern technological innovation increasingly

Table 1.2   Characteristics, forms and stages of knowledge production

Knowledge categories → Knowledge Phase of Institution or Firm ↓	Analytical	Synthetic	Symbolic
Exploration	Mathematical Reasoning	e.g. Gene Therapy	Experimental Art Work
Examination	Theorems to Test	Clinical Trial	Art Exhibition
Exploitation	e.g. Penrose Tiles*/Patterns	Therapeutic Treatment	Gallery Sale

Note: * Penrose Tiles are mathematically derived computer graphics.

progresses by means of the evolution of 'platforms' that combine many technologies that are, in increasing numbers of cases, adaptable across diverse industrial and technological contexts. A more penetrative analysis of the firm-level contribution to regional capabilities is then required. We return to our knowledge framework (as in Table 1.2) for consideration of distinct kinds of knowledge activity within firms in sectors in order to analyse their simply illustrated knowledge value chains for products evolved through interactive innovation processes.

The innovation process of firms and industries is strongly shaped by their specific knowledge base that can be grouped in three different epistemic categories of knowledge: analytical (scientific), synthetic (engineering) and symbolic (artistic). This is shown in Table 1.2, which analyses the exemplifications of the distinctive knowledge value chain in relation to different knowledge categories. This is done for purposes of illustration rather than to illustrate any particular relationship that such an analytical framework might have for considerations of, for example, proximity. The analysis shows that all kinds of knowledge pass through variants of the same three-stage transformation process as implicit knowledge is transformed into explicit or codified marketable new knowledge or innovations. In connection with this, firm behaviours can be mapped out in different arenas such as that of the region, and a further level of analysis can be added to include a regional knowledge domain dimension characterized by 'knowledge domain', 'knowledge capability' and 'innovation system' (Table 1.3).

Such categorization of relevant knowledge domains in regard to sectoral knowledge generation, testing and appropriation characteristics is represented in Table 1.3. Introduced here is the 'intermediary' knowledge process category of 'complicit' knowledge where a lot of value is created

Table 1.3   Knowledge: from implicit domain to digital innovation systems

Knowledge Phase of Institution or Firm → Region ↓	Implicit (Explore)	Complicit (Explore-Examine)	Explicit (Examine-Exploit)
Knowledge Domain	(Invention/ Discovery)	(Translator)	(Appropriation> IPR)
Knowledge Capability	(Talent)	(Research)	(Technique)
Innovation System	(Institutions)	(Networks)	(Digital, e.g. KMS**)

Note: ** KMS is knowledge management system.

by doing 'translational' and often creative or innovative advisory work assisting implicit knowledge to be made explicit or codifiable for exploitation. In Table 1.3 this is done by recognizing the importance of identifying implicit knowledge domains (for example post-genomics in Greater Boston) that are at least knowledge quasi-monopolies, mechanisms for extracting useful knowledge through complicit third-party mediation (for example incubation, intermediary technology institutes) and appropriation of rents from explicit knowledge (patents, licences). Then, the implantation of reproducible knowledge capabilities through the training of talent in the next generations that capably transfer as well as transform and evolve knowledge technically and commercially is a necessity. Finally, innovation systems take institutions and construct regional advantage through institutional networking that, in itself, embodies where appropriate and feasible digital knowledge flow platforms (DKFP) that systemically support knowledge exploration, and knowledge examination to knowledge exploitation interactions.

1.4.3   Worlds of Production

To characterize the basic variety of industrial organizational forms in regional space we now turn to consider the 'worlds of production' approach (Storper and Salais, 1997; Storper, 1997), a theoretical framework elaborated in the cited works that has proved most intellectually and practically penetrative in the decade since they were published. The central concept, of key importance to the analysis and investigational work proposed here, is that different forms of production organization are internally coherent in terms of their driving institutions, network interactions and conventions.

In the current era these resolve the four 'tensions' represented in Figure

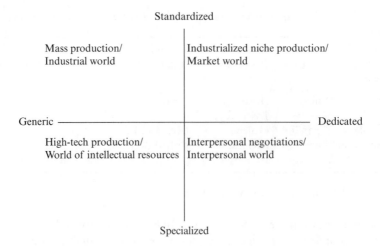

Standardized

Mass production/   Industrialized niche production/
Industrial world   Market world

Generic ─────────────────────────┼───────────────── Dedicated

High-tech production/   Interpersonal negotiations/
World of intellectual resources   Interpersonal world

Specialized

Source: After Storper and Salais (1997).

Figure 1.2   Regional 'worlds of production'

1.2. The first of these refers to 'standardized' production as practised in mass-production industries such as banking and automotives, in tension with a more 'specialized' production, in which the technology used and the know-how are restricted. On the second dimension is a 'dedicated' product that is customized to certain niche requirements such as luxury consumption (for example bespoke or customized tailoring) but also software or, increasingly 'designer drug solutions' in healthcare or personalized services of various kinds. Finally, 'generic' means products that carry well-known qualities, with predictable and foreseeable market. 'Specialization' involves generic products being produced in specialized ways, such as specialized forms of a generic tourism that might include, for example, archaeological cruises.

The reason for utilizing this approach is twofold. First, it underpins the mobilization of economic resources, the organization of production systems, factor markets, patterns of economic decision-making and forms of profitability. Second, it summarizes the diverse, economically viable action frameworks found in different industries, regions and nations.

1.5   CONCLUSIONS

Three things are clear from the foregoing analysis, each with great significance for the understanding of how knowledge exploration, examination and exploitation are organized and relate in business interactions under pronounced 'knowledge economy' regime conditions. First, although much research attention is devoted nowadays to investigation of contrasts between markets and networks, the state remains a significant factor in the knowledge economy not least because it is crucial for funding basic or fundamental exploration research. The new role of the state as prime funder of exploration knowledge could be seen in the context of KU Leuven's IMEC Centre (section 1.3.1; Hinoul, 2005) as well as more broadly in relation to the highly globally networked biotechnology field.

We further saw how some industry platforms like pharmaceuticals, biotechnology, chemicals and agro-food interact closely with universities in research, from which they produce co-publications which act as an indicator of accessing university knowledge. But many mature sectors like metals, electrical engineering and automotives do not do this, preferring a declining in-house knowledge base or purchasing knowledge from specialist firms or consultants. Surprisingly, there is little industry–university co-publishing even in software, but more in electronics. Thereafter we noticed how much financial markets are destabilized in the knowledge economy regime by 'fictitious' valuations of knowledge assets, especially symbolic ones like goodwill. Markets have generally found it harder to value firms by their knowledge assets and accountants have sometimes been complicit in approving distinctly unreliable balance sheets. Some have ended up in jail accordingly. By 2009 those caught up in illegal practices in the dot. com bust were joined in the US by others engaged in nefarious investment banking schemes.

Finally, we saw how network forms of knowledge exploration and examination now span the globe among 'megacentres' or, in the vein of this book 'platforms' of expertise linking 'knowledge domains' set in often unprepossessing and not always 'global cities'. Outsourcing of exploration and examination knowledge has become almost normal for firms in the energy, ICT and pharmaceuticals industries, also in mundane consumer products industries where, for example, Procter & Gamble matched its central R&D function with an outsourcing strategy and renamed the department in question the Connect & Develop (C&D) department in preference to the more traditional R&D departmental appellation. Networks are also pronounced in co-publishing and co-patenting on a global basis among network hubs, nodes or knowledge platform incumbents. Moreover industries differ in which others they seek proximity to for collaborative interaction. Thus ICT firms prefer the proximity of customers and suppliers clustering at the heart of the value chain, while biotechnology firms prefer proximate collaboration, with university research valued more highly. In general, we can conclude that the knowledge economy regime is highly asymmetric, destabilizing and globally networked. The state is crucial in funding knowledge generation, while markets still reign supreme for knowledge exploitation. But spanning all three knowledge phases are networks that are the glue that holds together the transformation of knowledge into innovation in the contemporary globalized economy.

The chapter concluded as it began with an exegesis of the theoretical and methodological frameworks that facilitated execution of the comparative research over a significant number of industries and regional economies across Europe. As we shall see in the next chapters, the studies conducted on the seven sectors show that each encompasses a multifaceted spectrum of knowledge categories (analytical, synthetic and symbolic) and different knowledge phases (exploration, examination, exploitation). This reflects, on the one hand, the complexity of these knowledge-intensive sectors and the composite nature of their knowledge products and, on the other, the particular tensions that arise from the interaction of different knowledge drivers (such as for example regulation, market structure, supply chain and corporate objectives) and knowledge responses (for example organizational, market, product/processes, professional) that the 'worlds of production' framework synthesizes.

A final cautionary note is that despite the criticisms of the notion of 'sector' highlighted above, much research into economic development must utilize such artifices and the following analysis recognizes this fact. Seven sectors were identified for Eurodite research and analysis based on their varying levels of knowledge intensity and use (Pavitt, 1984). Moreover, selection was based on their relevance to European knowledge economy objectives as expressed in the EU call to which this proposal was a successful response. The sectors investigated are the following:

1. Food and Drink.
2. Biotechnology.
3. ICT.
4. New Media.
5. Knowledge-intensive business services.
6. Automotives.
7. Tourism.

A full account of the knowledge dynamics of each is provided in the seven chapters from 3 to 9. In Chapter 2 we devote attention to the research objectives that Eurodite sought to pursue and fulfil. In Chapter 10, we summarize these findings in light of the developed regional knowledge capabilities model.

2. The rationale for Eurodite and an introduction to the sector studies

Stewart MacNeill and Chris Collinge

2.1 INTRODUCTION AND EURODITE OBJECTIVES

At the outset of the Eurodite project proposal stage in the early 2000s it was clear that the significance of knowledge for economic activity had grown exponentially since the 1980s. However, there was as yet little understanding of the nature and composition of the knowledge economy, especially at a regional level. The Eurodite project sought to address this deficiency by examining the dynamics of knowledge in the economies of European regions. A key aim, given that the client for the research was an important policy-framing body, was to generate findings that could be interpreted in ways that would inform policies seeking to promote the transition of Europe towards a knowledge-based society. The Lisbon Accords and aspirations would enshrine the policy importance of such a perspective for the rest of the decade. Questions in the minds of analysts and policy-makers alike included the following. What are the different trajectories towards the knowledge economy? Through what generative and communication pathways does knowledge flow into and within regional economies? Analytical frameworks would, as noted, be developed, enabling policy-makers to measure the intensity of regional knowledge use, and to identify appropriate practices for different regions given their respective economic base and level of knowledge development. Complementary activities ranging from workshops to websites were designed to ensure a high level of communication and take-up and validation of the project outputs.

The overall goal of Eurodite was to understand the role of knowledge in the economies of European regions in order to inform policies in these regions towards a knowledge-based economy with enhanced social cohesion (Table 2.1). The intention was to probe beneath the popular notion of the 'knowledge economy' by describing the diversity of learning processes, knowledge dynamics and knowledge trajectories across Europe. It was also intended to examine the assumption that regions and other spatial arrangements (such as 'clusters' or 'milieux') represented coherent units of explanation and intervention in the knowledge field. Such instruments and phenomena as these were, and remain, highly popular intervention mechanisms among policy-makers worldwide, and from the supranational level of the EU down to the implementation level of regions. Hence the emphasis upon regions came both from the theory that regions had become more important arenas for economic organization in a globalizing era of global nodes and networks, and the policy to optimize regional capabilities to support such imputed processes and gain regionally constructed advantage in the process. This involved the following research tasks:

1. Assessment of the current state of knowledge (stocks and flows) in European regional economies and identification of key trends within these and other aggregates (for example sectors, networks and markets, governance systems, education and science, social groups).
2. To produce a model of 'economic knowledge micro-dynamics' of the interaction over time of knowledge stocks and flows amongst networks of firms and others, starting in selected sectors and regions of Europe, and observing how these interactions extend organizationally and spatially. Key aspects of this are summarized in Chapter 1, though a much broader review with many contributors was conducted and papers can be consulted on the Eurodite website (http://www.eurodite.bham.ac.uk).
3. Development of methodologies to calibrate macro-level indicators as a diagnostic tool for policy-makers, for the measurement of regional knowledge stocks and flows. Research design and methodological issues are discussed in Chapter 1 and 'the matrix' as a diagnostic tool is presented in Chapter 12.
4. Evaluation of the contribution of these knowledge micro-dynamics to macro-level regional economic and social trajectories – to their performance in productivity growth and competitiveness as well as gender equality and social cohesion. These are considered in depth in the sectoral chapters 3 to 9 where gender issues are indicated, and key elements are summarized in Chapter 10.
5. Identification of the conditions that have created the observed knowledge dynamics – including positive and negative path-dependence – in different sectors and regions across Europe. These also form matters of key interest in Chapters 3–10 below.
6. Identification of key policy levers and coordinating activities available to the EU and other levels of governance to enhance knowledge dynamics and their contribution to regional development and competitiveness, economic and social cohesion. This is discussed in Chapter 12.

Table 2.1 Summary of project objectives, goals, means of achievement and baseline data

Objective	Operational goal and means of achievement	Baseline data
1	• Identify different types of knowledge stocks and flows • Select indicators for measuring these over time • Evaluate trends in knowledge stocks and flows	Current knowledge about the state of economic knowledge in European regional economies
2	• Identify and evaluate current models of economic knowledge micro-dynamics • Postulate model of these dynamics • Assemble data from studies of knowledge processes • Test and revise model	Current models of economic knowledge micro-dynamics in sectors and regions
3	• Evaluate current knowledge-relevant macro-level indicators • Propose alternative or additional indicators • Test and calibrate viable indicators	Range and value of current diagnostic indicators measuring regional knowledge stocks and flows
4	• Identify and evaluate current understandings of the contribution of micro-level dynamics to macro-trends • Propose a revised approach to this aggregation • Implement this approach in reference to data assembled from firms and other bodies	Current understandings of the contribution of micro-level dynamics to macro-trends
5	• Identify conditions – economic, institutional, governmental, social – currently postulated as relevant to these dynamics • Draw conclusions from findings about these postulates • Propose revised assessment of causal conditions	Current assessments of the causal conditions governing economic knowledge dynamics

Table 2.1   (continued)

Objective	Operational goal and means of achievement	Baseline data
6	• Evaluate current policy approaches employed to enhance knowledge dynamics in the light of research findings • Propose revised institutional frameworks and policy approaches	Current assessments of the most appropriate institutional frameworks and policy approaches

The ten-year strategic goal established at Lisbon was: 'that Europe should become the most competitive and dynamic knowledge-based economy in the world, capable of sustainable economic growth with more and better jobs and greater social cohesion'. However, it was widely considered that progress towards these goals had been slow. Even the EU's awakening to climate change issues and the need for regulation only really took form with the first Biofuels Directive in March 2007. On the other hand, the quest for an across-the-board 3 per cent statistic for expenditure of EU member state wealth (gross domestic product – GDP) on research and development (R&D) became something of an obsession and a self-invented stick with which to beat the European Commission. As with much Commission activity, many such headline-grabbing aspirations perform the function, at least to some extent, of raising consciousness among other stakeholders like businesses, member state and regional governments and, for example, universities. Nevertheless, in the early stages, despite good intentions, neither macro- nor micro-level policies were delivering innovation returns at the hoped-for rate. Perhaps because an inadequate conceptual model (Industrial Age) underlay the perspective of the Commission on how its aspirations might be at least part-fulfilled, it was important in this context to explore an alternative paradigm based upon knowledge dynamics, and to draw out the implications of this for future policy orientations.

Eurodite had two distinct types of baseline against which it would expect to be judged. The first was the current knowledge – from conceptual models to data sets – of the dynamics of economic knowledge as represented in academic literature and official statistics in various forms. The latter analyses were conducted at great length and with great care by the French team from Bordeaux but, perhaps predictably, yielded little of real value because the data collected at EU level is relentlessly sectoral and based on hard inputs like R&D expenditure and outputs like patents. Needless to say, these say little beyond the trivial about knowledge flows, nothing of value about innovation and little of consequence about the relationships between these and indicators of productivity, competitiveness and growth. As for assisting on questions like subcontracting, open innovation, and combinative compared to cumulative knowledge vectors, EU (and national) data are silent. Of course, these statistical archaisms also made few concessions to the presence throughout the EU of regions, the vehicles by means of which much EU policy, including innovation, is implemented.

What proved moderately approachable, as long as the above caveats regarding existing hard metrics were heeded, were small elements of the wish-list contained in the following:

1. The state of economic knowledge in the regions of Europe.
2. The micro-dynamics of knowledge in sectors and regions.
3. The contribution of micro-level dynamics to macro-trends.
4. The causal conditions governing economic knowledge dynamics.

In truth any progress, inevitably piecemeal, in these directions came from the tried and tested case studies approach which has always been central to regional innovation studies precisely because of inadequate official statistics to measure any of these important knowledge flows. This is signified in the recourse to the policy community as a baseline source in assessment of the prevailing state of the art. Thus the prevailing state of knowledge of these four factors, within the social sciences and amongst policy communities (established during reviews undertaken in the early work packages), would represent the baseline against which Eurodite progress would be reviewed and assessed.

2.2   POLICY ORIENTATIONS

Eurodite sought to identify impediments to the development of the knowledge economy in European regions, and to specify where in institutional and systemic terms these were located. The second set of baselines therefore relate to policy diagnoses and orientations designed to harness the economic benefits of knowledge to the economy at different spatial scales. The first of these, not surprisingly, could only be elicited piecemeal in relation to the case-based analysis of 28 regional economies conducted by the teams listed below in.

1. Current diagnostic indicators measuring regional knowledge stocks and flows.
2. The most appropriate policy approaches to enhance knowledge dynamics.

The project will therefore contribute both to current knowledge about economic knowledge dynamics, and to current policy understandings and orientations to the development of economic knowledge.

2.2.1   Outputs

Thus important outputs, against which the project could also be measured, were the changes to both the academic and policy debates that the research could engender. These contributions were to be delivered and monitored through:

- reports;
- publications subject to external review;
- policy discussions at different levels:
  - regional – through regional development agencies (RDAs) within the partnership and EURADA (the Association of Regional Development Agencies);
  - national – through RDA and partner links and via the dissemination events;
  - European – via links with Directorate General (DG) Regional Policy.

In this respect, the project partnership was interesting in bringing together heads of supranational membership associations like EURADA, which is the representative association of more than 300 regional development agencies in Europe, as well as representatives of specific regional development agencies from different member states such as the West Midlands (UK), Emilia-Romagna (Italy) and Styria (Austria). In this way Eurodite contained its own sounding-board, which frequently resonated, concerning the appropriateness, relevance and comprehensibility of specific academic debates. Equally, academic debate introduced knowledge of distinctive practices and the lineaments of new processes ongoing in the economy with which typical policy-makers were unfamiliar or hazy in understanding. Policy–academic interaction of this kind was expected to be, and generally worked as, a stimulus more than a barrier to communication and intellectual progress. This is, once again, because of the intersection of two kinds of perspective where academics scan widely and policy-makers deeply.

2.3   RELEVANCE OF EURODITE TO EU OBJECTIVES

The relevant EU priority for Eurodite was intended to mobilize social science and humanities research capacities to understand and address issues related to the emergence of the knowledge-based society in Europe, and new forms of relationships between its citizens, and of these to institutions. It was intended to contribute to the creation of a European Research Area (ERA) in the social sciences and humanities, a hot issue (on a fairly cold subject) at the time, culminating in vivid recommendations for enlivening the ERA scene by identifying research community energizing 'grand challenges' like climate change to stimulate greater cross-border knowledge flows among knowledge ecosystems and networks. This was rather against the Commission's own centralizing mindset as represented in the abortive concept of the European Institute of Technology (EIT) modelled – bizarrely, it might be thought – on the singular and eponymous entity founded in Massachusetts (EU, 2008).

Eurodite had a comparative focus across regions and sectors as well as member states, and sought to introduce a number of data and methodological innovations to the study of knowledge dynamics. Among these were 'innovation biographies' which were developed and widely used in the research, as indicated in Chapter 11. The partnership (Table 2.2) was extensive and multidisciplinary, and contributed directly to shared research methodologies, indicators, statistics and databases. The study aimed to extend and disseminate state-of-the-art reviews for policy-makers and general audiences, and make a contribution to the scientific basis of policy especially at the EU level. It would, in the process, generate an appreciation and mapping of the research competences in this field and link to, draw upon and contribute to national research programmes where relevant. The programme involved, as noted, not only the users and stakeholders in the partnership but, through the dissemination strategy, policy-makers, other researchers and the general public.

The topic addressed was specified by EU as: 'Improving the generation, distribution and use of knowledge and its impact on economic and social development.' A particular focus concerned the specified sub-area of 'Knowledge dynamics and economic and societal development in Europe and in its regions'. The objectives of the project, outlined above, related to the EU objectives for 'knowledge economy' study and advice as follows:

1. Assessing the current state of knowledge stocks and flows in European regional economies – contributes to understanding of the role of knowledge dynamics at the level of regions, sectors, social groups, institutions and organizations.
2. Producing a model of 'economic knowledge micro-dynamics' – will help understanding of how these relate to learning and competence building, and by this means the study addressed territorial,

Platforms of innovation

Table 2.2   *Participant list*

Participant role	Participant number	Participant name	Participant short name	Country	Date enter project	Date exit project
CO	1	University of Birmingham	CURS	UK	1	60
CR	2	Université Montequieu Bordeaux IV	IFREDE	F	1	60
CR	3	Université des Sciences Sociales de Toulouse 1	LEREPS-GRES	F	1	60
CR	4	Grenoble Ecole de Management	GEM	F	1	60
CR	5	University of Neuchâtel	UNINE	CH	1	60
CR	6	Institut Arbeit und Technik im Wissenschaftszentrum Nordrhein-Westfalen (IAT)	IAT	D	1	60
CR	7	University of Marburg	UMB	D	1	60
CR	8	Social Science Research Centre Berlin (WZB)	WZB	D	1	60
CR	9	Ålborg University	SPIRIT	DK	1	60
CR	10	Centre for Regional and Tourism Research	CRT	DK	1	60
CR	11	Fondazione Rosselli	FR	I	1	60
CR	12	Ca' Foscari University of Venice	Ca FOSCARI	I	1	60
CR	13	University of Lisbon	FUL	P	1	60
CR	14	Radboud University of Nijmegen	RUN	NL	1	60
CR	15	Nordic Centre for Spatial Development (Nordregio)	NORDREGIO	S	1	60
CR	16	Göteborg University	UGOT	S	1	60
CR	17	Advantage West Midlands	AWM	UK	1	60
CR	18	University of Economics, Bratislava	EUBA	SK	1	60
CR	19	Institute for Economic Research Ljubljana	IER	SL	1	60
CR	20	Polish Academy of Sciences	CIMPAN	PL	1	60
CR	21	Cardiff University	UWC	UK	1	60
CR	22	University of Rome 'Tor Vergata'	URTV	I	1	60
CR	23	Ludwig-Maximilians Universität München	L-M UM	D	1	60
CR	24	EURADA	EURADA	B	1	60
CR	25	ASTER	ASTER	I	1	60

Table 2.2   (continued)

Participant role	Participant number	Participant name	Participant short name	Country	Date enter project	Date exit project
CR	26	Universitat Autònoma de Barcelona	UAB	E	1	60
CR	27	Süleyman Demirel University	SDU	TU	1	60
CR	28	Styrian Development Agency	SFG	A	1	60

organizational and systemic configurations affecting the potential for innovation and economic development.

3. Developing methodologies and calibrating macro-level indicators as a diagnostic tool – leads to a practical understanding of the different engagements (and path-dependencies) within and between regions and sectors, social groups, and institutions and organizations.

4. Evaluating the contribution of such knowledge micro-dynamics to macro-level regional economic and social trajectories – facilitates examination of the relationship of knowledge dynamics to issues of innovation as well as competitiveness, regional development, and economic and social cohesion, including gender issues.

5. Identifying the conditions that have created the observed knowledge dynamics – including positive and negative path-dependence – addresses the processes of learning and competence building in different aggregates, and the territorial, organizational and systemic configurations affecting the potential for innovation and economic development.

6. Identifying policy levers and coordinating activities available to governance at different levels – contributes to policy thinking. The overall design of Eurodite project entails multidisciplinary teams engaged in comparative research across Europe.

A review of the state of the art of the area of research of the project had identified the following research topics in reference to which the project aims to make advances in understanding:

• Increasing returns to scale. The functioning and results of knowledge processes in different sectors and regions that may produce increasing returns to scale, giving rise to corporate and regional lock-in and path-dependence.

- Knowledge and innovation. The nature of the relationship between knowledge and innovation – the latter seen as exploitation and application of knowledge in some new or enhanced way.
- Localized learning and tacit knowledge. The processes of localized, incremental learning that build stocks of tacit knowledge within firms and how these relate to (occasional) 'heroic' innovation breakthroughs.
- Collective learning. The mechanisms of collective learning and the mechanisms of internal and external inputs to knowledge such as through networks and 'spillover' and the balance between trust and power in knowledge relationships.
- The knowledge trade-off. The extent of the trade-off in economic benefit between protecting knowledge as a requisite for exploitation and the perceived good occurring through spillover and availability.
- Regions as closed and open systems. The extent to which regions, largely defined by administrative boundaries, represent a realistic system or a spatial unit worthy of analysis.
- Regional capabilities and lock-in. The question as to why some 'places' are able to adapt new trajectories while others cannot escape previous 'lock-in' – and the role of linkages to other spatial scales.
- New firms, new markets. The appropriateness of conventional business and employment models to the knowledge industries and the societal impacts.

2.4   THE ANTICIPATED IMPACT OF EURODITE

The strategic policy context, at European level, derived from the recommendations of prevailing EU Summit declarations concerned with improving European competitiveness whilst accommodating enlargement, preserving sustainability and the European social model (Lisbon, 2000; Göteborg, 2001; Barcelona, 2002). In particular it concerned: 'preparing the transition to a knowledge-based economy and society' (European Council, 2002: 2). It is important to note that by no means all of the aims, methods, research and outputs achieved by Eurodite are written up in this book. The aim of this book is to report on the firm, sector and regional knowledge flows discovered and to identify conceptual, methodological and policy models pertinent to that task. Nevertheless, the broader impact of the whole Eurodite project could in respect of this strategic context be considered sequentially.

Firstly, the project would, through quantitative and qualitative methodologies, contribute to an understanding of the processes through which knowledge is generated and deployed.

Secondly, it would unpack existing data on knowledge and innovation by showing the variety of circumstances that are likely to be present within each region, and produce typologies that will allow knowledge data to be assembled and presented in a more relevant and helpful form.

Thirdly, by generating a model of knowledge micro-dynamics and linking this to macro-dynamics, it would contribute to the effectiveness of policies at different levels of government. It would, for example, illuminate the relationship between knowledge and learning (local and collective), innovation, competitive performance and gender equality. This would enable public policy resources to be applied more effectively to the Lisbon and associated agendas.

Fourthly, it would identify the conditions that create different aggregate knowledge trajectories – both micro-conditions and aggregate contextual factors – and would facilitate better forecasting and design of policy levers.

2.4.1 Output

The output of the Eurodite project will be a series of policy observations and proposals regarding support for the development of the knowledge economy at regional level. Pilot actions to implement and validate these recommendations will be undertaken by individual development agencies via the EURADA network of European development agencies. This will in turn contribute to the European and national strategies to move towards a knowledge-driven economy and knowledge-based society. The growing homogeneity and integration of European economies means that it is essential these issues are examined at that scale.

2.5 CONTRIBUTION TO POLICY DEVELOPMENTS

2.5.1 Links to the Policy Community

Eurodite's exploitation and dissemination actions thus included presenting project results to policy audiences, including regional development professionals, at all levels, a pledge that was fully implemented at numerous policy workshops throughout the EU. Eurodite also organized, in conjunction with the EURADA network, three small-scale conferences that were open to all of Europe's development agencies and the project partners, and promoted through the Regional Studies Association. The themes were decided as the project proceeded but covered such matters of interest to policy-makers as 'clusters and clustering policies', 'regional knowledge assets' and 'the knowledge-based economy'. A major international conference, open to both the policy and academic communities, was scheduled for the end of the project.

2.5.2   Policy Outputs

The project will produce reports which will be in easily readable (non-academic) form and available to the multilevel policy community. Aside from the Final Report and Policy Recommendations a number of Interim Reports will be produced. These may cover such topics as:

- State of the Art Review of the Knowledge Economy and Policy Initiatives.
- Regional Data Review including gaps and issues for policy-makers.
- Review of the seven target business sectors and the knowledge economy.
- Review of 'Regions in the Knowledge Economy' including Regional Indicators.
- Review of the Case Study 'Innovation Biographies' Method.
- Gender Issues in the Knowledge Economy.

The project website will be both a means of communication and dissemination for the partnership and the outside academic and policy communities.

2.6   RESEARCH, TECHNOLOGICAL DEVELOPMENT AND INNOVATION ACTIVITIES

What follows here is the detail of the bid proposal showing the steps ('work packages') by which the anticipated results were to be achieved. Since it was a successful proposal there is heuristic value in reading it for those interested in such things. For those with interest in getting at the meat of what was discovered, swift transit to Chapter 3 and subsequent chapters is recommended.

Eurodite examined knowledge processes in different European regional and sectoral settings in relation to five specific knowledge contexts: the firm, networks, governance structures, the education and science system, and society. It pursued its objectives through the following interconnected components:

- Conceptual work programmes to provide state-of-the-art reviews and generate questions and hypotheses to inform the research framework.
- A sectoral research programme that will examine knowledge trends and drivers in seven key sectors with a particular emphasis on understanding knowledge value chains.
- A quantitative regional research programme, based on the social systems of innovation approach, which will examine regional diversity in terms of knowledge accumulation and trajectories.
- A qualitative regional research programme that will explore the economic, technological and social dimensions of 24 regions with respect to the knowledge economy.
- Knowledge process case studies at the firm and network level that trace the processes and actors involved in the use of new knowledge and development of learning processes in firms or groups of firms.
- A series of synthesis programmes that will bring together the findings of the sectoral, regional and case study work in the light of the conceptual framework developed at the beginning of the programme.

Detailed accounts of each work package (WP), and outputs, are provided below. The lead partner for each WP is also given.

2.6.1   Input Work Packages

These will be completed at the beginning of the programme. They provide the framework and background for later research and set up the research questions and hypotheses.

Work Package 1: knowledge overview

Objectives   Work Package 1 provided a state of the art account of knowledge economy and knowledge in economics literature. Three sub-work packages examining concepts of knowledge as an economic factor, the development of the knowledge economy and the evolution of knowledge-related policy (particularly that developed and delivered regionally) were undertaken in the first phases of the programme. These work packages reviewed and developed the state of the art in each of these areas and provided a framework for the completion of the rest of the project.

Structure and participants   This work package was composed of three subpackages each with its own lead partner. These include:

- WP1a: Knowledge in the Economy (Leader: C. Antonelli, Rosselli Foundation).
- WP1b: The Knowledge Economy (Leader: C. Collinge, University of Birmingham).
- WP1c: Knowledge Economy Policy (Leader: H. Halkier, University of Ålborg).

The entire work package was coordinated and led by C. Antonelli, Rosselli Foundation

Research approach Work Package 1a described the state of the art regarding knowledge in the economy across a range of disciplines. A multitheoretical framework was designed (Chapters 1 & 10), which underpinned the taxonomical and analytical aspects of the project. It also assisted the interpretation project findings. It was theoretical and relied on the state of the art review.

Work Package 1b examined the growth, structures and tools of the knowledge economy and the roles of knowledge workers. Using secondary data and literature it explored the defining features of the knowledge economy. In particular, it examined what is distinctive about the creation and consumption of knowledge in the twenty-first century.

Work Package 1c reviewed the changing role of policy in a multilevel governance framework. This was done primarily through a review of the literature supplemented by primary research to identify and map new forms of regional policy emerging in support of the knowledge economy (Chapter 12). The subpackage developed a systematic approach to the evaluation of knowledge-based policy initiatives and ensured that the policy dimension was fully and importantly integrated in the project.

Outputs and contribution to the project It identified the different ways in which knowledge is conceptualized across different social science disciplines and showed ways in which the connection of concepts in these disciplines can be pursued. It further provided the theoretical framework to inform the structure of the Integrated Project as a whole. The outputs were:

- state-of-the-art reviews;
- a multi-theoretical framework;
- a series of definitions and a taxonomy regarding types of knowledge and knowledge processes;
- review of the changing role of policy in a multilevel governance framework;
- identification and mapping of new forms of regional policy;

- a series of research questions and hypotheses that will be explored in the rest of the programme.

Work Package 2: knowledge contexts

Objectives   To enable Eurodite to yield findings about different aspects of the dynamics of knowledge, these were addressed through a framework concerning the firm, firm networks and markets, and their relations with the governance system, the education and science system, and the socio-cultural milieu. These contexts of knowledge production and consumption have differing implications for knowledge dynamics and as such must feature as key arenas in the research (Chapter 1).

Structure and participants   Each context was pursued through a sub-work package led by acknowledged leaders in each field. These include:

- WP2a: The Firm (Leader: B. Dankbaar, Radboud University of Nijmegen).
- WP2b: Markets and Networks (Leader: P. Cooke, Cardiff University).
- WP2c: Governance (Leader: R. Cappellin, University of Rome 'Tor Vergata').
- WP2d: Education and Science System (Leader: C. Antonelli, Foundation Rosselli).
- WP2e: Society and Culture (Leader: J. Subirats, Universitat Autònoma de Barcelona).
- WP2eii: Gender Issues (Leader: T. Rees, Cardiff University).

The entire work package was coordinated and led by B. Dankbaar, Radboud University of Nijmegen.

Research approach   Eurodite again aimed to examine knowledge dynamics within these particular contexts through state of the art literature reviews. Some limited empirical work is also envisaged. These reviews were used to organize the later case study work through the identification of research questions and hypotheses, to design the different phases of each case study and to analyse and assemble findings. They represented concentric contexts of questioning permitting macroscopic implications to be derived from specific micro-level processes.

Outputs and contribution to the project   Each work package addressed issues specific to the particular knowledge context in question but a shared methodology and reporting system sought to ensure standardized results. The outputs were:

- State-of-the-art reviews with regard to knowledge in relation to each of these contexts.
- Research questions and hypotheses to inform the sectoral, regional and firm case studies, for example Templates for WP3.

Following the case studies a synthesis process will be undertaken that will allow for further comments to be made with regard to each of these contexts based upon this primary research.

Core Research Work Packages

The core research work packages of Eurodite comprised a sectoral research programme, a regional research programme and a firm-level case study programme in support of the conceptual work packages outlined above (the focus of this book). At the heart of the programme were firm-based case studies focusing on 'knowledge and learning biographies'. These were situated within the context of a variety of sectoral and regional studies each exploring the role of different organizational forms, institutions and spatial arrangements in knowledge dynamics. The specific details of each work package were as follows.

Work Package 3: sectoral contexts

Objectives This 'spine' of the project was the use of knowledge for economic purposes. Eurodite therefore took the firm as the starting point, as the location where knowledge is produced or deployed, and converted for economic gain. In order to identify firms for the research it was appropriate first to establish their sectors. It was also proposed that sectoral studies be undertaken in order to inform the firm-based studies. The aim was to understand the trends and drivers of knowledge use in each sector.

Structure and participants Seven sectors were selected for study within Eurodite and it is from within these sectors that firms were selected to form the basis of the case studies. Sectoral experts were identified from within the partnership to lead on each sectoral overview. They comprised:

1. Automotive (U. Jürgens, WZB Berlin; S MacNeill, University of Birmingham).

2. Biotechnology (P. Cooke, Cardiff University; R Kaiser, TU Munich).
3. New Media (C. Collinge, University of Birmingham).
4. Food and Drink (J. Manniche, Center for Regional and Tourism Research).
5. ICT (J. Vicente, Université des Sciences Sociales de Toulouse).
6. Knowledge-Intensive Business Services (S. Strambach, Philipps-University Marburg).
7. Tourism (H. Halkier, Ålborg University).

The entire work package was coordinated and led by P. Cooke, Cardiff University.

Research approach   The research in this work package was based upon interrogation of literature and data sources at a European level. A small amount of primary research was envisaged in each sector. Specific research was designed to address the different nature of each sector. However, a common framework and methodology was provided by the results of the input work programmes outlined above. This included:

- An examination of the structural characteristics of each sector in regional economies in European countries.
- An examination of spatial proximity and the significance of intraregional and interregional linkages for each sector and their innovation processes.
- An analysis of the different pathways through which firms are developing in different sectors.
- An examination of the different linkages within sectors.
- An analysis of gender differentiations by sector and by knowledge trajectory.
- An analysis of the manner in which knowledge value chains operate across each sector.

Outputs and contributions to the project   Through the shared research framework this research provided a sectoral context for the firm case studies. Specifically it will produce:

- Individual sectoral reviews structured around a set of shared research questions.
- A framework to inform the construction of the primary research in WP6.

Work Package 4: comparative analysis of European regions

Objectives   The goal of this work package was to shed light on European regional diversity in knowledge accumulation through an examination of regional socio-economic characteristics and trajectories. It sought to develop new quantitative methodologies to explore regional knowledge dynamics and to identify new indicators to measure regional performance within the knowledge economy. This led to the identification of knowledge flow indicators and the creation of a knowledge scoreboard. Findings from this programme also informed the selection of regions for the regional case study programme. This was the detailed examination and statistical synthesis of European hard metrics.

Structure and participants   This work package was led by C. Carrincazeaux and Y. Lung from Université Montequieu Bordeaux IV. Other members, particularly those in the Executive Group, made contributions as appropriate.

Research approach   The work package was undertaken through a statistical analysis of regional knowledge indicators and interregional data. Research was informed by the social systems of innovation (SSI) approach – a combination of different components referring to science, technology and industry, and financial systems, labour relations, education and training and economic characteristics – which examined regional diversity in terms of knowledge accumulation and trajectories. Combining the SSI model with local economic performance was intended to allow the research to define different regional configurations in order to identify regional trajectories and patterns of articulation between knowledge dynamics and performance.

This statistical package aimed to pursue a number of different tasks:

- Analysis of available regional data including public and private science capacity, industry specialization, education level, activity rate by gender and urban structure to identify differing regional configurations. This regional mapping will be used to inform the selection of regions for the regional case studies in Work Package 5.
- The identification of new knowledge-related regional indicators and data in order to address the limits of a regional scoreboard based only on high-tech and innovation indicators. Two questions will be addressed:
    - Identification of existing complementary data at the European level (going back to national statistics).

- Identification of new indicators to be used in future surveys or data collection processes.
- A search and analysis of more specific national databases including patents and scientific publication databases in order to introduce knowledge flows to the regional configurations. National dimensions will be considered in close cooperation with the European Socio-Economic Models of a Knowledge-based Society (ESEMK) STREP project.
- Econometric treatments in order to test hypotheses to link regional diversity with convergence studies and to examine the existence of knowledge spillovers between adjacent advanced and less advanced regions.

Outputs and contribution to the project   The statistical analysis in this work package aimed to produce:

- A typology of regions based on existing indicators – regional knowledge indicators.
- A review of indicators for further study – and for use in policy development.
- A review of data collection and measurement and identification of social and economic trajectories.
- Classification and selection of regions for case studies in Work Package 5.

Work Package 5: regional case studies

Objectives   A key outcome of Work Package 4 was intended to be the identification and classification of regions in which the firm-level case studies could be conducted. In order to enhance the regional analysis generated from European scale quantitative data, Work Package 5 undertook case studies of these target regions based on regional level quantitative and qualitative data. This aimed to enable the specifics of the firm case studies to be understood in the light of their regional socio-economic configurations and trajectories. This was to be achieved by thorough regional case studies exploring organizational structure, historical and cultural surroundings, and the established institutions for education and research within each target region.

Structure and participants   This work package was led by O. Crevoisier, University of Neuchâtel. It was anticipated that all academic partners will undertake at least one regional case study.

Research approach These case studies explored the current position of each region with regard to the knowledge economy. Case study regions varied according to their knowledge economy circumstances. The studies focused on each region's:

- Economic dimension (its degree of path-dependency and coherence as a system or several separate systems, its position in transition to the knowledge economy and capacity for change).
- Technological dimension (main sectors, technologies, products/ services markets, firms and networks – know-how and competences, training/research institutions).
- Social dimension (socio-professional groups, type of firms – for example: subsidiaries of large groups or networks of SMEs embedded locally; channels for the creation, diffusion, appropriation of knowledge; place of regional, national or European public actions).

Alongside the creation of a baseline knowledge economy picture for each region there would also be an examination on the possible future trajectories of each region. This included:

- Identification of the changes in production systems in the region.
- Simultaneous identification of the territorialities involved in these changes (local and external resources, migration of specific work-forces, capital flows, local anchoring or knowledge flows).
- Identification of the changes in the social systems.
- Simultaneous identification of the territorialities involved in these social dynamics (interplay between local and external players; anchoring and exit behaviour of multinational firms).

These studies were pursued through programmes of interviews, examination of professional documentation and validation and discussion with working groups.

Outputs and contribution to the project

- Case study documents for each region.
- Findings to inform the firm-level case studies to be undertaken in each region in Work Package 6.

The results from Work Package 5 and were combined with other Eurodite work packages to produce regional case study syntheses exploring processes of regional learning and addressing the research question and hypotheses described above.

Work Package 6: firm-level case studies

Objectives Work Package 6 examined important knowledge and learning processes occurring within individual firms and groups of firms. Selected firms were drawn from sectors and regions as above. The aim was to explore the nature of knowledge processes and dynamics within the target groups of firms and trace the process of their origin and interaction within the firm and also in external sources and agents.

The objective was to consider the total life span of a knowledge or learning process – a knowledge biography. Questions to be addressed included:

- What caused the firm to search for new knowledge?
- How and where did the firm search for new knowledge?
- Which parts of the firm have been participating?
- Which sectoral or regional external agents or agencies were involved?

A specific objective was to find out what the main internal and external sources of new knowledge (for example firm, sectoral, regional, global) were, and how the flows of knowledge within the firm and between the firm and these external agents or agencies took place.

The issues identified from the input work packages informed this method. Case studies examined the role of processes specific to the firm in the creation and use of knowledge within the firm, and considered the role of networks and markets, governance structures, the education and science system, and societal norms and conventions in these processes.

Structure and participants This work package was led by E. Helmstädter and B. Widmaier, IAT, Nordrhein-Westfalen; A. Larsson, Göteborg University; O. Crevoisier, IRER, University of Neuchâtel; A. Burfitt, University of Birmingham. Academic partners undertook at least three sets of firm-level case studies.

Research approach The case studies were undertaken through qualitative research methods. Shared, but not standardized, interview and research tools were developed and piloted in the early stages of the project and partners received common training and instruction in these new methods. These tools were informed by the hypotheses and questions generated in Work Packages 1–3.

The firm case studies involved:

- Biographies of historical knowledge, innovation and learning process in the selected firm or group of firms.
- Biographies of firms associated with the knowledge process – analysis and understanding of the existing networks and infrastructure, description of the various complementary networks existing in the cluster considered and identification of the elements of the value chain.
- Audit of knowledge assets – biographies of key types of player associated with the knowledge process, mapping networks of experts and identification and formal description of the explicit and tacit technological competencies existing within the firms in the study.
- Studies of regional institutional contexts supporting the network of firms (much of this should have covered in the preceding regional case studies).

WP6 was piloted in the early part of the project in order to explore and define the case study method. The methodology was, in itself, a significant output from the work package.

Outputs and contribution to the project

- Methodology for analysing knowledge processes at the levels of firms, sectors and regions.
- Model of knowledge flow and dynamics built around the firm.
- Standardized set of knowledge flow indicators.
- Comparisons between cases and typologies created where the main characteristics of each case are generalized, adopting an inductive approach. The techniques of time-geography can be helpful in creating typologies and will be adopted in this context.
- Conclusions about the significance of proximity in innovation processes in different sectors and types of firm and the influence, if any, of different types of region.
- A model of the micro-dynamics of knowledge flow.

These outputs would be contained in a series of reports produced for each region. They will also be used in final reports for each sector and in reports for each of the knowledge contexts identified in the conceptual framework.

Output Research Work Packages

Work Package 7: regional synthesis

Objectives   The aim of Work Package 7 was to classify and analyse the case study results in order to make generalized statements regarding knowledge processes in different settings and contexts and also to begin to distil policy lessons. The objective was to represent the detailed interview data in a general form that made it possible to compare processes in different firms, branches and regions. The adoption of a shared research language and method throughout the research was intended to support this process.

Structure and participants   This work package was to be led by R. Cappellin, University of Rome 'Tor Vergata'; O. Crevoisier, IRER, University of Neuchâtel; M. Vale, University of Lisbon.

Research approach   The core of the regional synthesis process involved the construction of a method and a framework through which to analyse the firm case studies in their regional contexts. It consisted of four key processes:

- Employing a shared research framework across different firms, sectors and regions throughout the research.
- Classification of processes by key characteristics.
- Typology construction.
- Construction of a model of knowledge dynamics in different firms and regions.

For instance it was thought possible to classify the findings of each case study of knowledge processes in a particular firm or group of firms in a region within a framework structured around its:

- Spatial dimension, stressing the importance of common experiences, face-to-face contacts, and common cultural values.
- Knowledge dimension, stressing the need for incentives directly related to the knowledge base – for example revealing tacit knowledge, routinizing the use of learning tools, or analysing the comparable knowledge position in the market.
- Management dimension, stressing the need for a systematic orientation of all institutions to a process of continuous stimulus–response feedback processes.

Within these broad dimensions further components, relating to knowledge creation and learning, could be classified allowing for the construction of detailed typologies of firms and regions and also allowing for the development of knowledge flow models in different contexts.

The framework described above was drawn from the territorial knowledge management (TKM) approach. In this model all business processes involve creation, dissemination, renewal and application of knowledge toward organizational sustenance and survival. TKM provides a conceptual and quantitative framework that can guide the collection of quantitative indicators on the knowledge creation process and it allows an easy integration with the 'knowledge biographies' proposed approach to be adopted in this project (Chapter 12 of this book).

It was possible to develop the TKM approach for use as an organizing tool within the Eurodite project, proving it likely, accordingly, to be suitable for use with other similar frameworks alongside or in developing alternatives to synthesize the findings of multiple case studies and draw conclusions of policy relevance. This was discussed and developed as the project developed.

Outputs and contribution to the project

- Methodology for analysing firm-level case studies.
- Detailed regional syntheses incorporating regional and firm-level case study data.
- A typology of regional knowledge trajectories.

Work Package 8: sectoral synthesis

Objectives   Whilst Work Package 7 attempted to read across case studies in order to formulate conclusions regarding of knowledge flow and dynamics in different types of firm in different types of region, Work Package 8 sought to generate similar statements but at a sectoral rather than a regional level.

Structure and participants   This work package was led by P. Cooke, Cardiff University; S. Strambach, Philipps University Marburg; S. MacNeill, University of Birmingham. (Chapter 10 reports results of WP8).

Research approach   A similar framework for synthesizing the results in sectoral terms was used as that employed in the regional synthesis process, namely:

- Employing a shared research framework across different firms, sectors and regions.
- Classification of processes by key characteristics.
- Typology construction.
- Construction of a model of knowledge dynamics in different firms and regions.

More complex frameworks such as that proposed under TKM were developed with regard to the sectoral findings.

Outputs and contribution to project

- Detailed sectoral syntheses incorporating regional and firm-level case study data.
- A typology of sectoral knowledge trajectories.

Work Package 9: project summation

Objectives   This work package was intended to:

- Undertake overall collation and assembly of project results.
- Ensure final publication.
- Ensure final dissemination of findings.
- Undertake other activities as necessary.

Structure and participants   The work package was to be led C. Collinge, University of Birmingham; C. Antonelli, Fondazione Rosselli; R. Cappellin, University of Rome 'Tor Vergata'; O. Crevoisier, IRER, University of Neuchâtel; J. Subirats, Universitat Autònoma de Barcelona.

2.6.2   Demonstration Activities

Pilot actions
The outputs of the Eurodite project were a series of policy proposals to support the development of the knowledge economy at regional level. Pilot actions to implement and validate these recommendations were to be undertaken by individual development agencies via the EURADA network.

A part of the budget was allocated to part fund pilot programmes. These were intended to occur in the final two years of the project which ends in August 2010.

Individual agencies were to provide funding to match that from the project. The offer to work with Eurodite to pilot policy proposals was to be extended, as appropriate, to additional regional development agencies via the EURADA Management Board.

It was not possible to anticipate the exact nature of the pilot activities but they were thought likely to include:

- New targeted business development grants for small and medium-sized (SMEs) entering or developing the knowledge economy.
- SME development 'contracts' for innovation and knowledge processes.
- Regional actions to link universities and business.
- Gender specific actions for women in the workforce or women 'returners' to the labour force.
- Area regeneration initiatives to encompass the knowledge economy and reduce exclusion.

The pilot actions were to be managed by the agencies concerned and overseen by the coordinators supported by the Executive Group. Evaluation of the pilots would be overseen by the implementing agencies and the Eurodite Executive Group. Independent consultants were to be appointed by the agencies to undertake evaluation and to produce assessments.

3. Production–consumption models and knowledge dynamics in the food and drinks sector

Jesper Manniche

3.1 INTRODUCTION

Until the 1970s the development of the economic and social systems through which food and drinks were grown, processed, marketed and sold was an uncontested productivist modernization project based on growing mass markets for standardized products. Neo-Marxist researchers in the 1970s presented a criticism of capitalist 'food commodity systems' and 'agro-industrial complexes' using analytical concepts in line with the 'agrarian question' problematic of classical Marxism (Watts and Goodman, 1997). However, since the beginning of the 1990s the prevailing industrial agro-food model has been subject to a much broader criticism and public debate. Food-related issues like obesity, health, lifestyle-related diseases, food safety, environment protection, animal welfare, the effects of genetically modified organisms on nature and humans, the decline of rural economies, protection of regional culinary traditions, global imbalances in food supplies and principles of international trade policies are all subjects for intensive political and ethical debates.

Furthermore, in economical business terms the dominating industrial food model has recently been challenged by the emergence and growth of a variety of new food markets, supplied by new types of businesses models and networks, emphasizing other definitions of quality than price, efficiency and standardization. Despite their limited economic weight these new food markets and business models represent important directions for the future development of the food and drinks (F&D) sector.

Two emerging business models seem to be relevant alongside the mainstream, industrial food model: the 'alternative' and the 'functional' food models. 'Alternative' food covers different products with rather fuzzy, symbol-laden qualities such as organic, local, speciality, high-quality, slow and fair trade food. Alternative food producers emphasize the abandonment or at least a reduced use of production inputs stemming from the industrial model of farming and food processing, and generally rely on traditional, often artisanal technologies. Functional food represents almost the opposite, a science-driven strategy of taking advantage of new biotechnologies and other advanced technologies in designing and producing food and drinks products with specific health, diet and nutritional benefits for consumers. Hence, the knowledge bases and knowledge dynamics of 'industrial', 'alternative' and 'functional' food networks seem to have significant differences.

The chapter is organized as follows. Section 3.2 describes the overall structures and change processes in the sector. Section 3.3 presents a theoretical framework for studying the emerging new food production–consumption models, depicts the main features of the three different food models, and outlines the typical innovation efforts and responses within the models. Section 3.4 looks at the specific knowledge categories and dynamics in the different models. Brief conclusions are provided in section 3.5.

3.2   OVERALL STRUCTURE AND TRENDS OF THE SECTOR

3.2.1   Structural Characteristics of the F&D Sector

The F&D sector is here defined as the food and drinks manufacturing industries at the two-digit level of the economic activity classification NACE-Rev. 1, that is, DA15. Sometimes a broader term, the 'agro-food sector/industry', is also used, including the whole food supply chain from agricultural and fishery activities to distribution and retailing.

The F&D sector is the largest manufacturing sector in the EU. In 2005 it accounted for 14 per cent of total turnover, 12 per cent of total value-added, and 13 per cent of total employment in manufacturing (CIAA, 2006). The activity of the F&D sector is less cyclical and more stable than manufacturing in general, due to the relatively static demand for food products. In general, however, employment in the industry is declining in Europe due to increased competition from low-income countries, technological development and restructuring initiatives of companies.

Four manufacturing industries dominate the sector: meat products accounts for 20 per cent, dairy products for 16 per cent, beverages for 15 per cent, and 'various food products' including bakery, chocolate and confectionary products, pasta and baby food for 26 per cent of total turnover

(CIAA, 2006). The industry of 'various food products' has experienced the highest growth rates since 1989 (CIAA, 2004). In terms of export figures, the beverages industry – including wine production – is the most important, in 2003 accounting for 31 per cent of all EU food and drink exports (CIAA, 2004).

The sector encompasses a diverse range of companies from multinationals such as Nestlé (the largest in Europe) with around 250 000 employees and a variety of product lines and production units, to micro family businesses employing only the owner and maybe a few family members and manufacturing only one product category. According to CIAA (2006), 99 per cent of the total 282 600 companies in Europe were small and medium-sized enterprises (SMEs) with less than 250 employed and accounting for 61 per cent of the total 3.8 million employees and 48 per cent of the total €836 billion turnover in the industry.

The sector is more labour-intensive than manufacturing as a whole. However, the labour productivity varies widely by country and the disparity has increased further with the accession of new member states. Labour productivity also varies highly by size of company – the largest companies have the highest productivity.

Despite the ongoing processes of globalization of food supply chains by which supplies of raw materials, ingredients and processed products are increasingly transported and distributed over long distances, the F&D sector still has a highly dispersed localization pattern in which rural areas play an important role. Moreover, in at least ten EU countries the sector is ranked as the number one manufacturing sector in terms of turnover (CIAA, 2006) and thus plays a significant role in maintaining industrial activities throughout Europe.

3.2.2   Trends and Drivers of Change

The main drivers of change in the sector are:

- new consumer demands.
- supply chain restructuring.
- technological development.
- new regulations and policies.

New consumer demands
Consumption of food and drinks is a central element of the cultures and everyday life of people all over the world. Eating and drinking plays a decisive role in the basic social and cultural rituals, traditions and communicational patterns within families; ethnic, territorial and religious

communities; and other social groups. Markets of food and drinks products are strongly interconnected with specific needs and the occasions of
customers' everyday and festive life. Despite a regular change characteristic of such consumption patterns and food cultures, overall growth in
incomes and trends in societies, cultures and lifestyles are changing the
demand for food and drinks. In the following, a number of consumer
trends affecting food markets are briefly described.

Demographic changes   The European population is expected to decrease
from 455.2 million in 2005 to 431.2 million in 2050, while the share that is
aged over 60 years will increase (EMCC, 2006a). This limits the potential
for growth but also increases the demand for products designed to match
special nutritional needs for older people.

New lifestyles and family patterns   The development towards longer
working hours, more leisure activities and more families with two working
parents has increased the demand for semi-prepared, convenience food
mainly in the form of fresh or frozen products rather than traditional
dehydrated and canned food products (EMCC, 2006b). Also eating out
(food services and catering) is a fast-growing market. In 2000, half of the
amount spent on food in the USA was spent on eating away from home,
while the share in most European countries was less than a third but
growing.

Food safety   Boosted by for example the BSE crisis in 1996, foot and
mouth disease in 2001, and avian flu in Europe in 2006, consumers have
become very aware of safety of food. For example, a 70 per cent drop in
poultry consumption was seen in Italy after the avian flu in 2006.[1] Other
more local safety problems are contaminated food bacteria such as salmo-
nella, campylobacter and E. coli. The sector experiences severe mistrust
from consumers, who expect industry and governments to come up with
solutions.

Healthy living   Consumers are increasingly concerned about problems
related to obesity, nutrition, food-related diseases, and the effects on
human health of genetically modified organisms (GMOs). Such concerns
have increased the demand for, for instance, organic food (KPMG, 2000).
Despite increased awareness of obesity and health, European consumers (compared to Americans) are still sceptical regarding GMOs and the
use of biotechnology in farming and food processing (Key Note, 2004).
Also regarding health issues, consumers expect industry to come up with
solutions.

Sustainability   Consumers are increasingly aware not only of quality of the food products as such but also of issues related to the production processes and globalization of supply chains, such as the environmental impact of production and distribution, degradation of local food cultures, animal welfare, safety, fair trade and working conditions.

Growth in niche markets   Food markets are increasingly segmented and specialized in the direction of, for instance, ethnic food, organic food vegetarian food, and local food, and this specialization trend also gives opportunities for small food producers.

Supply chain restructuring
The food supply chain consists basically of four links: (1) producers (farmers, fishermen and other suppliers); (2) processors (manufacturing industries); (3) retailers; and (4) consumers. The relationships between these four links and the dynamics and power structures that rule the actions of actors are under fundamental change (Hornibrook and Fearne 2005). According to Folkerts and Koehorst (1998), the food supply chain has been reversed from a production-driven (product push) chain with little coordination and loose relationships between the individual links, towards a market-driven (demand pull) chain with strong upstream vertical coordination mechanisms between the individual links.

One of the main factors driving this chain reversal and shifting the power balance from food processors to retailers is the ongoing concentration in the retail link, through which a relatively small number of supermarket chains have gained an immense importance in distribution and sale, and thus in the food supply chain as a whole. In 2002, supermarkets held the dominant position in sales of food, with 62 per cent of total sales in the USA and 56 per cent in Western Europe, and in most countries such sales figures are to a large extent the result of only a handful of huge retail companies. According to Millstone and Lang (2003), estimations from the UK show that half the food consumed by 57 million mouths is purchased in just 1000 stores.

The central role of supermarkets in the sale of food gives them negotiating power to influence suppliers' prices and in general to define the standards for product quality, safety and traceability, environmental impact, terms of delivery, and so on. The electronic point of sale barcode scanning system allows supermarkets to minimize their stocks and to order from suppliers only as is required and calculated on the basis of actual sales figures. Thereby supermarkets exert an enormous power over the food supply chain, which has changed from an economic system of 'selling what is produced' to one of 'producing what is sold'.

Technological development

Automation of plants and processes and new technologies are paving the way for more efficient forms of production and the development of new products. Mergers and acquisitions in the sector lead to increased investments in information and communication technology (ICT) tools to coordinate uniform data exchange across multiple production sites. Key new technologies in the sector are:

- biotechnology;
- new ICT tools for information sharing;
- e-business solutions;
- radio frequency identification;
- robotics and sensor technologies;
- nanotechnology.

Such technological development impacts on the workforce demand. The overall decrease in employment will continue in the coming years; however, some jobs will shift into services like customer services and logistics. There is increasing demand for more skilled types of labour including specialists in legislation, engineering and microbiology, and people with broader competences in reporting, communication, marketing and so on. At the lower end of the workforce there is a need for qualifications relevant to quality control and food safety.

New regulation and policies

The sector has historically been heavily embedded in national and regional agro-food policy and institutional frameworks regulating agricultural production, research and development (R&D) and innovation activities, education and training systems, working conditions, food safety control and so on. More recently, the international level of regulation has become highly important, reflecting the increasingly global character of the agro-food economic system as well as of the publicly debated problems and challenges. Relevant international regulation initiatives include:

- International trade liberalization facilitating market access, reducing export subsidies, import barriers and domestic subsidies.
- EU enlargement: for old EU states, EU enlargement means increased competition but also new markets.
- The 2004 reform of the EU Common Agricultural Policy (CAP). Policy instruments have been moved from price and production subsidies to more comprehensive farmer income support linked to

performance with respect to environmental standards, food safety, animal welfare standards, land use standards, and so on. In combination with globalization – that is, elimination of external trade barriers – this means increased competition and lower sales prices for the food industry, in particular for segments closest to agriculture such as sugar processing and dairies.

- EU and national legislation on food safety and hygiene standards are among the top issues of the political agenda, boosted by for example the BSE crisis in 1996, foot and mouth disease in 2001, and avian flu in Europe in 2006. National and EU initiatives have been launched to increase consumer confidence. They affect all links in the food supply chain, by requiring procedures to ensure that illnesses are not transmitted, food products are traceable and procedures are documented.
- EU environmental regulation regarding pollution, emission and disposal of waste, animal by-products, energy and resource savings and so on.
- EU animal welfare regulation sets requirements and standards for the breeding and transportation of living animals.
- EU certification and labelling schemes for the protection of food and drinks with a recognizable geographic origin, that is, the Protected Designation of Origin (PDO) and the Protected Geographical Indication (PGI).
- The EU LEADER programme for development and economic diversification in rural areas embodies the 'new rural policy paradigm' that is often emphasized as an important political framework supporting the emergence of 'alternative food networks' (Marsden, 1998; Marsden et al., 2000; Renting et al., 2003).

Implementation of the multifaceted range of new regulation demands in the food sector adds to costs in relation to administration and documentation as well as to investment in new equipment and adaptation of existing facilities to comply with requirements for hygiene standards, emission controls and so on. In general, large companies with administrative, technical and financial resources are better equipped than SMEs to implement the legislative requirements, while micro-firms are often exempted from regulations. Many food firms in the new EU member countries struggle to survive due to EU requirements and are subject to acquisition by Western firms. For example, according to EMCC (2006b), only 127 of 1513 meat processors in Poland in 2004 were licensed to export to the EU and no more than 1000 were expected to end up complying with EU safety regulations.

3.3　BUSINESS RESPONSES TO DRIVERS OF CHANGE

3.3.1　Emergence of New Food Production–Consumption Models

In many respects, including applied knowledge and technologies, the food sector is too diversified to describe and categorize as one homogenous type of economic activity with only one way of responding to changes in market conditions. In terms of economically important indicators like production outputs, turnover and employment, a paramount part of the food sector belongs to what is often analysed under the designation of the 'conventional' food industry (Sonnino and Marsden, 2006; Morgan and Murdoch, 2000; Green and Foster, 2005). However, one crucial driver of contemporary change in food markets is the so-called 'quality turn' of consumers in Western countries (Goodman, 2002; Goodman, 2004; Ilbery and Kneafsey, 2000; Hinrichs, 2000; Harvey et al., 2004), that has given rise to the emergence and growth of a variety of new food markets based on differentiation of the products from their mainstream, industrial 'cousins'.

In turn, this development has provoked a discussion in the academic literature about the question of a possible paradigm shift in agro-food systems, mainly with a point of departure in the proclamation of the rise of an 'alternative' food production–consumption model, and mainly stemming from rural sociology and economic and cultural geography (see for instance Marsden, 1998; Murdoch et al., 2000; Watts and Goodman, 1997; Watts et al., 2005; Renting et al., 2003; Ilbery and Kneafsey, 2000; Ilbery et al., 2005; Hein et al., 2006; Hinrichs, 2000; Winter, 2003; Sonnino and Marsden, 2006).

In order to understand and describe contemporary changes in agro-food economic systems such as the 'turn to quality' among consumers and food businesses, a growing number of agro-food scholars apply 'convention theory' (Murdoch and Miele, 2004; Murdoch et al., 2000; Ilbery and Kneafsey, 2000; Lindkvist and Sánchez, 2008). According to convention theory, which is related to actor-network theory, supply chains of farmers, processors, retailers, consumers, public authorities, R&D organizations, and so on are considered as 'network configurations, formed through processes of negotiation between differing entities and discursive formations' on the basis of differing 'repertoires of justification' (Murdoch and Miele, 2004). Hence, convention theory emphasizes that development, production, marketing and consumption of food is part of social and cultural discourses and interactive practices through which conventions regarding quality are constructed and justified. This, for example, could be the specific criteria for labelling products as 'organic' or 'local'. By looking at the conventions of quality that define food production and consumption systems, we are able to identify important keywords useful for specifying the categories of knowledge, technologies and learning processes prevailing in such systems.

Most scholars studying contemporary food networks seem to agree on the significance on the following quality conventions, originally suggested by Thevenot et al. (2000):

- 'Market worth', which evaluates worth based on the price, profitability, or commercial value of products in a competitive market.
- 'Industrial worth', which evaluates goods according to standards of technical efficiency and reliability.
- 'Civic worth', which refers to the worth of goods in terms of their general societal benefits.
- 'Domestic worth', which is largely based on trust and involves goods which can draw upon attachments to place and traditional modes of production.
- 'Inspiration worth', which refers to evaluations based on passion, emotion or creativity.
- 'Public opinion worth', which refers to the recognition and opinion that customers attach to trademarks, brands and packaging.
- 'Green' or 'environmental worth', which considers the general good of the collective to be dependent upon the general good of the environment.

Due to clearly identifiable differences in knowledge dynamics we will here look at three competing food production–consumption models, emphasizing different combinations of the above-listed quality conventions and with differing – though definitely not separate and contrary – knowledge and technology bases:

- 'Industrial food', in which the distinctive conventions of quality and competitive factors are price and efficiency and in which synthetic knowledge is decisive.
- 'Alternative food', in which domestic, green and inspiration qualities are crucial and in which symbolic knowledge plays a crucial role.
- 'Functional food', emphasizing health and nutritional effects and in which the core knowledge base is analytical.

These food models do not define non-overlapping segments of businesses and may not be useful in categorizing individual firms in all their activities and product lines. For instance, companies like Nestlé, Unilever and Kraft rely on brands of industrial commodity products but increasingly also engage in organic ('alternative') as well as functional food markets. Rather, the suggested models represent ideal types of food production and comsumption. The crucial factor lying behind the categorization is not necessarily connected with physical and tangible differences in products and productions as such, but rather with the somewhat fuzzy and socially constructed conventions of quality that are targeted in the development, production, marketing and consumption of 'industrial', 'alternative' and 'functional' food products.

The very emergence of alternative and functional food can be considered a business response to the changing production and market conditions in the sector outlined above. Alternative and functional food networks are two emerging production and business models that play rather insignificant roles in the total agro-food economy but nonetheless represent important directions for the future development of the food sector and already heavily influence the innovation efforts of mainstream, industrial producers in 'greener', 'healthier' and other directions.

In the following, the three food models are described in more detail. A particular focus is on those types of innovation efforts and responses to the drivers of change, outlined above, that characterize the models.

3.3.2 The Industrial Food Model: Characteristics and Responses to Change

Green and Foster (2005) highlight the following characteristics of the industrial food model that describe well the close relations between the production and consumption dimensions emphasized by convention theory: industrial food is based on raw materials produced by use of industrial agricultural practices exploiting advanced breeding techniques and major inputs of chemical fertilizers and pesticides, is transport-intensive, requires high-energy processing based on Fordist production technologies and organizational principles, relies on modern retailing systems and demands high-tech kitchens.

Among the different qualities that are embedded in products, price is the main distinctive quality on the basis of which industrial food products are produced, marketed and purchased.[2] Other qualities related to market performance and industrial efficiency, such as products' durability, safety and hygiene standard, seasonal uniformity and geographical accessibility, are important too however.

A number of factors such as increased liberalization of trade policies (not least relevant for firms closest to agriculture like sugar producers, dairies and meat producers), increased competition from low-income countries, the growing power of supermarkets, and technological developments, all together intensify the competition among industrial producers on price factors. This in turn enhances their focus on economics of scale and increases the advantages of large-scale technologies and distribution systems. This, in turn, leads to accelerated restructuring in the form of:

- Internal rationalization and productivity raising initiatives (automation of production, optimization of logistical infrastructure, energy savings and so on).
- Acquisitions and mergers to gain economics of scale and expand markets.
- Horizontal partnerships between food processing firms for delivery of supplies to retailers.
- Outsourcing and re-localization to low-income countries to focus on core competences and cut costs.

However, industrial food is not solely produced and consumed on the basis of efficiency and price factors. According to CIAA (2006), the targets for product innovation widely recognized as central by the F&D industry (CIAA, 2006) are qualities like 'pleasure', 'taste', 'sophistication', 'exotism', 'fun' and 'convenience'; that is, sensory and/or social attraction factors.[3] And in terms of product innovation, developing attraction factors such as taste, flavour, convenience and aesthetic aspects of the packaging is the main response of industrial food producers to survive in their markets.

Having said this, it must be emphasized that industrial food producers have to balance attraction factors with price and efficiency factors when deciding whether or not to introduce a new product or technology. Firms with specialized products are not to the same degree dependent on price factors and can, in the extreme case, focus one-sidedly on attraction factors.

Due to new regulative requirements and growing consumer awareness of environmental aspects of food production, 'green' conventions of quality are also increasingly important concerns for industrial food producers. These concerns are reflected in the adaptation and development of less polluting and resource-demanding processing technologies, for instance through use of new types of ingredients and additives as well as information technology (IT) and sensor systems for controlling processing. Awareness of green quality conventions are also reflected in firms' communication, public relations (PR) and marketing strategies, that increasingly put priority on specifying the raw materials and technologies used, the efforts of reducing the environmental impact, the environment-friendly principles and values of the business, and so on.

A similar background in the need for responses to new regulation and market demands is seen in relation to safety and hygiene issues, which can be classified as a quality convention linked to industrial efficiency and the technical reliability of products. As in firms' responses to green demands from regulation and consumers, the focus of responses to safety issues is not only on isolated working tasks and processes in the individual firm, but on the whole supply chain in which it takes part. Information systems for documentation of the fulfilment of quality standards in production, storage and distribution, and the demand for traceability of foodstuff along the whole supply chain, is of central importance for EU and national safety legislation as well as for the so-called Hazard Analysis and Critical Control Point (HACCP) certification that international supermarket chains have introduced and increasingly force their suppliers to comply with (Flynn et al., 2003).

Finally, the quality convention of 'public opinion' also has increasing importance. The segmentation of markets and consumers' general mistrust in the sector due to a number of recent food scandals, as well as their growing concerns for the environment and healthy living, challenge manufacturers to adjust and dedicate their products to diverse customer groups as well as to more strategic, interactive forms of communication and PR. For this they need to develop closer contact with customers to get information on market developments and to spot trends. Among the more innovative methods of building stronger and more trust-based relations with consumers is through electronic web-dialogue, e-logistic distribution systems and, maybe more relevant for small firms, direct sales.

The most frequently used strategy to ensure consumers' loyalty and trust, especially exploited among the large multinational corporations (MNCs) that in many respects dominate industrial food production–consumption networks, is the traditional one of product brands connecting certain features of the product with certain consumer lifestyles and aspirations, by use of marketing tools such as images and positioning in advertisements. Branding is a strategy that reflects the situation of industrial food production, confronted with many complicated and multifaceted quality demands, and through which firms try to integrate a number of quality conventions such as industrial efficiency reliability, inspiration, and green and civic qualities in one brand, one logo and so on. Branding, however, can also be risky. The value of a brand can quickly erode if associated with a scandal, or just with a negative consumer trend. In such cases firms need to refocus their brand. A successful example of this is Nestlé's recent change of its brand from a baby to a nutrition focus (CIAA, 2006).

3.3.3 The Alternative Food Model: Characteristics and Responses to Change

What is here grouped in one cluster of 'alternative food' in fact consists of several types of food networks with differing main conventions of quality like, for example, organic, local, high-quality, speciality, slow food and fair-trade food. The emergence of all these strongly symbol-laden and often premium-priced types of food is subject to a huge and fast-growing body of academic literature, often using 'alternative food networks' as a common designation (for example Marsden et al., 2000; Parrott et al., 2002; Renting et al., 2003; Ilbery et al., 2005; Watts et al., 2005; Sonnino and Marsden, 2006; Hein et al., 2006, Tesla and Massa, 2008).

The emerging alternative food networks represent a number of artisanal, entrepreneurial, social and territorially embedded business responses to growing public concerns about issues like environmental sustainability, health and food safety, the degeneration of territorial food cultures[4] and the decline of traditional agro-food economies in rural areas.

Producers of alternative food respond to new customer demands through differentiating their products from mainstream food commodities by claiming to provide 'alternative' qualities. These might stem from the raw materials, the production methods, the distribution channels or the principles for trading and payment of suppliers applied by the individual company or by the whole supply chain in which it takes part. This alternativeness results in those specific qualities that, according to the socially constructed conventions of quality prevailing in the production–consumption networks, are defined as attractive. This could be inspiration factors like better tastes and richer eating and drinking experiences (in particular emphasized in speciality products); domestic factors like preservation of gastronomic and culinary traditions and support to local economies and supply chains (emphasized by producers of local and regional food products); green qualities such as less pollution of the environment, more animal-friendly breeding methods and healthier products (the primary focus areas of organic producers); or civic qualities such as socially fairer payment principles and economic structures (in focus for 'fair trade' networks).

Nowadays, a common feature of producers of alternative food is the abandonment or at least a reduced use of production inputs stemming from the industrial model of farming and food processing. For example, this could be no or less use of pesticides and genetically modified organisms in the growing of crops; no or less chemical additives used in processing; no 'mistreating' of natural raw materials by use of industrial process technologies as in the homogenization of milk; and so on.

Instead of standardized, generic commodity inputs from global, industrial agro-food systems, alternative producers tend to rely on – at the risk of oversimplifying the findings from a number of research case studies (see for instance Ilbery and Kneafsey, 2000; Ilbery et al., 2005; Hinrichs, 2000; Hein et al., 2006; Parrott et al., 2002; Murdoch et al., 2000; Tesla et al., 2008) – local culinary traditions and knowledge; more dedicatedly grown and processed commodities; small-scale artisanal processing technologies in which the human senses are used for surveillance and quality control; and distribution systems that are local or otherwise alternative to international supermarket retailers such as direct sales, local retailers, tourist sites and delicatessen shops – all together signalling that products are handled with human care and attention.

The terms 'alternative', 'local', 'organic', 'fair trade' and so on, as well as the ways companies differentiate themselves according to diverse definitions of 'alternativeness', are indeed ambiguous and open to symbolic meanings and values rather than based on objective, scientifically measurable criteria such as specific requirements for hygiene standards or calorie content. This ambiguity is an important part of the reasoning behind applying convention theory in explaining contemporary trends in the food sector. How to define 'organic food', 'local food', 'slow food' and so on are continuously negotiated in the social networks of farmers, processors, retailers, consumers, distributors, researchers, public authorities, politicians and so on that constitute the production–consumption system.

One of the strategies for 'fixation' of the quality convention, which can be regarded as a form of protection of intellectual property rights similar to the use of brand trademarks or patents, is setting up certification schemes and formal criteria for the achievement of such regarding particular types of products. These could be government- or industry-defined labelling schemes for organic products; EU's schemes for protection of food and drinks with a recognizable geographic origin, the Protected Designation of Origin (PDO) and the Protected Geographical Indication (PGI); or supermarkets' introduction of private label brands to guarantee, for instance, certain health, safety and environmental standards or fair trade principles.

A number of analyses (Parrott et al., 2002; Marsden et al., 2000; Ilbery et al., 2005) have found big differences throughout Europe in firms' use of EU's PDO and PGI certificates. A total of 75 per cent of products granted a PDO or PGI certification in 2001 originated in peripheral, rural areas of the Southern and Mediterranean countries of France, Italy, Portugal, Greece and Spain, while only very few firms in Northern Europe such as the UK, the Netherlands and the Nordic countries had applied for and attained certification.

Parrott et al. (2002) provide two possible explanations of the varying popularity of territorial certification schemes: cultural-institutional and structural-economical. The cultural-institutional is related to the meaning and values, primarily prevailing in Southern Europe, attached to the territory as a combination of culture, history, tradition, production process, terrain, climate and local knowledge systems, and captured by the French concept of *terroir*. The EU certification schemes derive much of their reasoning and legitimacy from this concept (Watts et al., 2005). Parrot et al. also hypothesize the existence of two contrasting European food cultures: a 'Southern' with a wealth of local and regional food specialities, and a functional, commodity-driven 'Northern'.

The structural-economical explanation highlights the different economic structures and level of industrialization of the agro-food sectors in rural areas of Southern and Northern Europe. For small and technologically less-advanced farms and food processing firms in the South the PDO and PGI schemes seem to offer attractive new market opportunities and access to urban consumers, while they represent less attractive opportunities in rural areas of Northern Europe, characterized by an industrialized, technologically advanced and volume-oriented agro-food sector as well as by less rich – or maybe rather, not primarily locally defined – culinary traditions to exploit commercially.

Many alternative food firms and networks have been innovative in exploiting new technologies like ICT and the Internet in new forms of interactive sales and distribution channels where food and drinks are purchased on the Internet by customers and delivered directly to their door. Another innovative strategy regarding distribution and sales is opening of the manufacturing site to tourists and other visitors and providing it with, for instance, a shop for direct sales, exhibition facilities and possibilities for guided tours. Thus, parts of the alternative food sector develop inspiration factors through a sector shift towards tourism and take advantage of the trend towards the increased importance of storytelling in the emerging 'experience economy'.

Alternative food producers – and especially producers of local and regional food – often emphasize the local supply and knowledge base, that is, domestic qualities. It is often stated in the rapidly growing literature on alternative food networks that these can be seen as efforts to re-establish territorially embedded food supply chains and, thus, as a relocalization countertrend to the delocalization trend in industrial food provision systems (Marsden, 1998; Winter, 2003; Morgan and Murdoch, 2000; Watts et al., 2005).

However, there are indications that alternative products are increasingly sold via conventional retail systems and that supermarket chains are increasingly aware of the sales potential of more standardized types of alternative products like organic dairy, meat and vegetable products (Hein et al., 2006; Ilbery and Maye, 2006; Key Note, 2004; ACNielsen, 2005; Commission of the European Communities, 2004). More generally, there is increasing attention in research on alternative food networks to the question of to what extent and in which ways alternative products and productions are in fact alternative, and not just complementary to industrial food products (see for instance Sonnino and Marsden, 2006; Watts et al., 2005).

3.3.4   The Functional Food Model: Characteristics and Responses to Change

Functional food (or nutraceuticals) can be broadly classified into products naturally containing health-giving active ingredients, those fortified with extra levels to those already present, and those enriched with active ingredients not normally contained in them (Key Note, 2004).

According to Menrad (2003), in Germany functional food products have mainly been launched in markets for soft drinks, confectionary (for example chewing gum for dental hygiene), dairy, bakery, breakfast cereals, baby food and cholesterol-lowering spreads. The biggest product category on the European market for functional food is currently gut health products, in particular drink yogurts.

Compared to the artisanal, low-tech and somewhat 'return to nature' strategy employed by the diverse range of alternative food networks, functional food represents a 'forward to science' strategy. Functional food represents a science-driven model of food provision where new genomic and microbiology knowledge as well as bio- and nanotechnologies are used in the design and production of products. The critical convention of quality defining functional food markets is related to the health and nutritional effects of products, that is, specific technical functionalities of the products which can be placed under the quality convention of 'industrial worth'.

Hence, functional food does not entail a total break with the industrial food model (Menrad, 2003). On the contrary, as noted by Green and Foster (2005), functional food 'is still based on high outputs in agriculture and processing within internationally-organised production and trade'.

The importance of economics of scale factors (industrial efficiency) is clearly mirrored in the fact that the companies driving the emergence of functional foods to a large extent are large MNCs such as Unilever, Nestlé, Danone, Kellogg, Novartis and Quaker Oats, or national category leaders within, for instance, the dairy or ingredient sectors. Such companies have the needed financial resources, the R&D departments and the in-house expertise in nutrition and food technology to accomplish the long and demanding process of developing and marketing functional foods. According to Menrad (2003), the costs of product development and marketing of functional foods far exceed the costs related to the development and marketing of traditional food products. In addition to product development there are often huge costs and long-lasting procedures related to achieving proof of the efficacy of functional food through clinical tests such as intervention studies with high numbers of consumers or patients.

Besides qualities related to product functionality and industrial efficiency, green quality conventions related to environmental sustainability are also important for the emergence of functional food; however, interpreted and followed very differently compared to alternative food networks. The functional food model takes seriously the criticisms of the environmentally destructive nature of modern high-productivity agriculture, and claims to solve environmental and human health problems by using new genomic knowledge and 'smart' biotechnologies with less negative environmental side-effects.

Contrary to the alternative food model, however, the claim of green qualities and promotion of environmental sustainability seems to cause problems rather than growth potential. Consumers, particularly in Europe (Menrad, 2003; ACNielsen, 2005; EMCC, 2006a; Gehlhar and Regmi, 2005), generally have a negative view of the use of genetically modified crops and ingredients in the agro-food sector (while they are positive in relation to their use in the production of pharmaceutical products) and have fears about their effects on nature as well as on humans.

This situation means that winning bigger market shares might be an uphill struggle for functional food producers, and that public opinion and marketing initiatives will be crucially important. Contrary to alternative food products, which often seem to carry 'symbolic capital' in terms of green, inspiration and domestic qualities positively evaluated by major consumer segments, functional food needs targeted and strategic public information and marketing campaigns to gain a positive evaluation among consumers. Opinion leaders in the field of health and nutrition issues like medical doctors, dieticians and other nutritional advisors are a major target group for such campaigns (Menrad, 2003). On the other hand, the trends towards healthy living and the demographic development towards more aged people are in favour of functional food.

Finally, maybe unexpectedly considering the emphasis of functional food on their technical functionality in terms of health benefits, several studies indicate (for example Key Note, 2004; Menrad, 2003) that inspiration quality factors like taste, flavour, convenience and packaging are also important for consumers of functional food.

Table 3.1 sums up the main characteristics of the three models of

Table 3.1   Characteristics of food production–consumption models

	Industrial	Alternative	Functional
Quality conventions	• Price/ profitability • Industrial efficiency (e.g. safety, durability, accessibility) • Inspiration (taste, convenience) • Brand (public opinion)	• Domestic (gastronomy, culinary heritage, traditional production methods) • Green • Inspiration (taste, eating experience)	• Industrial efficiency and functionality in terms of health, well-being and nutrition • Green/ sustainability • Inspiration (taste, convenience)
Drivers of change	• Increased price competition • New customer demands (safety, green, convenience) • Supermarkets growing power • Regulation (safety, environment, working conditions)	• New customer demands/market opportunities • Regulation (new rural development policy)	• New bioscience and biotechnologies • New customer demands/ market opportunities
Responses	• Improvement of efficiency (profitability, safety, organizational restructuring) • Environmental initiatives • Targeted marketing, branding, communication • Creating inspiration	• Creating inspiration factors (taste, freshness, tourism-related) • Creating domestic factors (artisanal methods, local gastronomic traditions) • Development of green factors	• Improvement of technical functionality of products • Improvement of efficiency of technologies

Table 3.1 (continued)

	Industrial	Alternative	Functional
Responses	factors (taste, convenience)	• Marketing and public opinion initiatives (certification of products, close consumer relations, dedicated sales and distribution systems, storytelling)	
Dominating type of firms	• MNCs • Traditional SMEs	• Entrepreneurial micro-firms	• MNCs • Science-driven SMEs
Core technologies	• Large-scale industrial process systems • ICT systems (control, documentation, management, logistics etc.)	• Small-scale artisan technologies • Local production methods • Internet communication and distribution systems	• Biotechnology (outsourced to suppliers) • Large-scale industrial processing systems
Spatial organization	Global, dispersed location	Rural networks	Urban clusters
Regulation and policy framework	• Liberalization of world trade • Protectionism (EU CAP and national agricultural policy) • EU legislation on food safety and environment	New EU rural policy (CAP reforms and LEADER from sector to territory focus, geographical and organic certification schemes)	• Public health and obesity campaigns • Legislation and public debates on gene technologies and DNA patents

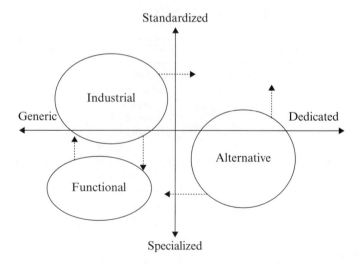

*Figure 3.1   The three food production–consumption models and main
            directions of innovation placed in 'worlds of production' of
            Storper and Salais (1997)*

industrial, alternative and functional food, including their typical strategic
responses to overall changes in food markets.

In Figure 3.1, the three food production–consumption models are
represented in the framework of Storper and Salais (1997), described in
Chapter 1 of this book. The arrows indicate directions of main innovation
efforts as responses to customer needs and show how the three models
tend to 'inspire' each other. As an example, the large international Danish
brewery, Carlsberg, recently opened a high-quality microbrewery and
visitor centre, Jacobsen Brewhouse, in order to regain the market shares
lost on the domestic market to the many microbreweries emerging in
Denmark.[5] In the alternative food model, innovation efforts are carried
out to standardize products and technologies without losing the dedicated
product qualities which differentiate them from mainstream products (for
instance via certification), that is, entering the standardized-dedicated
'market worlds of production'. Other development efforts within the alternative food industry are directed towards market expansion via developing more generic products. This strategy implies broadening of customer
bases and sales through larger-scale distribution channels like supermarket chains. In the long run this might compromise the dedicated product
profile that initially was the competitive advantage of most alternative
producers.

3.4 KNOWLEDGE DYNAMICS

In this section we will look more systematically at the knowledge characteristics and knowledge dynamics prevailing in the F&D sector. As described in the previous section, the three models of industrial, alternative and functional food emphasize different combinations of quality conventions and this has implications for the categories of knowledge searched for, developed and applied.

3.4.1 Analytical Knowledge

An early embryonic food innovation system developed in the nineteenth century on the basis of analytical types of knowledge explored within chemistry, thermodynamics, physics, plant biology, pharmacy and medicine. These bricks of analytical knowledge were exploited in the development of those industrial agricultural and processing technologies and machine systems that are today considered mature and standard. In the decades after the Second World War the knowledge dynamics in the agro-food sector were primarily related to the optimization and diffusion of well-known technologies and Fordist production principles (Green and Foster, 2005). Today, exploration of analytical knowledge plays a less important role in the R&D efforts of the food sector.

However, some changes towards science-driven knowledge dynamics and technological innovation have occurred recently. One of these changes is caused by the introduction of bioscience and genomic knowledge in the development of new agricultural, ingredient and food processing technologies. This analytical category of knowledge allows development of, for instance, new seed types through both genetic engineering and traditional breeding methods, enhanced by a better understanding of crops' molecular biology.

This new bioscience analytical knowledge is driving the emergence of the functional food sector. Through in-house R&D or partnership research with universities or biotech firms, mainly large food companies engage in exploration and codification of new bioscience knowledge as well as in examination of product possibilities and market potential (innovation of new products, technologies and ingredients). After a complicated process of testing and qualifying new products to market entrance, the resulting knowledge is exploited and applied in large-scale processing and distribution systems.

The future prospects of examination and exploitation of bioscience analytical knowledge are widespread for major parts of the agro-food sector, not least for what we here designate as the industrial food model. While the technical and certification features of the more pragmatic parts of the 'organic' strategy could incorporate a bioscience-driven strategy, this is however not the case regarding the 'bio-regionalist' parts of the organic movement.

3.4.2 Synthetic Knowledge

The manufacturing processes in the sector are performed mainly by use of traditional chemical and mechanical technologies through which agricultural raw materials and commodities are processed into food or drinks for household consumption or into semi-manufactured goods for use in other parts of the sector. The knowledge used is practice-oriented, combining disciplines such as chemistry, biology, physics, pharmacy and engineering, and applying different sorts of industry-specific technical knowledge.

Due to the increasing challenges concerning environmental effects, obesity and fatness, public healthcare costs, safety, and so on, the focus of food research and educational systems has been broadened since 1980 to cover not only manufacturing processing but also the whole food chain from 'soil to table' (ATV, 2003). As an effect, public and private food research of today also engages in social sciences and humanities, for instance regarding social and cultural phenomena and changes. Still, natural science and technical research are principal and dominant, not least in terms of expenditures and number of researchers as illustrated by Menrad (2004) in a study on the German food research system.

Development of basic food manufacturing technologies mainly consists in incremental innovations that optimize the efficiency and reliability, not least in terms of increasing economies of scale and decreasing inputs of labour. These innovations are primarily accomplished through knowledge examination and exploitation in the form of in-house R&D of mainly large companies within the industrial model, as well as R&D activities of private industry research centres and public agro-food universities, R&D centres, consultancy and control institutions and so on. From these often very large private and public research organizations, new innovations diffuse into the sector through imitation, adaptation and knowledge transfer systems.

The relevance and use of such synthetic types of engineering knowledge is typical to the industrial model but is also crucial for the alternative and functional food industry. For instance, the development and local adaptation of modern organic production methods relies on the examination and combination of diverse forms of synthetic knowledge.

3.4.3 Symbolic Knowledge

Although certainly not always consciously acknowledged and profession-ally exploited by individual firms, symbolic type of knowledge has funda-mental and widespread importance in the food sector, for instance related to creation of inspiration qualities. Cooking encompasses a clear element of artistic activity where tacit and codified knowledge about raw materi-als and processing techniques are combined in preparing food with, for example, an 'appetising appearance', a 'delicate taste', a 'crispy texture' and a 'bright flavour'. Description of foods and drinks is usually equipped with a huge vocabulary of associative and value-laden words and expres-sion, wine being the ultimate case. Also the importance of chemical addi-tives in giving food or drinks a more attractive colour, texture or flavour is an indication of the value of symbolic knowledge. Without tacit or codified symbolic knowledge a producer of food or beverages would not survive in the market in the longer run. This is the case for industrial, alternative and functional producers, but is absolutely crucial for alterna-tive food businesses for whom the opportunities of selling premium-priced products are connected with certain perceived product qualities additional to similar standard products.

This indicates the interconnectedness of knowledge of producers and consumers. By consuming and preparing food and drinks, consumers achieve the tacit knowledge needed to evaluate their qualities. And by consumers' purchasing of particular products and not others, produc-ers achieve information about consumers' tastes. Yet, pure sales figures only provide limited and often rather superficial information and codified knowledge about consumers' actual preferences. Closer contacts with con-sumers, such as face-to-face meetings, are needed for successful product innovation. Participation in trade fairs as well as diverse forms of market research methods can facilitate such meetings and provide invaluable inputs to innovation of products, markets and distribution.

At a more general level, Asheim et al. (2006) emphasize the central importance of 'buzzing' for creation of symbolic knowledge; that is, learning through social interaction in professional communities, learn-ing from youth and street culture or 'fine' culture and interaction with 'border' professional communities. Knowledge about food and drinks indeed seems to be an excellent example of this. Private dinners, res-taurant visits, shopping, social parties and celebrations, dialogue with customers and suppliers at fairs, professional interaction and network-ing, and so on, are all part of food and drinks producers' provision of symbolic knowledge.

Symbolic knowledge is needed not only in the development of food

and drinks products but also in the packaging, marketing and advertising of products and, more generally, in communication and public
relations with customers, suppliers and other stakeholders. The recent
emergence and growth of food products, marketed and branded with
designations like alternative, local, high-quality, organic, functional,
fair, fast, slow, discount, and so on, is an indication of food and drinks
products' increasingly symbol-laden dimension that firms need to target
and hit very precisely in advertising and communication. Business consultancy firms are crucial complicit actors in developing communication, marketing and advertising strategies of major parts of the sector.
The main characteristics of knowledge in the F&D sector are indicated
in Table 3.2.

3.5 CONCLUSIONS

This study has outlined the overall structural features, the main drivers
of change, the corresponding typical firm and network responses, and
the basic characteristics of knowledge dynamics prevailing in the F&D
sector. The analysis has illustrated that despite its mature and traditional
character, the sector is experiencing thorough processes of change due to
a number of reasons, such as new consumer demands, globalization, the
growing power of retailers in the supply chains, technological development and the introduction of new safety and environmental regulation. As
responses to changing markets and competition conditions, new 'alternative' and 'functional' business models are emerging in competition with
the mainstream 'industrial' food model. The three food provision models
emphasize different conventions of food quality, and hence have different
knowledge bases and dynamics.

The study has illustrated that the sector encompasses a multifaceted
spectrum of knowledge dynamics including:

- Laboratory-based exploration and codification of advanced types of
  analytical, bioscience knowledge.
- Plant-floor examination and testing of synthetic knowledge on new
  manufacturing equipment and methods that are more friendly to the
  environment and safer for workers and consumers.
- Socially and culturally mediated exploitation of symbolic knowledge of local culinary traditions in the development of new products
  and distribution channels appealing to the ever more demanding
  consumers.

Table 3.2   Knowledge characteristics of food production–consumption models

	Industrial food	Alternative food	Functional food
Core knowledge category	Synthetic (Symbolic)	Symbolic (Synthetic)	Analytical (Synthetic)
Important knowledge dynamics	• Exploitation of synthetic knowledge (productivity rising initiatives) • Exploitation of symbolic knowledge (product development & marketing) • Examination of synthetic knowledge (implementation of regulation)	• Examination and exploitation of symbolic knowledge in product development & marketing • Exploitation of synthetic knowledge on artisanal production technologies • Examination and exploitation of synthetic knowledge in development of modern 'alternative' production systems	• Exploration of analytical knowledge (codification of bioscience) • Examination of analytical knowledge (potentials and feasibility of biotech) • Exploitation of synthetic knowledge on industrial production systems
Learning methods	• In-house R&D • Public R&D transfer • Interaction with up- and downstream partners	• Local networking • Public R&D transfer • Dialogue with consumers	• University–science partnerships • In-house R&D
External sources for knowledge	• Supermarkets • Technology suppliers • Public/semi-public institutions (R&D, consultancy and control) • Marketing consultants	• Network partners (horizontal/ vertical) • Customers (e.g. tourists)	• Universities and research institutions • Ingredient suppliers

NOTES

1. Confederazione Italiana Agricoltori at http://www.meatprocess.com/news/ng.asp?id= 65866.
2. As pointed out by DEFRA (2006), from the point of view of consumers' purchasing it is maybe more correct to say value for money instead of price.
3. As noted by Murdoch and Miele (2004), the importance of inspiration and attraction factors in industrial food, as well as the social equality advantage connected with their affordable prices, is often neglected in Marxist political economy analyses of agro-food systems that analyse and explain the popularity of industrial food by use of concepts like 'fetishism' and 'alienation'.
4. For example, the 'slow food' movement started in Italy in 1986 as a response to the opening of the first McDonald's restaurant in Rome, which was seen as a threat to traditional Italian eating habits (Murdoch and Miele, 2004).
5. See http://www.jacobsen.com/core.html.

4. Comparative analysis of selected European biotechnology platforms

Philip Cooke, Carla De Laurentis, Robert Kaiser and Michael Liecke

4.1 INTRODUCTION

In this chapter a new knowledge-based theorization of economic geography is worked out, utilizing a variety of economic indicators regarding the medical biotechnology sector and bioscientific knowledge metrics. It will be shown that biotechnology has proved something of a pioneer sector that other industries emulate for its innovative industry organization. The medical biotechnology sector is only one of the bioscientific 'family' that together account for a significant share of gross domestic product (GDP) in the advanced countries, and a growing share in countries like India and China. Agro-food biotechnology has another significant share of many national GDP accounts, while environmental and energy biotechnology are of rising importance. Within such sectors, subsectors like bioprocessing,[1] bioengineering, bioinformatics, bioimaging and so on are also growing in significance in certain regional economies. It is a science-driven, knowledge-intensive and widely applicable group of interacting platforms that are already evolving certain pervasive characteristics for different functions, including health and safety testing and standardization (bioanalysis), civil and military security (DNA fingerprinting, biometrics) and applications in mechanical, electronic and civil engineering (nanobiotechnology), rather as information and communication technology (ICT) became pervasive during the 1990s.

To that extent they have the character of platform technologies and even general-purpose technologies (GPTs) as discussed by *inter alia* Helpman (1998). Traditional natural resource-based theories in economic geography explained the microeconomics of agglomerative economic activity relatively well. However, knowledge-based economic growth is less easy to explain and predict, although there are some aspects of knowledge economy agglomerations that are less uncertain than others. Thus this chapter is able to point with reasonable confidence at leading bioregions and offer a rationale for their current prominence. However, such regions may be said not to arise through a process of direct comparative or even competitive advantage, not least because markets do not explain much of the rationale for their existence. Rather, bioregions are exemplars of a modern tendency for regional accomplishment to be a product of 'constructed advantage' (Smith, 1776; Foray and Freeman, 1993). Constructed regional advantage occurs in substantial measure because of the influence of public goods upon a region.[2] Thus, in bioscience, a university and medical school is a key factor, not only for its role in the production of talent, but also for the innovative research and entrepreneurial businesses it sustains. Similarly, large research hospitals, for patient trials of new treatments, add to regional constructed advantage. Notably, most of these facilities are the product of initial public provision and are sustained by public teaching and research subventions. Thereafter, nearby pharmaceuticals and agro-chemical facilities may provide intermediate markets as they adjust to meet the new exigencies of 'open innovation' (Chesbrough, 2003).

In this chapter, section 4.2 discusses recent industry dynamics in medical biotechnology at the European and occasionally global scale, in relation to the knowledge categories utilized in framing the research. Section 4.3 begins the empirical accounting of key production and innovation platforms in Europe. This begins with a comparison of the two largest bioeconomies in Europe; Germany and the UK. These are assailed by knowledge, translational and commercialization deficits, more in Europe than the US. Nevertheless, even the latter is constrained by global shortage of capacity in bioprocessing, which further holds up the appearance of new products.[3] Finally, the rise of research and developmant (R&D) outsourcing from large to small firms, which is particularly pronounced in the US and Europe, leads to an investigation of the impact this has in the emergence of key 'spatial knowledge domains' and the extent to which this sustains biotechnology clusters and knowledge networks among them.

4.2   THEORETICAL AND CONCEPTUAL DIMENSIONS

As we showed in Chapter 1, this book attempts to evolve a theoretical framework for understanding the importance of regional knowledge capabilities, how they influence organizational practices of industries, and what these knowledge implications are for firms in various kinds of knowledge

Table 4.1   *Knowledge categories for medical biotechnology*

1. K. categories ➔ 2. K. phases	Analytical (Science-based)	Synthetic (Engineering)	Symbolic (e.g. Advertising)
Exploration (search, including research)	Small and, increasingly, large molecules	Gene therapy, bioengineering and diagnostics	Journals, co-publication 'ghost-writing'
Examination (e.g. trialling, testing, standard-setting or benchmarking)	Clinical research organizations, patient trials, pipeline trials	Good manufacturing and laboratory practice (GMP; GLP)	Patenting process
Exploitation (commercialization of innovation, sale on market, or socially useful & used)	Big pharma, venture capital, business angel finance investment in drugs etc.	Bioinformatics, combinatorial chemistry, biologics	Marketing distribution

value chains. Being an evolutionary growth process, successive increasing returns may be triggered from any point within or beyond the confines of Table 4.1. Thus, and briefly, in medical (and related variety) bio-technology, regional knowledge capabilities evolved from breakthrough research in describing the structure of DNA (Crick and Watson) gave the University of Cambridge an asymmetric knowledge endowment in research. This facilitated the later discovery of monoclonal antibodies (Mabs; Milstein and Köhler) albeit that the well-known patenting and commercial exploitation of the latter was performed by the University of California Medical School and Genentech in San Francisco. Strength in antibodies research nevertheless enabled Cambridge to evolve businesses, notably Cambridge Antibody Technologies (CAT) and others to become leading, globally networked dedicated biotechnology firms (DBFs). However, the relative absence in Cambridge of a strong biotechnology investor community and the combinatorial presence of extensive venture capital-related knowledge assets in San Francisco meant that the northern California region, including the University of California, Davis agro-food and bioenergy campus, gained and retained prominence after initial selection.

This constructed advantage arose, as it did not to the same extent in Cambridge, from the earlier evolution of new semiconductor, computing, communication and software start-ups in the broader region (Silicon Valley). This combination selected and retained the latter as the key regional knowledge domain for antibody-based treatments, particularly in oncology. The Cambridge region (Eastern England) and the research-focused Cambridge, Massachusetts city-region (including Greater Boston) have retained globally leading epistemic communities in genomics and post-genomics research, and innovative spin-out firms, though many more and faster-grown DBFs in the latter than the former. These exert club-goods effects and predominate as quasi-monopolies involving global knowledge exploration, and to varying degrees where the US clusters are strongest, knowledge exploitation capabilities (March, 1991). They are quasi-monopolies because although they generate most new knowledge, knowledge leaks from them in informal ways, as shown by Owen-Smith and Powell (2004). All evolved broader life science and agro-biotechnology capabilities; Cambridge MA in transgenics and some bioenergy, northern California in bioenergy and agro-food sciences. Cambridge, with its regional agro-food tradition, evolved expertise in crop science and bioenergy. Large agro-food, bioenergy and pharmaceuticals corporations routinely selected to outsource R&D to DBFs in these and other globally leading cluster-platforms, as we now denote them, according to the norms of efficiency and effectiveness referred to by Chesbrough (2003) as 'open innovation'. This process expresses increasing returns to such regional knowledge domains, which are enriched by the presence of related variety in the range and quality of biotechnology knowledges they offer. Accordingly, this reinforces the element of asymmetric knowledge endowment with which such regional platforms began.

Hence, as has been indicated, there is a question over the validity, reliability and even meaning of the notion of 'sector', but for now three criticisms can be made. First, the sector notion is mainly a statistician's artefact that is an increasingly misleading representation of reality. Second, sector classifications are little changed since their nineteenth-century origins, which hide identification of such activities as biotechnology, nanotechnology, clean technology or new media. Third, modern technological innovation increasingly progresses by means of the evolution of 'platforms' that combine many technologies that are, in increasing numbers of cases, adaptable across diverse industrial and technological contexts. A more penetrative analysis of the firm-level contribution to regional capabilities is then required. We return to our knowledge framework (as in Chapter 1) for consideration of distinct kinds of knowledge activity within firms in sectors to analyse their simply illustrated knowledge value chains for products evolved through interactive innovation processes.

The innovation process of firms and industries is strongly shaped by their specific knowledge base that can be grouped in three different epistemic categories of knowledge: analytical (scientific), synthetic (engineering) and symbolic (artistic). This is shown in Table 4.1, which analyses the distinctive knowledge value chain in relation to different knowledge categories in biotechnology. This demonstrates that knowledge flows in biotechnology, especially the medical variant, lean towards the analytical and synthetic (science and engineering) on the horizontal axis, and roughly equivalently to exploration (research), examination (testing and trialling) and exploitation (DBFs and big pharma commercializing research) on the vertical. Symbolic knowledge is by no means absent from the knowledge flows framework; indeed pharmaceuticals corporations and DBFs often prosper from their need to manipulate conclusions from trials positively, by employing ghost writers to write up results for tame academics to append their names to, give drug innovations sometimes spurious authenticity (Cooke, 2007a). This is not to mention the symbolic and real value of patenting, sometimes of the broadest kind possible, to protect, genetic sequences for example, nor the large advertising budgets that attend drug marketing. This analysis shows that in biotechnology all kinds of knowledge pass through variants of the same three-stage transformation process as implicit knowledge is transformed into explicit or codified, marketable new knowledge or innovations.

As has been done in relation to the other sectors studied for their combinatory versus cumulative knowledge flow dynamics, a further taxonomy is proposed in relation to the manner in which medical biotechnology businesses from DBFs to big pharma may be construed, this time in relation to their key drivers and responses to such dynamics (Table 4.2). This reveals a number of important characteristics, of which perhaps three may be highlighted. First, the healthcare market is one of the most highly regulated of all, a factor which adds enormous competitive burdens but is aimed at protecting the public from trialling disasters like thalidomide. Hence there are at least three pre-approval trialling stages followed by further regulatory controls as drugs reveal unsuspected side-effects that may require a cocktail of drugs to be taken to make the treatment safe. Second, and somewhat connected to this, drug and diagnostic markets, especially the former, are unusually oligopolistic and frequently oligopsonistic. In the latter dimension, observing countries like the UK with a single main purchaser, the National Health Science (NHS), it is hard to

Table 4.2   Analytical framework of medical biotechnology firm drivers and responses

1. K. ──▶ responses ╱ 2. K. drivers	Organizational	Market	Product/ Process	Professional
Regulation	Food & drug administrations & stock markets	Healthcare	Drugs & services	Medicine
Market structure	Oligopolistic & Oligopsonistic	Demand for higher quality & lower price	Increasingly outsourced to DBFs	'Open science'→ 'Open innovation
Supply chain (Networks)	Big pharma merger, licensing & acquisition	Customized designer drugs	Genomics	'Communities of practice'
Corporate objectives	Scale	Global	Innovation	Improve tarnished reputations

discern classic market drivers operating at all as deals are struck between drug provider and purchaser intermediated by the value-for-money intermediary the National Institute for Clinical Excellence (NICE). NICE has become notorious for establishing the practice of refusing to approve the expensive, often cancer, treatments produced by the likes of Genentech (for example, Herceptin, the anti-breast cancer drug), provoking the highly informed and active pressure groups that coalesce around such issues, who then lobby parliaments regional (as in Wales or Scotland) and national, where the NICE advice is frequently overturned by ministers. Finally, medical biotechnology is high profile in 'open innovation'. Since 1980, the first biotechnology firm, Genentech was majority owned (now wholly owned) by Swiss giant Roche, proving its major money-earner with a string of oncology treatment breakthroughs. So much so that by 2008 Roche was involved in seeking to purchase the outstanding equity in the first DBF in the world. Most big pharmas outsource knowledge-intensive biotechnology commercialization to DBFs, probably more as a share of total R&D and commercialization spend, because it is highly efficient and effective financially and scientifically so to do. In Cooke (2007a) it was

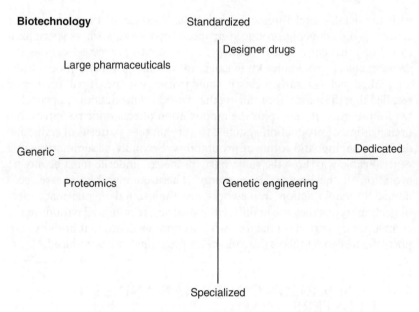

Figure 4.1   'Worlds of production' in medical biotechnology

shown that productivity by DBFs was in the mid-2000s some six times greater than in big pharmas, measured in terms of new chemical entities (NCEs) available for sale on the – albeit frequently oligopsonistic – health-care markets of the world.

Finally, to characterize the basic dynamics and variety of industrial organizational forms in regional space we now turn to consider the *Worlds of Production* approach (Storper and Salais, 1997; Storper, 1997), a theoretical framework elaborated in Chapter 1 that has proved most intellectually and practically advantageous for characterizing generic industry dynamics in the knowledge economy. The central concept, of key importance to the analysis and investigational work proposed here, is that different forms of production organization are internally coherent in terms of their driving institutions, network interactions and conventions. In the current era these involve the four 'tensions' represented in Figure 4.1.

It will be recalled that the first of these refers to 'standardized' produc- tion as practised in mass-production industries such as pharmaceuticals, in tension with a more 'specialized' production in which the technology and know-how utilized are restricted. On the second dimension there is a 'dedicated' product customized to certain niche requirements such as 'designer drug solutions' in healthcare or personalized services of various kinds. Finally, 'generic' means products that carry well-known qualities, with predictable and foreseeable markets. 'Dedicated' practice involves generic products being produced in specialized ways, such as specialized forms of genetically based treatments. It refers to processes, such as the deployment of proteomics knowledge, rather than a generic product like a flu jab, which is clearly a classic standardized vaccine. It will further be recalled that the reason for utilizing this 'worlds of production' approach is twofold. Firstly, it underpins the mobilization of economic resources, the organization of production systems, factor markets, patterns of economic decision-making, and forms of profitability. Secondly, it summarizes in a generalizable way how the same basic processes underlie most economic evolution in the knowledge economy. These comparably diverse, economically viable action frameworks are thus found in pharmaceutical biotechnology as they are in different industries, regions and nations in the contemporary period. In the following sections evidence that broadly supports the foregoing theoretical and conceptual analyses is adduced.

4.3 COMPARISON OF GERMAN AND UK CLUSTERS

In both these leading European bioeconomies, as more or less ubiquitously around the world, biotechnology organizes itself in clusters, with knowledge flowing locally to and from research institutes and globally among customers and other specialist research laboratories. In the following, the German platform of medical biotechnology is reviewed first.

4.3.1 Germany's Medical Biotechnology Clusters

Despite a growth in private venture capital associated with BioRegio, which kick-started German biotechnology commercialization from 1995, public funding remains important to the German venture capital industry and it is inconceivable that government intervention will not remain a central part of the future of German biotechnology industry development. German biotechnology firms and independent observers are in consensus that BioRegio helped close Germany's technology and, particularly, commercialization gap in biotechnology, and the view was widely expressed that government support should be continued after 2002. BioChance, BioProfile, BioFuture and other initiatives continued this trajectory from 1999 onwards. Weaknesses remain in Germany's biopharmaceutical industry and Bayer, for example, is far less significant globally than it once was, though in 2006 it grew through acquisition of Schering AG, while Hoechst was swallowed up in what is now the French firm Sanofi

Table 4.3   *Performance in core pharmaceutical biotechnology cluster*
              firms, 2002–05

	Rhineland	Heidelberg	Munich	Berlin
Number of firms				
2002	29	31	63	55
2003	28	27	63	50
2005	26	27	59	54
Drug candidates 2005				
Pre-clinical	8	8	47	44
Phase 1	4	2	19	5
Phase 2/3	4	3	17	12

Source: Ernst & Young (2005a).

that acquired Aventis, the merged Hoechst–Rhone-Poulenc entity, while BASF has withdrawn from medical biotechnology. Hence, for health-related biotechnology Germany's small business segment is relatively even more important than that in the UK where Glaxo is the second-ranked pharmaceuticals firm in the world and AstraZeneca is also a significant player. Thus the winning BioRegios of Rhineland, Rhein-Neckar–Dreieck and Munich are of particular interest and focus as Germany's leading biotechnology clusters. The strong biotechnology agglomeration in Berlin is profiled for comparative purposes. Berlin was not a BioRegio partner but, as can be seen from Table 4.3, it has the second-largest concentration of biotechnology firms in Germany.

4.3.2   Rhineland Biotechnology

Altogether the *Land* has some 167 research institutes, many employing relatively small numbers of researchers, but with representation across different elements of the biotechnology spectrum. In the early days of BioRegio, most federal funding went to expanding companies while land funding went directly into start-ups. As Table 4.3 shows, by 2005 Rhineland occupied a lagging position similar to Rhein-Neckar (mainly Heidelberg) compared to Munich and Berlin regarding both firm and drug candidate numbers. As of 2000 and the peak of the biotechnology boom, the sectoral distribution of companies working in the field of biotechnology meant that 22 per cent were in diagnostics, 12 per cent pharmarceuticals, 7 per cent agro-food biotechnology, 18 per cent in environmental protection, 9 per cent filtration engineering and 10 per cent bioanalysis, displaying apparently related platform variety. Within biotechnology the emphasis within Rhineland firms lies clearly on platform services and products (in the technological sense) and diagnostic technologies rather than drug production, as the meagre pipeline shown in Table 4.3 indicates. Rhineland is interesting primarily because it is not focused on one branch of biotechnology as tends to be the case in the others considered here, where healthcare predominates. According to Omland and Ernst (2004), Rhineland is successful as a mixed biosectoral region with a balance between bioremediation expertise, healthcare and agro-food biotechnology with several platform elements in proximity to the numerous research institutes. Until 2002 Rhineland also attracted more firms and applied for more patents than other German regions, but as everywhere, this performance was relatively short-lived after the 2000–2001 downturn. The BioRegio winner regions were the best-performing of all German agglomerations in biotechnology but many other non-BioRegio regions exploited their collective effort to grow more firms for a while on the back of their unsuccessful effort to win the contest.

4.3.3   Rhine-Neckar–Dreieck

Heidelberg is Germany's oldest university and has one of the best science bases for biotechnology. Two Max Planck Institutes, for Cell Biology and Medical Research are in the region, as is the German (Helmholtz) Cancer Research Centre (DKFZ). The European Molecular Biology Laboratory and the European Molecular Biology Organization are there, along with one of the four Gene Centres, the Resource Centre of the German Human Genome Project, two further medical genetics institutes and two plant genetics centres. Three other universities, Mannheim, Ludwigshafen and Kaiserslautern, and three polytechnics complete the research and training spectrum. There are two of Germany's leading big pharma firms nearby, namely Boehringer Mannheim Roche Diagnostics (Mannheim), and Merck (Darmstadt). But the heart of the BioRegio is the Heidelberg-based commercialization organization, the Biotechnology Centre Heidelberg (BTH). This is a three-tiered organization consisting of a commercial business consultancy, a seed capital fund and a non-profit biotechnology liaison and advisory service (Table 4.4).

4.3.4   Munich

The organization responsible for managing development of biotechnology, BioM, is located at Martinsried, in south-west Munich. The area has become a biomedical research campus with 5500 researchers working in

Table 4.4   Heidelberg diagnostics and genomics biotechnology firms

Expertise firms	No. of services	A Firms	B Firms	A/B
A				
Analytics/Services	10			2
Bioinformatics	6	2		2
Diagnostics	8	3		3
Custom Production	5			1
TOTAL	29			
B				
Genomics	3			2
Proteomics	7		1	
Therapeutics	8		1	1
Tissue engineering	3		2	
TOTAL	21	5	4	11

Source: Baden-Württemberg Government (2006).

biology, medicine, chemistry and pharmacy located there. BioM AG is a one-stop shop with seed financing, former administration of BioRegio awards and enterprise support policy under one roof. DBFs increased from 36 to 120 between 1996 and 2001 (Kaiser, 2003). BioM is a network organization, reliant on science, finance and industry expertise for its support committees. While at the 2002 peak there were 99 listed firms in Munich, by 2004 there were 93, over a quarter of the total number of core biotech companies in Germany (according to Ernst & Young's 2005 German biotechnology report (Ernst & Young, 2005b), there were 350 such companies in Germany in 2003). By 2005, 59 of these were core (therapeutics) biotechnology firms compared to 63 in 2002 (Table 4.5). In 2004, there were 13 insolvencies in Munich including several well-established companies, such as Axxima Pharmaceuticals, a drug discovery company founded in 1997. Axxima subsequently merged with GPC. Bio-M's annual report noted that venture capital for biotechnology had decreased in Germany from €243 million in 2003 to €226 million in 2004, when only some €50 million was invested in Munich. Many young companies had completed the first two rounds of financing but found it increasingly difficult to obtain further capital. The number of biotechnology jobs in the Munich region decreased to 2230 (compared to some 2600 in 2003). The average number of staff per company decreased from 27 to 24.

Nevertheless, pharmaceutical companies retained interest in the results of Munich's biotechnology research. Roche Diagnostics for example

Table 4.5   Core pharmaceutical biotechnology companies in the leading German clusters

Location	2002	2003	2005
Munich	63	63	59
Berlin	55	50	54
Rhein-Neckar	31	27	27
Rhineland	29	28	26

Source: Kaiser and Liecke (2006).

invested more than €140 million in enlarging its R&D facility in Penzberg near Munich. In 2006, 63 new drugs were in various phases of clinical development, with five of them in phase III, and one drug by Scil Technology in the approval phase. Medigene acquired the smaller Munich Biotech company, which was the first German company to bring a new drug onto the market. The Munich companies continue to focus mainly on therapeutics with turnover at €250 million in 2005, compared to €170 million in 2004.

4.3.5   Berlin

As the tables show, Berlin is a more significant 'critical mass' than anywhere outside Munich. The city of Berlin ranks today as Germany's number two biotechnology cluster. The emphasis however is not so clearly on pharmaceuticals as in Munich, but rather on several different areas such as bioinformatics, glycobiotechnology, DNA chips and regenerative medicine. To the region's disadvantage, however, may be its relative geographical distance from the principal actors in the industry. Yet the Berlin region (including Brandenburg) is host to seven largely public-funded founder and technology parks and more than 16 different research institutes. One comparative advantage of the city's location might be the existence of the largest research university hospital in Europe, the public Charité, which raises more than €100 million annually in third-party funds and which finances more than 3000 scientists working on some 1000 projects. It has 15000 employees, 3500 beds and an annual budget of €1 billion. Development of the life sciences is a strategic priority for Berlin. Key institutions include Berlin's three universities: Free University Berlin, Humboldt University and Technical University Berlin. Charité resulted from the merging of the US-founded Benjamin Franklin Medical Centre at the Free University in the former West Berlin, and Charité, part of Humboldt University in the former East Berlin.

Table 4.6   Core pharmaceutical biotechnology companies in the leading UK clusters

Location	2000	2004	2006
Cambridge Core Therap.	54	70	109
Cambridge Genomic	–	30	47
Oxford Core Therap.	46	50	63
Scotland Core Therap.	24	30	38

Sources: ERBI; Oxford Biosciences Network; Scottish Enterprise.

There is also a network of internationally recognized life science institutes, such as the Max Delbrück Centre for Molecular Medicine, the Max Planck Institute for Molecular Genetics, and the Max Planck Institute for Infection Biology. Berlin also is home to the Robert Koch Institute (Germany's version of the US Centers for Disease Control and Prevention), the Federal Research Ministry, Federal Health Ministry and life science-related trade organizations such as the German Association of Research-Based Pharmaceutical Companies. The number of DBFs is comparable to that in Munich, which is to say about 109 firms in 2004. VC investments reached a peak in 2000 with €150 million invested, followed by very meagre years with investments falling to €25 million in 2002, €45 million in 2003 and €53 million in 2004. In 2005, however, the accrued total of venture capital and other capital investments exceeded €100 million. The number of product candidates remains significantly lower than in Munich. The number of new firms being established in 2004 was also comparable to Munich, with about eight new start-ups.

4.3.6   Biotechnology Clusters in the UK

The main UK biotechnology clusters concentrate close to globally significant research universities at Cambridge, Oxford and, more regionally, Scotland (Table 4.6). There has never been a UK public support policy such as BioRegio, though there have been public technology initiatives for biotechnology such as the Department for Trade and Industry (DTI)'s Biotechnology Exploitation Platforms involving university collaboration with National Health Service trusts, *inter alia.* Cambridge has reached sufficient status that numerous international biopharmaceuticals laboratories have located nearby. Examples of inward investment include Amgen, Beacon, Chiron, Genzyme, Medivir and Millennium amongst others. However, while significant big pharma research infrastructure is less than that in, for example, Cambridge, Massachusetts, some are located within a 40 kilometre radius, such as Glaxo, Bristol-Myers Squibb, Dow Pharma, Merck, Sharp & Dohme, Novartis and Organon (Akzo-Nobel). Oxford's assets are mostly home-grown, but US firms Chiron, OSI Pharmaceuticals, Genzyme Therapeutics and Gilead are present in the cluster. Both Cambridge and Oxford, as will be shown, have leading public research institutes that complement the excellence of their university research centres and institutes. Scotland's platform has research excellence in universities and independent research institutes such as the Roslin Institute for transgenics research.

Cambridge's cluster
The Cambridge biocluster specializes in healthcare biotechnology. The two categories of 'biopharmarceuticals including vaccines' and 'pharmaceuticals largely from chemical synthesis' registered 14 and nine Cambridge firms respectively in 1998, reaching 47 and 20 respectively in 2006, evidence of the rapid rise of biotechnology over fine chemistry in the pharmaceuticals industry more generally. Examples of the former are Acambis, Alizyme, Amgen, Cambridge Antibody Technology (now acquired by AstraZeneca), Domantis and Xenova; and of the latter, Argenta, UBC and Mundipharma. In addition to these two key categories are direct biotechnology services like clinical trials, diagnostics and reagent supply.

Detailed research on Cambridge's genomics sector has revealed the collaborative aspect of biotechnology innovation to be strong. Regarding co-publication in journals, Casper and Karamanos (2003) showed only 36 per cent of firms were 'sole authors' while the majority partnered with firm founders, current incumbents and/or their laboratory. Academic collaborators are equally shared between Cambridge and the rest of the UK, with international partners a sizeable minority. Hence, biotechnology is associative in its interactive knowledge realization, at least in respect of the all-important publication of results that firms will likely seek to patent. Moreover, they will, in many cases, either have or anticipate milestone payments from pharma companies with which they expect to have licensing agreements.

Yet of all known genomics DBF foundings in 1990–2002, totalling 30, only nine were spin-outs from Cambridge University laboratories, a further five were spin-outs from the Medical Research Council's Cambridge Molecular Biology Laboratory, while others came from outside universities such as Imperial College, London (3), the University of Wales, Cardiff (2), others and industry (6). Casper and Karamanos (2003) hold that Cambridge functions as an 'ideas market' with a good scientific image and much scholarly collaboration as well as academic membership of DBF boards and advisory committees. Yet a third of interactions are with academic and entrepreneurial partners elsewhere in the UK, and a further third are abroad, mainly in the US.

The public infrastructure support for biotechnology in and around Cambridge is impressive, much of it deriving from the university and hospital research facilities. The Laboratory of Molecular Biology at Addenbrookes Hospital, funded by the Medical Research Council; Cambridge University's Institute of Biotechnology, Department of Genetics and Centre for Protein Engineering; the European Bioinformatics Institute; the Babraham Institute and Sanger Institute with their emphasis on functional genomics research and the Babraham and St John's incubators for biotechnology start-ups and commercialization, are all globally recognized facilities, particularly in biopharmaceuticals. However, in the Eastern region are also located important research institutes in the agro-food biotechnology field, such as the Institute for Food Research, John Innes Centre, Institute of Arable Crop Research and National Institute of Arable Botany. Thus in research and commercialization terms, Cambridge is well placed in biopharmaceuticals where it has high-grade basic and applied research. However it is not nowadays as strong in agro-food biotechnology commercialization.

The Oxford cluster

Oxford University has some 14 university research institutes in the life sciences. The Nuffield Department of Clinical Medicine is rated one of Europe's leading centres in functional genomics. Interdisciplinarity is pronounced and biochemistry, pharmacology and engineering, for example, conduct joint biotechnology research. Lawton Smith's (2004) survey found that while most of the bioregion's firms are mainly relatively new and small, the cluster is well established around a core of companies formed in the 1980s. The industry grew rapidly from the early 1990s. Sixty companies were established between 1991 and 2000 (70 per cent) compared to 25 between 1981 and 1990. The cumulative annual growth rate ran at over 14 per cent. Two-thirds employed between one and 50 people, but a quarter employed more than that. Some 17 per cent were still at the start-up and seedcorn stage, but over half (52 per cent) were in their second round of private funding. Oxford's DBFs are R&D-intensive with 42 per cent spending more than $1.8 million on this annually. Almost half anticipated doubling in R&D expenditure in the following year. The primary focus areas are biopharmaceuticals and diagnostics (34 per cent and 17 per cent respectively). The older companies mentioned above – like Oxagen and Xenova, each of which employs more than 250 people – trebled their employment between 1997 and 2001. The majority of these companies are independent while the rest include other independent companies, some of which are spin-outs from other universities including London University, Bath and Surrey. Yet others are foreign companies such as Genzyme. Some one-third of Oxford's DBFs are foreign-owned, with the majority owned in the USA (19 firms). Others have parents in France, Japan, Germany and Denmark.[4]

The public science base, mentioned earlier, is a key attraction and Lawton Smith (2004) saw this operating in three ways. First, Oxfordshire's clinical research strengths in medicine and medical research are echoed in the biopharmaceuticals and diagnostics DBF specializations. Diverse service firms occupy niche roles within pharmaceutical research, development and production, and some drug development DBFs conduct this alongside service functions. Those in the diagnostics subsector report little competition between co-located firms. Second, a quarter of the companies originated in Oxford University. Other firms like Prolifix were spin-outs from elsewhere, in this case the National Institute for Medical Research in London. Through Isis Innovation, the university's technology transfer office, Oxford University has spun out 17 firms in biopharmaceuticals out of a total of 32 spin-outs by 'star scientists' including Professors Ed Southern and Raymond Dwek (biochemistry), Brian Bellhouse and Mike Brady (engineering) and John Bell, Nuffield Department of Clinical Medicine. Of these, three are medical diagnostics and 14 are biotech firms.

Scotland's biotechnology platform

Biotechnology in Scotland is growing steadily, with more than 100 biotechnology companies employing some 3600 individuals. The vast majority of activity is highly geographically concentrated in the Dundee – Edinburgh – Glasgow triangle called the Scottish Biotech Cluster. Scottish Enterprise, the Scottish government's economic development agency, established a biotechnology team in 1994, and has pursued a focused policy of developing the biocluster on a number of fronts. By 2002, Scotland had already lured a few Boston, Massachusetts firms to its geographic 'triangle', including Braintree-based Haemonetics Corp., Bedford-based Millipore Corp., and Inverness Medical Ltd, a subsidiary of Inverness Medical Technology Inc. (itself a spin-off of Waltham-based Inverness Medical Innovations Inc. that was in 2002 sold to Johnson & Johnson). Hence a collaborative attitude among universities, between them and with R&D centres and among firms prevails in Scotland, considerably assisting the evolution of the biocluster. Examples of Scottish Enterprise support are the €40 million 'Proof of Concept' fund – this enables professors and other research leaders to access funding to 'buy out' their academic teaching and administration time to concentrate on the 'proof of concept' for the

Table 4.7   Composition of biotechnology sector in Scotland

Activity	Number of firms (core activity)	
	2000	2006
Biopharmaceutical therapeutics	24	38
Biopharmaceutical diagnostics	18	25
Biopharmaceutical clinical trials	10	15
Biopharmaceutical contract R&D	14	23
Bioprocessing	17	15
Environmental bioremediation	3	6
Environmental diagnostics	7	6
Environmental Waste Treatment	5	4
Agro-food therapeutics	1	6
Agro-food plant breeding	2	2
Agro-food diagnostics	4	5
Agro-food contract R&D	2	3
Supplies	23	47
Support services	26	181

Source: Scottish Enterprise (2000, 2006)

idea they are seeking to commercialize – and the Intermediary Technology Institutes. These aim to speed up commercialization by mediating the exploration–exploitation divide with resources, intellectual property rights (IPR) and spin-out formation.

Scotland is globally known as the home of the first transgenic animal, Dolly the sheep, developed at the Roslin Institute near Aberbeen. Other specialities include drug discovery, evaluation and clinical trial management in cancer research, cystic fibrosis, Alzheimer's and Parkinson's diseases. Scottish biotechnology also has a significant presence in agro-biotech, such as animal health and breeding, veterinary medicine, crop yields and pest control. Firms deploying environmental biotechnologies are also present. In all, Scottish Enterprise claims a platform of some 180 core and supply or service firms engaged to some degree in supporting it. By 2006 the support services industry was actually some 181 firms, while core therapeutics firms numbered 38 as may be seen from the relevant Scottish Enterprise annual data sourcebook summarized in Table 4.7. The industry in Scotland is made up broadly as follows (Table 4.7). It is clear that biopharmaceuticals is the strong, core part of the industry in Scotland, with a substantial number of firms in therapeutic product development, fewer in diagnostics, research and clinical trials (many of the contract R&D entries are universities, some with firms attached, others not). There is also a reasonably well-endowed supplies (reagents, chemicals and so on) and support services (legal, consultancy and so on) infrastructure. Hence, as a whole, Scotland has a robust basis for future growth in biotechnology, but it may lack, at present, the interactive capacities and more sophisticated private support arrangements found more extensively in Cambridge and Oxford. It is clear from much of the preceding material on Scotland's biotechnology cluster that it is both polynucleated and dependent on more public intervention and support than the clusters in Cambridge or Oxford.

4.3.7   Comparison: Germany–UK

It may easily be seen that those biotechnology clusters with thoroughgoing public policy support tend to be weaker than those that privately exploit high-quality publicly funded research that produces high-quality science. A full comparison of the cases examined is provided in Table 4.8, but by way of introduction it is important to stress the following three key points of comparison that are both qualiataive and quantitative. First, the German cluster firms are not as interactive at the firm level as those in the UK, and this may be problematic but it also may be a function of firm maturity. In leading bioclusters worldwide, there is a high degree of formal and informal interaction, sometimes collaboration, sometimes competition, among the same firms. This seems not to have developed in Germany – somewhat strangely given the concertation culture in business affairs more generally – and it may not evolve very much either in three of the four German clusters. In Heidelberg the 'creative destruction' of the early 2000s had destroyed many established linkages and new businesses were extremely small, immature and often in similar and competing fields (for example, diagnostics and platform technologies). In the cases of Rhineland and Berlin, firms are also small but in potential platform segments of biotechnology markets such as healthcare, agro-food and environmental biotechnologies where 'related diversity' is actually in need of more integration.

Second, too many German clusters specialize in low-value, highly competitive and rapidly changing diagnostics segments and insufficient numbers specialize in therapeutic biotechnology. This contrasts with the UK where numerous firms specialize not only in therapeutics but also in the most advanced post-genomic bioscientific innovation. This means that there is always likely to be rapid emergence and decline of market opportunities for these small German firms, although in some cases the fact that they are active in more than one line and that the extra line involves at

Table 4.8 Comparison of structural characteristics of German and UK biotechnology clusters

	Leading UK clusters			Leading German clusters			
	Cambridge	Oxford	Scotland	Rheinland	Heidelberg	Munich	Berlin
Recent dynamics in terms of start-ups and product pipeline	Strong	Strong	Strong	Weak	Weak	Strong	Strong
Focus	Therapeutics	Therapeutics and diagnostics	Therapeutics	Diagnostics	Diagnostics	Therapeutics	Diagnostics
Science base	World class	Strong	Strong	Strong	Strong	Strong	Strong
Commercialization of science	Relatively strong (in European comparison)	Strong	Moderate	Relatively weak	Relatively weak	Promising	Limited
Interaction between major firms	Strong	Strong	Dispersed firms without strong interaction	Dispersed firms without strong interaction	Dispersed firms without strong interaction	Strong/ promising	Weak
Share of DBFs in total firm population	High	High	High	High	High	High	High
Dependence on public funding	Low	Low	High	High	High	High	High
VC funding	High	Relatively high	Relatively low	Relatively low	Relatively low	High	High

Table 4.8 (continued)

	Leading UK clusters			Leading German clusters			
	Cambridge	Oxford	Scotland	Rheinland	Heidelberg	Munich	Berlin
Big pharma funding	High	High	High	Low	Low	Relatively low	Moderate
Number of life scientists	High	High	High	Low	High	Very high	High
Quality of innovation support infrastructure	Excellent	Excellent	Good	Moderate	Good	Good	Moderate
Life scientists	Medium	Medium	Medium	Modest	Medium	High	Medium
Firm numbers	Medium	Medium	Medium-to-low	Modest	Modest	High	High
Firm employment size	High	High	Medium	Low	Low	Low	Low
General assessment	Cluster of global importance	Leading European cluster	Still missing important elements of a leading European cluster	Still missing important elements of a leading European cluster	Still missing important elements of a leading European cluster	Leading European cluster	Leading European cluster

least therapeutics research is a promising indicator. To put it starkly, only Munich is remotely competitive in this regard in a European, let alone a global context. Other research on co-publications (Cooke, 2007a) shows clearly that German bioscientists are not active in biotechnology co-publication with scientists elsewhere in Europe, Asia or North America. Only Munich displays such connectivity in the leading European and US bioscience journals, and such links as Munich bioscientists demonstrate are few and far between. Finally, it is evident that Germany's biotechnology clusters demonstrate a marked dependence upon public support with purely private enterprise support being at a premium. This contrasts markedly with Cambridge and Oxford, but less so with Scotland. However, even in Scotland, which is located relatively peripherally to the main markets, there is active private venture capital and business angel activity.

4.4 PHARMACEUTICAL BIOTECHNOLOGY IN FRANCE AND SWITZERLAND

4.4.1 France

In contrast to Switzerland, France suffers from a lack of young innovative companies originating from either public research institutions or larger corporations. Even where public research organizations played a major role as a basis for commercialization in France, Switzerland remains a remarkable example of how traditional pharmaceutical companies can contribute to the birth of a new industry. Similarly to Germany and Switzerland, France has to cope with a second problem, which is the 'malfunction' of the public stock market as an exit channel for investors. However, the French situation seems to be even worse than in other countries since no biotech initial public offering (IPO) occurred between 1998 and 2004. Only in the late autumn of 2005 did two smaller French dedicated biotechnology firms (ExonHit Therapeutics and BioAlliance Pharma) make an IPO at Euronext (see Table 4.9).

To facilitate firm foundations, various policy measures have been implemented in France in recent years. The most salient ones were the implementation of the 'young innovative company' status and the establishment of geographical research focal points, the so-called 'Genopoles'. If a firm has qualified for the young innovative company status (so-called JEI – *jeune entreprise innovante*) it is completely exempt from contributing to the social system for R&D employees, comprising health programmes, unemployment insurance, pension funds and other benefits. The Genopoles were constructed to enhance the quality and output of biotechnology research

Table 4.9   Key data on French biotechnology

	2001	2002	2003	2004	2005
Number of firms	255	239	246	300	300
Raised capital in m EUR	254	238	179	268	165
Of which venture capital in m EUR	242	238	126	242	93
Of which follow on or IPO	12	0	53	26	72
Number of IPOs	0	0	0	0	2

Source: France Biotech.

on the one hand, and to facilitate and promote spin-offs on the other hand. The oldest, largest and most successful is situated in Evry, close to Paris, and was founded in 1998 by the French Research Ministry, private foundations, the University of Evry and several regional authorities.

In order to promote spin-offs, the Genopoles act as network nodes and organizations by providing several consulting services to potential (scientific) founders. In addition, founders gain privileged access to special public seed-funds, and they are further allowed to use laboratory space and facilities of the public research body for up to 24 months. Overall there are today seven Genopoles which were constituted in 1999 within the framework of the Génomique programme (see Tables 4.10 and 4.11).

4.4.2   Switzerland

Switzerland's main biotechnology cluster concentrations are at Zurich, Geneva and Basel, with close links to Roche and Novartis significantly influencing the focus in Basel. Not only does Novartis, for example, have globally competitive R&D but also its own incubator and venture capital (VC) fund. But Zurich and Geneva also have biotechnology, and university research is a key progenitor.

For many reasons, Swiss biotechnology is seen as somewhat of a special case. First, in relation to the country's population, Switzerland has the highest number of biotechnology firms in the world. Second, it is the only sector of its kind which is, in total, profitable. And third, three of the nine public firms are long-established companies that have diversified into the biotechnology business while four of the remaining six firms were founded out of the two pharmaceutical companies Novartis and Roche. Although even the Swiss platform entered a phase of consolidation, venture capital

Table 4.10   Clinical pipeline of French biotechs, 2004–05

Pipeline	2004	2005
Pre-clinical	103	108
Phase I	30	41
Phase II	32	39
Phase III	7	7

Source: France Biotech.

Table 4.11   Employees in French biotech companies

	Employees total	Employees in R&D
2004	3067	1890
2003	2890	1680
2002	2376	1514

Source: France Biotech.

Table 4.12   Key data on Swiss biotechnology

	2001	2002	2003	2004
Number of firms	119	129	139	133
Revenues in m EUR		2799	3279	3565
Venture Capital in m CHF	106	148	130	194
Number of IPOs	0	0	0	1

Source: Ernst & Young (2005a).

investments were still increasing (2001 – €106 million; 2004 – €194 million) (see Table 4.12). As a result, Switzerland in 2010 has the third-largest biotech-related venture capital market in Europe.

Apart from Novartis and Roche, Switzerland also hosted one of the world's largest biotechnology companies, Serono, which in 2001 had a market capitalization of $18 billion, ranking it third globally behind Amgen and Genentech. Serono and Amgen signed a licensing and commercialization deal for Serono to sell a multiple sclerosis drug in the US that it had developed with Immunex, a Cambridge, MA firm subsequently acquired by Amgen. In 2006 Serono was acquired by the German firm Merck. Other prominent firms are Actelion, Cytos, The Genetics

Table 4.13   Clinical pipeline of public Swiss DBFs, 2003–04

Pipeline	2003	2004
Pre-clinical	33	33
Phase I	8	9
Phase II	14	14
Phase III	20	24

Source: Ernst & Young (2005a).

Company, bio-T, CELLnTEC, Debiopharm, GeneBio and Solvias. In addition to Serono, Actelion, Berna Biotech, Debiopharm and Basilea have several pharmaceuticals in clinical testing. Lonza Biologics is also Swiss and one of the largest biosynthesis firms in the world. Debiopharm funds cancer research projects at Tulane University, New Orleans. Of Switzerland's 200 biotechnology companies 40 are pure DBFs, the others being instrumentation and services firms.

Some 22 per cent of the 200 are located in the Geneva–Lausanne 'BioAlps' region, approximately 26 per cent are in the Basel 'BioValley' region, and about 35 per cent are in the Greater Zurich region. Zurich has a Functional Genomics Research Centre. Since 2000, 45 new biotechnology businesses were established, 15 of which were spin-outs from the Swiss Federal Institute of Technology in Lausanne and Zurich and ten were spinouts from other Swiss universities. The remainder came from domestic and foreign subsidiary industry. Of the 30 or so public companies, many like Genedata (Basel), Cytos (Zurich) and GeneProt (Geneva), a proteomics DBF, have long-term collaborative research, opinion and licensing agreements with the likes of Novartis and Roche. International collaborations extend to the partnership between the University of Minnesota and the Swiss Federal Institute of Technology focused upon medical technology. This arises in part from Minneapolis devices firm Medtronic's subsidiary located in Switzerland and its collaboration with the likes of Disetronic, a leading Swiss insulin-pump manufacturer. In conclusion, Switzerland is a small, capable, knowledge-intensive biosciences economy (see Tables 4.13 and 4.14). It has leaders in 'big pharma', global DBF capability and numerous smaller DBFs and spin-outs concentrating on leading-edge proteomics and other post-genomics treatments. It is highly connected globally, but especially to the US megacentres through 'big pharma' and its leading clusters in Zurich, Basel and Geneva–Lausanne.

Finally, as in many other countries, the Swiss biotechnology industry has developed within regional agglomerations which have specific characteristics. The Zurich cluster, for example, counts the highest number

Table 4.14   Employees in Swiss DBFs

	Private Swiss biotechs	Public Swiss biotechs
2004	6063	7462
2003	5926	6920
2002	4883	6765

Source: Ernst & Young (2005c).

Table 4.15   Regional agglomerations in Swiss biotechnology

Cluster	Companies	Products	Employees
Zurich	65	5	2000
Geneva/Lausanne	30	29	5500
Basle	40	21	4000

Source: Ernst & Young (2005c).

of firms, but the lowest number of pharmaceutical product candidates, because most of the firms have been established at a very early stage out of public research organizations. In Geneva–Lausanne and Basle, though, a considerably lower number of firms have much more product candidates (see Table 4.15), which again reflects the role of the pharmaceutical industry as the origin of biotech firms that start with a much more comprehensive technology and product portfolio.

4.5   SWEDEN AND DENMARK

In this section we shall briefly examine developments in two smaller countries, more comparable to Switzerland, displaying a strong biotechnology cluster presence. Both Sweden and Denmark have developing network nodes, so how have these countries positioned themselves globally? What specialization, if any, characterizes their activity? To what extent do institutional and economic geography patterns involving clustering near major knowledge centres characterize the landscape of the sector? (Cooke, 2002a; Kaiser, 2003; Lemarié et el., 2001).

Sweden has its main concentrations in Stockholm–Uppsala and Lund–Malmö, now bridged formally to Denmark's nearby cluster in Copenhagen. This international complex is branded Medicon Valley for commercial purposes. (McKelvey et al., 2003; VINNOVA, 2003; Nelund and Norus, 2003). However, as will be shown, the trajectories by which these concentrations reached fruition are distinctive. In Sweden and Denmark corporate spin-out and supply were important even before Pharmacia's acquisition by Pfizer. Such spin-outs nevertheless combine with university research and associated start-up DBFs.

4.5.1 Sweden

The first commercial exploitation of modern biotechnology in Sweden was based on technology from Genentech, licensed by the Swedish company Kabi in 1978. Kabi merged with Pharmacia in 1990. Pharmacia later merged with two US companies, Upjohn and Monsanto, to form Pharmacia Corporation. In the spring of 2003 Pfizer, the US pharmaceutical company acquired Pharmacia Corporation. The other major pharmaceutical company in Sweden, Astra (now the Swedish–UK firm AstraZeneca) has headquarters in Södertälje near Stockholm with Swedish research based in Södertälje, Gothenburg and Lund started using recombinant DNA technology in the 1980s. From then, and increasingly in the 1990s, new DBFs were founded in Sweden. Most of these new companies were spin-offs either from university research or from existing large pharmaceutical companies. Swedish biotechnology ranks fourth in Europe in terms of number of companies, and number nine in the world according to the Swedish Trade Council in 2002.

The number of Swedish DBFs increased by 35 per cent from 135 in 1997 to 183 in 2001, and the number of employees increased by 48 per cent to about 4000 (VINNOVA, 2003). The two pharmaceutical companies AstraZeneca and Pharmacia Corporation were the dominant large companies engaged in biotechnology activities. Many Swedish DBFs serviced them in the biopharmaceuticals application sector, but also in such industries as food processing and agriculture.[5] These DBFs are highly research-led and knowledge-intensive. Between 10 and 20 per cent of employees in these companies have a doctoral degree. Of company presidents responding to VINNOVA's questionnaire, 93 per cent stated that their companies collaborated with academic research groups. From our earlier results, this appears to differentiate Swedish DBFs somewhat from those in the US and UK where research interactions are more among firms or distinctively among public research organizations (PROs). This is possibly an indicator of the relative immaturity of many Swedish DBFs formed as we have seen in the 1990s, for according to the VINNOVA study a majority of companies were small in 2001, that is, had fewer than 200 employees. Almost 90 per cent of the companies had less than 50 employees, and a good half had less than ten employees. However, the category of small and medium-sized biotech companies is growing such that in 2001 Swedish DBFs totalled about 4000 employees, a 35 per cent increase since 1997.

These are mostly found clustered in Sweden's metropolitan regions and in cities with large universities conducting substantial medical research. Fifty-six DBFs are located in the Stockholm region, followed by the Lund–Malmö and Uppsala regions, with 36 and 31 respectively. Twenty-four are located in the Gothenburg region. The smallest cluster is in the Umeå region, with fewer than ten biotech DBFs. The Swedish pharmaceutical industry annually spends around 25 per cent of its revenues on R&D, higher than the global standard of 17.5 per cent. This high percentage by international standards mainly reflects AstraZeneca's large expenditures in its Swedish research centres, with around one-third of the group's total R&D investments, $3.1 billion, occurring in Sweden. Of this some 20 per cent or $540 million is spent extramurally in Sweden (Benner and Sandström, 2000). Stockholm–Uppsala, in particular, contributes to Sweden's relative strength in biotechnology research, mainly through the Karolinska Institute, Uppsala University, Stockholm University, SLU[6] and the Royal Institute of Technology. These produce annually some 8000 publications, co-host some 4000 PhD students and employ some 2200 scientists.

However, on publication interactions, Sweden's collaborations revealed 70 per cent of co-authorships 1986–97 were with other Swedish PROs, while 12 per cent were with US institutions and an equivalent share with UK and German co-authors together. Regarding R&D projects, McKelvey et al. (2003) found the opposite: that is, of 215 collaborations made by 67 actors (firms, universities and research institutes), 52 were between Swedish institutions and the rest involved overseas partners, these again being mainly with the US and UK. This undoubtedly reflects the relative thinness of the pharmaceuticals and DBF market, particularly the former, in Sweden which perforce stimulates links for industrial research with larger economy incumbents. This is underlined to a limited degree for patenting where Swedish biotechnology patents registered in the US involved 62 jointly with US inventors. However 202 were products of Swedish-only collaborations; a similar pattern prevailed for pharmaceuticals joint-patenting (VINNOVA, 2003). Hence, Sweden may be said to display a relatively typical European introversion in much of its exploration or basic research activity, including to some extent patenting, but is more outgoing where applied research with industry is concerned. Stockholm–Uppsala is the stronger with 56 firms and 1126 employees, at least five strong research universities and around 1640 employees in smaller biotechnology businesses in four science parks. However, Lund–Malmö is a larger concentration, at 104, than Stockholm–Uppsala.

4.5.2 Denmark and Medicon Valley

Medicon Valley unites Lund–Malmö with Copenhagen and is well placed as a biotechnology cluster, being home to 11 universities, 70 biopharmaceuticals companies (60 per cent of the turnover of the Nordic pharmaceutical market) and 26 hospitals. Its academic institutions include, among others, Copenhagen and Lund universities, the Danish University of Pharmaceutical Sciences and the Royal Veterinary and Agricultural University, as well as centres for diabetes and stem cell research, and a multidisciplinary centre for stem cell biology and cell therapy. There are also 135000 students in the area, more than 300 research groups, 4000 life science employees and 27 local venture capital firms (Dorey, 2003). Pharmaceuticals firms have been key to growth on the Danish side through the likes of Hansen Laboratories, Carlsberg Laboratory and Novo Nordisk, a global insulin supplier and partner of Biogen the in the early bioengineering of human insulin. Medicon Valley Academy (MVA) was formed in 1997 to 'create, transfer, and exploit knowledge' with the aim of making it the most attractive bioregion in Europe by 2005. MVA is largely responsible for creating a sense of identity in the region, arranging networking events and also building relationships with other clusters in Scandinavia such as the Stockholm–Uppsala region. There is an emergent, small cluster around bioengineering and bioinformatics on the Aalborg University science park, counting some 20 start-up biotechnology businesses currently specializing in R&D and services rather than products.

4.6   CONCLUSIONS

We conclude that the European biotechnology presence is significant but immature compared to that prevailing in, for example, North America, especially the USA, where new biotechnology-based therapeutics continue to prove successful on world markets, notably as cancer treatments that are, nevertheless, often controversially expensive for oligopsonistic purchasers like the UK's National Health Servics (NHS) which seems unable or unwilling to drive hard bargains with pharmaceuticals giants like Pfizer, Roche and Wyeth *inter alia*, that are the main providers of such death-defying, or at least death-delaying, treatments. This is the key dilemma posed by the arrival of the rational drug design model that replaced 'chance discovery' with the onset of medical biotechnology as a major contributor to healthcare treatments. Such drugs often require less intensive care than predecessors utilizing chemotherapy and related care. This means that health services will logically require less massive centralized systems and, crucially, less intensive nursing staff and auxiliaries accordingly. Moderated somewhat by the rise in an aged population in most developed countries, the new biopharmaceuticals regime places tremendous pressures upon oligopsonistic systems, explaining why the threat of greater marketization in health services is politically so contentious. The platform nature of the evolution of biotechnology is captured in aspects of the drug production process where agro-food biotechnology enables antibodies to be grown in agricultural products such as maize, and even animals, although the latter approach remains highly expensive. Such plant waste that arises from what is known as 'pharming' may contribute to bioenergy from waste products.

European biotechnology firms remain on the whole small, vulnerable and undercapitalized mainly because their candidate products are, by and large, too limited in their scope to interest large-scale investors aiming to dominate world markets, notably pharmaceuticals firms, or they have selected or constrained to seek to exploit research that is too difficult to commercialize. This is because the 20-year lead in commercialization by US DBFs like *Genentech* means they captured the low-hanging fruit, leaving Europe with an eroding scientific lead and insufficient new research investment from the public sector and insufficient risk capital from the private sector because, to repeat, with a few exceptions, drug candidates have been insufficiently interesting to pharmaceuticals or venture capital companies. European DBFs are thus forced to occupy platform technology niches like diagnostic products, where global markets are highly competitive, rapidly evolving and with narrowing margins as a consequence. Only Switzerland, for a time, evolved DBF scale but Serono and others like Actelion are now absorbed into big pharmaceuticals companies. All in all, the knowledge flows future of European biotechnology as a serious competitor platform to that of the US seems to be in more serious doubt at the end of the 2000s than it has ever been before.

NOTES

1. A broad term that describes the use of microbial, plant or animal cells for the production of chemical compounds.
2. A number of key terms have been introduced. In definitional terms, their usage here is as follows. 'Region' is a governance unit between national and local levels. A 'regional economy' is 'the production, distribution and consumption of goods and services in a particular geographic region'. The 'knowledge economy' is measured, currently inadequately, as high-technology manufacturing added to knowledge-intensive services. A 'bioregion' has no standard definition, although regarding biotechnology 'clusters' a location quotient of 1.25 is considered sufficient. 'Knowledge' differs from 'information' in that it is creative and informed by meaning and understanding, whereas information

is passive and, without the application of knowledge, meaningless. To 'develop', as in 'regional development', means to evolve and augment, or enrich. Hence 'regional development' involves the cultural, economic and social enrichment of a region and its people. Here it mainly, but not exclusively, entails economic growth arising from increased efficiency and effectiveness in the use and exchange of the productive factors of an openly trading regional economy.

3. A drug from Immunex, a US biotechnology firm, was delayed in reaching the healthcare market because of a global shortage of bioprocessing capacity. Immunex's inability to produce sufficient quantities of its 'star' rheumatoid arthritis and psoriasis treatment Enbrel cost over \$200 million in lost revenue in 2001 alone; see Malik et al. (2002).

4. Thus PowderJect Pharmaceuticals is owned by Chiron, San Francisco (now owned fully by Novartis); part of British Biotech was bought by OSI Pharmaceuticals, Long Island, NY; Oxford Molecular is owned by Accelrys, San Diego,CA; Oxford Asymmetry was bought by Evotec OAI from Hamburg; and Oxford Glycosciences is owned by Union Belgique Chemie.

5. Swedish DBFs are noted suppliers and R&D partners to leading foreign pharmaceuticals firms (for example Carlsson Research and Merck; BioVitrum and Amgen; Kario Bio and Wyeth). However the official www.sweden.se website notes that: 'Both Astra-Zeneca and Pharmacia collaborate with numerous biotech companies, some of them Swedish . . . The pharmaceutical companies Astra (now AstraZeneca) and Pharmacia (today part of Pfizer) have stimulated the growth of the Swedish biotech industry, not only in the pharmaceutical and medical subsectors but also, for example, in biotech tools and supplies. Examples are Prevas Bioinformatics contract solutions for AstraZeneca, Biovitrum and GE Healthcare while blockbuster drugs like Losec (AstraZeneca) and Celebrex (Pharmacia) were clinically trialled by Swedish clinical research organizations (CROs) as were many others originating abroad (for example Lipitor, Norvasc & Zoloft for Pfizer; Lipovas for Merck; and Paxil for GlaxoSmithKline)'.

6. SLU is the Swedish University of Agricultural Sciences.

5. Knowledge phases, cognitive and relational distance in ICT alliance networks

Olivier Brossard and Jérôme Vicente

5.1 INTRODUCTION

There are several theoretical and empirical ways to study networks of innovators (Powell and Grodal, 2005). In this chapter, we focus mainly on the economic dimensions of knowledge dynamics in order to capture the reasons why firms engage in network relations. As a basic assumption, we suppose that knowledge is not only a public good – imperfect or impure though it may be – but also a complex and systemic good (Antonelli, 2005; Sorenson et al., 2006). Knowledge as an output is complex and systemic since it combines many interacting pieces of knowledge as inputs. Knowledge can be viewed as a 'recipe' which involves not just some peculiar combinations of 'ingredients', but also peculiar integration methods. Knowledge is therefore both complex and systemic insofar as its generation implies some systemic interdependencies between internal and external pieces of knowledge.

However, network strategies are not the panacea for knowledge-based firms' competitiveness. If firms improve their accessibility to external knowledge by establishing partnerships, they also face risks of appropriation defaults (Antonelli, 2006) in doing so. Network relations thus correspond to very peculiar strategies in which each participant considers that the benefits of accessibility exceed the risks of underappropriation. So that the relation may be of mutual advantage to them all, the partners establish collectively a specific network governance framework which especially defines the shared property rights structure.

The information and communication technology (ICT) sector will help us to carry out this study theoretically and empirically. This sector is particularly concerned by the role which networks play in the industrial organization. The questions of modularity, complementarity, compatibility and standardization are critical in the innovation diffusion process

(David, 1985; Aoki and Takizawa, 2002). These sectoral specificities entail some repercussions at the level of the firms' innovative and market performances. Successful firms are not necessarily the most innovative ones, but rather those which can have access to complementary knowledge resources. In this context, firms need to combine appropriation strategies designed to promote and exploit their knowledge in competitive markets with 'relational' strategies aimed at finding new opportunities and enhancing the integration of their knowledge into technical systems or platforms. Furthermore, in a complex and systemic view of knowledge dynamics, the ICT sector's network relations are more accurately analysed if they also include firms belonging to other sectors. Most high-tech industries are nowadays driven by technological convergence processes, and so by several cross-sector and technological windows. Most ICTs, as general-purpose technologies (David and Wright, 1999), are particularly concerned by these convergence processes, and network relations thus occur between ICT firms and media industries (web TV, mobile media, and so on), transport and aeronautics (on-board guidance systems), care industries (software for molecular information computation), banks and insurance companies (software for secure electronic transactions), and so on.

All these relations are typical of knowledge processes in which knowledge inputs are more or less fragmented into many technological areas. Moreover, the firms' motives for striking up these relations may differ strongly depending on their respective position in the knowledge value chain (Cooke, 2006a). Firms can explore new technological fields by combining complementary bits of knowledge in an upstream research and development (R&D) phase: the goal here focuses on technological feasibility. Firms can examine the technological integration of an innovation into an existing technological system, or examine the potentiality of shaping collectively a technological standard: the goal here goes from feasibility to the capture of network externalities to potential tradability. Firms can also exploit collectively a new technology on a market in an attempt to achieve scale economies collectively. Obviously, the network's governance structure will depend on the knowledge phase in which the firms are involved. It will also differ according to each partner's knowledge base, as well as according to the cognitive distance between them (Nooteboom, 2000; Wuyts et al., 2005). Such an assumption is consistent with the knowledge trade-off between accessibility and appropriation. Too strong a cognitive proximity may give rise to uncontrolled knowledge spillovers and thus weaken the respective knowledge appropriation capabilities. So, the strength of the relation – that is to say, relational proximity or distance – will depend on the private knowledge that firms are led to share with other partners, as well as on the specification of the collective property rights that they defined with a view to extracting rents from the knowledge output.

This chapter is divided as follows: section 5.2 provides definitions of cognitive and relational distance and shows that firms develop positioning strategies in this two-dimension space with a view to handling the appropriation–accessibility trade-off. In section 5.3, we show that the firms' motives for shaping alliances and partnerships differ depending on the phases of the knowledge value chain. In section 5.4, we develop a theoretical typology of network relations in the ICT sector. Section 5.5 presents the data set, the empirical methodology and the results. Section 5.6 concludes and develops further theoretical and empirical research issues.

5.2 COGNITIVE AND RELATIONAL PROXIMITY (AND DISTANCE) IN KNOWLEDGE NETWORKS

Following Nooteboom (2000), Boschma (2005) and Bouba and Grossetti (2006), we may define the level of cognitive proximity between firms according to their respective knowledge bases and paths. Firms are cognitively close when they share close capabilities, not only concerning technological knowledge, but also in relation to marketing or business knowledge. Firms belonging to the same technological fields[1] tend to be cognitively close, whereas those which do not have any technological similarity tend to be cognitively distant. Nevertheless, it would be too simplistic to reduce cognitive proximity (or distance) to the only technological dimension (Nooteboom, 2000). For instance, firms operating in the same technological fields can differ strongly if they do not share and develop the same business models or marketing knowledge (research-oriented or market-oriented).[2] Business, manufacturing and marketing practices are also forms of knowledge which are sometimes procedural, at other times declarative.

Relational proximity refers to the notion of interaction structure. Firms are relationally close when they have an interaction structure at their disposal which allows them to make transactions on knowledge. The fact that agents are cognitively close does not necessarily imply that they interact (Vicente and Suire, 2007). Relational proximity does not exist without a communication or an interaction structure. Interactions can be strong and frequent, or weak and scarce; they can be purely cooperative and horizontal, or hierarchical and vertical. A prerequisite for such analyses would be the construction of relational databases using for example data on financial relations, joint ventures and strategic alliances (Hagedoorn et al., 2000), co-patents and co-publications (Audretsch and Feldman, 1996; Breschi, and Lissoni, 2001), social capital provided by friendships and scholarship (Boschma, 2005), and so on. In this chapter, which is mainly focused on knowledge phases and cognitive distance, we shall only propose here a more qualitative assessment of relational distance in strategic alliances (see section 5.5.2).

Furthermore, we should underline that, most of the time, cognitive proximity and relational proximity are not pure strategic substitutes, nor pure strategic complements. There are several possible situations where relational proximity can match cognitive proximity efficiently, and other situations where relational proximity can perform better with a certain amount of cognitive distance. The critical parameter which determines the efficiency of cognitive and relational proximity combinations is the balance between knowledge spillovers and network spillovers. On the one hand, firms face risks of unintended knowledge spillovers when they share knowledge with other partners. On the other hand, the necessity of acquiring complementary modules of knowledge requires such knowledge-sharing processes, when compatibility and interoperability between systemic and network technologies are the rule of competitiveness (Economides, 1996; Jaffe, 1996). The risks of unintended knowledge spillovers are even more important when cognitive proximity between partners is strong, each partner's technological absorptive capabilities being very similar as a result of the proximity in their respective knowledge paths (Nooteboom, 2000), and the weak differentiation of the markets on which they compete (Vicente and Suire, 2007). In this case, firms can be affected by appropriation defaults which constitute, *ceteris paribus*, a weak incentive for them to form partnerships, and so to enhance their relational proximity. Nevertheless, in many technological fields in which knowledge is complex and systemic, these risks are largely offset by the benefits that firms may derive from network externalities (direct and indirect) at the demand level. The ICT sector is, of course, one of those most concerned by such a phenomenon. The consumers' willingness to pay for a technology depends strongly on the interoperability and compatibility between competing technologies (direct externalities). It also depends on the integration of a specific technology into a larger technological system and so on the vertical integration of technologies coming from different firms (indirect externalities). The firms' necessity of capturing these externalities requires a certain amount of relational proximity to shape a technological standard or to solve compatibility or interoperability problems. The more or less reciprocal accessibility to knowledge is, in this case, coupled with some appropriate property rights (such as licensing or cross-licensing agreements) in order to favour accessibility and reduce appropriation defaults.

The above argumentation leads to the following propositions:

Proposition 1: firms deal with the knowledge trade-off between accessibility to and appropriation of knowledge by embedding their knowledge strategies within a cognitive and relational space.

Proposition 2: in a complex and systemic view of knowledge, the firms' incentives to form partnerships depend on the balance between the benefits of network externalities encapsulation and the risks of unintended knowledge spillovers. The weight of unintended spillovers is even more important when cognitive proximity between partners is strong.

Nooteboom (2000) argues that there is an optimal cognitive distance which generates a maximum level of learning through interaction. Too strong a cognitive distance causes an excess of mutual misunderstanding between partners. On the contrary, too strong a cognitive proximity lowers the novelty value of the mutual learning process. Beyond the difficult question of the different ways to measure cognitive distance and to infer an optimal one, we would like to develop further the debate about cognitive distance through two interconnected arguments. Firstly, if we acknowledge that too strong a cognitive proximity does not bring enough novelty to produce new knowledge, we want to emphasize that it can, however, play an important role in the diffusion of new knowledge on markets. This is particularly true in the ICT sector as a consequence of the systemic characteristics of knowledge. The balance in partnerships between cognitive proximity and cognitive distance will be different depending on whether firms cooperate with a view to experimenting with cross-sector and cross-technological knowledge, or with a view to capturing direct or indirect network externalities. Secondly, we also admit that too strong a cognitive proximity restrains the firms' incentives to cooperate on account of the risks of unintended knowledge spillovers. Nevertheless, property rights are available to enable firms to control these risks and internalize these spillovers. The strength of the property rights governing partnerships thus proves to be one of the critical parameters of the variety of knowledge networks.

5.3 THE KNOWLEDGE VALUE CHAIN AND ALLIANCES STRATEGIES IN THE ICT SECTOR

The balance between knowledge appropriability and accessibility, and consequently between network spillovers and knowledge spillovers, may be highlighted by focusing more specifically on the different phases of the knowledge value chain (Cooke, 2006a). The combinations and the respective levels of relational and cognitive proximity will differ according to the knowledge phases. As a result, knowledge phases represent decisive determinants of the variety of knowledge networks.

The literature generally puts forward two main phases in the knowledge value chain (Gilsing and Nooteboom, 2006): (1) a phase of exploration, based on a strategy of radical innovation through research and experimentation; (2) a phase of exploitation, based on a strategy of incremental innovation through product development and adaptation to market change. Though this simple breakdown of the knowledge value chain still remains relevant at the firm level, it fails to grasp the complexity of knowledge generation and diffusion when knowledge inputs are fragmented and when knowledge outputs depend on network effects. Therefore, following Cooke (2006a), we propose introducing a third and intermediary phase of knowledge examination.

In network-based exploration phases, a certain amount of cognitive distance in knowledge exchange is necessary for the generation of knowledge, as knowledge is cumulative and emerges from the complementarity between 'distant' bits of knowledge. Cognitive distance between partners is thus one of the key parameters of the probability of innovative success in the exploration phase, even if too strong a cognitive distance may bring about misunderstandings between partners. The intensity of relational proximity therefore has to be stronger in this case than in pure exploitation phases insofar as interactive learning through communication is crucial to reach mutual understanding.

Such a postulate is all the more important in the ICT sector since it includes a wide range of general-purpose technologies (David and Wright, 1999), that is to say technologies with potential for innovation in many other more or less adjacent sectors. This explains why ICT firms' partnerships often include firms from other sectors such as aeronautics and aerospace, the defence and military, transport, automotive industries, chemistry, business services, and so on. In the very upstream phase of the knowledge value chain, firms try to explore new technological fields by forming alliances with partners from other sectors for two main reasons. The first reason – extensively evidenced by the evolutionary theory of the firm – consists in the preservation of diversity and technological options for the future. The second reason, which is more specific to the ICT sector or at least to general-purpose technologies, relates to firms' strategies in the field of 'convergent technologies'. These situations are typical of knowledge processes in which knowledge inputs are fragmented into many technological areas. The exploration phase thus consists in knowledge combination strategies through more or less formal R&D agreements within the framework of a very upstream technological feasibility research (prototype definition). In this phase, accessibility to external knowledge is the partners' main objective, which has to be supported by a high degree of relational proximity and a certain amount of openness and cooperative behaviour (Cooke, 2006b; Gilsing and Nooteboom, 2006). The difference between the partners' absorptive capabilities justifies the intensity of relational proximity insofar as it implies both frequent meetings and engineers' mobility. Such a proximity is facilitated by the fact that firms do not originally compete in the same markets, which means that the risks of unintended knowledge spillovers are lower in this case than in pure exploitation phases.[3] The typical 'mutual hostage' situation of technological partnerships is thus compatible with 'loose' and 'trust-based' research alliances (Gilsing and Nooteboom, 2006). Nevertheless, if the network-based exploration phase succeeds and leads to new knowledge, co-patenting appears to be an appropriate tool to solve the appropriation–accessibility trade-off (Breschi and Lissoni, 2001).

The intermediate phase between exploration and exploitation is examination (Cooke, 2006a). In this phase, appropriation and accessibility interplay in a complex property rights game. If cognitive proximity can possibly be as weak in this case as in the exploration phase, the focus here is not on feasibility, but rather on potential tradability. That is why the solving of compatibility problems between complementary bits of knowledge constitutes an additional phase of the dynamic knowledge generation process. This phase may be divided into two distinct subphases depending on whether firms form alliances with a view to capturing indirect or direct network externalities.

In the first subphase, relational proximity still remains important, even if contacts and face-to-face interactions can be lower than in pure exploration phases as a result of the progress in the knowledge codification process. Firms need to integrate different modules of knowledge and make sure that these are compatible. When the knowledge produced by a firm generates increasing consumer satisfaction only if this knowledge is integrated into existing technologies, the firm in question must pursue a double objective. Firstly, it has to ascertain the compatibility between its module and the technological base into which this module will be introduced. Secondly, in order to capture indirect network externalities at the demand level, it needs to choose its partner according to the breadth of the so-called 'installed base'. The tradability of complementary modules of knowledge requires these two conditions. Licensing agreements are generally implemented in these situations as, in contrast to exploration phases, knowledge already exists and has to be controlled by the innovative firm.

In this examination phase, relational proximity is favoured by the necessity of combining the partners' respective technological expertise (through engineers' mobility for instance). Each partner draws an advantage from this relational proximity: the licensor finds a potential for trade opportunities as far as its technological output is concerned, while the licensee may find some opportunities to enhance its technological installed base and improve its products' functionalities.

The second examination subphase rests on a stronger cognitive proximity. If cognitive proximity between firms can favour their respective absorptive capabilities, it reduces the probability of new knowledge generation. Nevertheless, strong cognitive proximity can be compatible with partnerships when firms focus their efforts on defining a technological standard. Such efforts require reaching a critical mass so that direct network externalities may play their role and reduce the uncertainty that firms are confronted with in emergent markets (Hill, 1997). This can be facilitated by the guarantee firms may obtain when they are provided with a public licence or when clearly identified common property rights are defined. However, cognitively close firms may maintain a relational distance if: (1) they want to keep a high degree of appropriation over their knowledge; and (2) they consider that the benefits of shaping compatible technologies do not exceed the risks of uncontrolled knowledge spillovers (and the compatibility process costs as well). In the latter case, 'standards war' will prevail over cooperation and collective appropriation. Cognitive proximity can prove very useful in terms of knowledge diffusion when firms seek to combine their knowledge with a view to shaping a new technological standard. In doing so, firms capture the benefits resulting from network externalities at the demand level, even if they thus take the risk of losing private control over their inventions. As regards the ICT sector, we can draw an enlightening parallel between the knowledge appropriation–accessibility trade-off and the network externalities–knowledge externalities trade-off (Jaffe, 1996). Nevertheless, relational proximity in this case tends to be weaker than in the exploration phase since relations focus more specifically on highly codified knowledge exchanges, rather than on research capabilities and tacit knowledge. Most of the time, the latter had previously been built by each of the firms, or in the context of exploration relations with other firms.

The exploitation phase combines cognitive proximity with a certain amount of relational distance. Following Gilsing and Nooteboom (2006), alliance-based exploitation strategies are particularly well suited to the purpose of technological generalization. Once the industry standard has been established, firms need to consolidate this standard into a dominant design by enlarging the scale of diffusion not only in the geographical space, but also in the application space. In this context, firms develop manufacturing agreements, marketing agreements and joint ventures in order to extract rents from scale economies and increase their market power. The interaction structure in this phase requires weak ties as the risks of unintended knowledge spillovers are strong due to the high level of cognitive proximity between partners. Firms only share their production or marketing capabilities and maintain a high level of appropriation over their knowledge capabilities through a formal specification of their respective intellectual property rights. The extreme case of contract specification and monitoring is the joint venture strategy in which partners integrate their production or marketing capabilities into a special purpose entity so that they may maintain a strong relational distance between their knowledge capabilities.

The above argumentation leads to the following three propositions:

Proposition 3: the level of cognitive and relational proximity between firms depends on the phases of the knowledge value chain in the ICT sector.

Proposition 4: the intensity of relational proximity is positively correlated with cognitive distance.

Proposition 5: the strength of property rights schemes increases with cognitive proximity, reducing the risks of unintended knowledge spillovers along the knowledge value chain.

5.4 A THEORETICAL TYPOLOGY OF KNOWLEDGE PARTNERSHIPS IN THE ICT SECTOR

Before we move on to the statistical test of the above-mentioned propositions, we suggest summarizing the explanations of the variety of knowledge relations through a typology and a few empirical examples. The typology crosses the cognitive and relational proximity axes with the identified knowledge phases. Empirical examples are extracted from the SDC Platinum database – a powerful database of strategic alliances and joint ventures. It is widely admitted that strategic alliances may be considered as monitoring systems for knowledge sharing and exchange (Mowery et al., 1996; Gulati and Singh, 1998). Alliances can take the form of licensing or cross-licensing agreements, technology transfers, customer–supplier partnerships, joint development agreements, R&D contracts, equity joint ventures, and so on. Most alliances actually combine several of these characteristics to support complex strategies of knowledge network positioning. Consequently, to understand these strategies, it might be useful to consider the technological specificities of the ICT sector and place strategic alliances within the bidimensional space of cognitive and relational distance, as well as within the framework of the three knowledge phases. This will help us to understand alliances as devices for the implementation of complex collective knowledge accumulation and generation processes (Antonelli, 2006). This will also allow us to show that these are flexible tools that may be customized to fit the different phases of the knowledge value chain (Cooke, 2006a).

The two axes of the typology cross the respective levels of cognitive and relational proximity and display different combinations corresponding to specific knowledge relations – from no relation to competition, including other cooperative and 'coopetitive' agreements and strategies. The top left-hand side of Figure 5.1 symbolizes the absence of interactions between firms. The excess of cognitive distance and the absence of technological convergence opportunities imply the non-existence of knowledge or strategic interactions. Cognitive distance may yet generate knowledge interactions when cross-sector opportunities occur and technological windows are opened. The bottom left-hand side of Figure 5.1 displays the particular situation of collective knowledge exploration. In this phase, the firms' main motive is to access external modules of knowledge in order to develop a 'differentiation through exploration' strategy (Gilsing and Nooteboom, 2006). The purpose in this phase is not the direct tradability, but the feasibility of technology combinations. R&D agreements are generally implemented here and co-patents are the natural output of such a collective process. Relational proximity can be strong in this phase due to the level of cognitive distance between partners which requires the construction of a mutual understanding and, consequently, frequent meetings between engineers and other employees. This strong relational proximity is, however, compatible with 'loose' contracts, that is to say agreements in which the *ex ante* definition of property rights is not necessary insofar as the risks of unintended knowledge spillovers between so cognitively distant partners are not very high. The strategic alliance signed between Philips Electronics and Levi Strauss & Co. in August 2000 is characteristic of such a situation:

> Levi Strauss & Co., a unit of Levi Strauss Associates, and Philips Electronics NV formed a strategic alliance to provide research and development services in United States and Netherlands. The alliance was to develop electronic clothing. The clothes were fully equipped with fully integrated computer networks. (SDC Platinum database, deal n°1038365045, August 2000)

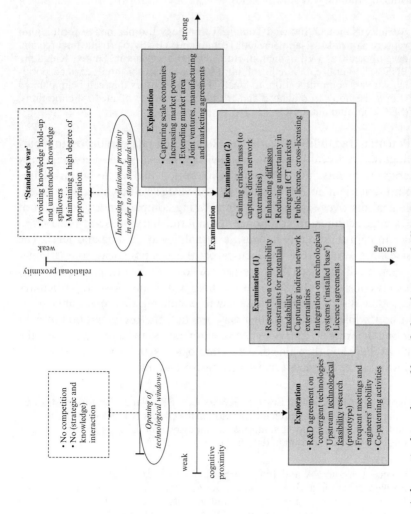

Figure 5.1   A theoretical typology of knowledge phases and alliance strategies in the ICT sector

Beyond the surprising but very illustrative character of this alliance, many other such partnerships occur between firms from different sectors, thus confirming the fact that ICTs are general-purpose technologies which give rise to technological convergence processes. The technology combinations taking place between ICTs, biotechnologies and nanotechnologies are among the most recurrent ones:

> Advance Nanotech Inc. and Toumaz Technology Ltd planned to form a joint venture named Bio-Nano Sensium Technologies (BNS) to provide research and development, as well as manufacture bio-nano sensors in United Kingdom. BNS was to utilize an intelligent, ultra-low power sensor interface, incorporating wireless communication, to create bio-nano sensors that can be implanted within the body to diagnose and treat a wide variety of medical conditions. (SDC Platinum database)

Potential tradability concerns the examination phase in the bottom part of Figure 5.1. Recall that when knowledge is fragmented between many interacting agents, the traditional exploration and exploitation phases are not sufficient to understand the knowledge value chain, from technological discovery to diffusion. Integrating complementary modules of knowledge requires an additional and intermediary phase of research in order to capture indirect network externalities at the demand level. The first examination subphase focuses on the technological compatibility between modules. Each firm's respective goal differs: one partner's objective may consist in integrating its technology into another complementary and widely installed one with a view to enhancing the potentiality of its diffusion; while the other partner may benefit from this integration by augmenting the variety of services and functionalities, and so by increasing the installed base and the value of the technological standard (Hill, 1997). The following three alliances furnish illustrative examples:

> Nokia Oy AB (NO) and Eastman Kodak Co. (EK) planned to form a strategic alliance to provide research and development services of kiosk printing services and other retail printing solutions to empower mobile users to turn pictures into prints. (SDC Platinum database)

> France Telecom SA and Intel Corp. planned to form a strategic alliance to provide research and development services of wireless household devices. Under terms of the agreement, FT and IC were to set up a joint development team to research image, video, music, photo and games devices and share intellectual property resulting from the transaction. (SDC Platinum database)

Compatibility and interoperability are at the centre of the second examination subphase. In this case, the alliance prospects are typical of 'coopetition' situations where competing firms cooperate in order to impose a technological standard. In these situations, cognitive proximity is strong due to each partner's knowledge paths, but the risk of knowledge drain does not exceed the collective benefit that firms can gain from the collective capture of direct network externalities, whether these are technological or social. In particular, knowledge stealing is limited when public licences exist (like in the mobile phone industry) or if a collective shared and mutual property rights strategy has been defined. The risks of unintended knowledge spillovers are also reduced when the alliance is not research-intensive, that is to say when technologies exist and the additional research phase focuses only on technological interoperability and the collective marketing strategy. The mobile phone industry is typical of these partnerships:

> Ericsson Radio Systems and Motorola agreed to cross-license technologies related to the global system for mobile communications (GSM). The companies also agreed to design and manufacture their own cellular equipment, but will conform to specifications set by a 17-country European consortium. Ericsson and Motorola also agreed to a program which enabled Motorola's GSM base station equipment to operate with Ericsson's switching platform. The agreement was extended to Orbitel Mobile Communications, an Ericsson GSM equipment venture. (SDC Platinum database)

> Nokia Oy AB and Sony Corp. planned to form a strategic alliance to provide telecommunications services. The alliance was to develop and create a set of open standards for interoperability between mobile devices. (SDC Platinum database)

On the right-hand side of Figure 5.1, we find the joint exploitation phase in which firms form alliances or joint ventures in order to consolidate their standard or technology into a dominant design. These partnerships are dedicated to the manufacturing and marketing of new products developed in the first two phases. Since appropriability is the main concern here, partners have to find agreements which both diminish relational proximity and delineate precisely property rights. Consequently, joint ventures are the privileged form of alliance used to implement these manufacturing and marketing agreements. Moreover, these kinds of alliances are characterized by low cognitive distance. The two following well-known examples are typical of this collective exploitation phase:

> Fujitsu Ltd (FL) and Siemens AG (SA) formed a joint venture named Fujitsu Siemens Computers (FSC) to manufacture, retail and wholesale computers and peripherals for the European market. FSC was based in the Netherlands. Under terms of the agreement, FSC manufactured personal computers and

peripherals for corporate users and sold them under FL's and SA's brand names. FL and SA each held a 50% interest in FSC. FL's Fujitsu Computer (Europe) Ltd and SA's Siemens Computer Systems division were combined into FSC. *(SDC Platinum database)*

Finally, on the top right-hand side of Figure 5.1, we find the 'standards war' situations, where firms compete on incompatible and non-interoperable technologies. Cognitively close firms can maintain a relational distance if they want to keep a high degree of appropriation in the exploitation of their knowledge and if they judge that the benefits of shaping compatible technologies do not exceed the risks of uncontrolled knowledge spillovers (and also the costs of the compatibility and interoperability processes). In this case, 'standards war' prevails over alliances. The coexistence of technologies in the video game industry constitutes a good example.

These predictions imply in fact that alliance characteristics are not randomly distributed: there should be a typology of alliances in keeping with the knowledge phases. We shall now proceed to implement a cluster analysis on the ICT sector's alliances in Europe with a view to testing whether these predictions are valid or not.

5.5   DATA AND EMPIRICAL ASSESSMENT

5.5.1   The Data on ICT Alliances in EU-25

We used the well-known SDC Platinum database operated by Thomson Financial. We extracted all effective alliances with at least one participant from the ICT sector and one European (EU-25) participant between 1997 and 2006. We deliberately adopted a broad definition of the ICT industry including not only hardware, software and telecommunication sectors, but also audio and video equipment, navigational instruments, ICT-related commercial services, communication services, media broadcasting, and so on. This definition is roughly the same as the official Organisation for Economic Co-operation and Development (OECD) definition of the ICT sector that has recently been extended (see Bourassa, 2006). It is even broader insofar as we also integrate 'Content Activities' such as radio and TV broadcasting. These network-based activities are integrated as well since we think they are very similar to the ICT activities in terms of their knowledge production and diffusion processes.

The choice of SDC Platinum as the data source may raise several difficulties. First of all, we must acknowledge that this database is certainly not exhaustive. Furthermore, it would have been misleading to conclude that other well-known alliance databases such as CATI, CORE and NCRA-RJV were more relevant for the kind of study we proposed to undertake.[4] We could not, indeed, use CATI because it is restricted to technological partnerships and excludes manufacturing and marketing agreements. We, in fact, need information about these kinds of non-technological agreements insofar as we set out to identify knowledge value chain phases and we think that there also are some knowledge flows in the exploitation phase. Neither could we use CORE or NCRA-RJV because their data come from the US Department of Justice and are consequently focused on US rather than on European alliances.

So, SDC Platinum appeared to be the most relevant data source for a study of non-technological and technological alliances focusing on the ICT sector in Europe. The data set is split into two subperiods, namely 1997–2002 and 2003–06. This will allow us to account for a possible structural instability resulting from the bursting of the dot-com bubble and its aftermath.

For the period between 1997 and 2002, there were 2390 alliances reported to which 5231 firms were party. Over the period 2003–06, 876 alliances occurred with 1793 firms involved. It thus appears obvious that the Internet crash strongly decreased the activity of strategic partnerships in Europe's ICT sector. By way of illustration, there were on average 398 alliances reported per year between 1997 and 2002, and only 219 alliances per year over the period 2003–06.

Whatever the period, alliance participants mainly come from five subsectors: computer programming and data processing; telephone communications; communications equipment; electronic components and accessories; and computer and office equipment.[5] The Internet crash did not change this hierarchy, but it affected some sectors more strongly than others: for example, the share of alliance participants from the telephone communications sector dropped while that of computer programming and data processing increased. The share of alliance participants from Media Broadcasting and other TV services has experienced a significant drop too, as well as that of Miscellaneous Investing activities. On the contrary, the share of alliance participants from the research, development, and testing services, and drugs sectors went up significantly. However, it is necessary to be cautious when interpreting these changes insofar as we do not know whether these are due to the crash of the dot-com bubble or to some other – more structural – changes.

We shall now proceed to describe the different kinds of alliances encountered in these two periods. In SDC Platinum, alliances are primarily characterized in terms of institutional arrangement: an alliance

Platforms of innovation

Table 5.1   Alliance characteristics

	Number of alliances	Frequency (%)	Number of alliances	Frequency (%)
	1997–2002		2003–06	
Alliance form				
Strategic alliance	1763	*73.77*	790	*90.18*
Joint venture	627	*26.23*	86	*9.82*
Total	2390	*100.00*	876	*100.00*
Alliance characteristics				
Alliance with cross-border participants	1952	*81.67*	793	*90.53*
Services agreement	1350	*56.49*	414	*47.26*
Marketing agreement	327	*13.68*	155	*17.69*
Licensing agreement	311	*13.01*	87	*9.93*
Manufacturing agreement	232	*9.71*	71	*8.11*
R&D agreement	189	*7.91*	49	*5.59*
Technology transfer	120	*5.02*	168	*19.18*
Supply agreement	84	*3.51*	3	*0.34*
Cross-technology transfer	51	*2.13*	130	*14.84*
OEM/VAR* agreement	24	*1.00*	6	*0.68*
Exclusive licensing agreement	15	*0.63*	6	*0.68*
Spinout	10	*0.42*	4	*0.46*
Royalties	7	*0.29*	0	*0.00*
Equity stake purchase	4	*0.17*	0	*0.00*
Equity transfer	3	*0.13*	0	*0.00*
Cross-licensing agreement	2	*0.08*	2	*0.23*
Cross-equity transfer	1	*0.04*	0	*0.00*
Joint venture stake option	1	*0.04*	0	*0.00*

Note: * OEM/VAR: original equipment manufacture/value-added reseller.

is either a 'joint venture' or a 'strategic alliance'. It is a joint venture if it involves the creation of a special-purpose entity – with or without equity participation from the partners – dedicated to the implementation of common activities. Conversely, it is a strategic alliance if no independent entity is created. Either kind of alliance can then be characterized by its aims as well as by the tools it uses to achieve them. We are thus provided with several binary variables describing the alliances' characteristics. The full list is given in Table 5.1.

A great majority of alliances are simple strategic alliances with a low level of irreversibility. It is worth stressing that this figure is even bigger after the crash of the dot-com bubble (from 73.8 per cent to 90.2 per cent). Financial uncertainty in the post-crash era appears to be a strong barrier to the forming of joint ventures.[6] A great majority of alliances involve participants from different countries (82 per cent), this figure being even bigger in the second subperiod (91 per cent).

Concerning the means and goals of alliances, we can see that services, marketing, manufacturing, licensing, technology transfer and R&D agreements are the most frequent types of arrangements. All these characteristics are directly available as binary variables in the SDC Platinum database,[7] except for the category 'services agreements'. We ourselves created this category to describe alliances which have none of the other characteristics as coded by the SDC Platinum staff. A thorough check of these alliances' deal documents led us to describe them as 'services agreements'. Most of the time, these concern alliances by which a firm offers some services to other firms – computer, programming, multimedia or Internet services very frequently. The other kinds of services often provided are broadcasting or telecommunication services, and commercial or environmental services.

Many alliances combine several of the characteristics described in Table 5.1 (for example, manufacturing and marketing agreements or R&D and marketing agreements). Consequently, it is worth assessing whether some combinations of characteristics tend to be recurrent in the sample. In relation to section 5.3 where we underlined the probable existence of different phases in the knowledge value chain, we expect the combinations of agreements characteristics to correspond to the different phases of the knowledge value chain. Moreover, we expect the alliance participants to be characterized by different degrees of cognitive proximity from one phase of the knowledge value chain to another.

5.5.2 Measures of Cognitive and Relational Distances

In section 5.2, we defined cognitive proximity as the sharing of common knowledge bases, that is to say close technological capabilities, as well as close business and marketing practices. Consequently, cognitive proximity is not restricted to the sole technological aspect of firms' knowledge. What is important to point out here is that common cognition processes between alliance participants generate a higher risk of unintended knowledge spillovers, and therefore require the alliance to protect knowledge property rights more efficiently. There are several ways to measure cognitive proximity but, as underlined by Wuyts et al. (2005), it is first necessary to account for organizational and strategic cognition, as well as technological cognition. Technological aspects may be captured through patent field codes or R&D budget allocations across technological fields, but it is more difficult to find information about strategic and organizational practices. Inasmuch as we do not have such information at our disposal, we decided to use SIC and VEIC codes to build our cognitive proximity indicators. Indeed, they are both available in the SDC Platinum database and have the great advantage of being overall indicators capturing both the technological focus and the business characteristics of the firms. SIC codes are well-known US industrial classification codes ('Standard Industrial Classification'). VEIC codes rather describe firms' technological fields. They were originally created by the Venture Economics subsidiary of Securities Data to track venture capital-backed companies.

Our measures of cognitive distance are derived from a count of the number of common digits between the primary SIC or VEIC codes of alliance participants. We build two variables. The one based on SIC codes is labelled *distk_SIC*, and the one based on VEIC codes is labelled *distk_VEIC*. They are computed in the following way: if the first digit of the codes considered is common, a score of 1 is assigned; if the first two digits are equal, a score of 2 is assigned; if the first three digits are equal, a score of 3 is assigned; and finally, if the first four digits are equal, a score of 4 is assigned. Consequently, each cognitive distance variable varies between 0 and 4. Yet, this count measure is not satisfactory since it implies a linear increase in cognitive proximity with the number of common codes. For example, the measure's growth is the same when we move from a 'first digit in common' alliance to a 'first two digits in common' alliance, and when we move from a 'first two digits in common' alliance to a 'first three digits in common' alliance. In the latter case though, the real increase in the intensity of cognitive proximity is much higher. To account for the probable non-linearity, we decided to compute the squared scores and the scores' exponential values. These variables are then labelled *distk2_SIC*, *distk_exp_SIC*, *distk2_VEIC* and *distk_exp_VEIC*.

Relational proximity is much more difficult to synthesize into a single measure insofar as firms and their stakeholders are embedded in many different interaction structures: financial relationships, interlocking directorates, specialized job markets, social networks, and so on. Consequently, it seems to be nearly impossible to compute a meaningful overall measure of the degree of relational proximity between alliance participants. Nevertheless, what is important here is to have an idea of the relational proximity which the alliance itself creates, which is feasible to a certain extent. We cannot say that a manufacturing agreement implies more or less relational proximity than a marketing agreement. But there are some other alliances' characteristics for which it is much easier to determine whether they create a high level or a low level of relational proximity.

Table 5.2   Qualitative assessment of relational proximity in alliances

Type of alliance	R&D	Licensing, technology transfer	OEM/VAR, supply	Marketing/ manufacturing/ services	JV
Relational proximity	+++	++	+	−	−−

Firstly, R&D agreements certainly imply a high level of relational proximity because the exchange of new ideas is not possible without frequent contacts. Licensing agreements or technology transfers also imply a certain degree of relational proximity, at least at the beginning of the agreement, because it is necessary to explain how to use the transferred knowledge. However, this relational proximity will last less time than in the case of an R&D agreement. OEM/VAR agreements and supply agreements also necessitate a certain degree of relational proximity since it is necessary to make sure that the product supplied by one participant to another fits the final product. Some interactions between firms' engineers will consequently be necessary to adjust the products. Finally, we can certainly conclude that OEM/VAR agreements, licensing or technology transfer agreements and R&D agreements all imply a phase of technological adjustment between the participant firms in which their engineers exchange knowledge in order to develop efficient joint products. In these cases, relational proximity is much more necessary than in the case of simple manufacturing, marketing or services agreements.

Relational proximity also varies depending on the alliance's form: a joint venture (JV) is certainly a case of lower relational proximity than any strategic alliance since it implies the creation of a separate entity. Thus, in the case of a joint venture, the partners of the original firms do not interact any longer. The interactions are internalized in a distinct entity where only the members of the JV interact, while those that remained members of the original firms do not.

To sum up, we can propose a qualitative measure of the relational proximity created by some characteristics of strategic alliances (Table 5.2).

We are now in a position to combine these quantitative and qualitative measures of cognitive and relational proximity with the above-described alliance characteristics in order to assess the existence of knowledge-related phases in alliances strategies. As already underlined, we expect these phases to be characterized by specific types of alliances creating different levels of cognitive and relational proximity.

We propose testing this hypothesis through the use of a specific classificatory procedure. We shall also have to check whether these specific combinations of agreements are stable across the two subperiods. This is indeed a matter of concern since the statistics in Table 5.1 show us that some kinds of agreements clearly dropped after the crash (licensing, services, manufacturing, R&D agreements) while others, on the contrary, went up significantly (technology and cross-technology transfers).

Since a priori there are many possible combinations of agreement types, it is necessary to use a specific statistical methodology to identify a limited number of meaningful alliance clusters and characterize them. We expect that some specific kinds of agreements are implemented in the exploration phase of the knowledge value chain, while others are rather used in the examination and exploitation phases. But is this assumption validated by the data? To put it differently, are the combinations of alliance characteristics distributed randomly between alliances or, on the contrary, is it possible to uncover some recurrent types of combinations of alliance characteristics? And, if so, do they make sense in terms of what the theoretical literature has taught us about the aims of partnership in the different phases of the knowledge generation process?

We use a classification procedure with the following steps. First of all, we exclude from the list of variables alliance characteristics with low variance or with low communality. The first criterion amounts to cutting out the characteristics that have too few occurrences (see Table 5.1) such as equity transfer, royalties, spinout, and so on. The second criterion leads us to exclude the variables which have a low correlation with the factors retained in the principal components analysis or which have a significant correlation with several factors so that they cannot be clearly related to any specific factor. This selection of relevant variables leaves 11 alliance characteristics which we combine with our measure of cognitive distance *distk_exp_VEIC*[8] with a view to implementing the principal components analysis (Table 5.3).

It is worth recalling that even if the frequency of most characteristics is rather stable between the two periods, a few of them experience a significant change between the first and the second period. Most noticeably, the shares of cross-sector alliances and supply agreements, respectively, drop from 46 per cent to 36 per cent and from 5 per cent to 1 per cent. There is also a significant drop in the percentage of alliances with more than two participants (from 12 per cent to 4 per cent). On the contrary, the share of technological transfers rises from 7 per cent to 20 per cent, and the share of strategic alliances rises from 74 per cent to 90 per cent. All these changes may generate differences in the alliance typologies between 1997–2002 on the one hand and 2003–06 on the other.

The principal components analysis conducted on these variables gives

Table 5.3 Descriptive statistics of the variables used in the classification procedure

Variable	Definition	Type	Min	Max	Mean	Std Dev.	Mean	Std Dev.
Servicesagree	Whether the alliance is a services agreement or not	Binary (Yes = 1; No = 0)	0	1	0.57	0.50	0.47	0.50
R_Dagree	Whether the alliance is a R&D agreement or not	Binary	0	1	0.08	0.27	0.06	0.23
techtransf_all	Whether the alliance implies technological transfer (unilateral or cross-) or not	Binary	0	1	0.07	0.26	0.20	0.40
licagree_all	Whether the alliance is a licensing agreement (simple, cross-, exclusive) or not	Binary	0	1	0.12	0.33	0.10	0.30
Allsupplyagree	Whether the alliance is a supply or an OEM/VAR agreement or not	Binary	0	1	0.05	0.21	0.01	0.10
manufagree	Whether the alliance is a manufacturing agreement or not	Binary	0	1	0.10	0.30	0.08	0.27
Mkgagree	Whether the alliance is a marketing agreement or not	Binary	0	1	0.14	0.34	0.18	0.38
Jv	Whether the alliance is a joint venture or not	Binary	0	1	0.26	0.44	0.10	0.30

Table 5.3 (continued)

Variable	Definition	Type	Min	Max	Mean	Std Dev.	Mean	Std Dev.
strategicall	Whether the alliance is a strategic alliance or not	Binary	0	1	0.74	0.44	0.90	0.30
numberofpart_r	Whether the alliance involves more than two participants or not	Binary	0	1	0.12	0.32	0.04	0.21
crosssector	Whether the alliance involves participants from non-ICT sectors or not	Binary	0	1	0.46	0.50	0.36	0.48
distk_exp_veic	Exponential value of the number of common digits of participants' VEIC codes	Numerical	1	54.60	5.80	13.13	8.61	16.24

Table 5.4   Principal components analysis results

Component	1997–2002			2003–06		
	Initial Eigen-values	% of explained variance	Cumu-lative %	Initial Eigen-values	% of explained variance	Cumu-lative %
1	2.36	19.65	19.65	2.34	21.23	21.23
2	1.86	15.46	35.11	1.74	15.86	37.09
3	1.28	10.68	45.79	1.36	12.37	49.46
4	1.20	10.00	55.79	1.20	10.87	60.32
5	1.02	8.48	64.27	1.01	9.21	69.54

the following results (Table 5.4). We can see that the percentage of explained variance is, whatever the period, very satisfactory, which means that the information contained in the 12 alliance characteristics variables can in fact be synthesized into five factors which are able to account for 64 per cent to 70 per cent of the total variance of alliance characteristics.

We then perform two non-hierarchical cluster analyses – one for each period – based on the scores of the principal components analysis. To put it differently, we classify the alliances into clusters of statistically meaningful alliance types, combining not the 12 alliance characteristics but the five factors extracted from the principal components analysis. In order to determine the final number of alliance clusters, we use three usual criteria: (1) the statistical accuracy of the classification measured by the ratio of within-cluster and between-cluster variances (Fisher's test); (2) the number of firms per cluster; and (3) the economic meaning of the clusters identified. According to these criteria, we are able to discern four alliance clusters in the first subperiod and five in the second subperiod. To interpret the categories, we compute the mean of each alliance characteristics indicator in each of these clusters (Tables 5.5 and 5.6).

For the period 1997–2002, the application of the above-described three criteria provides an alliance classification with four clusters. For each alliance characteristics variable, we check whether there is any cluster for which the score is significantly higher (or lower) than the average across all alliances. If such is the case, we use the variable to qualify the cluster. As an example, we can see in Table 5 that Cluster 1 is mainly made up of joint ventures (73 per cent) and is characterized by a higher than average proportion of manufacturing agreements (34 per cent), a lower than average proportion of cross-sector alliances (only 20 per cent) and high levels of cognitive proximity measures (21.16 and 19.64 per cent respectively). So, we may qualify Cluster 1 as the category of 'joint ventures with a high

Table 5.5   Mean value of the characteristics variables in each cluster of the alliance typology

Cluster (N = number of alliances)	1997–2002												
	Servicesagree	R_Dagree	techtransf_all	licagree_all	Allsupplyagree	manufagree	Mkgagree	Jv	strategicall	numberofpart_r	crosssector	distk_exp_sic	distk_exp_vcic
1 (N = 399)	0.53	0.01	0.05	0.06	0.00	**0.34**	0.09	**0.73**	0.27	0.03	**0.20**	**21.16**	**19.64**
2 (N = 224)	0.42	0.03	**0.12**	0.06	**0.48**	0.04	0.12	0.53	0.47	**0.56**	0.58	9.09	6.83
3 (N = 1322)	**0.80**	0.00	0.08	**0.18**	0.00	0.00	0.00	0.12	**0.88**	0.08	0.50	**6.94**	**2.41**
4 (N = 445)	0.00	**0.40**	0.04	0.05	0.00	0.18	**0.59**	0.14	**0.86**	0.09	0.53	**7.87**	**2.50**
Average across all alliances (N = 2390)	0.57	0.08	0.07	0.12	0.05	0.10	0.14	0.26	0.74	0.12	0.46	9.83	5.80

Table 5.6   Mean value of the characteristics variables in each cluster of the alliance typology

Cluster (N = number of alliances)	2003–06												
	Servicesagree	*R_Dagree*	*techtransf_all*	*licagree_all*	*Allsupplyagree*	*manufagree*	*Mkgagree*	*Jv*	*strategicall*	*numberofpart_y*	*crosssector*	*distk_exp_yeic*	*distk_exp_sic*
1 (N = 76)	0.49	0.04	0.07	0.01	0.00	**0.38**	0.09	**1.00**	0.00	0.01	**0.61**	8.36	10.94
2 (N = 69)	0.32	**0.54**	0.07	0.06	0.00	0.07	0.09	0.14	**0.86**	**0.55**	**0.67**	**3.88**	**5.65**
3 (N = 166)	0.00	0.04	0.06	0.04	0.01	**0.20**	**0.85**	0.00	**1.00**	0.00	0.34	**10.48**	16.93
4 (N = 363)	**0.98**	0.00	0.00	0.00	0.02	0.00	0.00	0.00	**1.00**	0.00	0.28	7.79	16.15
5 (N = 202)	0.00	0.01	**0.75**	**0.37**	0.00	0.01	0.00	0.00	**1.00**	0.00	0.32	9.37	**19.69**
Average across all alliances (N = 876)	0.47	0.06	0.20	0.10	0.01	0.08	0.18	0.10	0.90	0.04	0.36	8.61	16.30

level of cognitive proximity and dedicated to manufacturing and services exchange'. We may summarize the clusters' characterization for the period 1997–2002 as follows:

- Cluster 1: 'Joint ventures dedicated to manufacturing and services exchange essentially inside the ICT sector, with a high level of cognitive proximity'.
- Cluster 2: 'Supply or services agreements with a higher proportion of technology transfers, a high number of participants and average cognitive proximity'.
- Cluster 3: 'Strategic alliances dedicated to services exchange or to licensing agreements, with a low level of cognitive proximity'.
- Cluster 4: 'Strategic alliances dedicated to R&D and marketing, often cross-sector and with low cognitive proximity'.

Concerning the period 2003–06, we obtain five significant clusters with the following characterization:

- Cluster 1: 'Joint ventures dedicated to manufacturing or services exchange, often involving ICT and non-ICT firms and with average cognitive proximity'.
- Cluster 2 : 'Strategic alliances dedicated to R&D or to services exchange, with a high number of participants, often cross-sector and with low cognitive proximity'.
- Cluster 3: 'Strategic alliances dedicated to manufacturing and/or marketing with high cognitive proximity (VEIC)'.
- Cluster 4: 'Strategic alliances dedicated to services exchange with average cognitive proximity'.
- Cluster 5: 'Strategic alliances dedicated to technology transfers and licensing agreements with average cognitive proximity (VEIC)'.

Several points are worth noticing about these results. First of all, some alliance types are very similar across the two periods:

- Cluster 4 (period 1) and Cluster 2 (period 2) are both characterized by alliances that are often cross-sector, R&D-focused and with a high level of cognitive distance;
- Cluster 1 (period 1) and Cluster 1 (period 2) are both characterized by manufacturing and services alliances most often in the form of joint ventures. These alliances' cognitive proximity is very high in the first period and only average in the second. Nevertheless, there is also, in period 2, a cluster (Cluster 3) made up of strategic alliances

which are dedicated as well to manufacturing (and/or marketing) and characterized by high cognitive proximity. This suggests that the high level of cognitive proximity is a rather robust attribute of manufacturing agreements;
- Cluster 2 (period 1) and Cluster 5 (period 2) are both characterized by technology transfers and average cognitive proximity.

These results allow us to position the types of alliances on the axes of relational and cognitive distance with a view to comparing them with the theoretical model as proposed in Figure 5.1.

First of all, the hypothesis of a knowledge exploration phase is empirically validated by the existence, in the two subperiods, of an R&D alliances cluster clearly positioned in the bottom left-hand side of Figure 5.2, which means that R&D alliances are characterized by low cognitive proximity[9] and high relational proximity between partners.

Secondly, the existence of a knowledge exploitation phase is also validated in our data since the presence of manufacturing joint venture clusters with high cognitive proximity and low relational proximity is effective in the two subperiods.

Thirdly, there also seems to be at least partial empirical validation for the hypothesis of an intermediate 'knowledge examination phase' where alliances are dedicated to technology transfers between partners of average cognitive and relational proximity. Nevertheless, we must acknowledge that licensing agreements and marketing agreements cannot be clearly assigned to any phase of the knowledge value chain insofar as their position changes between the two periods.

This cluster analysis does not invalidate our theoretical propositions or the theoretical typology of alliances (Figure 5.1) we proposed above. Firstly, our general Propositions 1 and 3 are clearly supported by the statistical analysis. In a systemic and complex view of knowledge, the bidimensional space of learning strategies (relational and cognitive dimensions) appears to be relevant to classify firms with regards to the way they use alliances to control the knowledge trade-off between accessibility and appropriability (Proposition 1). We also obtain evidence that the different phases of the knowledge value chain are characterized by specific levels of relational and cognitive distances: high cognitive distance and relational proximity in the exploration phase; average cognitive distance and relational proximity in the examination phase; low cognitive distance and relational proximity in the exploitation phase (Proposition 3 and Figure 5.1). It is true however that the examination phase is just partially validated insofar as only technology transfer agreements are persistently positioned in the middle of Figure 5.1 (average cognitive

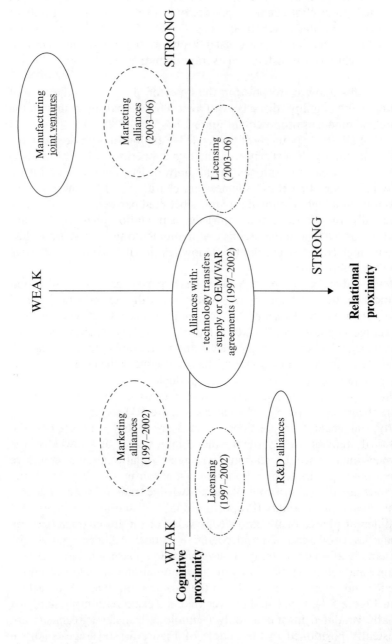

Figure 5.2   An empirical typology of knowledge phases and alliance strategies in the ICT sector

distance and proximity). Yet, in the theoretical part of this chapter, we had argued that technology transfers as well as licensing and marketing agreements could be used in the examination phase of the knowledge value chain where firms seek to solve compatibility and interoperability problems with a view to imposing new technology standards or to maximizing their installed bases. To explain why licensing and marketing agreements are not positioned where expected, we can argue that the ICT sector was in a phase of technological convergence in the 1990s and that it is now in a phase of maturity where the main concern is to market and diffuse technologies. The purpose of marketing and licensing agreements may thus have changed between the two subperiods: they may have been used as exploration tools between cognitively distant partners in the first subperiod, and as exploitation tools between cognitively similar partners in the second subperiod.

The empirical analysis also validates in a satisfactory way our more specific Propositions 2 and 4. Indeed, if our relational distance qualitative index is to be accepted, the balance between the benefits of network externalities encapsulation and the risks of unintended knowledge spillovers seems to generate a negative correlation between cognitive and relational distance along the knowledge value chain.

The validation of Proposition 5 is more ambiguous and calls for more theoretical and empirical developments, as well as more data on the property rights schemes of strategic alliances. On the one hand, it is true that the agreements where property rights are the most strictly defined (joint ventures) are characterized by the highest levels of cognitive proximity. On the other hand, though, licensing agreements – which are specially designed to ensure the protection of knowledge property rights – are not permanently positioned on the right-hand side of the cognitive proximity axis (Figure 5.2), as we have already acknowledged. Such an ambiguity could actually result from the duality of property rights exchange tools (licensing agreements): besides their traditional appropriation and tradability function, licensing agreements can also be used to explore new possibilities of knowledge combinations between cognitively distant partners (technological convergence and integration). The balance between these two purposes of licensing agreements may therefore have changed between the two periods under consideration in the present chapter. Further empirical assessments would be required to validate this conjecture. Nevertheless, these first results encourage us to develop further the analysis on the knowledge examination phase.

5.6 CONCLUDING REMARKS

In this chapter, we analysed – theoretically and empirically – the phases of the knowledge value chain in the European ICT sector. We suggested that the trade-off between the appropriation of and accessibility to new knowledge compels innovative firms to develop specific strategies oriented towards the creation of relevant alliance networks. These strategies are conceived in such a way that firms are positioned in three different knowledge phases: the exploration phase, the examination phase and the exploitation phase.

We began with some theoretical considerations of the role of cognitive and relational proximity in knowledge networks. This led us to put forward propositions which we may sum up as follows: the accessibility–appropriation trade-off can be managed thanks to positioning strategies in a two-dimensional space, that is, the dimension of cognitive distance and that of relational distance. Firms choose their position in this space in relation to their needs in terms of access to new knowledge, as well as in relation to their fears in the face of the risks of unintended knowledge spillovers. Of course, this chapter deliberately focuses on the relational and cognitive dimensions of these positioning strategies, but the geographical dimension should not be neglected either. Our view, however, is that this dimension has already been thoroughly explored in the literature. We therefore believe that it would now be relevant to centre the research programme on the assessment of the relative importance of geographical, cognitive and relational proximity in knowledge generation processes.

Though still preliminary, these results are very encouraging insofar as they suggest that it might be relevant to focus on alliance networks as a means of positioning the firm at the optimal point of cognitive and relational strategy. This might pave the way for a new research programme in which innovation would not be solely explained by R&D, property rights schemes and geographical proximity, but also by some network positioning strategies. We therefore suggest going further in the exploration of this perspective through three avenues of research: (1) exploring other types of networks where knowledge can be exchanged (for example financial networks), and comparing network proximities with geographical proximities as sources of knowledge spillovers; (2) conducting a more thorough analysis of the structural properties of networks of innovators in relation to the knowledge trade-off; (3) introducing variables capturing the properties of these knowledge networks in the econometrics of innovation production functions.

NOTES

1. Mowery et al. (1996, 1998) have introduced the concept of 'technological overlap' which is partly similar to our concept of cognitive proximity as far as the technological dimension of this proximity is concerned.
2. We discuss below the way SIC and VEIC codes can prove helpful in measuring cognitive distance in terms of both its technological and its organizational dimension.
3. Cantwell and Santangelo (2002) develop a similar argument which is, however, related to geographical instead of relational proximity.
4. For a description of these databases, see for example Hagedoorn et al. (2000).
5. Supplementary descriptive statistics can be made available on request.
6. JV in the sequel.
7. A thorough description of each variable can be found on the SDC Platinum server.
8. We preferred to use the measure based on VEIC codes (*distk_exp_VEIC*) rather than the one based on SIC codes as it is more precisely focused on the firm's knowledge base. Nevertheless, the measure based on SIC codes is also introduced below to characterize the alliances' types. We selected the measure computed with the exponential formula since it stresses more strongly the differences in cognitive distance. However, the results remain unchanged whether we use the simple count of the number of common VEIC codes (*distk_VEIC*) or the squared variable *distk2_VEIC*.
9. Please note that this result may explain why Mowery et al. (1998) could not obtain empirical validation for their hypothesis H5 according to which: 'Partners in alliances at early stages of the innovation process (that is, research alliances) will exhibit greater technological overlap than partners in production or marketing alliances'. We have provided both theoretical and empirical arguments here which show that the reverse hypothesis might be much more relevant.

6. Distributed knowledge and creativity in the European new media sector

Adreene Staines and Chris Collinge

6.1 INTRODUCTION

New media is an important sector in the context of the knowledge economy, not least because of its intimate relationship with knowledge production, dissemination and consumption (Klein, 1998; Pratt 2000; de Aquino et al., 2002). One of the main delineating features of the current economy is the emergence of knowledge as an important driver of economic development alongside traditional factors of production such as land, capital and labour.

The new media sector is at the centre of this process of structural transformation and economic dynamism; indeed new media exemplifies the convergence of digital platforms (from digital TV and radio, through mobile phones, to Wi-Fi and the Internet), causing not only an increase in the volume of communication but also the interweaving of media, with content of all sorts passing more and more easily from one format or platform to another (Pratt, 2000; Backlund and Sandberg, 2002).

An important question, which is now being debated, is the degree to which it is possible to think about new media in sectoral terms at all, and the role of the platform concept in this context. Some authors suggest that it may be difficult to identify new media as a distinct industrial sector, especially as it overlaps greatly with other sectors including old media. They feel that new media is simply the name for the convergence of old media around a common technological platform.

On the other hand, some have interpreted 'new media' as a convenient fiction and suggest that its study provides a useful opportunity for us to observe 'an ongoing political and sociocultural project to construct an industry with a distinct identity, one that is capable of lobbying governments and administrative bodies to obtain support' (Backlund and Sandberg: 87). Another issue concerns the relationship between medium and message, between technology and content, and whether they should be considered together or separately. Is new media the message or is it the medium? Is new media a platform?

Nevertheless, despite the conceptual and methodological difficulties in identifying the boundaries of new media, it is important to remember that new media firms are like any other business, with a range of organizational forms, business models, knowledge domains and knowledge practices that must be examined and understood. Therefore, in this chapter, we assume that new media is a sector defined in terms of its particular set of products or services and that it involves an interaction of changing technological platforms and media contents. We describe new media as it currently exists, its structure, trace its relationship to the knowledge economy and identify the knowledge domains and trajectories that are relevant to new media. We are interested in the processes through which knowledge is created, applied and distributed in new media activities.

6.2   NEW MEDIA: OVERVIEW

New media is a growing dynamic economic segment in many European countries. It is also one of the key sectors in the emerging knowledge-based economy and has become an important focus for regional economic development strategies (Backlund and Sandberg, 2002). Still, the question is often asked: 'What is new about new media?' (Cooke, 2002b, Livingstone, 1999). While the term 'media' is easy to grasp and understand, the addition of the prefix 'new' changes its underlying dynamics and definition. It describes much more than a simple broadcast of information and knowledge to a large number of people. New media differs from traditional media in many respects although there is a strong tendency to focus on the technological developments that have made possible the emergence of new media.

In 1990, media denoted mainly terrestrial television, analogue radio, newspapers and other forms of print media, telephone and, to a small extent, the emergence of the personal computer. Media content and platforms were largely controlled by large media and telecommunications empires owned by governments or private individuals. The media industry was an intermediary which collected information and made this available to citizens and consumers. However, the proliferation of information technologies, especially the extension of digitization, has changed the media landscape considerably. New media differs from traditional media in three main respects.

Firstly, diversification of media forms, content and channels. It is often suggested that the new thing about new media is its convergent nature, evident in its technological capability previously unavailable to traditional media (Lewis, 2000). But the term 'new media' is also associated with the proliferation of new media formats and channels, including the iPod, e-mail, viral advertising and so on. New media is the capability to produce media which integrates still and moving images, text, graphics, pictures, sound and data electronically on a CD-ROM or the Internet (Cooke, 2002b; Leisink, 2000):

> Content is rapidly being transformed from a prepackaged combination of text, audio and video delivered in linear stories on a predetermined schedule by ana-logue media such as newspapers, magazines, television and radio. Emerging is content that is a dynamic blend of on-demand information mixing text, audio, video, graphics, animation and interactivity. (Pavlik and Powell 2003: 229)

Digitization also offers new opportunities for the transmission of media content. New media represents changes in the delivery of media content driven by developments in broadband transmission technologies through the fixed line (xDSL, cable modem, powerline) and the emergence of wire-less technologies (WLAN, WiMax). Broadband access to multimedia content provides many opportunities for print – online newspapers and magazines; television – digital and interactive TV; and radio – digital radio and podcasts. New forms of media platforms have emerged such as the Internet, mobile phones and iPods.

Secondly, personalization of media content. Another major transformation in the media landscape is the demand by users of interactive and specialized programming. Traditional media has had to change its media offerings to reflect the needs of its users, evident especially in its offering of TV programmes. Viewers are not only demanding a vast choice of channels, but also want the choice of compiling their own personalized programmes from digital content and watching them when they please, irrespective of the actual broadcast time. New media content is increas-ingly customized to meet the needs of its users. For example, gender-oriented content, such as fashion updates and news, are available as podcasts, text and video messages for access on mobile phones and PDAs. Further, new media are not exclusively mass media, which suggests that viewers are mere consumers of media content. Rather it offers opportuni-ties for users to create websites and CD-ROM applications and to make them available to others. The open architecture of the Internet means that an individual's media content is just as accessible as that from large media professionals (Bolter, 2001).

Thirdly, shift from consumption to production. New media has radically changed the media communication channel. Traditional media audiences were mainly passive consumers of content created and controlled by professional media editors who offer mass information. Conventionally, media audiences consume TV and radio broadcasts, and newspapers, all of which were produced by the media industry and offered negligible or non-existent control to the viewer. New media represents a shift from one-way mass communication to specialized and interactive communication between medium and user. In the new economy, characterized by blog-ging, user-controlled websites such as YouTube, MySpace and Wipikedia, the media audience is now vocal. The development of Web 2.0 offered audiences a platform to create and shape media content. Recipients are active participants on discussion boards, sharing information and shaping events. The role of traditional media is evolving from 'omnipotent com-municator to experienced and often critical guide. The role of the citizen is changing from absorber of facts to discoverer, interpreter, and synthesizer of knowledge' (Pavlik and Powell, 2003: 230). The Internet has created a platform where the line between content creator and user is blurred. New media are not rigidly unidirectional, nor do they require the same level of capital investment as mass media. Audiences as users are increasingly to be understood as plural (that is, multiple, diverse, fragmented), as active (that is, selective, self-directed, producers as well as consumers of texts), and as both embedded in and distanced from specific contexts of use (Livingstone, 1999: 64).

'Media' is an explosive term denoting anything from traditional print and broadcasting media forms to new media forms made possible through technological developments in information communication. Yet, although we cannot avoid the fundamental dichotomies – a few were mentioned earlier – between old and new media, in some respects new media can be viewed as a continuum with rather than a departure from traditional media forms. New media, like traditional media, is concerned with the transmission of information and knowledge albeit through new mediums, and in new forms and contexts.

The lack of a clear sectoral boundary examined above makes it difficult to map the sector (Fuchs, 2000). It is often proposed that research in new media concentrate on the providers of new media content. Although this approach has its benefits, it also engenders the risk of undermining the key role of providers of information and communication technology (ICT) platforms in new media, particularly in areas such as the games content segment, where it has been shown that developers of computer games are dependent upon technological advances in consoles and PCs. To a large extent, new media content is dependent upon and intertwined with the ICT sector. We accept that many firms involved in new media, as provid-ers of enabling technologies and users of new media products and services, are not inherently new media firms. However, these actors are key players in the new media value chain and cannot be excluded from an overview of the sector.

For our statistical mapping of the sector, 'new media' refers to content that has been created for interactive use on several digital media platforms and is not limited to content produced and delivered by a publisher. We will focus on content creation, that is, content published online rather than the infrastructure itself. In this context, new media content will mean: websites, intranets and extranets; multimedia CD-ROMs and DVDs; computer games; interactive elements of traditional television; fully interactive TV programmes; interactive elements for video DVDs; interactive elements for use within websites; and interactive content for mobile devices. Similarly, new media content platforms will include: web and Internet (desktop computers, mobile devices, TVs via set-up boxes, broadband, wireless); offline multimedia (desktop computers, TVs via CD-ROM, DVD, other magneto optical media); interactive TV (via set-up boxes, integrated digital TV); and electronic games (desktop computers, TV consoles, mobile devices). Our mapping of new media will focus on new media content providers active mainly in the entertainment, media and information and communication industries. Subsectors of interest are wireless services, computer games and animation and interactive television and radio.

6.2.1   Structure of New Media

Although we know that new media is closely related to the ICT and media industries, and that its firms are mainly small enterprises which often operate in networks and have a highly educated labour force, mapping the sector is still a difficult task. Its convergent nature makes it a kaleidoscope of different platforms, content, players and activities – yet this very nature is what makes it uniquely 'new media' and is an important aspect of what is involved in this dynamic sector. New media represents a convergence of telecommunications, computing and traditional media. It embraces a wide range of technologies, ranging from the Internet to mobile phones, global positioning systems and high-definition television (Pavlik and Powell, 2003).

To understand the structure of new media is to identify first the activities and actors that are key components of this sector. Lash and Wittel (2002) suggest that the sector is divided among firms that emphasize the front-end services, those that emphasize the back-end services and those that are closer to advertising, design and brand building. Yet, the boundaries for these categories are not sharply defined as there are new media

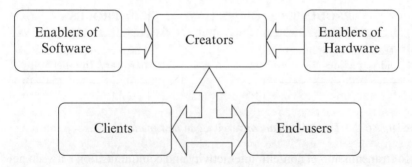

Figure 6.1   New media value chain

firms involved in all three areas. The new media value chain (Figure 6.1) includes four main types of actors:

- Creators: firms, organizations, departments and individuals that create new media products as their primary activity (for example games developers).
- Enablers: those firms that provide infrastructure, technologies or services to support the creation and deployment of new media products (for example PC providers).
- Clients: those organizations or departments that commission or use new media products as part of a wider set of activities (for example knowledge-intensive business services – KIBS).
- End-users: final consumers who purchase or experience new media.

Therefore, a complete new media production value network includes creators of media content, hardware and software developers, consultants and service providers as well as final users who sometimes modify new media content. Three main areas of activities can be identified: the provision of enabling technologies; the creation of new media content; and the use of new media products and services as intermediary and final goods.

Infrastructure and applications
Technology is the fundamental enabler of new media. New media is the point at which media content and different layers of information and communication technologies converge. New media products and services are the outcome of an integrative effort including hardware providers of computing and communication components, software providers of applications, and creators of media content. Software makes it possible to create new communication applications in order for individuals or organizations to collaborate and compete. Hardware provides the physical infrastructure

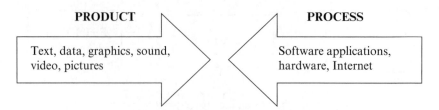

PRODUCT	PROCESS
Text, data, graphics, sound, video, pictures	Software applications, hardware, Internet

Figure 6.2   Technological convergence in new media

for transmission of content, interactivity and communication between new media users and between users and information. Pavlik and Powell (2003) identify five main functions performed by new media technologies:

- information gathering, searching, sorting and communicating;
- production, editing and design;
- storage, representation and retrieval;
- distribution; and
- access, design and display.

The convergent nature of new media technologies, comprising an interface of telecommunications, ICT and media, often means that these functions are integrated into a single device, such as the Nokia N95 mobile phone which offers advanced computing services, regular mobile communication, video and sound recording and display, and a digital camera, as well as such diverse functions as global positioning system technology. New media technologies reflect convergence in media forms as well as in technology (Figure 6.2).

Technology is the backend of the new media value chain that offers functionality and interactivity for the digital transmission of content. Active in this area are ICT and telecommunications firms which provide the Internet infrastructure and the Internet infrastructure applications used to transmit new media content (Lash and Wittel, 2002). These actors involve Internet service providers, Internet backbone carriers, manufacturers of end-user equipment and many software application providers. Apple Inc., Microsoft, Adobe, Cisco and Oracle are a few firms active in this group. Egan and Saxenian (1999) outline some of the hardware and software technologies that are key aspects of new media. They include operating systems software at 32 and 64 MB for PCs, audio and video processing on PC, storage growth from CD to DVD, high-resolution and flat panel displays, colour laser printing, software applications for desktop publishing, image processing and editing for audio and video, interface devices like touch screens, graphic scanners, digital cameras and multimedia projectors, and networking through Internet and WWW accessed through TV, PC and handheld devices (Cooke, 2002b).

Broadband technologies and wireless communication infrastructure are also emerging as key enablers in new media. Wireless technologies offer new avenues for the distribution of new media services and products. Technologies such as Global System for Mobile Communications (GSM), General Packet Radio Services (GPRS), third generation networks (3G), wireless fidelity (WiFi), Worldwide Interoperability for Microwave access (WiMax), wireless local area network (WLAN) and Bluetooth are major enablers of new media. The transition to digital television technology (DTV) allows broadcasters to offer television with movie quality picture and sound.

Then there are also the many technologies that facilitate the protection of content as it is distributed and accessed through digital means. Content management technologies such as digital rights management (DRM), and protection measures such as copy controls, access control, electronic envelopes, encryption and watermarking to safeguard transactions are important aspects of the infrastructure in the new media value chain.

New media service providers

The provision of business-to-business (B2B), business-to-consumer (B2C) or e-commerce services is a major component of the new media value chain. Lash and Wittel (2002) argue that new media agencies facilitated the Internet revolution by teaching clients how to use the Internet for commerce. New media service providers were often contracted to create websites allowing clients to have an Internet presence. However, new media service providers have evolved from mere web designers to becoming techno-consultants. These firms now advise clients on how to develop a corporate strategy using the web as its main platform. They assist clients in using the Internet to provide new kinds of information on customers, to establish new supplier relationships, to extend the network of information gathering and to create new markets (Girard and Stark, 2002). Thus, the new media landscape witnessed a transition from a focus on interactive content for websites towards technological consultancy and the provision of 'interactive communication solutions' (Lash and Wittel, 2002). These firms are concerned with giving clients' customers a cross-platform brand experience, offering e-commerce solutions. European new media service providers include firms such as Razorfish, Inconmedialab, Sapient, ConcreteMedia and Modem Media. Their client base includes firms from a cross-section of sectors, from manufacturing to financial services to education. New media consultancy is a significant part of this sector and the use of new media services for marketing, distribution and communication is an important corporate strategy for many firms.

The use of new media content spans many industries including financial services, pharmaceuticals, automotive, consumer goods, health and education. Digital media is becoming a significant part of strategic business content, influencing several business processes such as marketing, product development and customer service. In particular, for sectors such as consumer goods and pharmaceuticals, there is a close relationship between product assets and digital media assets (Trippe and Guenette, 2007).

New media interacts with management and business consultancy, design and advertising; the boundary between knowledge-intensive business firms and new media becomes blurred. For new media firms to identify and provide the best possible service, they require intimate knowledge of the organizational structure and operations of their clients, not unlike KIBS. They have now moved into the category of new media consultants and to the extent that these firms provide communication solutions to client firms, they may be regarded as KIBS.

New media content

If technology is the backbone of new media, then media content is in its foreground (Fuchs, 2000). Creators develop new media content; enablers provide the hardware and software platforms for delivering new media content; clients use new media content as intermediary goods or services; and end-users are final consumers of new media content. The provision of new media content is the main function of the sector. Whilst there has been a strong emphasis in the literature on the technological infrastructure that has facilitated new media, there is now an emerging emphasis on the importance of new media content. Preston and Kerr (2001: 112) argue that traditional research in new media 'stress[es] the potential of new technologies to provide increased communication and information exchange without any attempt at delineating the types of information which might be exchanged, the quality of that exchange or its implications'. They argue for a shift in the nature of research to include the development and delivery of new media content, which is also an important area.

Digital content first emerged in the context of the media industry where the first attempts were made to repackage media content for digital transmission. Digital content, and the delivery of digital content and information, are becoming increasingly ubiquitous. This is driven in part by the rapid penetration of broadband technology, the improved performance of hardware and software, and the expanding capabilities of delivery platforms. The digital content market includes several non-media providers of

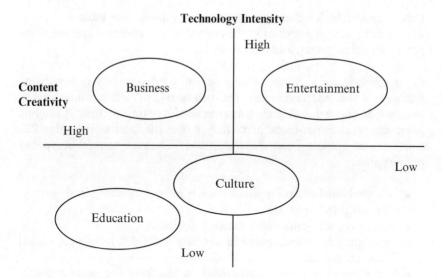

Figure 6.3   New media content segments

digital content such as cultural institutions, governments, financial firms and entertainment firms, amongst others.

The content market is highly heterogeneous, with different developers providing content for various market segments, such as gamers and students. Moreover, within each content segment, there is further differentiation of the type of content offered. For example, in the games content segment, developers provide more advanced games for core gamers (for example MMORPG) compared with simple online games (for example poker and solitaire) offered by services such as Yahoo and MSN.

Further, our research indicates that each content segment has a unique relationship with ICT in terms of level of technological intensity and use of sophisticated new media platforms. For the providers of interactive software, advances in technological hardware and software are key drivers of growth. However, in other segments such as the provision of educational content, standard technology is often used; thus the main objective is to provide creative content. We propose that the new media content industry may be categorized based on a combination of technological intensity and content innovation as shown in Figure 6.3. We will examine two content segments that are located at extreme points of this continuum: the entertainment content market with a high technological focus but low content innovations; and the educational content or e-learning market with high content innovation but low technological intensity.

Entertainment: high technology intensity, low content innovation
There are two main activities in the entertainment content segment: computer and video games, and online music.

Computer and video games   Computer and video games is a growing segment of the entertainment content industry, of which online games, and mobile and wireless games, are the most dynamic sectors. An online game is any computer-based game played over the Internet including PC, consoles and wireless games (OECD, 2005a). There are four main types of online games:

- classic board and card games, mostly offered by web portals such as Yahoo, MSN and AOL;
- PC or console games with network options;
- multiplayer games where players play individually or in a virtual evolving world;
- entertainment games that provide a platform for other types of learning, training and interactive applications.

There is a symbiotic relationship between game developers and the technologies used for these games, particularly the providers of game consoles. Developers incorporate cutting-edge technological advances, such as three-dimensional (3D) animations, sound and graphics, from the upstream hardware and software suppliers in their game development process. Suppliers of game consoles rely on developers to create games that are compatible with their device. This relationship is unique, as game developers have to negotiate to get their content onto particular platforms since console manufacturers have exclusive control over titles for their hardware. Therefore, it is critical that developers create more than one game per platform, particularly as the computer game development process is often long, very research and development (R&D)-intensive and costly. Moreover, developers are often constrained in their ability to develop games for cross-platform use, given the significant difference in the technologies of each console. Thus, they spend considerable time and investment adapting games to new platforms.

The European games industry is a major world player and strongest in PC games (EPA, 2004). Interactive software firms are mainly located in the United Kingdom, France and Germany (Figure 6.4). Some of the major European games firms include Infogames/Atari, Ubisoft, Eidos, Vivendi Universal Games and Codemasters. Many popular world games are European such as the *Harry Potter* and *Lord of the Rings* series, *Tomb Raider*, *GoldenEye* and *Rollercoaster Tycoon*.

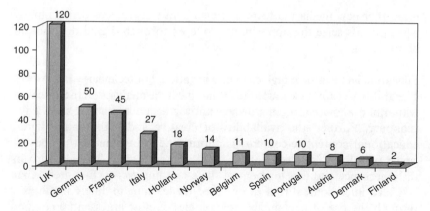

Source: OECD (2005b).

Figure 6.4 Number of game developers by country

Online music Music is an area where the transformative impact of digital distribution is strong for both the supply side (artists and the music industry) and the demand side (new music consumption styles, consumer choice and network users as creators) (OECD, 2005b). Broadband and technological developments in software and hardware have facilitated the emergence of a strong online music industry which has changed the way music is accessed and consumed. Increased broadband penetration has stimulated an increase in the innovative creation, interaction and use of online music. The rapid growth of the online music sector has also stimulated the emergence of new technologies in consumer electronics (that is, portable audio and video players) and media carrier technology (OECD, 2005b).

The rise of online music attracts many new entrants and new intermediaries, creates new business models and generates new forms of product and process innovations. Although the creation of sound recording to a large extent still rests with artists and publishers, in the new digital music model new forms of distribution and business functions have emerged. The creation of an online music store requires content creation and production, the digitization of content, the clearing of rights, the settling of technological issues including digital rights management systems (DRMs), the creation of online music storefronts, secure billing systems and delivery networks.

The impact of digital distribution of music is not however limited to the creation and distribution functions. Spillover effects have occurred on the supply side through developments in music software (music player software, digital rights management software) and hardware such as portable audio players, cellphones or personal computers. The online music sector is another new media platform in which convergence is evident as many new entrants seize the opportunities offered through digital distribution of music.

Education and learning: high content innovation, low technology intensity
The ability to capture knowledge so that it can be analysed, reused, shared with others and used to generate new knowledge underpins the knowledge economy. Further, the availability of creative and high-quality digital educational content (e-content) is another key outcome of the convergence of information technologies and content, which has also driven the emergence and development of the e-learning sector. E-content, that is, educational content that can be used for learning in different contexts through the use of new media technologies, is now an essential component of the education and learning system. The use of digital educational content is evident in traditional formal education, professional training programmes and non-formal education such as vocational training as well as self-learning.

The e-content market is growing and offers many opportunities for traditional content providers, teachers and learners. In Europe, there are three main types of e-content providers: educational publishers such as Pearson Group and Reed Elsevier; professional training providers; and operators in the educational software market such as Berlitz and Aurolog. Traditional publishers offer custom content, which is closely linked to curricula, online as well as on CD-ROMs to complement existing texts (Massey, 2004). Non-publishing players, such as professional training providers, have expertise in specialized subject, occupational and sectoral areas and therefore offer content such as software and simulations for professional and compliance training in fields such as engineering and financial services. The public sector is a large consumer of content from these suppliers. Other e-content providers are multimedia and software houses, which offer mainly multimedia educational content. These three types of educational content providers are not purely e-content suppliers, but rather have added e-content to their core operations. As is typical of the new media sector, the e-content segment is another area where firms that were in previously separate industries have converged to exploit the opportunities offered by digitization.

While the focus as been on traditional subject-based content, the e-content segment is moving towards a demand for innovative and high-quality digital content. There is a difference between content created specifically for use on an e-learning media platform, and content that is distributed within an e-learning platform but not necessarily created for such a platform, as in the case of print texts that are published online. Innovation in organization and deployment of content is the key factor for the growth of this segment rather than technological innovation. As the e-learning market moves towards standardized technologies and applications that are interoperable, the key issue becomes one of providing e-content that is relevant to education and learning. Digital educational content has to be pedagogically effective, market-compliant and relevant to the user. The technological platforms to provide e-content are standard learning management systems such as WEbCT or open source e-learning technologies that have been developed by academics for academics. Technology occupies a very low-key role in the e-content market in comparison to its dominant influence in the entertainment content segment. For the European e-content market, where localization and customization are key factors influencing the demand and supply of e-learning content and services, content innovation is very important and e-content providers are expected to supply high-quality, innovative and specialized content for users.

As information technologies become more prevalent in the education system, there is also a correspondent demand for high-quality, media-rich content that can be effectively repurposed and reversioned for different devices, platforms and infrastructure (eLIG).

Another area of the e-learning market of particular relevance to new media firms is the provision of e-learning services. In many cases, e-learning providers supply full services including content as well as service and technology. There are three main components in the e-learning service market: training services, brokerage services and technical services (Kastis, 2006).

6.3 KNOWLEDGE DYNAMICS IN NEW MEDIA

The acquisition of new knowledge is crucial to new media firms since they operate in a market that is characterized by an increasing demand for new and innovative media content and applications, rapid turnover of technological developments and high levels of uncertainty. Further, the development of new media products and services is a process of collaboration between different platforms, disciplines and sectors and is fundamentally a social process (Preston and Kerr, 2001; Banks et al., 2002). The concept of newness or innovation in new media firms may refers to several things, including new web design content, new websites and web services for business clients, new commercial applications of Internet technology in the new media service providers, or the adoption of organizational innovations such as temporary products and extensive interfirm networking (Heydebrand and Miron, 2002).

New media firms draw upon several knowledge bases reflecting the interactivity of technology, industry and media functions. Although new media firms draw heavily on the scientific knowledge base of technology, tacit knowledge also plays an important role in driving creativity and innovation. Moreover, new media firms tap into an external knowledge base that offers new ideas and expertise in order to enhance their internal knowledge management processes. New media knowledge workers are active in local, regional and national networks. They work in close proximity to each other, sharing strategic information, tacit knowledge and know-how (Arora and Arthreye, 2001; Batt and Christopherson, 2001; Heydebrand and Miron, 2002).

6.3.1 Knowledge Domains in New Media

Technological knowledge has traditionally taken pre-eminence in new media research, as technology is the backbone of the sector, providing access, hardware and software. Nevertheless, it has become increasingly evident that new media firms draw upon other knowledge domains that are just as important as technological knowledge. Equally important are soft knowledges – knowledge domains such as media and business skills – which also influence content innovation in new media. The development of new content is a form of product innovation that is facilitated by new media technology. But where process innovation depends on scientific knowledge, the production of new content is often dependent upon tacit knowledge embodied in the members of the project team (Dolfsma, 2004).

The relevant knowledge domain is also closely related to the new media value chain. Content creation requires the knowledge functions of scripting, authoring, editing and designing. On the distribution side, knowledge of how to package different forms of media content into new products and services is critical. Consequently, new media activities require the use of combinatory knowledge. Our research suggests that new media draws upon three main knowledge domains: technology, creativity and business. However the extent to which any single knowledge domain is regarded as more important than others is to a large extent determined by a combination of factors such as the specialization of the firm, its core market and the priorities of its owners and managers. Those from a traditional media background such as journalism, broadcasting, advertising or graphics are interested in how they can use new media platforms to transmit information and data. These are typically the creative thinkers in the industry. Other media actors from an information technology (IT), telecommunications and engineering background are more interested in the hardware and software involved in the delivery of content. They approach new media from the capabilities of its media platforms.

Technology

Technological knowledge is an important knowledge base for this sector, particularly in the entertainment segment of new media. Game developers require knowledge of cutting-edge technologies, such as 3D animations, to develop and publish games and other interactive content on media platforms. Hence, there has always been a very strong relationship between the entertainment content segment and ICT. Technological knowledge is also important for new media service providers who offer business and communication solutions to clients. Thus, technology is critical to the service that they offer, since the core of their operations is the convergence of ICT with industry.

There are two aspects to the technological knowledge required in new media. First, new media firms need the technical knowledge of how to deliver media content to different platforms, such as the Internet, but also including new mediums such as mobile phones, iPods, PDAs and MP3 players. Second, they require knowledge of how to create content for different platforms. These two areas of competency are very critical to the sector, as each platform has particular characteristics which influence the type of media content created and the methods used to transfer media content to the platform. For example, WAP content for mobile phones cannot accommodate the same amount of textual and graphical displays as web-based contents.

Technological knowledge is typically situated in the project's technical team and comes from programming, media production and content development. Programmers develop the technical structure for the publishing of media content. Media production specialists are concerned with the design and development of media forms such as text, video, moving images, graphics and animation.

Creativity

Creativity has been defined as the production of novel, useful products, services, ideas, procedures or processes (Woodman et al., 1993; Amabile et al., 1996). That creativity is an important knowledge base for new media is no surprise, as new media is regarded as one of the creative industries. Caves (2000) defines creative industries as those 'in which the product or service contains a substantial element of artistic or creative endeavour'. Nevertheless, as creativity is ubiquitous and by no means the preserve of 'creative industries', the focus here is on the development of new media content, whether informative, educational or entertaining. Further, as new media technology becomes more mainstream, the value of creative content increases as content becomes the key source of innovation. For new media, the pertinent knowledge base is not merely knowledge of technology but rather knowledge of how to use new technological knowledge in the development of content. Preston (2002) argues that technical ICT skills, competencies and expertise are 'necessary but not sufficient' for successful industrial innovation strategies in the digital media sector (Preston, 2002). In cases where the technologies underlying the production of new media products are standardized, innovation in media content and media delivery become the sources of competitive advantage. Creativity, in this context, is the ability to use both technological knowledge and media-related skills in a way that generates new ideas for new media products and services.

The notion of creative knowledge signals different things for new media firms. Banks et al. (2002) in their study of creativity in new media small and medium-sized enterprises find that overall creativity is perceived as a combination of individual skill, personal attributes, organizational capacity and managerial capability. This composite knowledge base is essential to generate innovation in product development and to enable problem-solving.

In new media firms that are mainly content providers, such as those firms providing e-learning and education-based services, creativity involves innovative ways of developing content and using media platforms to promote new knowledge and understanding. For the technologically intensive new media firms, such as graphic designers, games developers and e-commerce providers, creativity is less important in terms of content, but more so in terms of providing an enhanced product based on the available cutting-edge technology. Creativity is about pushing the boundary of artistic creation and using technology in a clever way.

Creative knowledge is not always exclusive to a single individual but may also be the outcome of a process of social interaction. What is often seen as a discrete innovation of the creative mind may be defined and socially structured through organizations and forms of group interaction (Banks et al., 2002).

Business

In this sector, where several knowledge domains interact and combine to provide new products and services, organizational or strategic knowledge is also very important. Business expertise is critical in identifying and managing the relevant knowledge domains of this sector. In this respect, new media relies on knowledge that is general to firms and organizations. This includes:

- knowledge of first-order management functions such as design, marketing, research and development (R&D), finance, internationalization, entrepreneurship; and
- knowledge involved in second-order management functions such as strategic management, business modelling, knowledge management, project management and competence management.

Strategic knowledge is an important knowledge domain that determines the existence of the firm from its outset. New media firms require operational flexibility as well as the strategic knowledge to recognize opportunities, whether in the form of a new technology (wireless technology) or new form of content (WAP-enabled content) (Girard and Stark, 2002). Moreover, new media firms rely upon certain specialist knowledge related to the regulatory system and policy developments. These firms operate in an emerging regulatory environment as legislators attempt to address the deficiencies in current regulations regarding new digital media content and technology. Knowledge of developments in intellectual property rights, digital rights management and other relevant areas is important to meet compliance requirements.

New media firms also draw upon an external knowledge base of freelancers, market experts and technical specialists who are an important source of new knowledge. The demand for sophisticated and innovative new media products and services means that these firms have to source and exploit content, skills, knowledge and expertise external to their boundaries.

The knowledge base of new media is a combination of creative knowledge and technical knowledge and there is no reason to expect that the latter will be more relevant. Our interview with a new media expert in the West Midlands of the UK confirms the importance of a combination of technical, creative and business knowledge for the success of new media firms (Table 6.1, Figure 6.5). The interviewee made frequent references to the importance of the 'creative individual' to the emergence of innovative products and services in new media. He also emphasized the increasing demand by new media employees for soft skills. New media employers are looking for workers with non-technical skills, such as communication, marketing and networking. The successful new media firm is able to identify and use the appropriate combinations of technology, creativity and business skills. Our interviewee responded that:

> if creativity and technology are not in that organisation we found an awful lot of organisations collapse because they don't know how to collaborate, how to protect intellectual property and how to actually find new markets.

In the digital media domain, putting the technologies in place often comprises only the first and easiest step in the overall innovation process.

Table 6.1   Main knowledge base for new media firms

Type of new media firm	Main knowledge	Secondary knowledge
Technical firms	Technological	Business, Creative
Service providers	Business	Technological, Creative
Content providers	Creative	Technological, Business

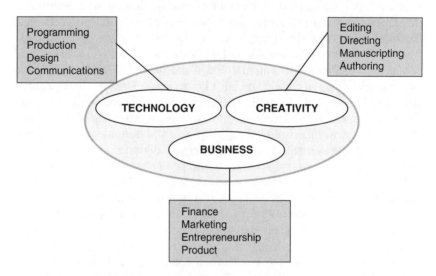

Figure 6.5   Knowledge domains in new media

6.3.2   Knowledge Phases

As knowledge is the most important asset of new media firms, which they exploit and use in their production of knowledge products and services, these firms are also actively involved in a process of knowledge generation and exchange. The knowledge phases of exploration, examination and exploitation differ however for new media firms compared to sectors such as biotechnology and food. Nevertheless, we attempt to trace the different phases of knowledge in new media using the provided framework (see Table 6.2).

Exploration
Exploration involves an active search for new knowledge, products and processes. New media firms do not usually have distinct research and development departments as do most manufacturing firms. However,

Table 6.2   Examples of new media activities using knowledge framework

K. Categories \ K. Phases	Analytical	Synthetic	Symbolic
Exploration	• analysis of media regulations (EC. TV Without Frontiers Directive) • research on business environment	• developing technologies • developing software • designing content	• market research • exploring new clients
Examination	• market research • beta testing (e.g. Yahoo and Hotmail trial versions of messenger and email)	• testing of content using platforms and software	
Exploitation	• income returns • validation by external agents (e.g. census status for games) • media reviews	• offering content on different platforms (e.g. weather forecast on mobile phones) • providing enhanced versions of products (iterations of existing games)	• marketing to new markets (health and education) • offering digital content management services to firms

high levels of uncertainty and frequent changes in technology and customer needs mean that these firms are actively and continually exploring
new sources of knowledge. Moreover, unlike biotechnology firms where
patents are often used to protect intellectual property, new media firms
operate in an industry where new technology and new innovation are
easily replicated because of low barriers to entry and limited opportunities
for future rents. Thus, new media firms are forced to innovate continually.
In their exploration of new knowledge, these firms are searching rather
than researching, designing rather than developing, outward-looking

rather than inward-facing. They adopt a pull rather than a push strategy in which market demand is the underlying motivation for new knowledge exploration. They develop systems and structures that facilitate the generation of new knowledge and creativity, which often involves finding new ways of using existing knowledge.

Interactivity is a key method of acquiring knowledge in new media (Heydebrand and Miron, 2002). Knowledge exploration occurs through a process of internal interaction among and between new media knowledge workers as well as being the outcome of interaction with external new media technical, design and market specialists. Heydebrand and Miron (2002: 1955) observe that innovation in new media firms: 'is not so much the result of thought and action of an isolated individual or genius, but the result of social interaction and learning among participants in diverse situations and heterogeneous networks, groups, and organisations'. Often new media offices are organized in such a way that staff work in small groups, within close proximity to facilitate the exchange of ideas and knowledge.

New media firms also have an extensive external knowledge base on which they draw. In this sector, both specific and tacit knowledge play a key role. Often a new media firm is unable to internalize all its knowledge bases because either they do not fit with its core activities, or it is financially constrained. Therefore developing a network of external new media specialists, mainly freelancers, is vital for firms to access knowledge.

Frequent changes in information and communication technologies mean that the sector is always acquiring new technological knowledge to develop new products and use new distribution. This process of exploration promotes continuous evolution and learning of competencies.

Examination

Examination is not an important knowledge phase for new media, since the nature of their products and the speed with which the technology changes do not allow firms to conduct product trials and testing. Rather, the trend in the sector is to reduce the time required to transform media content into a format that will allow it to be published on different media platforms. As mentioned earlier, in many respects the sector is characterized by a pull rather than a push strategy. Consumers and end-users are the drivers of new content and influence the nature of media content provided. Consumer demand for more customized and localized content has been a strong influence on new media offerings. The Internet is a dominant source of information on the changes and direction of consumer new media demands.

Exploitation

The form and outcome of new knowledge in new media is to a large extent reliant on the specific objectives of the firm. Heydebrand and Miron (2002) identify three main types of new media innovation: problem-solving innovation – a deliberate problem solving process; client-oriented innovation – where the client's needs are the source of innovation; and executable innovation – where innovation leads to business development and business success. It is often the case that new media innovation is reflected in a redefinition of an old problem, using new technologies, rather than an invention of new technology or new design. For example, in the entertainment segment, innovation may mean new iterations of an existing game, using new technologies, rather than developing a new game. Technological knowledge is not used to invent the technology, since this is the domain of hardware and software providers; rather, new media firms will use knowledge of new technologies to provide enhanced and more advanced versions of existing products. This was also evident in our interview where the interviewee responded that:

> I mean in the games arena they're looking very much forward to things like DX10, that'll allow new things to be done. But it's interesting, some of the companies are different. For example Cordmasters which tends to concentrate on iterations of their previous games . . . It's very risky to be creative in games when you know, the average game now costs eight, nine, ten million pounds and if it fails, it fails. So people like Cordmaster, and I don't blame them, would tend to stick to their existing franchise.

Business profits are increasingly becoming a major factor in the sector as the novelty of new technology wears and the reality of achieving a bottom line emerges. MUDIA (2003) observes that one of the most important drivers of news media industries currently is finding a profitable revenue model. The main concern is developing a healthy business from new media innovation. New media innovation is valuable to the extent that it can be effectively deigned, executed, marketed and sold to the client or provider of venture capital (Heydebrand and Miron, 2002: 1962).

Knowledge exploitation is equally as important as knowledge generation. Nevertheless, the phases of exploration and exploitation are not separated in new media firms but instead occur simultaneously rather than sequentially. Instead of having specialized search routines where one department is dedicated to exploration and another to exploiting existing knowledge, these two processes are distributed throughout the firm and become the responsibilities of all departments. Thus, departments, divisions and work teams are interdependent in the knowledge exploration and exploitation process.

6.3.3   Knowledge Drivers

There are several drivers of innovation and performance in new media: increased penetration of broadband technologies; disintermediation in the value chain as digitization opens new windows of opportunities for entrants; persistent advances in the quality, efficiency and number of media platforms; as well as changing consumer needs work together to drive change and development in this sector. Also, frequent developments in intellectual property rights regulations exert a strong influence on the development and availability of media content. These drivers of change shape the way knowledge is created, accessed and used in new media. In this section, we focus on three knowledge drivers of particular significance for the European new media sector: regulation, market structure and the supply of media content.

Regulation
In the knowledge economy, rapid technological change, a proliferation of media content, greater user control, and costless and seamless transmission of knowledge and information over different media platforms place severe pressure on existing EU and member state media and telecommunications regulations. Traditional media regulations are finding it difficult to cope with the speed of technological, economic and social change facilitated by new media technologies. Consequently, there have been several calls for modernization of media regulations, which has serious implications for new media. Compared to the traditional media industry, new media is distinct to the extent that it represents a converged space on which media, ICT and telecommunications interact, thus rendering obsolete previous technology-specific regulations that were based on the distinction between telecommunication and media. In the past, telecommunications, media, broadcasting and content legislations were developed separately; however the convergence of previously separate industries in new media makes it necessary to reassess the existing regulatory framework. There is now a shift from a vertical to a horizontal regulatory framework where regulation is no longer separated along sectoral boundaries but instead is based on a distinction between content and transmission (Valcke and Stevens, 2007).

The first step in modernizing the old EU regulatory framework was concerned with the transmission layer and illustrated by the New Regulatory Framework Directive, 2002/21/EC on electronic communications networks and services. In the late 2000s, the EU has moved on to the second layer – media content – and has revised its Television without Frontiers Directive to regulate media content. The main objective is to provide regulations of media content that are 'technology-neutral' and impose the same obligations on all providers of new media services irrespective of the underlying platform or distribution means (Valcke and Stevens, 2007). This approach was previously applied to the audiovisual media sector. Extending this framework to cover all media content has far-reaching implications for the new media sector.

One the one hand, modernization of media regulations to cover new media services provides a level playing field for traditional media firms who currently face intense competition from several non-media firms offering the same or similar forms of content in the same market, while being subject to a different regulatory environment. Nevertheless, many new media firms fear that new regulations to cover all new media content and not just television services will constrain investment and market developments. Thus, while there is a need for pluralistic regulation of new media, a broad-brushed approach may inhibit innovation and development, particularly as many new media firms are small and medium-sized enterprises. There is also a risk of greater concentration of market power as small new media service providers may be unable to cover high regulatory costs. Valcke and Stevens (2007) observe that the indirect costs of higher regulation may dampen the growth of many emerging new media service areas such as online gaming and content hosting, thereby causing delays in investment and reducing competitiveness.

Another important regulatory driver for the sector are rules governing intellectual property rights (IPRs), as new media facilitates and promotes the development and sharing of media content that is decentralized from a unilateral source, as was typical of traditional media. Intellectual property rights and digital rights management are crucial regulations influencing innovation and product development in new media. IPRs facilitate or constrain the availability and digital distribution of new media content. They are intended to regulate unauthorized use of copyright material, but in many cases grey areas are quite common as original contracts of ownership rights were drawn up before broadband became prevalent and thus silent on digital distribution (Cawley and Preston, 2007). Moreover, because digital distribution of content is now a part of every aspect of society, IPR regulation is not only concerned with entertainment and information content for consumers, but also business content and government content. Intellectual property rights become a key issue as it becomes easier for users to download media content.

The development of new 'on-demand content', distributed over wireless platforms such as mobile phones, creates special difficulties for regulation. Current (late 2000) European regulation is mainly focused on traditional broadcasting and may not be applicable to new platforms for content distribution. Currently, it is suggested that the EU uses self- and co-regulatory models to govern and manage digital content. Regulation of digital content has to find a balance between protecting owner rights of content and allowing new media firms to respond quickly to the changes that are characteristic of the sector.

Digital rights management exerts a greater influence on the sale and distribution of media content than intellectual property rights. Intellectual property rights protect ownership of media content; however DRM is concerned with identifying and describing digital content that is protected by intellectual property rights. The notion of 'digital rights' refers to copyrights and other related rights in the digital environment. DRM technologies are used to manage digital rights by enforcing rules of usage set by content owners or determined by regulation. DRM is also an emerging legal area, involving complex and technical issues, and is developing at a much slower rate compared to the opportunities being made available for digital distribution. In the presence of uncertain DRM regulations, content development and distribution becomes constrained. Moreover, in the absence of transparent DRM regulation and where regulations actually exist but are rigid, there is the fear that users may minimize their use of digital content.

Market structure
The market structure of new media is characterized by two main types of firms (Braczyk et al., 1998; Wirtz, 2001; Backlund and Sandberg, 2002). First, there are firms that are strictly new media-oriented, offering innovative products and services. These firms take advantage of the benefits offered by developments in information and communication technologies, digitization and the Internet. Many of them were first-movers in new media and their corporate strategy revolves around providing interactive media content and services for a wide range of customers. They specialize in different segments of new media, mainly as content developers and service providers. These firms include Internet service providers (IPS), e-commerce firms, developers of interactive digital content and new media service providers such as web designers. The other class of firms are established companies which previously specialized in telecommunications, media or computer technology but have now moved into new media. Many of these firms have added new media services and products as a part of their core activities, through alliances, mergers and acquisitions. This latter group comprise mainly large global entities such as AOL Time Warner, Bertelsmann and Microsoft. The former group is more diverse with many small and medium-sized firms that cater mainly to regional or local markets, as well as a few large firms which have an

established global presence through the Internet such as Google, Yahoo, MSN and eBay.

Convergence has not only created new sales opportunities, but it has also changed the nature of the value chain of the media and communications sectors, and significantly impacted upon the nature of competition in new media, which was previously dominated by a few large Internet-based companies. Industry convergence has eroded the first-mover advantage enjoyed by many pioneer new media actors and has fostered intensive competition in the sector from media giants and telecommunications firms (Wirtz, 2001).

The new market strategy of new media firms is to take advantage of the opportunities for combining their services with complementary value-added elements of the media and information and communication sectors. Knowledge exploitation will depend upon how effective these firms are at collaborating with other firms in providing products and services which integrate the various elements of the media and telecommunications sectors into a united system.

Supply chains

The role of supply networks in driving knowledge processes in new media is closely related to changes in the market structure such as technological and industry convergence, which allow many new entrants to compete in new media. The availability of new media technologies and media content is transforming the supply chain for distributing new media products and services. There is a shift towards new methods of distribution, new ways of accessing and using digital content, and new types of content. Moreover, the supply of media content is being driven by the demands of consumers for innovative and personal content that can be accessed across a wide range of new media platforms.

Technological development has eroded the market power of many established access providers (ISPs). It has also made many small new media firms disappear and generated a wave of alliances, mergers and acquisitions (Susaria et al., 2000). Greater competition in the supply function has encouraged increased provision of innovative digital media products and services, particularly personalized content, to meet the growing demand of new media users.

The suppliers of enabling infrastructure, whether software, hardware or telecommunications networks, have been relatively stable, with a few large firms dominating this aspect of the new media value chain, largely because of the high sunk costs associated with infrastructure investment. Nevertheless, with increased deregulation and liberalization in the telecommunications market, many small ISP providers have emerged. In most instances, however, these firms are eventually acquired by larger providers. For example, in the UK, BT recently acquired Plusnet – a young dynamic ISP provider that had corned a significant share of the UK's broadband market.

Currently, there is a trend towards providing value-added bundled products and services, combining access and content into a single product. New media firms are being driven to supply content that is operable over a large range of platforms. Users demand content – weather, news, sports, financial news or directions – that may be accessed through their personal computers, mobile phones, iPods, game consoles and PDAs. The new media supply chain has to be responsive, making content available quickly for an increasing range of distribution models and consumer formats and devices.

With the entry of many ISPs into the content market, greater collaboration between ISP providers and content developers is encouraged. ISP firms are restructuring their business models from being mere providers of a portal service to being aggregators and suppliers of new media content. They have taken over several of the supply chain functions such as distribution, pricing, billing, product and network management that were previously controlled by retailers. For example, the BT Yahoo broadband service is a collaboration of game developers and Internet portal. To a large extent this has disrupted the traditional supply chain for new media content and created a flatter supply structure.

Managing the digital media supply chain from creation to delivery is an important strategy for new media firms. It influences their ability to gain and maintain market share as well as reduce costs. Innovation in the supply chain is an effective way of managing this process. The development of digital asset management solutions enables new media firms to manage the supply chain effectively. Digital asset management solutions reduce the costs associated with the digital media supply process, such as replication, agency fees, shipping and file transformation. Thus, by taking advantage of these technologies new media firms are able to provide more innovative content, which can be quickly processed through the supply chain and made available to customers.

6.4   CONCLUSIONS

The issues of how new media firms respond to the changing regulatory environment, intense competition from non-media actors and changing consumer needs will determine their survival and development. Assessment of these will form part of this concluding section. Many small new media firms have been taken over by larger entities in order to increase market share and competitiveness; nevertheless it is becoming increasingly clear that innovation and creativity are key determinants of the ability of new media firms to survive in the uncertain environment in which they operate. One of the most significant characteristics of the new media sector is its flexibility as well as its adaptability in a rapidly changing environment (Lash and Wittel, 2002). Below we look at a few of the responses of new media firms.

6.4.1 Organizational Responses

It was mentioned earlier that technological convergence stimulated a demand for value-added new media products and services which offer several capabilities and are operable on different media platforms. This has also stimulated a wave of alliances, mergers and acquisitions in the new media industry. As new media firms are constrained in their ability to focus on core competencies, since their products and services require a combination of knowledge from different disciplines, there has been increased emphasis on project networks and interfirm networks. There is a growing trend towards collaboration and networking for knowledge sharing as new media firms at different stages of the value chain collaborate to supply bundled products and services. Recent acquisitions and mergers between telecommunication firms, Internet providers and content developers are testimony to this trend. For example, AOL's acquisition of Time Warner provided rich and varying media content for its portals, thus increasing its product and service offerings. Similarly with this merger, Time Warner obtained a new marketing avenue for its media content, facilitating innovation in content development.

Girard and Stark (2002) argue that new media firms have become 'heterarchies' – a mode of organizing that is neither market nor hierarchy (Powell, 1996; Grabher and Stark, 1997). Heterarchies involve relations of interdependence, which is important for new media firms which rely on knowledge domains that are external to the firm, and are continually searching for new knowledge while attempting to exploit the benefits from their existing knowledge stock. In the uncertain environment in which they operate, these firms, instead of delegating knowledge exploration and exploitation to specialized units, have decentralized the knowledge process throughout the organization so that innovation and new knowledge acquisition becomes the domain of every unit. As heterarchies, new media firms are continually searching: 'as part of their reflexivity they are continually scanning the environment, continually coping with unpredictable strategy horizons' (Girard and Stark, 2002).

Lash and Wittel (2002) also observe that there is a trend towards consultancy, from interdependence to client dependency. They argue that many new media firms are moving from project-based networks to establishing long-term relations with clients. This is particularly evident in the organization and strategies of new media service providers.

On the one hand, there is a growing importance of interfirm networking and collaboration to cope with the demands of the market as well as to provide bundled products and services. Yet, in another respect, the sector is also moving towards greater consultancy, to exploit fully the opportunities offered by the Internet and information and communication technologies. But, while there has indeed been a trend towards consultancy, the new media industry remains dependent on distributed knowledge bases that are interdependent. However, this interdependence is less on the basis of collaboration between new media companies and clients, and more in terms of collaboration between content, technology and access. New media firms, particularly content providers, are now engaging in intensive interfirm networking with other providers in the value chain, particularly those of new media technologies and Internet service providers. Thus, while the heterarchy still exists, its nature may have changed to reflect vertical and horizontal alliances between different aspects of the new media value chain.

6.4.2   Product and Process

The business model of new media firms evolves around three main questions: What type of content? What delivery platform? and What opportunities? The type of content demanded and the available platform determine the products and processes that are core in the sector. With an increased usage of personal media technologies, users are demanding media content that is personal, localized and available at their convenience. Hence, new media firms respond to their market by changing the way they offer media content. New media firms also respond to new communication technologies by modifying the product and service that they offer.

For instance, the advent of wireless technologies has created a new market segment offering new opportunities for new media products. Content developers are now able to provide content across the wireless platform, while wireless access providers can now source content from many providers for their platforms. Nevertheless, as new media firms respond to the new wireless technologies, they need to be aware of the differences in the wireless market. The profile of the wireless market differs from traditional segments such as PC users; therefore firms modify their content to appeal to the wireless market, which is constrained by limited

Table 6.3   Summary of new media knowledge drivers and responses

K. Responses / K. Drivers	Organizational	Market	Product/Process
Regulation	• alliances and mergers	• developing technologies • developing software • designing content	• customized content • pay for content business models
Market structure	• alliances and mergers • heterarchy • consultancy	• testing of content using platforms and software	• bundled products and services • new products for broadband and wireless platforms
Supply chain	• disintermediation • interfirm networking at different layers of value chain	• offering content on different platforms (e.g. weather forecast on mobile phones)	• bundled products • alliances with ISPs to provide content • offering products directly to end users

bandwidth and low storage capacity. In particular, wireless customers are more sensitive to price in choosing their content, than PC users are. Content must be translated into a wireless format as wireless technology opens up the market demand for an entirely new set of products. Many traditional game developers are rolling out interactive, knowledge-based games that are wireless-ready. These examples are presented in Table 6.3.

7. Knowledge-intensive business services (KIBS)

Simone Strambach

7.1 INTRODUCTION

Knowledge-intensive business services firms are organizations that are particularly representative for knowledge-based economies (Gallouj, 2002). Knowledge is not only the key production factor of these service firms, it is also the 'good' they sell. Professional service firms, including management consultancy, technical engineering services, research and development, software and information processing services, or advertising and marketing services, mainly provide non-material services. The primary value-added activities consist of the creation, accumulation and dissemination of knowledge for the purpose of developing customized intangible service solutions (Bettencourt et al., 2002). The commodities these firms trade on the market are to a large extent intangible and knowledge-intensive. They are involved in the exchange and conversion of knowledge for economic gain and value-added processes.

The knowledge-intensive business services (KIBS) industries have been among the most dynamic segments of the service sector in European countries since the mid-1980s. Initially this growth was primarily seen as a demand-led, cost-driven, outsourcing phenomenon. However, KIBS also play an increasingly important role for the performance of their clients' sectors, as they provide 'vital input to the performance of other sectors of the economy' (EMCC, 2005: 19; cf. den Hertog and Bilderbeek, 2000; Hauknes, 2000; Miles, 2005). This emphasizes the relevance and benefits of KIBS for the knowledge dynamics of their different client industries, often referred to as indirect effects on the system level. Studies of innovation systems and research in service innovation have especially outlined the more central role that KIBS firms are playing in innovation – as knowledge carriers, producers and mediators in national and regional economics (cf. Bessant and Rush, 2000; Hipp and Grupp, 2005, Miles, 2001; Wood, 2002). KIBS research to date (2010) is mainly conducted using an innovation perspective. However, with respect to knowledge processes of this service sector the understanding is still limited. Some backgrounds are described while the nature and the characteristics of these processes remain in part unclear (Howells, 2001).

The intention of the chapter is to sort out, with an analytical focus on knowledge processes, the unique and essential way KIBS contribute to knowledge dynamics in firm, sector and territorial contexts. The particularity of KIBS is their interconnectedness with other sectors and the distinct contribution to knowledge dynamics resulting out of this. Knowledge dynamics arise through the changes in knowledge itself and are the driving force behind innovation. These processes are strongly influenced both by the specific knowledge base of agents and by the context in which these processes take place. The intention of the chapter is twofold:

- to identify the sector-specific way in which KIBS drive knowledge dynamics at multiple levels;
- to distinguish the essential knowledge drivers for the KIBS sector itself and which resulting responses and typical changes can be stated in the European KIBS sector.

These services seem to be on the path towards developing into a knowledge-processing and -producing industry. In section 7.2, a short insight in quantitative terms is provided into the structure and growth of KIBS in European countries between 2000 and 2005. The special contribution of KIBS to knowledge dynamics resulting from both their products and the mode in which they are producing knowledge-intensive services is discussed in section 7.3. Based on this analysis section 7.4 shifts to an empirical focus on the KIBS sector itself and identifies key drivers stemming from the changing international business environment and their influence on the European KIBS sector. How the sector responds to these driving factors is outlined in section 7.5. Finally, section 7.6 draws conclusions and outlines some open research questions.

7.2 STRUCTURE AND GROWTH OF KIBS IN EUROPE

Business services in general terms are those services demanded by firms and public organizations, not for private consumption. What differentiate KIBS from other services are the demand side and the knowledge intensity. The term 'KIBS' has been used to refer to predominantly non-routine service firms that are characterized by their high knowledge intensity and the orientation of their services to other firms and organizations (Muller and Doloreux, 2007). In international research they are known also as 'advanced producer services' (Moulaert and Tödtling, 1995), or 'strategic business services' (OECD, 1999a). Miles et al. (1996) define KIBS as: 'business units which involve economic activities which are intended to result in the creation, accumulation or dissemination of knowledge'. Wood (2002) refers to them as profit-making private sector companies or partnerships, which provide knowledge-based services to other business and non-business organizations. The indicator for knowledge intensity is a matter of debate. These firms are most commonly characterized by the proxy of a large degree of highly skilled employees (cf. Rubalcaba-Bermejo, 1999).

As it is mostly the case for new emerging sectors, the KIBS sector crosses the conventional statistical definitions and classifications of economic activities. The Eurostat statistical definition of the knowledge-intensive service sector, for instance, is not concerned with a distinction between business and private services and is therefore rather broad.[1]

Regarding subsectors, it contains valuable segmentation in market services, high-technology services, financial services and other knowledge-intensive services. Since Eurostat provides harmonized statistical data at the European level, it can be used for a short quantitative insight into the economic structure of the KIBS sector in Europe (see Tables 7.2, 7.3 and 7.4). Despite every effort, uniform definitions of firms or activities that can be classified as providing knowledge-intensive business services are not available. Nevertheless, most definitions include a core of activities that are professional services – like chartered accountancy, tax consultancy, management consultancy and human resource development services – but also technical engineering services, research and development, computer software and information processing services, as well as advertising and marketing services. These segments – often referred to as KIBS in the narrow sense (Table 7.1) – will be focused on in the qualitative analysis of the chapter (sections 7.3, 7.4 and 7.5).

Following the perspective of institutional approaches, sectors can also be differentiated in relation to their specific economic and technological conditions, their knowledge base, and their types and structures of interactions among firms and non-firm organizations as well as with respect to sector-specific institutions (Malerba, 2005; Hall and Soskice, 2001). Firms in a sector have some communality and, at the same time, they are heterogeneous (Malerba, 2005). Common characteristics of KIBS can be clearly identified from the research which allows these firms to be considered as a definable sector. There are three main features that provide the links between the heterogeneous KIBS subsectors:

Table 7.1   KIBS definition in the narrow sense

NACE	Branch	Branch aggregation
72	Computer and related services	Computer services
72.1	Hardware consultancy	
72.2	Software consultancy and supply	
72.3	Data processing	
72.4	Database processing	
72.5	Maintenance, office equipment repair	
72.6	Other services related to data processing	
73	Research and development	Research &
73.1	Research and development in natural sciences	development
73.2	Research and development in social and economic sciences	
74	Other business activities	Economic services
74.1	Legal services, tax consultancy, management consultancy, market research . . .	
74.2	Architecture and engineering offices	Technical services
74.3	Technical, physical, chemical analysis	
74.4	Advertising	Advertising

- Knowledge is not only a key production factor of the firms, it is also the 'good' they sell. For the most part the firms provide non-material intangible services.
- The provision of these knowledge-intensive services requires in-depth interaction between supplier and user and both parties are involved in cumulative learning processes. The utilization of knowledge-intensive services cannot simply be equated with the purchase of standardized external services.
- The activity of consulting, understood as a process of problem solving or problem framing in which KIBS adapt their expertise and expert knowledge to the needs of the client, makes up, to different degrees, the content of the interaction process between KIBS and their customers.

Empirically well documented in international research are specific governance mechanisms which coordinate the transactions and interactions within and across the borders of the sector. Formal and informal network relationships, references, reputation and long-term relationships together make up a key function as coordination mechanisms in interaction

Table 7.2 Knowledge-intensive and less-knowledge-intensive services in Europe, 2005

		Services (2005)			Knowledge-intensive (2005)			Less-knowledge-intensive (2005)		
		Total (thousands)	Share of total employm. (%)	Growth (%) 2000–2005	Total (thousands)	Share of total employm. (%)	Growth (%) 2000–2005	Total (thousands)	Share of total employm. (%)	Growth (%) 2000–2005
EU:	*EU-15*	116259.9	69,5	9.8	58050.4	34.7	12.9	58209.5	34.8	6.9
be	Belgium	3096.6	73.5	4.0	1598.4	38.0	5.5	1498.2	35.6	2.5
dk	Denmark	1985.7	72.5	3.3	1172.7	42.8	2.5	813.0	29.7	4.6
de	Germany	24532.5	67.8	5.8	12096.6	33.4	9.7	12435.9	34.4	2.3
ie	Ireland	1278.9	66.3	21.6	654.7	33.9	23.7	624.2	32.4	19.4
gr	Greece	2854.2	65.1	19.6	1074.1	24.5	22.8	1780.1	40.6	17.7
es	Spain	12306.3	65.1	28.9	5095.0	27.0	35.7	7211.3	38.2	24.6
fr	France	17498.4	72.0	8.8	8821.9	36.3	10.0	8676.5	35.7	7.6
it	Italy	14779.8	65.3	12.1	6755.3	29.8	21.0	8024.6	35.4	5.6
lu	Luxembourg	156.5	80.9	12.9	81.2	42.0	26.5	75.3	38.9	1.2
nl	Netherlands	5876.2	72.4	6.2	3401.3	41.9	10.3	2474.9	30.5	1.0
at	Austria	2544.2	67.7	8.1	1163.5	31.0	12.3	1380.7	36.8	4.7
pt	Portugal	2961.5	57.7	11.6	1166.5	22.7	21.8	1795.0	35.0	5.8
fi	Finland	1673.6	69.0	7.6	982.6	40.5	9.5	691.0	28.5	5.1
se	Sweden	3287.0	75.4	9.6	2083.3	47.8	10.5	1203.7	27.6	8.2
uk	United Kingdom	21428.5	76.3	5.5	11903.2	42.4	7.7	9525.2	33.9	2.8

New member countries

bg	Bulgaria	1700.8	56.5	10.3	662.0	22.0	8.9	1038.8	34.5	11.2
cz	Czech Republic	2680.5	56.4	4.6	1188.3	25.0	5.7	1492.2	31.4	3.8
ee	Estonia	366.0	60.1	9.8	176.4	29.0	15.5	189.6	31.1	5.0
cy	Cyprus	246.8	71.0	25.4	93.3	26.8	32.7	153.5	44.1	21.3
lv	Latvia	634.9	61.8	11.6	265.3	25.8	10.6	369.6	36.0	12.4
lt	Lithuania	845.5	57.4	2.3	376.4	25.6	−6.0	469.0	31.8	10.1
hu	Hungary	2443.7	62.8	7.4	1100.3	28.3	9.1	1343.4	34.5	6.1
mt	Malta	101.0	68.1	–	45.1	30.4	–	56.0	37.7	–
pl	Poland	7387.4	53.0	–	3375.6	24.2	–	4011.9	28.8	–
ro	Romania	3391.6	36.5	7.3	1275.9	13.7	8.1	2115.7	22.7	6.9
si	Slovenia	506.0	53.4	8.0	236.2	24.9	16.4	269.8	28.5	1.6
sk	Slovakia	1230.6	56.0	5.9	562.1	25.6	10.3	668.6	30.5	2.5

Other European countries

hr	Croatia	848.1	54.2	–	325.8	20.8	–	522.2	33.4	–
is	Iceland	114.8	70.6	6.0	70.1	43.1	14.0	44.7	27.5	−4.5
no	Norway	1732.2	76.0	3.3	1041.7	45.7	8.5	690.5	30.3	−3.8
ch	Switzerland	2822.2	71.0	7.8	1590.5	40.0	13.5	1231.7	31.0	1.3

Source: Eurostat (2007); author's calculations.

Table 7.3 Knowledge-intensive high-tech and market services, 2005

		Knowledge-intensive (2005)			Knowledge-intensive (high-tech) (2005)			Knowledge-intensive (market services) (2005)		
		Total (thousands)	Share of total employm. (%)	Growth (%) 2000–2005	Total (thousands)	Share of total employm. (%)	Growth (%) 2000–2005	Total (thousands)	Share of total employm. (%)	Growth (%) 2000–2005
EU:	*EU-15*	58050.4	34.7	12.9	5833.3	3.5	8.2	14404.0	8.6	20.5
be	Belgium	1598.4	38.0	5.4	149.5	3.6	0.7	308.0	7.3	-0.1
dk	Denmark	1172.7	42.8	2.5	128.3	4.7	-6.3	207.8	7.6	2.7
de	Germany	12096.6	33.4	9.7	1217.9	3.4	10.8	2984.2	8.2	19.0
ie	Ireland	654.7	33.9	23.7	68.5	3.6	1.9	146.9	7.6	20.9
gr	Greece	1074.1	24.5	22.8	76.0	1.7	18.8	289.9	6.6	33.8
es	Spain	5095.0	27.0	35.6	518.9	2.8	47.9	1510.7	8.0	44.4
fr	France	8821.9	36.3	10.0	953.9	3.9	6.8	2086.7	8.6	13.4
it	Italy	6755.3	29.8	21.0	655.3	2.9	7.2	2068.9	9.1	60.4
lu	Luxembourg	81.2	42.0	26.5	6.4	3.3	34.0	17.3	8.9	34.8
nl	Netherlands	3401.3	41.9	10.3	328.2	4.1	1.2	837.7	10.3	5.6
at	Austria	1163.5	31.0	12.3	101.9	2.7	-1.0	283.0	7.5	24.9
pt	Portugal	1166.5	22.7	21.8	94.3	1.8	60.2	270.3	5.3	30.0
fi	Finland	982.6	40.5	9.5	109.3	4.5	5.2	230.1	9.5	14.6
se	Sweden	2083.3	47.8	10.5	223.7	5.1	5.6	466.1	10.7	18.6
uk	United Kingdom	11903.2	42.4	7.7	1201.2	4.3	-1.1	2696.7	9.6	4.4

New member countries

bg	Bulgaria	662.0	22.0	8.9	86.3	2.9	19.7	130.5	4.3	59.8
cz	Czech Republic	1188.3	25.0	5.7	147.4	3.1	3.6	231.3	4.9	5.6
ee	Estonia	176.4	29.0	15.4	17.2	2.8	5.4	43.8	7.2	24.8
cy	Cyprus	93.3	26.8	32.7	7.1	2.0	52.4	23.0	6.6	20.5
lv	Latvia	265.3	25.8	10.6	27.2	2.7	23.1	47.8	4.7	−3.0
lt	Lithuania	376.4	25.6	−6.0	31.3	2.1	−8.1	49.3	3.4	15.1
hu	Hungary	1100.3	28.3	9.1	117.7	3.0	0.2	234.5	6.0	31.6
mt	Malta	45.1	30.4	–	4.0	2.7	–	8.6	5.8	–
pl	Poland	3375.6	24.2	–	299.6	2.2	–	712.2	5.1	–
ro	Romania	1275.9	13.7	8.0	127.1	1.4	−13.8	204.3	2.2	91.7
si	Slovenia	236.2	24.9	16.4	27.8	2.9	23.3	49.0	5.2	26.6
sk	Slovakia	562.1	25.6	10.3	60.1	2.7	−2.8	104.6	4.8	51.7

Other European countries

hr	Croatia	325.8	20.8	–	31.6	2.0	–	76.5	4.9	–
is	Iceland	70.1	43.1	14.0	8.1	5.0	16.8	13.7	8.4	8.6
no	Norway	1041.7	45.7	8.5	90.9	4.0	6.3	205.5	9.0	3.9
ch	Switzerland	1590.5	40.0	13.5	151.5	3.8	5.0	369.1	9.3	22.8

Source: Eurostat (2007), author's calculations.

Table 7.4 Enterprises, employees and turnover in KIBS subsectors of selected European countries, 2004

Size classes (number of employees)	IT services Share (%) in:			Economic services Share (%) in:			Technical services Share (%) in:			Marketing/Advertising Share (%) in:		
	Enter-prises	Employ-ees	Turn-over	Enter-prises	Employ-ees	Turn-over	Enter-prises	Employ-ees	Turn-over	Enter-prises	Employ-ees	Turn-over
Denmark ≤ 9	93.2	18.3	23.7	95.7	29.9	40.9	93.1	16.6	22.5	91.5	24.5	31.9
10–49	5.5	21.9	17.5	3.7	28.7	21.0	5.7	21.3	18.2	7.2	33.7	30.0
50–249	1.0	22.6	21.1	0.4	19.2	16.3	0.9	17.2	15.6	1.2	28.5	32.3
≥ 250	0.3	37.2	37.6	0.1	22.2	21.8	0.4	44.9	43.7	0.1	13.3	5.8
Finland ≤ 9	84.5	13.6	13.9	95.8	46.3	49.7	90.2	26.4	31.7	91.8	43.6	30.3
10–49	11.5	18.6	18.0	3.6	25.9	23.5	8.1	27.5	24.9	7.3	36.6	42.7
50–249	3.4	31.5	32.3	0.5	–	–	1.4	–	–	1.0	–	–
≥ 250	0.5	36.3	35.7	0.1	–	–	0.2	–	–	0.0	0.0	0.0
Germany ≤ 9	88.7	16.1	12.8	87.1	35.9	35.5	91.8	32.0	36.9	90.3	16.4	34.3
10–49	9.4	24.3	16.4	12.2	40.6	33.3	7.5	35.4	30.4	8.4	20.6	36.1
50–249	1.6	21.3	17.3	0.5	10.2	11.9	0.6	15.3	15.8	1.0	13.9	20.9
≥ 250	0.3	38.3	53.5	0.1	13.3	19.3	0.1	17.3	16.9	0.3	49.1	8.6
Norway ≤ 9	94.6	21.3	22.7	96.4	49.9	50.1	94.4	32.0	34.6	94.4	43.6	31.4
10–49	4.5	26.1	20.6	3.4	24.9	21.2	4.9	28.3	–	5.2	39.6	–
50–249	0.7	21.1	20.2	0.2	10.1	–	0.5	15.1	17.9	0.4	12.1	17.0
≥ 250	0.2	31.6	36.5	0.1	15.1	–	0.1	24.6	–	0.04	4.7	–

Spain	≤ 9	91.6	14.0	13.8	96.9	51.5	55.2	97.4	33.1	47.0	93.3	25.1	24.7
	10–49	6.7	20.7	13.5	2.9	28.4	26.5	2.2	24.9	17.6	5.7	24.0	21.9
	50–249	1.3	21.3	15.5	0.2	10.1	10.1	0.3	19.3	16.5	0.9	23.0	45.3
	≥ 250	0.3	44.0	57.3	0.03	10.0	8.2	0.1	22.8	18.8	0.1	27.9	8.0
Sweden	≤ 9	96.3	20.5	21.2	98.7	51.6	55.2	97.0	35.5	43.1	96.9	44.7	38.0
	10–49	2.9	21.0	19.8	1.1	–	–	2.6	21.3	20.9	2.8	33.8	34.1
	50–249	0.6	21.9	18.6	0.1	13.0	13.1	0.4	17.1	15.0	0.3	14.0	24.7
	≥ 250	0.2	36.6	40.5	0.02	–	–	0.1	26.1	20.9	0.03	7.6	3.2
United Kingdom	≤ 9	94.4	28.4	0.3	91.8	28.3	1.2	90.8	28.8	0.3	88.8	22.8	1.2
	10–49	0.1	37.8	5.6	0.2	29.6	0.7	0.2	31.7	1.6	0.3	31.0	10.0
	50–249	4.6	17.6	8.0	7.1	24.0	1.5	8.0	23.7	4.3	9.3	24.6	12.8
	≥ 250	0.8	16.2	86.0	1.0	18.1	96.6	1.0	15.8	93.9	1.6	21.7	76.1

Note: Subsectors correspond to NACE Rev. 1.1: 72 (IT-Services), 74.1 (Economic Services), 74.2/74.3 (Technical Services) and 74.4 (Marketing/Advertising).

Source: Eurostat (2008); author's calculations.

processes between KIBS and their customers as well as among KIBS firms themselves (Boden and Miles, 2000; Glückler and Armbruster, 2003; Wood, 2002). Project-based work is the dominant form of work organization, due to the need for a high degree of flexibility and the provision of client-specific and, at the same time, comprehensive solutions. Even though networking and project organization are becoming more important in many industrial sectors, for KIBS firms they have always been the conventional form.

7.2.1 Varieties and Specializations in National Contexts

In terms of employment, KIBS growth is one of the main drivers of the creation of new jobs and the continued shift towards the service economy in Europe. From 2000 to 2005, all business services – referring to the subsectors of real estate, renting and business activities in Labour Force Statistics (EC, 2006a: 62) – accounted for one-third (3.5 million) of the net employment creation of 11.5 million in the service sector. Measured as the change in gross value-added, the growth of KIBS has even outperformed the European average for all sectors in recent years in most European countries (EMCC, 2006a: 3).

Drawing upon employment data from Eurostat, knowledge-intensive services (KIS) had growth rates almost twice as high as less-knowledge-intensive services in the EU during the 2000–2005 period. The higher dynamic of KIS compared to the so-called less-knowledge-intensive services holds true for all EU countries except Denmark and for most other European countries (Table 7.2). Despite this general trend, growth rates and the share of total employment differ substantially between particular EU countries. The service sector employs, for instance, 75.4 per cent of the workforce in Sweden, and similarly 76.3 per cent in the UK. But while in Sweden knowledge-intensive services make up 47.8 per cent of the total employment (and 42.4 per cent in the UK), in the UK less-knowledge-intensive services have a relatively higher share of service sector employment. In contrast to economies with a high share of KIS on total employment, all new member states are falling below the EU-15 average with a very low KIS share (13.7–30.4 per cent). In 2005, also countries belonging to the EU-15 like Germany, Italy, Ireland, Greece, Spain, Portugal and Austria did not reach the EU average share in knowledge-intensive services.

International investigations into the spatial organization of KIBS in different European countries show not only country-specific levels of KIBS involvement, but also country-specific specialization patterns of KIBS subsectors. For instance, technical services are more important in Germany than in other European countries, while Luxembourg's KIBS specialization in 2001 was biased towards legal, accounting and management services (Eurostat, 2004a: 365). Moreover, there is evidence that KIBS branches accumulate in particular countries and regions, as for example law firms are most prevalent in the UK (EMCC, 2006b: 12; cf. Keeble and Nachum, 2002). In addition to these selected examples, it is worth taking a closer comparative look at the subsectors of the knowledge-intensive service sector in all European countries. For instance, the distinction between high-technology KIS and market KIS shows further national differences in the importance of these two subsectors (cf. Table 7.3). Most notably, the dynamics of growth (2000–2005) differ to a large degree between countries. In Denmark, for example, high-tech KIS have a relatively high share of total employment (4.7 per cent compared to 3.5 per cent for the EU-15), while in Italy this subsector is of minor importance (2.9 per cent) compared to the subsector of market KIS (9.1 per cent compared to 8.6 per cent in the EU-15). Furthermore, Denmark's high-tech KIS showed a decline (-6.3 per cent) in employment growth (the EU-15 average is 8.2 per cent), while in Italy the market KIS were able to grow dynamically over the period specified (+60.4 per cent; EU-15 average 20.5 per cent).

In summary, the structure and growth of knowledge-intensive services differ substantially throughout the national economies of the European Union and even more between EU-15 and new member states. The development of professional services is not directly linked to the country's level of development measured by its income; rather, various determinants of these national specializations should be taken into account (Noyelle, 1996). In particular, institutional effects on KIBS client sector interactions seem to play an important role for the evolution of specialization patterns in European countries over time.

7.2.2   Regional Concentrations

Empirically it is clear that KIBS are concentrated strongly in fast-growing urban areas and that their remarkable growth throughout European city regions within only a few decades was paralleled by positive overall economic growth. As a result of their tendency to accumulate (cf. Moulaert and Tödtling, 1995; Strambach, 2001; Wood, 2002), core metropolitan regions are the spatial units in which knowledge dynamics of KIBS are most likely to unfold. In Finland for instance their concentration is remarkably high, with around half of all Finnish KIBS (in terms of employment and turnover) being located in the Helsinki metropolitan area (Toivonen, 2002: 208). In Germany more than 70 per cent of KIBS employees are located in only a few large urban clusters (Strambach, 2004). Unfortunately, detailed statistical material following the preferred definition of KIBS cannot be used here, but aggregated data points towards regional disparities throughout Europe can be substituted. For instance, employment figures on NUTS 2 give further evidence of the concentration of KIBS in rapidly growing city regions. The highest concentration of KIBS can be found in the Ile-de-France and Rhône-Alpes regions in France, in the South-East and London region in the UK, as well as in other city regions like Stockholm, Oslo, Barcelona and Prague. Certainly, the causality is not clear, although there is a definite correlation between these growth regions and the strong base of KIBS.

In addition to country-specific specialization patterns of KIBS subsectors, investigations into the spatial organization of KIBS in European countries also show considerable variations in regional importance of individual KIBS segments in different urban regions. However, empirical evidence of this trend is restricted due to the shortcomings of statistical data available for KIBS. Since the term 'KIBS' does not constitute an aggregation of official statistics, available data on services often cannot provide a clear picture on the developments in service subsectors (cf. Toivonen, 2004).

7.2.3   Segmentation of the KIBS Sector

Three common structural features of the KIBS sector in European countries have not changed much since 1980. Besides the dynamic growth and the regional concentrations already outlined, the segmentation of the KIBS sector is the third characteristic. National and regional-based small and very small firms constitute the largest part of the sector. In most of the KIBS subsectors, more than 90 per cent of the firms have up to nine employees (see Table 7.4). These firms provide knowledge-intensive services chiefly for national and regional markets, while a few large, mainly multinational, KIBS firms, which can be found in all KIBS subsectors, operate at the global scale. In Denmark, Finland, Germany, Norway, Spain and Sweden just under 1 per cent of all KIBS firms reach a size of more than 250 employees. The UK is the only country where the share of large firms in two KIBS subsectors – economic services with 1 per cent, and marketing and advertising services with 1.6 per cent – exceeds this.

The segmentation of knowledge-intensive business services indicates that transforming knowledge into tradable goods has its limits. The knowledge markets in which KIBS act are highly fluid, rapidly changing and characterized by a high degree of uncertainty resulting from ambiguity with regard to performance, quality and appropriateness, and marked heterogeneity of the competencies involved.

The low formal constraints on market access allow for fast market entries; which, however, are accompanied by a high ratio of market exits. Additionally, the delay in internationalization processes of KIBS compared to industrial manufacturing firms indicates difficulties in trading knowledge-intensive services across cultural borders. Many knowledge-intensive services still require face-to-face contact between the provider and the customer, at least in some phases of the service production process, even though information technologies enhance possibilities for decoupling the synchronization of time and location between service provider and customer, a major characteristic of services.

This brief analysis of available statistical data on KIBS in Europe was meant to provide a broad background on the macro-level in which knowledge dynamics in the KIBS sector are embedded. To understand processes and changes in knowledge dynamics, the micro-level of KIBS inevitably needs to come into play, which will be dealt with in the following section.

7.3 THE CONTRIBUTION OF KIBS TO MULTILEVEL KNOWLEDGE DYNAMICS OF FIRMS AND SECTORS

The dynamic growth of economic transactions related to knowledge itself, and the more systematic generation and commodification of knowledge, are the main underlying characteristics of the knowledge-based economy. The understanding of the dynamics of knowledge processes, knowledge products, knowledge contexts and their interrelationship is a key issue in the globalizing economy.

The visible results of knowledge dynamics are innovations in products, services or processes. In the following knowledge dynamics is understood as the dynamics unfolding from processes of the creation, using, transforming, moving and diffusing of knowledge. These processes are strongly influenced by both the specific knowledge base of agents and the context in which these processes take place. The competencies of agents, understood as the way through which knowledge is elicited, used and applied to specific contexts and domains (Malerba and Orsenigo, 2000: 297) are therefore a major factor shaping knowledge dynamics. How KIBS induce knowledge dynamics in different contexts, by contributing to the change of knowledge bases and competencies and to the capability building of agents, will be discussed in more detail in the next section.

7.3.1 Knowledge Bases and Composite Knowledge Products

Evolutionary innovation research focusing on industrial dynamics and evolution of industries provides theoretical and empirical evidence that industrial sectors tend to vary systematically with regard to their knowledge bases which, in turn, tend to shape strongly the innovation processes of firms. The firm's knowledge base determines both what it actually produces and where new search processes are directed (Patel and Pavitt, 1997; Pavitt, 1984). The knowledge base refers to the key dimension of knowledge considered relevant for innovative activities of an industry (Malerbra and Orsenigo, 2000). Three different categories of knowledge can be distinguished by their epistemic content, characterizing particular knowledge bases: analytical, synthetic and symbolic knowledge.

An analytical knowledge base dominates in industrial settings in which science-based knowledge is highly important, and in which knowledge creation is often based on formal models, codified science and rational search processes. Industrial sectors with predominantly analytical knowledge bases include pharmaceuticals and biotechnology, for example. In the KIBS sector this kind of knowledge creation is of minor importance, except for research and development (R&D) service firms which in recent years have been a small but dynamically growing subsector in European countries. Small, highly specialized R&D service firms providing contract research for large multinational pharmaceutical corporations are empirically documented examples.

The KIBS sectors that are more dominant in Europe in quantitative terms – technical engineering and data processing services, also called t-KIBS (technological-based KIBS; cf. Miles et al., 1996) – focus instead on synthetic knowledge. Examples are technical engineering firms providing product development services or prototype development for the automotive industry, or software firms that provide visualization tools of finite element calculations. The knowledge processes of these subsectors correspond to that described by Asheim and Gertler (2005) for industrial settings with a dominant synthetic knowledge base. The third type of knowledge which is particularly important for KIBS industries is symbolic knowledge. KIBS subsectors like marketing and advertising are heavily dependent on symbolic knowledge, dealing with ideas, symbols and socially constructed commodities. The cultural embeddedness of interpretations, habits and norms is made responsible for the strong tacit component that characterizes this type of knowledge base (Mariussen and Asheim, 2003). As a result of this differentiation, the knowledge types mainly dealt with by KIBS are those of synthetic, symbolic and, to a lesser degree, analytical knowledge.

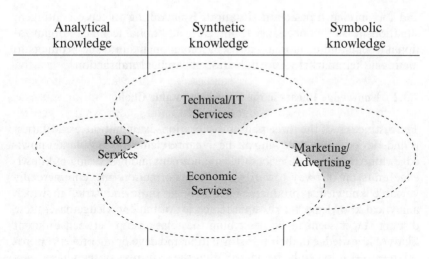

Source: Strambach (2008).

Figure 7.1 The focal points of KIBS subsectors in the different knowledge categories

Although KIBS subsectors have a focal point in one type of knowledge base, as shown in Figure 7.1, most KIBS subsectors have amalgamated knowledge bases that combine and join different knowledge categories at different scales (illustrated by the outer circles in the figure). Architectural services, for instance, exemplify how closely technical engineering knowledge and symbolic knowledge are intertwined. There are broad overlaps and intersections of knowledge types in the multitude of KIBS operations and knowledge-based products. In many traditional segments of knowledge-intensive services, the introduction of new information and communication technology (ICT) has brought about major structural changes. Management consultants, for example, have integrated information and communication technology consulting services, advertising agencies also offer multimedia services, and technological services such as software firms provide management consulting.

A tendency towards convergence among KIBS can logically be induced from the need to provide comprehensive solutions whilst being simultaneously highly specialized. This balance is a strong driver for KIBS to integrate knowledge units from diverse categories on different scales into their knowledge base in order to deliver composite knowledge products (cf. section 7.5). The use and market value of knowledge products is to a large extent context-sensitive, depending on the context of the particular client and the specific transaction situation. By adapting to these contingent situations it is often necessary to integrate additional technical, organizational, social and economic knowledge components into the products to maintain their market value in the respective client transaction.

7.3.2   Knowledge Phases in the Knowledge Value Chain

The distinction of the three phases exploration–examination–exploitation is understood in the following as the dynamic element of a general knowledge value chain and describes the enhancement and processing of knowledge units on the way towards their transformation into commercially valuable knowledge products. Especially in those industries in which analytical knowledge makes up a large part of the knowledge base, these distinct stages seem to be describing the relationship between different kinds of knowledge in their transformation and developing process appropriately. Yet it has to be recognized that the sequences of the phases may overlap and feature multiple feedback loops.

According to March (1991), knowledge exploration is a process of finding new economic opportunities in order to profit from them. This approach inherently contains search and discovery activities as well as risk-taking. Knowledge in the exploration phase is bound to involve some uncertainties and requires dealing with risks, considering that economic returns are systematically less certain in comparison to knowledge in the exploitation phase. Cooke (2006c) proposes examination as a third necessary step between exploration and exploitation. The examination phase, including testing, experimentation and validation activities, is aimed at improving the knowledge content towards its appropriateness for commercial value-added.

The knowledge products of the different KIBS subsectors have different focal points in the knowledge value chain (Figure 7.2). The major share of the products of technical services and information technology (IT) services, and also economic and marketing services, are located in the examination and exploitation stage of the knowledge value chain. The knowledge products contribute to an often very complex application context or to applied problem-solving processes. In particular, research on innovation in services underlines that KIBS operate in all three knowledge phases (see Table 7.5) and correspond to all knowledge categories, even those with a focal point in synthetic and symbolic knowledge domains.

Epistemic rules in exploring analytical, synthetic and symbolic knowledge seem to be highly distinct. Knowledge in the exploration stage has long been determined by the R&D approach, with the dominant focus on the creation of new science and technological knowledge. According to

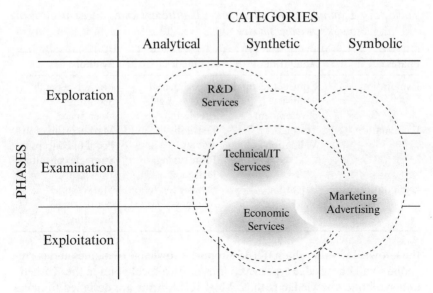

Source: Strambach (2008).

Figure 7.2 The focal points of KIBS subsectors in knowledge categories and phases

Djellal et al. (2003), the concept of R&D is to a large degree responsible for the underestimation of knowledge exploration in services. The systematic nature of knowledge creation through scientific methods, and an appreciable element of novelty in the knowledge product, are the fundamental principles underlying the R&D concept. With this focus, the approach is directed to capture the epistemic rules of knowledge creation in analytical and synthetic knowledge fields, but to a large part ignores these rules in terms of symbolic knowledge.

Internal processes of knowledge creation are only weakly formalised, as has been shown by research in service innovation (Hauknes, 2000; Sundbo, 2000; Marklund, 2000).[2] In contrast to manufacturing firms, most KIBS firms do not distinguish R&D activities systematically in organizational terms. A project-based, ad hoc development of new knowledge in customer relations and for the interaction with customers is characteristic for knowledge-intensive service firms (cf. section 7.3.4). Thus knowledge exploration, examination and exploitation often overlap or take place simultaneously, while some phases may be skipped by this mode of knowledge production.

To summarize, due to their operation in all three knowledge phases of

Table 7.5   *Examples of KIBS activities in different knowledge categories and knowledge phases*

Phases	Analytical	Synthetic	Symbolic
Exploration	Contract research Contract development	Experimental engineering Pre-design	Market research Scouting Open space
Examination	Testing Validation	Feasibility studies Prototyping Design	Market estimation Proof of concept Strategic consulting
Exploitation	Patenting	Series-production readiness	Marketing campaign Branding

the knowledge value chain, KIBS support knowledge dynamics and correspond to all knowledge types, even those with a focal point in the synthetic and symbolic knowledge realms. Most KIBS firms are designed to make heterogeneous knowledge bases available to their clients in an integrated way with their composite knowledge products.

7.3.3   Knowledge Domains: the Interconnection with Sector Contexts

Knowledge domains are an important dimension of firms' and industrial evolution, because domains of knowledge affect the type of competencies and the competition in an industry (Malerba and Orsenigo, 2000). Over time, firms develop competencies that are highly sector- and technology-specific and they also develop competencies which are related to the specific features of users and demand. We introduce the distinction between horizontal and vertical knowledge domains (Figure 7.3) and claim that these are important for the understanding of KIBS evolution and the special knowledge dynamics within, and in interaction with, KIBS at the sector level. KIBS operate in complex horizontal and vertical knowledge domains and their own knowledge bases are located in these domains. Horizontal knowledge domains are related to business functions, and vertical knowledge domains contain sector-specific knowledge.

The ongoing restructuring of the value chain, combined with the increasing interdependence of technological and organizational change at the corporate level (Tidd et al., 2005), is leading to the increasing complexity of horizontal and vertical knowledge domains. KIBS appear to be responding to the increasing need for coordination, communication and organization caused by these developments, with both their

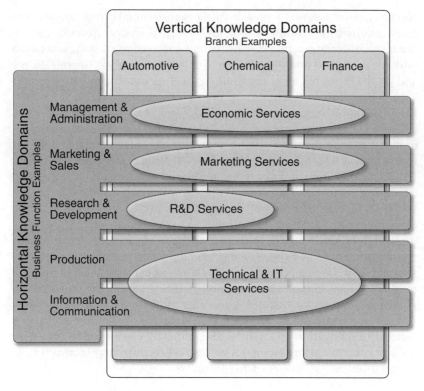

Source: Strambach (2008).

Figure 7.3 KIBS linkages to vertical and horizontal knowledge domains

composite knowledge products and the mode they use in producing their services.

Horizontal knowledge domains (or functional knowledge domains) connected to business functions have been undergoing an increasing technological and organizational complexity. Business functions like production, R&D, marketing, financial and data processing, or human resource management are generic in the sense that they apply across many different sectors and industries. The vertical disintegration in production has been going on for a long time (cf. Dicken, 2003), whereas the increasing organizational decomposition of more intangible business service processes, enabled through ICT, is a recent development that is leading to further fragmentation of value chains. Modularization and externalization processes in intangible business services and recently in R&D, and thus in knowledge creation processes, have led to the further break-up of company structures and to new hybrid organizational forms. These processes reinforce the complexity of knowledge domains around business functions, thereby creating new proximity–distance relationships between multiple intra- and interorganizational actors – not only in organizational and spatial terms but also, above all, in institutional and cognitive terms.

In addition to fragmentation processes, the ongoing vertical specialization of industries is driven by the dynamic reconfiguration of value chains (cf. Humphrey and Schmitz, 2004). Vertical specialization displays industry-specific characteristics that seem to be rooted in related different technological and market characteristics (Macher and Mowery, 2004). Hence, vertical domain knowledge becomes more complex as sector specialization continues to advance. Vertical disintegration and specialization processes in industries, as well as modularity and standardization at the corporate level, generate more interfaces between diverse knowledge-using and -producing units, thus creating the need for communication and coordination of knowledge exchange and implicit and explicit knowledge-sharing. KIBS are responding to this development with their knowledge product specialization, and even new KIBS are beginning to emerge, typically along sector-oriented knowledge domains. Examples are software firms, specialized in services for the financial or telecommunications sectors. In innovation research KIBS are mostly considered to be a unit, but like other maturing sectors, KIBS are characterized by increasing differentiation and specialization in subsectors.

7.3.4   Knowledge Processing and Knowledge Producing in Client Interaction

Client participation in the delivery process of the knowledge-intensive service product is a fundamental characteristic for KIBS and is very different from the production process in other industries. It is different insofar as clients are directly involved in the added-value activities. Three processes – the contextualization, de- and recontextualization of knowledge – play an important role in exploring general linkages between knowledge processes and knowledge dynamics in KIBS–client interactions. These processes are especially shaping the contribution to multilevel knowledge dynamics.

KIBS are specialists in the contextualization of knowledge; this is evident implicitly from substantial empirical and theoretical research in the field. Contributions from innovation in services and systems of innovation research are emphasizing KIBS firms as innovation or knowledge agents (for example Bessant and Rush, 2000; Miles et al., 1996, Muller and Doloreux, 2007; Strambach, 2001; Wood, 2002). Important functions are described, such as transferring technological knowledge and management know-how, exchanging experience-based knowledge and best practice from different branch contexts, integrating different stocks of knowledge and competencies and adapting existing knowledge to the specific needs of the clients. These functions refer to the knowledge contextualization as an essential process that fosters knowledge dynamics by being conducive to the change of knowledge bases of client firms.

Turning from the processing of knowledge within a given service relationship to the knowledge production of KIBS firms, the process of decontextualization is a main mechanism. KIBS have the capability for producing new knowledge from this accumulated and experience based knowledge through decontextualization. We define decontextualization as the deliberate process of extracting experience-based and procedural-based knowledge from its client and project-specific contexts, to combine and reconfigure it with the pre-existing knowledge base in order to develop new knowledge products. KIBS firms acquire explicit and tacit knowledge from a variety of client contexts in the course of the provision of the service. They learn the main characteristics of their customers over time, and develop competencies that are related to the specific contexts of clients' vertical as well as horizontal knowledge domains.

There has been little exploration of the decontextualization process in KIBS research itself. KIBS are companies that work mainly on a project base (section 7.2) – repeated tasks are not the norm. Therefore these organizations' learning and capability development usually takes place during projects. The recently developing literature strand on innovation in project-based environments throws some light on the decontextualization process even if not explicitly named as such. As Acha et al. (2005) show for project-based firms, capabilities are often located at the organizational edges of the firms. A common practice for KIBS firms is to carry out knowledge processing in cross-functional and interdisciplinary project teams and communities of practice composed of both client and KIBS staff. Project learning, or episodic learning (Acha et al., 2005), involves relationships between learning by individuals and project teams as well as learning across project-based firms and sectors. These firms operate in a multi-actor environment and thus the decontextualization process entails the unleashing of dispersed experience-based knowledge components bound to practice contexts of individual and collective knowledge agents in complex project configurations, or what Grabher (2004) called 'project ecologies'. The decontextualization implies knowledge codification of accumulated experience-based knowledge and procedural-based knowledge mainly attained by group-level learning in projects. The formation of new knowledge products through decontextualization in turn opens up new opportunities for KIBS to interact with their customers. In a certain sense, KIBS create their own markets (Strambach, 2001).

A third process, which we call recontextualization, plays an important role for the contribution of the KIBS sector to knowledge dynamics. Recontextualization can be understood as the process of direct contextualization of individual or collective tacit knowledge without being transformed through codification.[3] Knowledge codification aims at the conversion of knowledge into explicit knowledge, and facilitates its exchange and valorization. It is, however, widely acknowledged that knowledge can be transferred without codification. As Cohendet and Meyer-Krahmer (2001: 1565) point out, codification processes themselves are context-dependent. There are contexts in which agents are willing to invest more into codifying knowledge and others in which they use and reinforce their tacit knowledge. The discontinuous and temporary nature of project-based service production by KIBS firms acts as a significant brake on knowledge codification and, in turn, fosters recontextualization processes. For project-based firms, the costs for codification are high and hinder the exploitation of systematic knowledge. The highly customized service solutions and the multiplicity and collective dimension of decontextualization processes increase the use of tacit knowledge and its exploitation in the application. Knowledge creation in the mode of the interactive (social) construction of a solution to a particular client problem in a complex application context is typical for KIBS. The term 'ad hoc innovation' is used in service innovation research for describing this result (Gallouj, 2002).

Furthermore, new complex projects provide the opportunity to build up new capabilities in fast-changing knowledge markets. Thus it is more attractive for KIBS firms to engage in new projects than to invest in knowledge codification of organizational dispersed implicit knowledge for capturing and storing it. Hence, under these conditions, the direct contextualization of experience-based tacit knowledge is supported through its adaptation in project contexts and project learning.

7.4   KNOWLEDGE DRIVERS FOR THE KIBS SECTOR

Based on the analysis of knowledge processes taking place in KIBS firms themselves and in interaction processes with their clients, the aim of this section is to outline key drivers stemming from the changing international business environment (Figure 7.4.), as well as the influence of and reactions to these changes in the European KIBS sector.

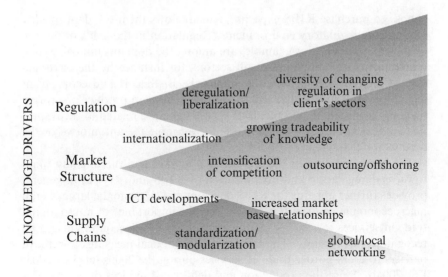

Figure 7.4   Knowledge drivers for the KIBS sector

With its dynamic growth and increasing maturity, the KIBS sector has become subject to the factors and drivers shaping the emerging knowledge-based economy as a whole. Today's growing KIBS sector has therefore risen due to the interrelated dynamics of internationalization, information and communication technologies, and the restructuring of value chains and firm organization. These essential drivers are exerted primarily by the forces of regulation – the market and supply chains – whereas regulation is understood in a broad sense, encompassing both direct and indirect regulative measures. Each of the drivers has its specific implications in terms of knowledge dynamics for KIBS, without the need to describe the basic differences between the KIBS branches again. The drivers outlined in this section consequently point out key factors with overall significance.

7.4.1   Regulation

To meet the requirements of increasing and complex regulation, special-ist knowledge and expertise is needed both for the provision of explicit knowledge and for assistance in the organizational processes of imple-mentation. For quality and cost-efficiency reasons, many organizations choose to purchase KIBS expertise, which allows them to adapt quickly to changing regulatory environments. Regulation in the fields of finance or the environment, for example, are among the domains imposing high requirements on companies of all sectors, for instance by the introduction of international accounting standards, BASEL II and eco-efficient technologies. Additionally, sector-specific changes in product or process regulations initiate requirements of special expertise related to the respective vertical knowledge domains (see for example the automotive or the food sector chapters in this book).

The harmonization of the EU internal market and the ongoing trend towards deregulation and liberalization of KIBS and services in general provides further impetus for KIBS development. Despite the large overall macroeconomic contribution of services, the importance of international trade in services for the competitiveness of the whole economy has been recognized just recently. The EU has taken political measures to remove barriers to cross-border trade of services during the 2000s (cf. EC, 2003; EC, 2004b). Since the production and delivery of services often contains more complex rules than is the case for tangible goods, services still face many obstacles to international trade, at both the intra-European and the global level. This indicates that there remains a large potential both for opening up new international KIBS markets applying knowledge-intensive services on a new scope, and in various niches (cf. OECD, 2005a).

KIBS are also affected by regulation in a direct way because they are themselves embedded in regulatory environments, which vary considerably due to the wide spectrum of sectors they operate in. High levels of regulation – exerted by either governmental or professional bodies – can mainly be found in liberal professions such as lawyers, notaries, accountants, architects, engineers and pharmacists (EC, 2004a). According to Robertson et al. (2003: 834f.), regulation and standards are critical to knowledge creation in professional contexts. Thus, deliberate change and removal of such barriers to competition as are subject to the Lisbon Agenda could essentially open up new courses of action and interaction. Furthermore, all KIBS segments are affected by employment law because they rely heavily on human resources, while the adaptation to foreign national human resource practices poses a challenge for operating in foreign markets, especially for smaller KIBS. Ambiguous as these development trends are, the other side of the coin is that every deficiency and shortfall of information, expertise and knowledge triggers new KIBS to develop.

Regulation also serves the important function of removing legal uncertainties and installing proper framework conditions for newly emerging markets, and thus for new KIBS branches. Regulating property rights

– particularly in knowledge products, which do not involve technical artefacts or processes but include symbolic knowledge to a large
extent – presents a major challenge in the knowledge-based economy.
Consequently, changes in the regulation of the non-uniform patent practice of EU countries can be observed. On the one hand, efforts are made
for the harmonization of proceedings. On the other, attempts to widen
the scope of intellectual property rights to rapidly emerging new fields of
knowledge and innovation are also being made, as so far these cannot be
covered by present patent law (cf. OECD, 2001).

7.4.2 Markets and Technology

The ongoing internationalization of the economy is driving KIBS development by opening up new markets and learning opportunities, while at
the same time strongly intensifying competitive pressures from abroad
(cf. Kuusisto and Meyer, 2003) and the presence of competitors, especially from emerging markets such as India and China. Frequently, the
internationalization of clients is a trigger for KIBS to follow the broadening of operations on an international level (Roberts, 1998). In terms of
industrial production, the internationalization of physical production was
first observed, while the scope of the international division of labour has
further widened to more knowledge-intensive R&D functions. Recently,
subcontractors like system or component suppliers are additionally acting
as clients of KIBS since they increasingly exercise sophisticated functions
in innovation processes and thereby also face a need for external sources
of knowledge – as can be seen in the automotive sector (cf. Jürgens, 2004;
Jürgens, Blöcker and MacNeill, Chapter 8 in this book).

As internationalization strategies are not restricted to the manufacturing sector, this trend is supplemented by proactive internationalization strategies of service firms in recent years, which further adds a new
customer segment and internationalized demand for KIBS. Thanks to
the growing tradability of knowledge, a multitude of services are now
increasingly globalizing in ways similar to the manufacturing sector for
several decades. As new information technologies facilitate the increasing divisibility of information and allow it to be communicated instantly
and without spatial limits, more and more services can be split into components and single service components are shifted globally (UNCTAD,
2004: 96). The rapid expansion of ICT benefits KIBS by creating the scope
for an increased division of labour through specialized functions and at
the same time creates demand for new competences and expertise as well
(Hauknes, 2000). The growing tradability of knowledge has also favoured
the expansion of outsourcing activities for service functions in general,

as well as for sophisticated business functions relating to innovation in particular. The contracting of services has significantly shaped the KIBS industry and is one of its key drivers.

At present, some particularities of the labour market also act as driving factors for KIBS growth, including market shortages of highly skilled labour. This renders the acquisition of external services more appealing, and increases demand for the flexible management of labour resources previously met by providers of human resource development services or personnel leasing. Additionally, aspects of lifestyle gain in importance for employment decisions in favour of KIBS, which can offer alternatives to traditional choices (EMCC, 2006a: 6).

The need for knowledge-intensive services is not limited to private business. The restructuring of the public sector and the introduction of market mechanisms can induce further demand for knowledge-intensive services and stimulus for new KIBS segments. Apart from this, the public sector begins to act as a supplier of knowledge-intensive services when, for example, public or semi-public research and technology institutions start to offer consultancy services to private businesses (cf. OECD, 2006). On the other hand, KIBS increasingly complement and compete with public sector institutions in the supply of R&D activities as a 'second knowledge infrastructure' (den Hertog and Bilderbeek, 2000). The common trait of these trends is a blurring of the boundaries between public sector and private KIBS and a remarkable intensification of competition, which presents another knowledge driver for KIBS.

7.4.3   Restructuring of Value Chains

Predominantly flexible coordination mechanisms can be found in the KIBS sector; therefore driving forces emanating from supply chains are relatively weak. Nevertheless the ongoing fragmentation of the supply chain tends to affect KIBS themselves. Standardization and modulariza-tion – even of mainly intangible goods like KIBS services – are triggered by clear architecture, clear interfaces and a well-defined set of functional tests, in order that small subsystems can be designed and produced inde-pendently. A modular production system enables KIBS to source parts of their knowledge input from suppliers or to establish network structures for the division of knowledge creation (cf. Baldwin and Clark, 2000; Miozzo and Grimshaw, 2006).

In the course of restructuring of value chains, growing competition within the KIBS sector also results from the increasing presence of com-petitors, not only from emerging markets but also from companies from other sectors that are moving into the KIBS market to offer more KIBS-type services. New market entrants like formerly internal units of manufacturing firms now act as profit-oriented KIBS providers which leverage their internally acquired expertise (IBM, Siemens or Porsche Engineering being prominent examples).

The ongoing decomposition of innovation processes (Chesbrough, 2003; Schmitz and Strambach, 2008) and the more widely distributed knowledge production between multiple intraorganizational and interorganizational actors being established at present, indicates other main drivers underlying the development of KIBS. In this respect, the importance of communities of practice and networks of innovation need to be acknowledged (Brown and Duguid, 2001; Wenger, 1999). Given the further fragmentation of the value chain, and the distributed knowledge generation accordingly, new demand for integrative and coordinative knowledge-intensive services is created, presenting a counterpart to other disintegrating tendencies. However, KIBS themselves enable the breaking-up of the value chain and the ongoing decomposition of innovation processes, as outlined in section 7.3, and consequently can be seen as both an outcome and a prerequisite of the further fragmentation of value chains. This follows the main argument that KIBS can be considered as drivers of knowledge dynamics in general.

7.5   KNOWLEDGE RESPONSES OF THE KIBS SECTOR

Responses to these actual drivers and developments are diverse and partly contradictory. On the one hand a range of communalities in KIBS sector responses can be observed in how to deal with multiple changes in regulations, markets and networks; while on the other hand each single KIBS segment develops on distinct paths to meet clients' requirements.

7.5.1   Organizational Response

KIBS in general are facing opposing poles, including specialization versus comprehensive solutions; the strategic choice to focus on standardization or on client-specific solutions; or the creation of competitive advantages through the mixture of both (Figure 7.5). Knowledge drivers and knowledge responses induce change processes which often lead to innovation.

The growth economies of scope and scale on an international level foster large KIBS firms on the one hand, while specialization in particular knowledge domains is attractive for rather small and medium-sized KIBS on the other (Morgan et al., 2006). Business models are changing

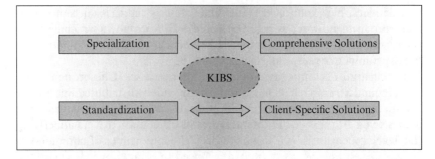

*Figure 7.5   Fields of tension for KIBS-related horizontal and vertical
            knowledge domains*

as clients become more demanding, require more expertise in their knowledge domain, and insist on flexibility and speed. KIBS firms are therefore changing the way they serve their clients, engaging in more vertical and horizontal knowledge domain specialization, building and improving networks, adjusting the way projects are staffed, and altering compensation systems. They rely on both the knowledge to understand the client's business as well as their own professional and specialized knowledge base. In this regard, long-term collaborations and more actively managed knowledge input of KIBS are occurring. The relationships within KIBS companies and between them and their clients may therefore be characterized by deeper interaction under high uncertainty (Toivonen, 2004: 140). However, closer relationships on a transnational basis often face the challenge of lacking cultural and social knowledge and common understanding (Roberts, 1998). Therefore, in the KIBS–client relationship the pattern of proximity and distance is diversifying and this is likely to increase further due to developments in ICT and the different forms of proximity possibly emerging with them.

In many cases (for example manufacturing, finance and retail), the maturity of the sector is accompanied by a long-term trend towards the concentration of a higher share of added value in the largest firms. However, the KIBS sector is less concentrated than the entire economy, as it is made up of many small firms in regional or specialized niches, together with a small number of very large firms operating transnationally. Empirical evidence for the territorial and subsectoral concentration of KIBS emphasizes the obvious need for closer examination (Eurostat, 2004b; cf. section 7.2). The ongoing concentration is a result of intensified competition in the KIBS sector and the resulting pressure on costs. Therefore, KIBS make use of rationalization of their processes and knowledge flows, mainly enabled and supported by the application of ICT. Knowledge management tools for efficient storage, diffusion and reuse of knowledge; project management economization; and internal process quality standards are just a few common information management processes in large KIBS, and trickling down to small and medium-sized firms. One consequence of the restructuring and rationalization tendencies is that KIBS use more flexible staffing models that result in a leaner workforce (Kennedy Information, 2005). Additionally, access to new implicit and embedded knowledge is improved through flexible recruitment on a market or network basis (Howells, 2006).

Changes in KIBS–client relationships are multifaceted and partly counterintuitive, ranging from establishing close personal interaction or collaboration, to independent forms of informal relationships. The latter refers to pressure within many KIBS subsectors towards distant relationships with client companies in which the KIBS firm is largely a contractor performing a predefined task. Distant relationships are possible due to ICT and new workflows in the context of globalization; thus market-based transactions gain in importance. In particular, if surveying knowledge is needed from the KIBS firm, tasks can often be specified, isolated and – if proper standardized interfaces are in place – externalized. This can be observed in software development, laboratory analysing and testing, and other subsectors of KIBS. However, different patterns of development in client relationships are possible in relation to various KIBS sectors and firms. Virtual proximity via ICT can substitute spatial proximity associated with face-to-face contacts in particular phases of the KIBS–client relationship. As a result, the obligatory concurrence of production and consumption – typically a feature of services – disappears partially, and simultaneously gives rise to mass customization and a lower degree of uniqueness, even of intangible goods like knowledge-intensive services.

As a response to the uncertainty and low degree of transparency due to the difficulties in assessing the quality of intangible service products in the KIBS market, many KIBS firms have established two means to improve quality of services. Firstly, internal quality standards are in place and signalled to potential clients, either as proof of process quality (for example, CIMM-Levels in software development, ISO 9000 certification) or as de-facto standards of service management quality (for example ISO 20000 and ITIL V3).[4] So far, standardization and modularization can mainly be observed in the software sector. At the same time, more market-based relationships could be established. Recently, the role of standardization and modularization has been increasing in other KIBS subsectors as well, particularly in those dealing with synthetic knowledge. Secondly, quality-level agreements with clients and flexible fees coupled with assessments of added value through the use of KIBS formalize the client–KIBS relationship and complement trust-based and subjective validation of the KIBS–client interaction (cf. Schweitzer and Rajes, 2006).

Moreover, deficits in quality of services and the lack of transparency can be reduced by the introduction of standards not only for the services themselves, but also for the KIBS professions. This is reflected in professional standards like Management Consultancies Association's (MCA) UK certified consultants, or certifications of skills in the software administrator profession, for instance. Finally, quality assurance in professions and in the services themselves is facilitated by the initiatives of professional associations (as associations either in subsector terms or in regional terms). They provide training, skill enhancements and other forms of qualifications that are essential in a knowledge-based business like the KIBS sector. The development of an awareness of future needs within the KIBS sector is a crucial policy action of professional associations to increase effectiveness, efficiency and competitiveness of the KIBS sector (EMCC, 2006b).

7.5.2 Product and Process

As mentioned above, the ongoing complexity of knowledge domains creates the necessity for specialization of KIBS into a particular set of knowledge domains. Thus, KIBS seek to facilitate their expertise in their niches or core competence fields to provide their clients with a unique set of knowledge products. Concerning their service products, many KIBS clients are seeking increasingly high levels of specific knowledge, requiring niche or so-called 'boutique' offerings. As a result, smaller, specialized KIBS firms are favoured in these cases. At the same time, however, KIBS broaden the range of services they provide, as a response to the flexible and volatile market demand for comprehensive services and solutions. Service firms try to compete by integrating competencies of neighbouring knowledge domains (for example, legal services integrating management consultancy functions). Another example is the development of new capabilities on a meta-level, like engineering KIBS moving towards a project management expert whilst subcontracting and outsourcing engineering tasks (Schamp et al., 2003). Thus, convergence in the knowledge domains among KIBS firms can be recognized to some extent, as their services often overlap (Strambach, 2001). Such convergence is a trend across many KIBS sectors, as traditionally distinct KIBS subsectors increasingly offer services that were previously only provided by each of them individually. While larger KIBS have developed a multisectoral direction through acquisitions to offer comprehensive solutions, smaller KIBS rely more commonly on networks to deliver a set of specialized solutions. The traditional segmentation of a few big KIBS firms and many very small to medium-sized KIBS is therefore prevailing if not increasing.

In accordance with quality and cost considerations on the market level, KIBS are also driven to provide more standardized and modularized service solutions to common problems. They are increasingly looking for ways to standardize services to benefit from economies of scale and repetition, perhaps through the introduction of modular solutions for common problems that can be customized to the client's needs. This can particularly be observed in IT services dealing mainly with synthetic knowledge. This intensification of competition and technological progress – especially in ICT – forces KIBS to develop service innovations and new delivery models. Associated with this is the tendency to provide comprehensive solutions, which nevertheless are based on a bundle of specialized domain knowledge.

Finally, concepts (fostered by policies) emerge sporadically, which put dedicated R&D sections and the introduction of analytical methods in the development of new services in focus. For instance, the application of systematic, engineering-type procedures in the planning and development of new services, particularly if they rely on synthetic knowledge ('service engineering'), is an approach to improving efficiency and effectiveness of service development and to elevate quality.

7.5.3 Internationalization

Like other maturing sectors, KIBS are restructuring to focus on their core competencies. One response to this development is the outsourcing and/or offshoring of less-knowledge-intensive services (business process outsourcing) and even modular knowledge-intensive tasks (knowledge process outsourcing), which affects large to medium-sized KIBS as well. Examples for the offshoring of knowledge-intensive services can be seen in offshore centres of consultancies, or offshore financial research departments in the investment and banking sector.

In the course of this development, the internationalization of KIBS firms is one response to the increasing internationalization of their clients as well as the globalization of KIBS services themselves. Multinational clients are demanding the same service provider around the world. As a result, some formerly nationally focused KIBS are expanding their international horizons to satisfy these new client demands (cf. Roberts, 1998) and therefore need to access the necessary combinations of internal and local knowledge. Furthermore, changes in the business environment and the distribution of knowledge due to globalization also affect KIBS not directly operating in international markets. In general, the role of large transnational service companies is expanding (UNCTAD, 2004: 105). However, internationalization does not only concern large firms. Simultaneously to the emergence of large multinational KIBS, some small and medium-sized companies are also becoming more active on an international scale. Controversially, some small KIBS operate on an international basis right from the start, especially if their business is based on Internet or software services (EMCC, 2005). However, often this is only possible because they benefit from the support of professional bodies and they rely on partnerships with other KIBS or even are part of a 'virtual firm', a network of loosely coupled small KIBS (Morgan et al., 2006).

The distribution of knowledge production is evolving further in this regard. The restructuring of knowledge value chains facilitates distant relationships to suppliers, employees and clients as a workable and applicable way to create knowledge-intensive services. Therefore, the ability of KIBS to work together virtually and in reality promotes a division of labour based on interaction and on mutual benefits (FIDIC, 2006). Simultaneously, deregulation and new occupational images lower the market protection of professional bodies. Consequently, competition within and between occupations is increasingly fuelled even more by the internationalization of labour markets.

In summary, a versatile mix of new direct and indirect forms of internationalization can be observed, while their correlation with knowledge creation remains at present unclear (Toivonen, 2002).

7.6   CONCLUSIONS

The KIBS sector is particularly representative of the knowledge economy because knowledge products and knowledge inputs are essential to ensure competitiveness in the marketplace. The commodities these firms trade on the market are to a large extent intangible and knowledge-intensive services. These firms are developing into a knowledge-processing and knowledge-producing industry. They are involved in the interaction of the use of knowledge for economic purposes and the conversion and configuration of knowledge for economic gain and added value. Changes in knowledge make up the driving force behind innovation. KIBS fosters multilevel knowledge dynamics in firms and sector contexts by influencing knowledge bases and competencies of agents through both the specific characteristic of their composite knowledge products and the way in which these are produced.

In innovation research KIBS are mostly considered as a unit, but these services are becoming more and more diversified as the sector is maturing.

The application of different knowledge categories (analytic, synthetic, symbolic) enables the identification of distinct knowledge bases of the KIBS subsectors and the composite nature of their knowledge-based service products. With these products KIBS act as drivers of knowledge dynamics at the firm level by complementing or changing the knowledge base of their clients. Even if the KIBS subsectors are focused on particular knowledge categories, as shown, they are not limited to these. Most KIBS subsectors have merged knowledge bases composed of highly skilled staff that combine and join different knowledge categories at different scales. They integrate various knowledge units into composite knowledge-based service products and this enables them to deliver knowledge from contexts in which their clients are not usually embedded. KIBS foster knowledge dynamics by contributing to problem identification and problem solving and thus subsequently to knowledge articulation, sharing and reconfiguration. In these interaction processes KIBS are carrying out communication and coordination functions by using and establishing linkages and networks, and spanning diverse organizational, institutional and spatial boundaries. KIBS firms operate in all knowledge phases along the generic knowledge value chain.

Furthermore, they directly and indirectly contribute to the knowledge dynamics at a sectoral level. The dominant feature of the KIBS sector is its dynamic interconnections with other sectoral contexts. Co-evolution processes with client sectors are leading to cumulativeness of knowledge and specialization of KIBS subsectors in horizontal and vertical knowledge domains. By extracting knowledge from different sectors and recombining it in different sectoral contexts they contribute at the same time to specialization and diversification. Besides being specialists in the contextualization and reconfiguring of existing knowledge units, these firms are characterized by their dynamic capability to decontextualize knowledge and to transfer it to new contexts using mixed types of horizontal and vertical knowledge domains. Additionally the recontextualization of implicit knowledge is a special competence of KIBS firms which accelerates the diffusion of implicit knowledge among sectoral contexts.

Turning to a spatial perspective, KIBS are likely to have indirect rather than direct effects on territorial knowledge dynamics. While they surely directly drive what Cooke calls 'dynamic regional capabilities' (Cooke, 2005a), it is nevertheless difficult to estimate, or even quantify, the extent of such direct contributions. What we do know is that the majority of KIBS are small to medium-sized firms and act primarily in regional and national contexts. However, as internationalization is becoming more important, the transfer of local knowledge to other regional and national contexts is being promoted by KIBS, due to both their capabilities for

spanning different territorial and sectoral contexts and their own internationalization that has recently been observed (cf. Toivonen, 2002). We
suggest advancing the questioning beyond present KIBS research and
focusing on the interplay of KIBS and regional economical trajectories in
order to get new insights into the implications of KIBS involvement for
territorial knowledge dynamics. Addressing this relationship in theoretical
and empirical terms is also an important issue from a political perspective. Several impacts of KIBS on the performance of territorial knowledge
dynamics can be assumed, given that the KIBS sector evolution depends
very much on complex, often long-term relationships with client firms in
other sectors of the economy:

- KIBS may facilitate regional trajectories and drive knowledge
  dynamics in a particular direction, reinforcing the existing uneven
  knowledge endowment of well-established innovating regions. In
  this way they contribute to 'dynamic stability' and the renewal of
  regional trajectories.
- KIBS also have the potential to open up established regional knowledge trajectories and to create new paths, as they are not limited to
  one single knowledge domain.
- KIBS contribute to the decontextualization of knowledge, promoting particularly the mobility of tacit and implicit knowledge, and
  thus make the migration of knowledge and its spatial dispersion
  easier.

However, there is still a lack of empirical evidence that illustrates the
spatial variation in the subsectoral configuration of the KIBS industry
and the need for in-depth cross-regional comparisons. Thus, the extent to
which KIBS knowledge dynamics are determined by regional and local
factors largely remains an open question. The same holds true for the
knowledge processes in the interrelation of KIBS and regional economies.
In particular, research linking quantitative and qualitative analysis could
provide new insights into these issues.

NOTES

1. The Eurostat classification includes the NACE Rev. 1.1 sectors 61, 62, 64–67, 70–74, 80,
   85 and 92.
2. For detailed discussion of service specificities in innovation and innovation processes see
   Hipp and Grupp (2005).
3. For this aspect I appreciate particularly the discussions with Ernst Helmstädter.
4. A best-practice collection for IT operations with a focus on the service lifecycle.

8. Knowledge processes and networks in the automotive sector

Ulrich Jürgens, Antje Blöcker and Stewart MacNeill

8.1 INTRODUCTION

The automotive industry holds a special place in the hearts and minds of the public and is viewed as a 'flagship' by policy-makers, politicians and academics alike. It is highly competitive and more structured than any other industry and has thus been the focus of considerable study in economics, management, environment and other fields. Since the early part of the twentieth century the industry has set the paradigms for work organization and business models, such as 'Fordism', 'Taylorism', 'Toyotaism' and 'lean manufacturing' and has been a base for wider economic thinking.

Its history dates back more than 100 years to when Karl Benz produced his first car at Mannheim, in Germany, in 1885. Large numbers of manufacturers sprang up in the 20 or so years that followed, producing vehicles based on 'short runs' of individual models largely carrying out assembly of 'craft-based' components which were often subcontracted to different workshops. Some of these became car makers in their own right or developed as suppliers. Most early companies were absorbed through mergers and acquisitions but some remained to the present, including Daimler (1890 – later Mercedes-Benz), Fiat (1899), Austin (1905) and Ford (1903). In the course of this history the industry has experienced radical changes discussed in terms of three 'industrial revolutions' (Womack et al., 1990), the first two being the introduction of assembly line production by Henry Ford and lean production by Toyota. Since 1970, the industry has experienced further radical changes affecting the entire value chain, from manufacturers and suppliers to service providers and dealers (Chanaron, 2004; MacNeill and Chanaron, 2005; Roth, 2006) and, since the mid-1990s, has been undergoing a 'third revolution' focused on change through flexibility, primarily affecting product cycles and the consequent new forms of product creation and production.

The main drivers of change are cost pressures, driven by intense competition, environmental concern and the regulatory regimens that result, and consumer choice which, in particular, drives market breadth and specialization but also contributes to safety and environmental responses. The most important of these is cost pressure which, together with intense competition, has encouraged economies of scale and led to the main production paradigms. Cost pressure has driven successive waves of mergers, the standardization of components, trends towards outsourcing to specialist suppliers and the imperative for manufacturers to increase the high-value content of vehicles by the addition of electrical, electronic and communications componentry. Pressure from regulators and consumers has led to a drive for more efficient powertrains, reduced emissions and the development of technologies for reduced weight, hybrid or electric vehicles and biofuels. In addition, consumer pressures have led to the growth of new market segments, such as minivans or small 'city' cars, and the need to offer increasing numbers of radical variations whilst maintaining common 'under-skin' platforms.

These factors have given the industry its present-day characteristics. The most obvious feature is its size, with 2006 global production of more than 70 million cars and light trucks and a turnover of €1500 billion. Consolidation has seen the number of large car makers reduced to some 13 global players with just seven companies accounting for 70 per cent of global sales. In Europe alone the industry has some 2.3 million direct employees, and 12.6 million if employment in supply, distribution, retail, fuel and related trades such as advertising and insurance is taken into account (ACEA, 2006). However, with a total worldwide capacity of around 80 million vehicles the above figures represent only 75 per cent plant utilization. In addition the trend towards outsourcing means that car makers retain smaller proportions of value in each vehicle (approximately 30 per cent in 2010) and are losing some of their technological lead to major suppliers, especially in areas such as plastics, electronics and communications. OEMs[1] can be characterized as large and relatively stable but often with poor profitability, especially in the small and medium range car segments.

The challenges and consequences of these factors for knowledge dynamics in the industry are examined with the aid of the following questions:

- What knowledge dynamics characterize the industry, and how and by what means have knowledge flows changed since the 1990s?
- What are the essential knowledge drivers, what are the responses, what changes are typical for the sector in this context? Has knowledge as a whole increased, and how do the various factors interrelate?

- What categories of knowledge predominate, and are there any differences with regard to the phases of knowledge creation?
- What actors are particularly important in relation to drivers and responses, and phases and categories?
- What knowledge contexts are problematic or conflictual?

The following four characteristics are particularly important: Firstly, the industry is a multi-technology industry with no specific analytical base or scientific discipline, but drawing on thermodynamics, mechanics, hydraulics or pneumatics (the traditional science base) as well as electronics, communications, nanotechnology and so on. A specific requirement is the capability to integrate different technologies since modern vehicles contain innovations in all aspects, components, and functionalities. To an increasing extent, OEM's specialize in integrating new knowledge identified inside and outside the industry. The multi-technology nature also holds true for the range of process-related technologies needed in development and production.

Secondly, it is a multi-actor industry, comprising a multitude of specialists and with a trend towards further specialization (new business models) in which some companies have gained a clearly identifiable science base (such as electronics experts, nanotechnology, paint experts and so on). Many of the actors or employees are outside the formal industry classification.

The multitude of interfaces is a third characteristic deriving from the previous two. The following are crucial for knowledge flows and for communication and cooperation within the industry:

- Interfaces between academic disciplines. Differences in the methods and mindsets of people with a background in mechanics and electrics or electronics play an increasingly important role (not least as a source of problems).
- Interfaces between functional organizations within firms – classically between development and production.
- Interfaces between firms and other external actors involved in different processes.
- Interfaces between hierarchical levels and between planners and executors of work (as exemplified by the classical Taylorist divide).

The well-known symbolic supply chain, illustrating these interfaces, is shown in Figure 8.1. However the increasing reality is of a more complex series of back-and-fore interactions in a modern supply matrix rather than a linear 'tiered' chain. The compexity of interactions, which we discuss in the sections below, requires one strong area of knowledge, shared between

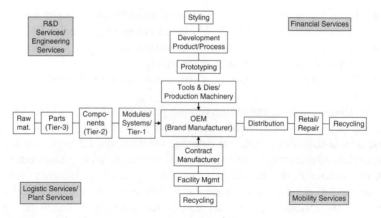

Figure 8.1   Automotive supply and distribution 'chain'

different players at many different parts of this matrix, to be that of how to organize and manage interfaces.

The many contradictory goals and interests are a fourth characteristic. These are partly a functional element of the technical and organizational needs and partly a covert dimension of micro-policy, which can distort or block knowledge flows. For example, there is pressure to save fuel and reduce emissions by weight reduction whilst at the same time manufacturers, driven by economic imperatives and consumer expectations, increase vehicle weights though the addition of high-value components and extra 'trim and luxury'.

8.2   KNOWLEDGE DRIVERS AND KNOWLEDGE RESPONSES

Based upon the grid discussed in Chapter1, the factors considered here are regulation, market structure, supply chain (networks) and corporate objectives under which four types, or areas, of knowledge response are discussed: organization, market, product and process, and professional. The confrontation of these drivers and responses furthers the process of change, leading in many cases to innovation.

8.2.1   Regulation

Regulation is a key force for change, although actors and regulatory areas are heterogeneous and largely unconnected. The most important areas are safety, emissions, and resource or fuel consumption which, primarily, make technical demands. Other important fields concern vehicle use, costs and pricing policies, the control of intellectual property rights (IPR), the downstream dealer and market structures, and the changing conditions of the industry's block exemption from European competition policy.

Regulation – organizational

The heterogeneous nature of regulation also leads to contradictory goals. In the EU, the Cars 21 Initiative, 'Competitive Automotive Regulatory System for the 21st Century' (European Commission, 2006c), has made recommendations for a competitive regulatory framework with a ten-year roadmap covering better regulation, environment, road safety, trade, research and development, taxation and fiscal incentives, intellectual property and competition. Given its importance, companies have taken steps to influence regulatory processes through associations and direct lobbying at the EU and national levels.

Currently most important, as far as organizational response is concerned, is regulation of distribution structures, especially the European Commission Block Exemption Regulations. This aims to strengthen the position of independent dealers and repair shops and affects the fundamental and growing interests of OEMs in brand presentation and direct contact with customers. The intermediary role played by independent dealers affects knowledge processes concerning customer complaints, requirements and demands. The spread of direct sales and the establishment of business-to-customer (B2C) channels aim to ameliorate the situation. This is a field in which power interests overlap with knowledge dynamics, resulting in conflicts. Abolishing the special rules about relations between OEMs and dealers and repair shops would open the way to new business models like setting up multibrand dealerships or selling vehicles through outsiders such as insurance companies and department stores, with far-reaching consequences for the sector's hierarchical decision-making structures and downstream knowledge dynamics.

Regulation – market

While the structural impacts of regulation on the market are of great importance, the knowledge dynamics (learning processes) that result can lead to significant regulation-induced impacts, for example regarding specialization. One example is the divergence of markets during the 1990s, which was of crucial significance for the different development of the industry in the United States, Europe and Japan. Contrary to the expected 'world-car concepts', driven by platform strategies and harmonization of technical standards, different regulations in trade, taxation, safety and emissions encouraged differentiation. Thus, in North America, a protected light truck segment developed which, for a good decade, almost exclusively benefited North American firms. A comparable development in Western Europe was the diesel boom in the second half of the 1990s, whereas in Japan growth of the mini-vehicle sector can be partly attributed to regulatory issues.

Regulation – product and process
Product-related regulation plays a key role in innovation and competition processes. Each of the three central regulatory areas (safety, emissions and resource consumption) makes 'integrative' demands on vehicle concept and design. Regulation hence makes a crucial contribution to the closed, proprietary nature of the product and thus to the knowledge architecture of vehicles. This has major consequences for the innovation model (largely hierarchically, OEM-controlled, fewer open interfaces onto which suppliers can dock with independent propositions).

Apart from the centralizing effect, regulation fosters technological developments to address increasingly stringent emissions targets. These include the development of hybrid drives, biofuels and alternatives such as natural gas or hydrogen, and the move towards electrically operated auxiliaries that enable the optimization of drive and chassis, without which targets and upper limiting values, particularly for CO_2, cannot be attained. Regulation thus plays a key role in technology development and the associated knowledge processes. Although less important as a driving force of process innovation, here too secondary knowledge dynamics can be generated. For instance, new tacit knowledge connects process automation and safety requirements (crash results) in body-in-white (basic structure) processes; and requirements about new materials for reducing emissions and fuel consumption (for example, aluminium or composite processing).

Regulation – professional
In some countries regulation influences standards and structures in employment. For example in Germany, with professional qualifications for engineers and others, and the transition to the bachelor and master degree system in universities, there is a fear of decline in qualification standards which would necessitate special knowledge responses. Simultaneous changes in the vocational training system for blue-collar occupations offer a further example.

8.2.2   Market Structure

Market structure covers individual customer requirements for product characteristics, performance, comfort, prices and range of uses; as well as different customer groups (demography, income) and markets (internationalization). Despite the changes described above, the large car makers continue to control the market as both oligopsonistic, upstream, buyers of components and oligopolistic sellers to the consumer through strictly controlled dealer networks. This market structure is highly competitive and innovative and, at face value at least, brings ever-increasing capability and value to consumers.

Market structure – organizational
Organizational responses to changes in market structure often concern corporate organization. Some companies adopt divisional structures, as in General Motors (and recently, with new divisions like Smart at Daimler Benz or Mini at BMW). In contrast, other firms, like Toyota, have so far preferred a strongly integrated structure. The organizational distribution of functions has far-reaching consequences for knowledge dynamics where organizational boundaries permit specialization on customer groups but makes transfer of tacit knowledge difficult. Another organizational response concerns the internationalization of production and research and development (R&D). This is preceded by the creation of market observation posts, especially in lead markets for certain segments (such as California).

A third reaction is mergers and acquisitions or, as an alternative, the creation of alliances to broaden product ranges, achieve scale economies or to help resist aggressive takeovers. Knowledge about specific product markets and related competencies can thus be bought or acquired.

A fourth response, driven by weak financial returns on sales, is to expand OEM-specific functional areas to finance, leasing, fleet management and other services. This broadens the knowledge base of classical, production-centred firms. On the one hand, knowledge about the traditional customer base is gained in new business segments, for example through loan financing of vehicle purchases; while on the other hand, new areas of knowledge are opened up.

Market structure – markets
Sales forecasting is a major zone of uncertainty. Companies use their own surveys but external studies provide additional feedback. These include those by J.D. Powers on customer (and dealer) satisfaction where, since the 1990s, the Powers Index has dominated the North American market as a quality benchmark. The Index is also becoming important in Europe alongside traditional tests and expert assessments published by the specialist press. The basis for both systems is a comparison between competing products, thus furthering a degree of 'herd behaviour' towards benchmark products and firms.

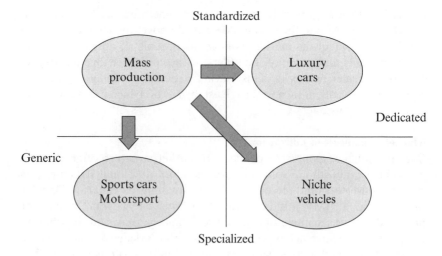

Figure 8.2   'Worlds of production' model: market trends

In terms of the overall trends in vehicle sales, and therefore production, we have trends towards products which are dedicated to particular groups of consumers whilst, at the same time, retaining as much 'under skin' commonality as possible. We can also observe the need of manufacturers to maximize returns on sales though the addition of high-value technologies or additional trim and luxury. Figure 8.2 illustrates this overall trend using the 'worlds of production' model (Storper and Salais, 1997). The block arrows show the trend away from mass 'push-based' manufacture towards more specialized, higher-value production.

Future market structures are influenced by a mixture of hard (relatively predictable) and soft factors. The former include demographic developments and income distribution; the latter, fashions and culture. Others include expectations about future regulation and political and economic developments regarding fuel, raw materials, and so on. Tacit knowledge is important alongside 'hard' observations. Setting up producer market observation posts in important markets (for example California) and presenting vehicle concepts at international exhibitions, as well as consulting market research institutes, are important responses to market uncertainty alongside scenario techniques. However, this information gathering and modelling, as repeated real-world flops testify, is not always successful.

Market structure – product and process
Firms react to feedback by means of product and process design with a measure of trade-off between the two. In the past, the longer life of

models meant that responses often took the form of periodic facelifts with bundles of improvements to existing products. The shorter model cycles of recent years are themselves a reaction to changing market structures, enabling larger packages of improvements to be introduced, and organization focusing more strongly on the next generation. Shorter cycles also mean shorter development times (time-to-market). Thus products are designed and developed closer to launch – probably the most important process (and organizational) response to changing market structures. One measure to reduce time-to-market is to decouple component development from the rhythm of model cycles. New components are held ready until a new total package is prepared. This requires greater standardization at interfaces and a certain opening up of product architectures.

Another response is to involve marketing in the early stages of product and concept development. Representatives of marketing and distribution are thus included in cross-functional development groups.

Apart from time reductions, the main way to anticipate changes in market structure has been expansion of the product spectrum. Thus since the beginning of the 1990s product ranges have grown massively. For the organization of development processes, this means extreme fragmentation, requiring new responses in process and organizational design. The kernel of the new procedural organization was a transition to project-type organization instead of, or in conjunction with, traditional functional organization, the parallelization of activities which in the past had been dealt with sequentially (simultaneous engineering) and working in cross-functional teams under the influence of suppliers (see Jürgens, 2000). The issue of shorter lead times also includes efforts to reduce individual customer delivery times by building to order as far as possible. A third area concerning knowledge responses to market structures is the use of information and communication technology (ICT), especially the Internet, with knowledge transfer processes shifting from customer–dealer relations directly to the customer.

Market structure – professional
There are fewer opportunities for standardizing and structuring as regards qualifications, specialization patterns, and so on. Shifts are caused especially by process reorganization (front-loading of market information in product development), cross-functional cooperation, and by ICT (B2C, customer relationship management – CRM, and so on.). Overall, white-collar work, which is difficult to coordinate through OEM hierarchies, continues to grow. A central problem in reorganizing knowledge processes arises from shortening the product development processes. Knowledge management systems face crucial challenges in transferring knowledge

and experience horizontally between different vehicles and projects, and vertically from preceding projects, to succeeding projects, and in organizing knowledge transfer processes.

The growth of KIBS in the sector
A notable phenomenon, present in all the arenas discussed above, is the growth of knowledge-intensive business services (KIBS; see preceding KIBS chapter). Commercial providers are represented in the supply matrix at almost every point. They are thus present as:

1. Upstream engineering and aesthetic design companies – such as the Italian company Pininfarina – which will also manufacture small-volume variants of mass market models.
2. Specialist engineering and test companies with high skills and knowledge in specific areas – such as the Austrian engine design and testing company AVL.
3. Consultancy companies, or automotive divisions of the major accountancy firms, that offer supply chain management, logistics, market intelligence, market analysis, promotional activities and other services.

8.2.3   Supply Matrix Networks

Upstream structures and processes have been subject to fundamental transformation since the 1990s (cf. Florida and Sturgeon, 2000; Humphrey and Memedovic, 2003). The forces driving this process are globalization, capital markets and the OEM strategies.

Supply chain – organizational
'Tiering' is the term typically used to describe supply structures. Given the complexity of the matrix (see Figure 8.1), one explicit aim of outsourcing has been to reduce OEM requirements to manage upstream process chains. The coordination of upstream purchasing and associated knowledge processes is shifted to large-scale systems and module integrators known as 0.5th or 1st tier suppliers, which in turn outsource functions to second-tier suppliers, and so on. The growth of KIBS is part of the increasing division of knowledge accompanying the traditional division of labour. An inherent contradiction is highlighted by need to balance the value outsourced against the efficient utilization of companies' own resources and competences.

A second element of restructuring supplier relations is change in selection processes. In corporate procurement organization, units for forward sourcing, and selection and certification of preferred suppliers, have been established on the lines of the 'extended enterprise' or Japanese *keiretsu* model. A particular issue is the balance between competitive and cooperative goals and requirements. Thus there has been an attempt to integrate suppliers into a 'lean manufacturing' model which seeks to optimize supply quality, costs and delivery (QCD). Companies balance the advantages of social capital, trust, cooperative experience, and mutual knowledge of organizational and corporate cultures against path-dependent restrictions on obtaining new capabilities and knowledge.

As with market surveillance, the procurement function establishes observation posts around the world to monitor supply capability developments and sources. The search for new sources is to some extent also behind the formation of alliances with competing firms, such as the joint venture between PSA and Toyota in the Czech Republic (TPSA in Kolin established 2005).

A third issue is functional and regional cluster formation. Examples are found in the different variants of supplier sites with different organizational and spatial forms such as the supplier parks approach, OEM–supplier condominium approach, consortium approach (Jürgens, 2003; 24) and regional R&D centre for simultaneous engineering. A key aspect is the importance of geographical proximity for knowledge processes, knowledge development and knowledge transfer (Preissl and Solimene, 2003).

Supply chain networks – market

Two crucial aspects are the opening up of new markets, and customer areas, through specific combinations of technology and prices, achieved through specific supplier relations and the contribution of 'follow-sourcing' where suppliers set up plants adjacent to new OEM sites.

Regarding the first, knowledge responses are concerned with both the screening and selection of suppliers and with questions of cooperation and the protection, or shared exploitation, of new knowledge. Suppliers must consider how to exploit knowledge acquired in cooperative projects outside their relationship with the OEM, whereas OEMs seek to delay diffusion in order to prolong 'first-mover' advantages. The second, 'follow-sourcing', is concerned with the suppliers' role in OEM globalization. Together with their own parallel low-cost sourcing, global footprints of suppliers have become strongly differentiated and fragmented – more so than those of the vehicle makers.

Supply chain networks – product and process

The reorganization of supplier relations has a crucial impact on products and product development, and on production. There has been an increase in the value of bought-in parts alongside a significant reduction in the number of individual components and suppliers. During the 1990s, changes were made to product architecture under the modularization and platform approaches. These require standardization at interfaces, which induces opening up of product architectures to counter the closure processes discussed above. Such approaches are open but proprietary, for while OEMs retain their oligopsonistic position they decide which suppliers and development firms are trusted with module development or production. Thus, product modularization is also a driving force in reorganizing supply matrices but, with the exception of its effects on architecture and changes in technology–price combinations made possible by suppliers, the product-related effects of these changes are small.

The impacts on processes, however, are far-reaching. Outsourcing functions and responsibilities to suppliers (including engineering service firms) has a major impact on the organization and processes of product development. Selected, innovative suppliers are closely integrated into the process of concept development and the development of on-the-shelf products. We have already discussed the associated problems in systems where there is no long-term commitment to a supplier, with regard to knowledge protection and sharing exploitation of jointly generated knowledge.

In series development, suppliers are increasingly integrated through cross-functional and cross-company teams. Suppliers' representatives liaise with the relevant functional areas in their own firms and defend their demands and strategies. Vice versa, in view of the outsourced functions, OEM employees assume greater responsibility for controlling and supervising outsourced activities instead of themselves developing and planning products.

Supply chain networks – professional
Changes in process chains result in depreciation of the OEMs' knowledge and the restructuring of requirements away from technical or functional orientations, for instance in computer-aided technologies (CAx)-aided work in favour of supervisory and coordinating activities. Combinations of engineering business administration know-how and management knowledge are, therefore, at a premium. Shifts in knowledge requirements, and the type of knowledge generated, also result from the work of cross-functional teams. Instead of concentrating purely on technical matters, teams address other requirements and contexts, not least those concerned with production.

8.2.4 Labour Demands and Requirements

Labour is a classical zone of uncertainty in capital exploitation yet, with a widening knowledge base, it is the most important success factor. Exploitable knowledge can only be described as such when it resides in people. Personnel policy, human resources management, and industrial relations are tradition-ally important, but recent developments have seemed to weaken this role. The influence of trade unions has declined, and process standardization, outsourcing and offshoring have eroded the power base of both blue- and white-collar labour and the number of disputes has fallen. At the same time, however, the sensitivity of process chains to disruption has grown. New demands also arise from the need for greater flexibility in labour input. Labour continues to be the primary target of downsizing and rationaliza-tion, where competitive pressures alone lead to a year-on-year reduction in employment of around 5 per cent throughout the industry (MacNeill and Chanaron, 2005). Implications for knowledge responses include:

- problems in knowledge transfer owing to the growing use of agency work – as high as 15 per cent of the workforce in some major companies;
- problems in knowledge and experience transfer owing to personnel cutbacks;
- involvement of the workforce in continuous improvement and organizational learning;
- the extent and direction of continuing training.

8.2.5 Corporate Objectives

Many of the developments discussed above can be revisited in this context. One important factor, since the 1990s, has been the capital market. Mergers and acquisitions raise expectations of greater profitability and shareholder value, and of risks and opportunities, which can have a far-reaching effect on corporate objectives. To sum up:

1. The objective of concentrating on core competencies is a major driving force of organizational change, especially in supply chain networks. This is also the case with outsourcing and offshoring.
2. Corporate objectives regarding markets are concerned primarily with aspects like product quality, product positioning and market position-ing in the global environment.
3. There is an imperative for vehicle makers, and their suppliers, to maintain planned production volumes in order to utilize plant

capacity and maintain low unit costs. Hence, where sales fail to meet expectations, OEMs will offer showroom discounts or deals to fleet and car-hire companies. These strategies not only add to the price pressure throughout the supply matrix, and ultimately reinforce many companies' weak financial position, but also require an expansion of the knowledge base.

4. Product and process-related objectives – quality, productivity, time-to-market – have already been discussed. Below we look at objectives concerning the attractiveness of work assignments, job design and personnel development.

5. Corporate objectives concerning the 'professional' field seem at present to be largely dominated by downsizing strategies, at least in Western Europe. Commitment, loyalty and personnel development rank low, to the middle-term detriment of enterprises.

8.2.6 Summary

The key knowledge drivers discussed above have been regulation, market structure and supply chain networks. An important aspect for knowledge responses is control over zones of uncertainty such as predicted sales and the technical and organizational attainability of product and production goals. Labour is also an important zone of uncertainty with regard to the success of productive exploitation (Crozier and Friedberg, 1993; Boyer and Freyssinet, 2003).

Each knowledge driver is associated with specific knowledge responses. From a knowledge point of view, regulation is concerned primarily with product-related innovations and new professional capabilities, market structure with the product and process-related restructuring of knowledge processes, and supply chain networks with the dissolution of boundaries for knowledge intensification in cross-functional and cross-organizational transfer, involving risks of depreciation, misappropriation, and so on.

8.3   KNOWLEDGE PHASES AND CATEGORIES

We can distinguish three phases of knowledge: exploration, examination and exploitation, within the categories of analytical, synthetic or symbolic. Like Cooke (2006a), Gerybazde (2004) and other scholars, we see the 'three Ex's' (exploration – examination – exploitation) not as a linear sequence but as an overlapping and reflexive process.

In the industry, product development is an important reference process which structures many knowledge processes. Figure 8.3 gives a schematic

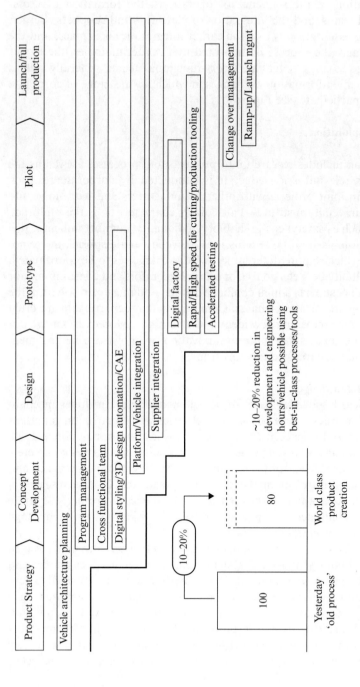

Source: Berger (2004): 18.

Figure 8.3 Product development process

representation of the sequence of operations, the formation of cross-functional teams, and the integration of platforms and suppliers (Berger, 2004). The assumption is that the earlier integration takes place, and the more strongly the process is supported by CAx technologies, the higher will be the savings potential. Cross-functional teams generally act as intracompany information exchanges in which a wide range of corporate functions participate (see Figure 8.3).

8.3.1 Exploration

Exploration includes research into products and processes as well as the search for relevant knowledge. It is conducted by corporate research facilities, in joint projects with other manufacturers and with university and non-university institutes. Particularly characteristic is the multitude of goals such as safety, cost, reliability and quality, comfort, mileage, fuel consumption, gas and noise emissions, recycling and disposal, and 'emotionality' which require different knowledge categories to be coordinated. Incompatibility between goals (for example, comfort and consumption, or quality and costs) has a high conflict potential and must be resolved in the goal-setting and strategy phases. Company patent departments are often responsible for screening new ideas and inventions. Moreover, knowledge screening occupies a key place in innovation or knowledge management functions now established in many firms.

Analytical knowledge
The classical knowledge base for vehicle manufacture includes mechanics, aerodynamics, thermodynamics, electrics and electronics, materials engineering and science, fuel science, acoustics and optics. Since 1990, basic physics has been supplemented by additional, sometimes completely new knowledge. Microphysics, molecular physics, thermodynamics and materials science are among the most widespread areas of basic research in the mathematical and natural sciences, not least because formerly separate fields have combined into new disciplines like microsystems technology (MST) or nanotechnology.

Internal facilities rarely conduct basic research. Therefore in fields such as nanotechnology and microsystems joint projects between public and semi-public institutions and enterprises are important in knowledge generation – and often rely on personal and financial links. The staffing profile of vehicle technology institutes at key universities, as well as the staff of research institutions (for instance, the German Fraunhofer and Max Planck Institutes), often reveal close personnel ties, with many professors previously employed in the sector (and vice versa). Links can thus occur between geographically remote loci of analytical knowledge production. Alumni networks are also an important source of knowledge, especially in recruiting. In view of the anticipated scarcity of engineers, students are integrated at an early stage through involvement in joint projects.

Only exceptionally does analytical knowledge pass through a phased process from exploration to exploitation. The general rule is integration and synthesis in connection with specific applications and component areas, with a range of disciplines meeting in the process. The 'interested parties' are both product and process development. Vehicle manufacturing also shows extraordinary heterogeneity: mechanical engineering, tool making, forming and moulding technologies, painting technology, automation technology, robotics, measurement and control engineering, quality control technology, and so on.

Synthetic knowledge
Synthetic knowledge is the predominant type in the sector, but in a wide range of combinations:

- a synthesis of different types of analytical knowledge (for example, mechatronics);
- a synthesis of synthetic and symbolic knowledge;
- a synthesis of tacit or implicit and explicit knowledge;
- a synthesis of phase-specific knowledge (the 'three Ex's').

Owing partly to the interdependencies, disciplines are integrating in increasing measure, for example mechanics, electronics and informatics which together constitute mechatronics, described as the current mainspring in the industry where 30 per cent of production costs and 90 per cent of all innovation for new passenger vehicles are now located (McKinsey/ PTW, 2003; Mercer/FhG, 2004).[2] Present-day cars are the outcome of 25 years of mechatronic evolution with driver assistance systems like: traction control (anti-block braking – ABS; automatic stability control – ASC; electronic stability programme – ESP; electronic differential lock – EDL); light (adaptive curve light, high beam assistance, night vision); comfort and safety (Tempomat car control system, parking aid, brake assistant – BAS; ACC – adaptive cruise control; lane departure warning; lane keeping support; ISA – intelligent speed adaption).

Future systems might include object recognition and pedestrian protection, accident recognition, automatic emergency braking and 'automatic avoidance manoeuvres'. Propulsion technology offers further new challenges in knowledge generation such as sensor technology for energy management. Knowledge about new materials (aluminium, magnesium, and new lightweight steels) in engines and bodywork, as well as the exterior and interior use of biopolymers, is also required.

These examples demonstrate how independent technologies and products, with their own lifecycles, may be developed and produced by different suppliers. Almost every module in the vehicle is being rendered 'more intelligent'. In order to link up the multiplicity of electronic components and vehicle systems, software control has become a key competence where bus systems, operating system and application software have to be intelligently interconnected. This makes standard-setting extremely important.

Symbolic knowledge
OEM research divisions focus on societal trends (future mobility, demography and health, cultural taste patterns, brand image, technology trends, patent trends, and so on) and set up observation posts in trend cities. The quest for knowledge is undertaken by marketing experts and social and cultural scientists. Intercultural learning is important. Normative and cognitive expectations about changing driving behaviour feed into this complex. Political knowledge, financing expertise and intercultural learning pose major challenges. Symbolic knowledge – image knowledge, for instance – becomes important in assessing the risks of mergers and acquisitions or developing the brand value of a model. Widely differing types of symbolic knowledge thus feed into idea generation. In the 1980s and 1990s, some OEMs spun off their facilities for investigating societal and cultural trends from their central research and development divisions, and established them in the geographical vicinity of trendsetters (megacities). Many work very closely with large, specialized marketing firms.

Exploration actors
Unlike science-based sectors such as the chemical and pharmaceutical industries and electrical engineering, the auto industry set up research departments at a relatively late stage. German producers did so only in the late 1960s (cf. Hack and Hack, 2005: 44ff.) in response to new sets of issues such as emissions, vehicle safety and electronization. Central research was often deliberately accommodated in separate premises where creative forces could be better mobilized. Moreover, it was often distributed among several different locations. For example, DaimlerChrysler 'Research and Technology' in 2003 comprised three research directorates with a total of 14 laboratories and 65 departments.

Apart from internal research, companies screen external knowledge developments and potentials. From an organizational point of view, this takes place in the context of corporate innovation management. It involves analysing and evaluating worldwide trends, and technology scouting. Intranet and Internet play an increasing role and many producers have virtual communities 'open idea' portals. In addition, aspects of technological R&D are outsourced in the same way as component production. However, not all car makers operate the same, highlighting another organizational issue. How much knowledge should be retained versus the savings in personnel costs and the advantages of specialization? In addition, use is made of research and forecast studies on issues of demography, life worlds, technology and science, mobility, politics and the environment, as well as studies on trends and scenarios in the development of the motor vehicle industry.

Forwarding, synthetic knowledge, exploration
The industry distinguishes between unspecific R&D or advanced engineering, and phases of vehicle-specific development. The former ends when concept development for a new vehicle begins. With shorter product cycles and development times it is important to reach decisions at the earliest possible stage to eliminate potential goal conflicts. This requires different functional areas in the company, and supplier firms, to be involved as early as possible in concept development. Thus, knowledge is assembled at an early stage to be 'synthesized' by committees and project teams.

Compared with categories of synthetic knowledge, like mechatronics, which in integrated form can still be represented by single individuals, synthesizing is experiencing decreasing personnel integration. This is accompanied by growing potential for interpersonal, interspecialization and interorganizational conflict. The exchange of information in concept-finding, development forums and functional groups are to a very large extent conflict processes, for example between product development and marketing, or between development and production. Production, too, has hitherto had problems if asserting that a given concept could be difficult and expensive to realize.

8.3.2 Examination

Examination is a core process and integral to all phases in product development and marketing. There is therefore no separate examination phase, but there are many specialised organizations and activity groups engaging in examination processes, like the test construction process in product development or quality assurance.

Being a core process, examination is a major issue in the relationship between tacit and explicit knowledge (Nonaka and Takeuchi, 1997). The background is the growing digitization of all product-to-market process phases. Computer-aided or fully computerized processes have had a far-reaching impact on traditional organizational structures, activity groups and competencies. However, the limits of these changes have yet to be analysed. Tacit knowledge and trial and error continue to play a central role, and the anticipated risks and opportunities of digitization are still controversial.

However, through the digitization of formerly personal tacit knowledge, some examination processes have merely been transferred to the new medium, while in other cases new knowledge has been gained through the medium. An example is knowledge from bionics, used for modelling driving behaviour and finite element computation of materials performance. In any case, knowledge now stored with the aid of computer programs enables the product or process developer to check and secure solutions, and reduces the number of interfaces with examination specialists and test construction.

Since the early 1990s, benchmark comparisons have played an important role in the weighting and exploration of examination knowledge, inspired by the 'after Japan' movement (Clark and Fujimoto, 1991). Comparison with the structures, processes and performance of other firms throws light on a company's own structures and processes, to some extent providing knowledge about alternative solutions to problems, and organizational models. 'Reverse engineering' has been vital for the development of catch-up economies, Japan being a prominent past example and now China. Product teardowns allow manufacturers and suppliers to evaluate their own designs and cost structures (see Jürgens, 2000).

In terms of new product development (NPD), the concept phase is characterized by a strong concentration of knowledge from various sections of the process chain. For this examination, not only is computer-accessed knowledge crucial but also personal knowledge. Personnel from different functional areas are therefore integrated into the processes as project members and members of product committees. Important examination processes address the producibility and suitability of design solutions for manufacture and assembly, as well as marketing. In the construction phase, producibility is dealt with in greater detail, leading to close cooperation (simultaneous engineering) between product development and tool and process development, where the latter functions as an examination process for efficient and cost-effective construction design.

Even if the virtual examination of concept and construction design has increased, the use of models and prototypes continues to play a major role in the iteration process of design – build – test cycles. Theoretical knowledge, synthesized in the form of specific (paper- or computer-based) designs and practical production knowledge, confront one another. An important intermediate step is the production of (thousands) of tools and dies – often requiring periods of up to a year. Once the special tools and equipment have been built and the first prototype vehicle or parts produced, a wide range of tests follows, the most spectacular being crash tests. There is interaction between 'theoreticians' in development and 'practitioners' in test construction and test laboratories. Here explicit and tacit knowledge meet directly and often conflict.

All manufacturers organize product development similarly, with decisions based on a series of design – build – test cycles or iterations (Clark or Fujimoto 1991: 120ff.). The importance of trial and error as a principle of knowledge development and examination is shown by the extraordinary effort still put into prototype building and crash testing. However, compared to previous systems, digitization permits major simplifications, thus saving time and expense. Advanced CAx systems make it possible to produce digital mock-ups and to carry out virtual tests, rendering many high-skill blue-collar activities, like constructing tools and test facilities, unnecessary. Development is hence taking on an increasingly theoretical bias with tacit knowledge being displaced.

Other aspects of digitization are the increasing importance of software development and the growing number of software-based systems on the vehicle. Whereas in the past it was still possible to dock electronic subsystems additively onto existing bus systems or to increase the number of bus systems (in VW vehicles in the late 2000s there are nine different ones), integration in the sense of developing integrated electronic architectures has now become indispensable for reasons of safety and energy management. This requires system designers to obtain knowledge of the source codes of mechatronic components, which means suppliers disclosing critical know-how. With the motor vehicle being increasingly electronized and software-based, the existing balance between the knowledge domains of producers and suppliers is upset; power issues overlap knowledge issues.

One way to resolve this situation would be to develop standards for the design of electronic architectures and interfaces for subcomponents. Such standards would make it possible to dock on subsystems with ease, as with current simple infotainment systems. The Autosar Initiative (Automotive Open System Architecture), set up by BMW, Daimler, Bosch, Continental, Volkswagen and Siemens VDO in 2003, seeks to set standards to overcome the increasing incompatibility of components with the overall vehicle system. In 2004 Ford, General Motors, Toyota and Peugeot were accepted as further partners.

In the planning of series production, a similar process of displacing tacit knowledge is apparent, associated with the concept of the 'digital factory'. Through the digitization of product and process data, including the modelling of human movement sequences, the production process can be more

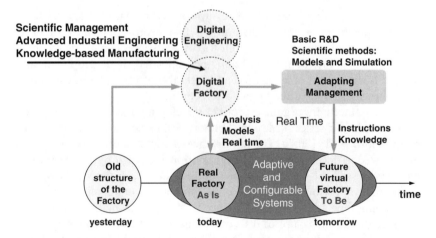

Source: Westkämper (2006).

Figure 8.4 *Transition model from the real factory to the future virtual factory*

and more realistically simulated. The knowledge of production planners, hitherto predominantly tacit, appears to be becoming redundant under these conditions. Figure 8.4 shows this transition from the engineer's perspective. However, in actual work organization and procedures, digital factory planning (still) plays only a minor role. In view of the many factors involved, these techniques are also highly controversial.

The knowledge processes of exploration and examination also play a key role in production and assembly. Particularly in Japanese firms, knowledge transformation and exchange processes are subjects of systematic analysis and the basis for the development of independent production systems. An important outcome of the debate on Japanese management systems was to open the eyes of Western management to microprocesses of knowledge creation and knowledge exchange (Nonaka and Takeuchi, 1997).

Just as the conceptualization of production can be construed as examination of the upstream construction and planning phases, use by customers, the drivers of the new vehicles, can be interpreted similarly.

8.3.3 Exploitation

Analytical and synthetic knowledge
As in the case of examination processes, the three categories of knowledge – analytical, synthetic and symbolic – are highly integrated. Exploitation

in the sense of using knowledge embodied in people and machines as well as explicit knowledge contained in databases, manuals, and so on raises many questions about production systems, provoking debate and dispute (Boyer and Freyssinet, 2003). One key aspect is the use made of employees' formal and tacit knowledge. Fordism, and the preprogramming of work flows, making for a quasi-mechanical process, has been a classical subject of debate. The acquisition of tacit shop-floor knowledge by experts (industry engineers, and so on) is a precondition since studies have shown that a system of this type (that seems to remove the knowledge content) can only operate with the input of informal knowledge and autonomous shop-floor problem-solving.

A second aspect of the production system debate addresses the maintenance and upgrading of existing knowledge, and thus the conduciveness of production and work organization to learning. Toyotism, Volvoism and other systems offer various approaches to promoting learning and upgrading knowledge (one variant is the 'VW 5000' production system: cf. Schumann et al., 2006).

Production systems bundle, use and develop knowledge in different ways. In weighting categories of knowledge, different degrees of automation need to be taken into account. The digitization of control processes enhances the importance of analytical knowledge in automated fields, but here too, symbolic knowledge continues to play an important role in communication and cooperation.

The design of process chains across various divisions, production sites, firms and countries lends increasing weight to this latter aspect of communication and cooperation. The transfer and transformation of knowledge at interfaces pose growing challenges (Bargigli, 2005; Winter, 2006). Face-to-face communication and spatial proximity clearly play an important part in many processes in the industry, more so than, for example, in the electronics sector. This is likely to be because of the high proportion of tacit knowledge (Rentmeister, 2002; Preissl and Solimene, 2003). An open question is whether electronization and the spread of software-based systems will diminish the importance of face-to-face communication and proximity. In any case, the increase in software activities modifies qualification requirements. It is often necessary to recruit specialists from outside the firm, thus provoking conflict between 'old' and 'new' engineers, between hardware and software specialists, between general software and embedded software specialists

In the past, OEMs had few software specialists at their disposal where 'old' functional divisions were staffed by traditional vehicle technology engineers responsible for specific disciplines. Only with the mechatronization and electronization of vehicles have their competencies expanded to include software and CAx technologies. New competence has been developed by the BMW's CAR IT GmbH (2002), Daimler's Virtual Design Center in Ulm (1995), and especially by the MB Technology GmbH. Other companies like VW and Opel, which in the 1990s had relied strongly on specialized emergency safety functions (ESFs), have followed the premium sector lead, founding their own subsidiaries (for example, VW Carmeq GmbH 2003 in Berlin).

Major electronics suppliers (for example, Bosch, Siemens, Sumitomo, Mitsubishi Electric), providing most of the embedded software for OEMs, have pursued a different approach. Standardization of embedded software is meanwhile extremely advanced, so that development in Europe is under strong offshore pressure. For example, Bosch has a workforce of some 1200 in this field in Bangalore, India.

The second form or stage in knowledge exploitation is marketing. A key aspect is the patenting of analytical and/or synthetic knowledge created in a firm or in cooperation with others. Patents have traditionally played a comparatively minor role in the automotive industry. The closed, proprietary nature of product architectures and the dominance of vehicle assemblers – with the exception of some key suppliers that have managed to secure dominance in certain fields – had meant little interest in patenting (Jürgens and Meißner, 2005). Patents also involved the risk of calling competitors' attention to important developments, hence undermining first-mover advantages.

However, this situation changed fundamentally with outsourcing and the reorganization of supplier relations. In the new 'co-opetition', patents are strategic tools for safeguarding independence vis-à-vis business partners and where necessary, bringing pressure to bear in the event of conflict. It is instructive that in this period there has been an increase in the compositeness (combination) of technologies represented by each patent (for example mechatronics) and that the numbers of patents related to product or to process have been roughly equal in number (Antonelli and Calderini, 2006), illustrating the importance of interface management and process in supply matrices.

Other market-related knowledge processes in exploitation include:

- increasing division of knowledge external to the OEMs with new players and increasing technological complexity;
- increasing compositeness of knowledge and the widening of the industry's knowledge base;
- increasing complexity of knowledge management and the need for OEMs and major suppliers to protect 'unique knowledge' while letting go of ubiquitous knowledge via outsourcing;

- multiple use of knowledge through generic technologies, platforms and modules, and identical parts;
- synthesis of market and customer knowledge and financial knowledge (commercialization through financing, loans, leasing, and so on).

The other aspect of knowledge exploitation is in downstream functional areas by using knowledge in financing, fleet management, vehicle leasing, and so on. Another form of the multiple knowledge use is spinning off consulting entities or setting up consulting firms like Porsche Consulting GmbH.

Symbolic knowledge
We have highlighted the declining proportion of value, and technology, retained by the OEMs. However, as we have also discussed, they retain control over both the upstream supply matrix of goods and services and downstream distribution and sales. This dominance comes from their position as the end suppliers to the market, a position of power embodied in branding restricted to the OEMs themselves. Brands, and their protection and promotion, are critical – as reflected in annual calculations of brand values (Interbrand, 2006) and the proportion of market capitalization represented by the brand, for example: BMW, 61 per cent; Mercedes, 49 per cent; and Ford, 70 per cent. Thus in 2009 it is only in limited circumstances that suppliers' brands appear as part of marketing. OEM brands carry the weight of company image and history, and convey the qualities of the product (Lury, 2004). A significant case study of brand protection, and care about image, can be observed in the OEMs' negotiations on the new Block Exemption Regulations (NBE), as discussed in section 8.2.1 above, governing how vehicle manufacturers distribute their products in Europe. The OEMs resisted attempts to open the distribution system, for example through multibrand outlets, and largely retained control of how their vehicles should be displayed and sold through dealerships (MacNeill and Chanaron, 2005).

8.4   CONCLUSIONS

As we have illustrated, the automotive industry is complex and multifaceted. The summary grid shown in Table 8.1 illustrates the multiple aspects of knowledge in the industry in terms of the knowledge stages and types highlighted in the preceding sections. However, as we have also discussed, there is considerable overlap and interplay between the different areas. To

Table 8.1 Automotive knowledge grid

	Analytical	Synthetic	Symbolic
Exploration (Search and research)	Basic physics, chemistry • Thermodynamics • Acoustics • Metallurgy	Product related e.g., mechatronics • Sensors • Electronics • Vehicle systems analysis • Hybrids Process related • Systems design • Integration teams • Supply matrix Downstream relations • Market research	Societal and political trends Brand image and perception (values) Demography, Health
Examination (Trialling, testing, standard setting, benchmarking)	Test/trial • Dynamics • Safety/crash • Noise and vibration • Fuels/efficiency • Catalysts • Emissions	Product and process trialling Regulation • Safety • Environment • (homologation process) Production methods e.g., QCD Logistics – upstream and downstream	Styling Concepts – aesthetic and 'hard' innovations interaction with dealers and customers
Exploitation (Commercializing)	Specialist firms • e.g., engine, chassis, body + • Universities and research institutes	Commercialization • Product mix • Supply matrix and logistics management • Patenting – specialist firms and research institutes	Branding, brand values • Communication, PR, (selling) • Presentation Downstream • Dealerships • Specialist Consultants

sum up, we can identify five key characteristics of automotive 'knowledge landscapes' and the dynamics they develop.

8.4.1   Diversity and Distribution

As we have seen, the automotive landscape shows extraordinary diversity of knowledge bases and knowledge agents. Sources are spatially and organizationally widely distributed and must be brought together anew for each project and bundled for the given product and process. The tendency for fragmentation in process chains has increased the importance of external knowledge but the newly emerging networks are still strongly asymmetrical in structure.

8.4.2   Closed Proprietary Knowledge

Product architecture in the sector is largely 'open but proprietary'. Standards are strongly dominated by OEMs. Counter-tendencies manifest themselves in modularization, outsourcing and standardization efforts with regard to electronic architecture. The background is the wish of OEMs to maintain dominance.

8.4.3   Front-Loading

In endeavouring to reduce lead times, OEMs mobilize knowledge within and outside the organization at the earliest possible stage before investing in hardware, in order to secure concepts as comprehensively as possible. Knowledge processes are condensed by bringing together phase-specific knowledge at an early point, generating a paradoxical configuration. On the one hand, this front-loading offers opportunities for participation – by downstream areas of production, too – in strategic product development decisions (settling conflicts between development, planning and implementation).

8.4.4   Protection of Knowledge

Protection of intellectual property in the form of patents, trade secrets and customer data, and control over standardization, are sources of power. The protection of intangibles has so far depended largely on patents for product and process technologies. The debate about knowledge property rights manifests itself primarily in the context of cooperation with suppliers. Since protection as a form of appropriating knowledge is becoming much more important, there is a growing danger of innovation processes being blocked by disputes about IPR.

8.4.5 Digitization

The increasing diffusion of computer-aided systems and virtualization, and the growing use of electronics and software-based technologies, are degrading the status of tacit knowledge. This causes major reorganization of workforce structures, especially in relations between white-collar and blue-collar workers. Digitization, together with front-loading, are furthering the transformation of the sector into a science-based industry.

NOTES

1. OEMs are original equipment manufactures (vehicles manufactures as final assemblers and system integrators).
2. In 2005, the average figure for driver assistance systems per vehicle sold in Germany, for instance, was about €900 (mainly for ABS, ESP (Electronic Stability Programme), brake assistant, tyre pressure control, ACC, adaptive light). For 2010, studies predict an average figure of €3200, and for 2015, €4300 (McKinsey/PTW, 2003).

9. Tourism knowledge dynamics

Henrik Halkier[1]

9.1 INTRODUCTION

Several good reasons present themselves for taking a closer look at tourism knowledge dynamics. Firstly, in order to produce a rounded view of regional knowledge dynamics in Europe, the economic and political salience of tourism is obvious: this part of the service sector has traditionally involved large numbers of low-skill jobs, it has a significant presence in many peripheral areas, and it has been heralded as a potential driver of future economic growth in both peripheral and urban areas across Europe. Secondly, because of the inherently spatial and often international nature of tourism – normally defined in terms of staying some distance away from home – it would seem to present a promising area in which to study the relationship between 'local versus non-local' forms of knowledge because operating successfully in the market for tourism experiences will require an understanding of both the regions with potential customers – what are the prevailing notions of ideal ways of spending time away from home – and the regions which attempt to attract tourists in connection with leisure or business activities. Thirdly, while the existing academic literature on knowledge processes in tourism is fairly limited, it has suggested low levels of formalized research and development (R&D) within the sector and hence a dependence on knowledge imported via the application of new technologies and organizational forms developed elsewhere (Malerba, 2004; Orfila-Sintes et al. 2005; OECD, 2006a; Weiermair, 2006), and a spatial pattern where tourism destinations, despite involving the co-location of large number of actors involved in tourist services, do not appear to operate in ways similar to that of traditional manufacturing clusters (Tremblay, 1998; Hjalager, 2000a, 2001, 2002; Shaw and Williams, 2004). Finally, from a policy perspective the need to move towards a better understanding of the specific knowledge dynamics within tourism would seem to be pressing. While stimulating innovation and learning has gradually become somewhat more important both in tourism policy (Fayos-Sola, 1996; Hall, 2000; Commission of the European Communities, 2006) and in regional development policies at large (Cooke, 2004; Halkier, 2006), this would seem to have occurred on a trial-and-error basis in a policy environment giving priority to other concerns, for example EU policies using tourism as a vehicle for rural development, and a tourism policy community which has traditionally favoured place promotion as a means to boost visitor numbers (Lundtorp, 1997; Hall, 2000). In short, from a policy perspective knowing more about knowledge dynamics in tourism would seem to be a prerequisite for designing strategies that would be able to address the specific problems in what is clearly an important area of economic activity, and make tourism an integrated part of a future European knowledge society and economy.

This chapter takes a first step in this direction by undertaking a literature review on the basis of shared Eurodite conceptualizations in order to tease out current thinking about knowledge generation, geographies and dynamics within tourism as an economic activity – and on the basis of this to discuss the possible position of tourism in a future knowledge economy and society in Europe. The text proceeds in three steps: first a short section provides background on tourism as a diverse area of economic activity in Europe, then the main section explores three key aspects of tourism knowledge dynamics, namely the generation and geographies of different types of knowledge, and the dynamics of these processes in terms of drivers and responses within the sector. Finally, the political economy of tourism knowledge dynamics is discussed, taking into account the regional and national positions of tourism in the ongoing process of globalization.

9.2   STRUCTURE AND SCALE OF THE SECTOR: FROM TOURISM TO TOURISMS

In order to be able to illuminate processes within tourism in the context of regional trajectories to the knowledge economy, it will be important to be precise about three things: global development trends; the spatially uneven character of tourism activities in Europe; and the existence of different touristic paradigms that makes it possible to identify commonalities with regard to trends and drivers in what may appear to be an extremely diverse area of social activity. But before doing so, it is worth briefly revisiting a much-debated issue, namely the delimitation of tourism as a socioeconomic activity. This has been the subject of much academic debate over the years (Debbage and Daniels, 1998; Tremblay, 1998; Hall, 2000; Hjalager, 2001; Therkelsen and Halkier, 2004; Kvistgaard, 2006; 17–23), and although some of these discussions may appear to be less productive, from a theoretical perspective they have highlighted the complex nature of tourism as a service which can entail a vast number of components (for example, transport, accommodation, catering, shopping facilities, man-made attractions, natural sights), many of which are also used by local residents for non-touristic purposes (for example commuting, family events, spending sprees, education, leisure). When studying tourism from the perspective of knowledge processes at different organizational and territorial scales, the precise delimitation of the sector is, however, less important, and thus for pragmatic reasons tourism will be defined as 'travel and activity away from one's usual environment' (Stephen Smith, quoted by Kvistgaard, 2006: 20) involving at least one overnight stay or crossing of international borders – differentiating tourism from home-based leisure activities but including day-trips abroad – and thus the tourism sector can be defined as those private or public providers of services or infrastructure involved in facilitating these activities. This fairly traditional definition is needed in order to get an inclusive approach to the tourism phenomenon, unlike recent attempts to reinterpret tourism as part of the 'experience economy' (for example Ooi, 2005): while the notion of experience is undoubtedly central to many forms of (leisure) tourism (Kvistgaard and Smed, 2005; O'Dell, 2005; Mossberg and Johansen, 2006), using it as a defining characteristic of tourism as such would seem to exclude many forms of, for example, business travel, which are driven by external commitments rather than expectations of individual experiences.

9.2.1 Tourism as an Economic Activity in Europe and Beyond

Tourism is a sizeable economic activity in Europe, with international tourism alone accounting for 2.2 per cent of gross domestic product (GDP) in 30 European countries in 2004 according to the UNWTO (calculated on the basis of the UN World Tourism Organization, 2006) and experiencing growth rates generally exceeding that of GDP since the boom in mass tourism began in earnest in the 1960s.[2] Although this figure is below some of the more exuberant claims made by tourism trade organizations attempting to enhance the public standing of the activities of their members (for example the World Travel and Tourism Council)[3] and involve considerable data difficulties with regard to, for example, unorganized forms of tourism that do not involve commercial accommodation (for example visiting friends and relatives) and are not registered as international travel due to the absence of border formalities within the Schengen and Nordic subregions of Europe (Nyberg, 1995), it still presents a clear indication of the overall importance of touristic activities from an economic perspective. Moreover, the vast majority of touristic activity undertaken by Europeans – 86 per cent of all international trips in 2004

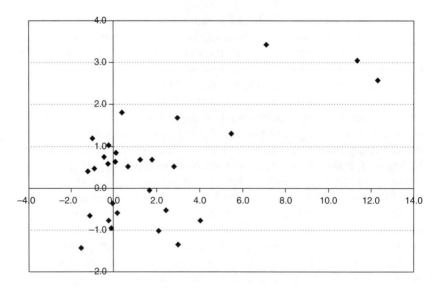

Source: Calculated on the basis of World Tourism Organization (2006).

Figure 9.1   International tourism in Europe

(World Tourism Organization, 2006: 47) – is undertaken within Europe,
and although the share of non-European destinations for European tourists has increased and the annual growth rate of inbound international
tourism has been lower in Europe than the rest of the world since 1990,[4]
the overall balance between inbound and outbound tourism for Europe as
a whole is still roughly in balance because of the popularity of 'old-world
destinations' with non-European tourists.

   Having established the overall importance of tourism in Europe, it
must however at the same time also be stressed that this activity has a very
uneven geography, something which is extremely important not only from
an economic and socio-cultural perspective, but also in terms of policy
implications. Expenditure on international tourism varies between 0.8 per
cent (Romania, Turkey) and more than 5 per cent (Cyprus, Bulgaria[5]) of
GDP, while receipts from international tourism vary even more, from 1 per
cent or below (Romania, Germany) to nearly 15 per cent (Cyprus, Malta).[6]
By presenting the same data as deviations from the European average,
Figure 9.1 allows us to identify four main country groups, namely:

● High-exchange countries where international tourism plays an
   important role in society, both as a generator of income and as an
   activity for citizens, typically small southern seaside countries (Malta,

Cyprus, Bulgaria); relatively rich countries specializing in particular types of tourism like skiing (Austria, Slovenia, Switzerland); temperate seaside tourism (Denmark); heritage and city breaks (Ireland); business tourism (Belgium); city breaks, sea cruises and lake-side tourism (Estonia, Hungary).

- Recipient countries where international tourism plays a significant role as a generator of income but plays a more limited role for citizens, typically traditional Mediterranean seaside destinations (Spain, Portugal, Greece, Turkey).
- Generating countries where international tourism plays a significant role in society with above-average expenditure by citizens, but which are less important as destinations for foreign tourists; typically wealthy North-Western countries (Germany, UK, Sweden, Norway).
- Low-exchange countries where international tourism plays a relatively limited role in society, both as a generator of income and as an activity for citizens; typically geographically peripheral countries (Finland, Slovakia, Romania) and, perhaps rather more surprising, countries with complex and traditional tourist destinations and high levels of domestic tourism (France, Italy) (Bovagnet, 2006; 2).[7]

Given the uneven importance of tourism as a social and economic activity across Europe and the predominance of interplace competition as an inherent part of the industry's mode of operation (for example Hall, 2000: 139ff.), it is hardly surprising that for example EU member states have found it difficult to agree on tourism policy measures, not even in the form of common promotional measures overseas (Anastasiadou, 2006).

These country-level differences will, however, in practice in most cases reflect the presence of particular tourist destinations within the national territory – for example ski resorts, picturesque towns, global economic nodes, coastal resorts – and thus in terms of the on-site production and consumption of services and experiences, the geography of tourism is regional and local rather than national (Hall, 2000; Weaver and Lawton, 2002; Spörel, 2006). In terms of the relative intensity of commercial accommodation this is clearly very uneven, with traditional tourist areas like Mediterranean seaside resorts, Alpine and Swedish skiing, the Anglo-French Atlantic coast, and the rejuvenated German Baltic seaside being clearly visible at the NUTS 2 level; cf Figure 9.2. But in terms of absolute numbers, the list of the 20 regions with the most overnight stays by tourists also includes regions which have traditionally been less central from the perspective of international tourism, such as Denmark, Rhône-Alpes and Languedoc-Roussillon in France, and German coastal and mountain regions. This uneven spatial

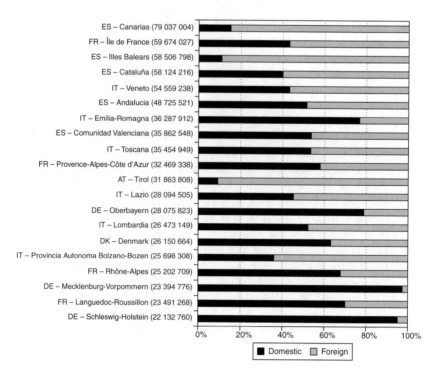

Source: Spörel (2006): 5.

*Figure 9.2   TOP 20 EU/25 NUTS 2 tourist regions: nights spent by
             tourist origin*

character probably explains why tourism is often on the regional political agenda also in countries where this activity barely registers in national
politics (Hall, 2000; Chapter 6; Kvistgaard, 2006: 36ff.), and along similar
lines it also hints at why, at least in financial terms, the most significant EU
policy involvement can be found in the use of funds from regional and other
spatial policy programmes for tourism development in, for example, rural
areas (Hall, 2000: 125ff. Anastasiadou, 2006). And from the perspective of
knowledge processes it underlines why the notion of clusters in tourism has
had an obvious appeal to policy-makers: specific forms of tourist activities
tend to be spatially concentrated because they rely on particular natural or
cultural phenomena to provide input to the overall tourism experience (cf.
Hjalager, 2000b), and hence the idea of adopting cluster-type policies along
the well-tried lines pursued by national or regional authorities for more than
a decade clearly has a certain intuitive appeal.

9.2.2 Tourism Complexities: An Institutionalist Perspective on Trends and Drivers

An obvious and oft-noted feature of the tourism product is its multifaceted nature, consisting of a wide variety of distinct services which need to be present in order for tourism to take place; and one way of attempting to create an overview of the activities involved is to adopt an institutionalist perspective on tourism as an area of social activity (Hall, 2000; Weaver and Lawton, 2002; Therkelsen and Halkier, 2004) by focusing on the rules according to which different actors interact (cf. Halkier, 2006: Chapter 3). In the following this approach is first translated into a heterogeneous set of tourism 'production chains', and these are then reassembled in the form of four basic tourism paradigms which can be used as points of departure for the ensuing overview of knowledge processes in tourism.

When transposed from its original industrial environment, three important adjustments will have to be made to the conceptualization of the key elements of the 'production chain' within tourism. Firstly, like other services tourism is an intangible product that cannot be tested before being produced, making market communication and, for example, place branding central features of the positioning of particular products in the marketplace. Secondly, the tourism product is produced and consumed at the same time, because while the capacity to deliver a service must be established in advance, there is no way that empty plane seats, hotel rooms or pool chairs can be stored and resold come the next season (Weaver and Lawton, 2002: 206ff.), and thus perishability is a basic rule that conditions the activities of tourism actors and tends to make the selling of existing capacity a principal preoccupation (Tremblay, 1998). Thirdly, the heterogeneous nature of the services that when combined constitute the tourism product is evident (Hall, 2000; Gunn and Var, 2002; Shaw and Williams, 2004: Chapter 2). According to the definition above, tourists require:

- travel services in the form of private or public transport companies and/or the use of (mostly public) infrastructure in order to get from the place of origin to where tourism takes place;
- on-site services to provide for, for example, shelter and sustenance while away from home; and
- on-site activities that are the *raison d'être* of the journey, that is, specific activities that can only be accessed through corporeal presence such as visiting museums or cool down-town bars, or participating in business meetings or religious gatherings.

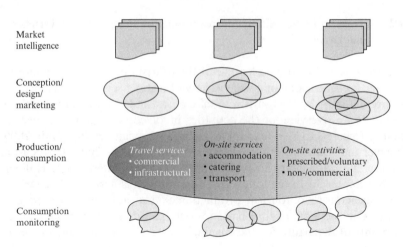

Market
intelligence

Conception/
design/
marketing

Production/
consumption

Travel services
• commercial
• infrastructural

On-site services
• accommodation
• catering
• transport

On-site activities
• prescribed/voluntary
• non-/commercial

Consumption
monitoring

Figure 9.3   Producing tourism: products, phases and actors

As illustrated by Figure 9.3,[8] the tourism production process can be
subdivided into four main phases, and all of them are likely to involve a
wide range of actors (Halkier, 2002): private and public service providers; promotional bodies attempting to bridge the gap between supply and
demand; and, not least, the tourists themselves who in many cases take an
active role in assembling the product by drawing on independent service
providers at home and on-site in order to be able to engage in the on-site
activities that were the driving force behind going away in the first place.
Besides this organizational complexity, tourism as an area of economic
activity is also characterized by the fact that that all the actors involved
in specific forms of tourism will not be located in one and the same place,
simply because moving physically from A to B is a defining characteristic
and thus at least the tourists will originate outside the area in which they
undertake tourist activities. In practice this means that distance – not being
close to all other actors involved in the production process – is a basic condition which gives the issue of coordination of activities, and hence knowledge processes within tourism, an inherently spatial character.

In order to understand knowledge processes in an area in which many
production chains are intertwined, it is useful to focus on four basic paradigms of tourism which can be defined as specific combinations of rules
and actors which taken together constitute the process through which
tourism as a social activity unfolds. From an institutionalist perspective an
obvious starting point for trying to make sense of tourism would seem to
be two types of institutions, namely the purpose of going away (what rules
and incentives make people tourists) and how this activity is organized

(what rules and incentives govern the production of services that constitute tourism). On the one hand tourists are driven to travel for different reasons (see for example Weaver and Lawton, 2002: 28ff.): some travel primarily for individual pleasure in order to experience other places and people, and others travel because they are fulfilling an obligation of 'co-presence' (Shaw and Williams, 2004: 2) to a collective entity, for example their family or place of work. On the other hand their period away from home can be brought about in very different ways: while some people organize their own journeys by buying separate services and indulging in discrete experiences on a piecemeal basis, other forms of tourism are organized by corporate entities offering a more or less complete package of activities, whether for pleasure or business. Obviously both dimensions are most usefully seen as continuous scales rather than dichotomies: the extent of the packaging by tour operators can vary; some forms of accommodation may include add-on experiences such as the exoticism of the Jukkasjärvi ice hotel or the trans-Siberian railway; and someone attending a family or religious gathering may see this as an act of pleasurable self-fulfilment or as a duty that goes with belonging to a particular group. But by combining these two dimensions, it is possible to identify four basic tourism paradigms, as illustrated by Figure 9.4. Some of this involves creating opportunities by identifying appropriate relatives to visit or business cycles influencing the need for 'accidental' individual business travel, but at the same time these are also likely to reflect developments of a more touristic nature, for example, the introduction of low-cost airlines making travel cheaper, or budget hotels making business travel more affordable for small and medium-sized enterprises (SMEs). In contrast to Keith Pavitt's famous sweeping classification of individual services like tourism as 'supplier-dominated' with regard to technology development (Orfila-Sintes et al., 2005; Decelle, 2006), the nature of the wider knowledge processes is therefore likely to reflect not only various ways of organizing tourism activities, but also the heterogeneous social and economic drivers that propel different forms of tourism. In the following section knowledge processes associated with three forms of tourism will be analysed, focusing on the distinct sets of actors and interaction processes involved.

9.3   TOURISM KNOWLEDGE DYNAMICS: DRIVERS AND RESPONSES

This section attempts to summarize the existing state of research on knowledge processes in tourism, focusing on types of tourist activity representing three of the four paradigms identified in Figure 9.4.[9] The individual

Purpose

		Pleasure	Duty
	Individual	Leisure travel Pilgrimage	Accidental tourism Visiting relatives
Organization	Corporate	Package tours Trekking, cruises	MICE (meetings, incentives, conferences, exhibitions)

Figure 9.4   Drivers and organization of tourism activities

types have been chosen because they are important from an economic and social perspective in Europe as a whole or in particular parts thereof:

- leisure travel organized by individual tourists accounts for a very large share of tourism in the more temperate parts of the Continent, from seaside destinations like Blackpool and Rügen to ski resorts like Les Deux Alpes and Zakopane, as well as the growing market for city breaks;
- package tours still account for a very large share of the south-bound seaside tourism concentrated around the Mediterranean coasts, constituting more than half the holidays in both Germany and the UK in 2001 (Medina-Munoz et al., 2003); and
- conferencing has been a growing form of business tourism, especially in larger European cities with promotional agencies fiercely contesting major events (Therkelsen, 2002).

For each of these tourism types, a three-step procedure will be followed: first the main actors involved in the various elements and stages of the production processes will be identified using Figure 9.3 as a starting point; then the characteristics of knowledge types and phases will be identified on the basis of existing literature; and finally the key drivers and organizational responses involved in knowledge dynamics processes will be discussed.

9.3.1   Individual Pleasures: Knowledge Processes in Leisure Travel

Beginning the survey with leisure travel has a double rationale: tourism has often primarily been associated with leisure and pleasure, and from a historical perspective self-organized genteel travel, the Grand Tour, has often been seen as a prototype for modern-day tourism (Weaver and Lawton, 2002: 62f.). Leisure travel is characterized by a very visible complexity because the various services that in combination constitute the holiday experience are assembled by the tourists themselves through a host of different providers, public and private, at home and while at the destination.

In terms of knowledge generation, key actors within leisure travel are polarized. On the one hand some major actors – transport companies, hotel chains, major visitor attractions and large promotional bodies – occasionally sponsor gathering of market intelligence via consultants or public knowledge institutions, are regular customers of knowledge-intensive business services (KIBS) for a variety of purposes, and often monitor consumption through customer surveys. On the other hand the numerically dominant SME providers of on-site services and activities tend to use external providers of knowledge, public as well as private, only to a limited extent (Herslund and Nyberg, 2001), and instead rely primarily on more informal feedback and interaction with existing customers (Bærenholdt et al., 2004: Chapter 1), something that is facilitated by the integrated nature of service production and consumption but which is also likely to increase their path-dependency with regard to the services provided. Leisure travel would in other words seem to be dominated by knowledge exploitation, while examination and especially knowledge exploration play more limited roles. At the same time it is also worth noting that the dominant types of knowledge, unsurprisingly, are synthetic and symbolic because of the importance of organizational change – for example establishing of SME networks – and market communication in developing activities (Bramwell and Sharman, 1999; Hjalager, 2000b; Hjalager and Jensen, 2001; Decelle, 2006; Dredge, 2006). Moreover, and probably even more importantly, these knowledge types are intimately linked because of the intangible nature of the various services involved and, indeed, the exotic experiences associated with leisure tourism (cf. Therkelsen and Halkier, 2004): improving existing products or developing new ones are of limited use until this has been brought to the attention of potential customers through, for example, market communication or branding initiatives. All in all, the prevailing knowledge generation processes in leisure travel are in other words characterized by the dominance of knowledge exploitation, and an intimate link between synthetic and symbolic types of knowledge.

In terms of drivers of change and the responses of private and public actors within leisure tourism, it is possible to identify three different types of processes which are likely to be prominent, depending on the nature of the destination in question. In leisure-oriented destinations such as seaside resorts the predominance of SMEs is a general characteristic, and here two types of drivers of firm-level change are prominent (Goméz and

Rebollo, 1995; Jamal and Getz, 1995; Shaw and Williams, 1998; Bramwell and Sharman, 1999; Hall, 2000; Hjalager, 2000a, 2000b; Russell and Faulkner, 2004; Decelle, 2006; Dredge, 2006): on the one hand changing market trends are important, especially in the negative sense of responding to a declining number of visitors. On the other hand they act as a public policy response to a manifest crisis in the sector. Finally, policy may act as a proactive attempt to make the most of perceived opportunities in the growing 'experience economy' in, for example the form of 'green' or 'sustainable' tourism. Either way around, responses have often revolved around creating networks for promotional or product innovation purposes, with more or less extensive involvement of promotional bodies or backing of public authorities in the form of, for example, quality certification schemes, both of which would appear to be based on the assumption that individual tourism SMEs are likely to be either unwilling or unable to bring about major changes even in their own activities (Buhalis and Cooper, 1998; Ioannides and Debbage, 1998; Hjalager, 2000a, 2000b; Bastakis et al., 2004; Getz and Nilsson, 2004; Shaw and Williams, 2004: Chapter 3; Christensen, 2006), but still involving a fairly limited reliance on market research in order to make sense of current and future trends. In addition to this, two other types of dynamics have been evident in recent years (Bieger and Wittmer, 2006): the gradual spread of national and international hotel chains that trade on using their brand to expand their market shares by establishing a presence in especially important city-break destinations; and the increasing role of air travel in relation to individual holidays, through the emergence of low-cost airlines and the proliferation of loyalty schemes among networking airlines and the resulting bring-the-spouse short breaks. The relative importance of these three types of dynamics is difficult to establish, especially because of their mutual dependence. Both hotels and airlines offer services that are integrated parts of leisure travel but none of them are 'reasons to go' and thus piggy-back on either the promotional efforts of the localities themselves or – in the case of, for example, Paris or Rome – the pre-existing images of particular destinations. On the other hand, the attractiveness of particular destinations also depend on the services which potential customers can avail themselves of with regard to travel and accommodation, and thus, for example, having Ryanair flying to a disused military airport will do wonders for the adjoining Baltic seaside resort.

9.3.2 Organized Pleasures: Knowledge Processes in Packaged Tourism

For obvious reasons the immediate impression of complexity is greatly reduced when we turn to consider package tours, simply because one private firm, the tour operator, takes on the role of an 'intermediate assembler' (Ioannides, 1998) that brings together at least a significant part of, if not all, the services and activities involved in leisure tourism. Being frequently associated with sheep-like or hooligan-hedonistic patterns of behaviour depending on the age of the dominant customer groups, this 'Fordist' mass production of tourism remains massively important (Ioannides and Debbage, 1998), both socially as the single most important form of holiday engaged in by Northern Europeans, and as a crucially important economic activity in the coastal parts of Southern European which have become the preferred 'leisure space' of the urbanized north (Goméz and Rebollo, 1995), and it is therefore more than a little surprising that packaged tourism has received relatively little scholarly attention (Ioannides, 1998: 139).

Compared to leisure travel, the number of actors involved in producing package tours is smaller, but while this will certainly be the case from the perspective of the prospective tourist perusing brochures and leaflets, a central role of the tour operator is to undertake the combination of a host of services from a wide range of subcontractors in the country of origin, internationally, and at the locality where tourism will eventually take place. From this perspective, the level of complexity has of course been reduced somewhat through the selective choices made by the tour operator when deciding the programme for the coming season, but in effect what has happened is simply that the managing of what is still a complex product has to a large extent been internalized within a private firm, thereby making it easier for tourists to decide because services and activities have been bundled, while in the process making holidays in the South more affordable through, for example bulk-buying from charter airlines and local hotels (Goméz and Rebollo, 1995; Ioannides, 1998; Medina-Munoz et al., 2003).

With regard to knowledge generation, continuity in relation to leisure travel with regard to the various components of the overall product also implies that the same knowledge types, synthetic and symbolic, also dominate with regard to package tours. What is perhaps more surprising is the fact that existing research would seem to suggest that despite the central role of large private firms, still relatively little market research is being undertaken except in the form of formal monitoring of subcontractor performance and customer satisfaction (cf Reimer, 1990; Ioannides, 1998) – although compared to other parts of the tourism industry such as accommodation and catering, tour operators would still seem to be relatively innovative in the quest for maintaining their market share and in keeping up with consumer demands for more differentiated products (Fayos-Sola et al., 1994; Jensen et al., 2002; Medina-Munoz et al., 2003;

Stamboulis and Skyannis, 2003; Bastakis et al., 2004; Orfila-Sintes et al., 2005; Decelle, 2006; Weiermair, 2006).

In terms of knowledge dynamics, two trends have been in evidence recently and would seem to be likely to continue in the foreseeable future. Firstly, a development towards the creation of larger and larger national and international companies through a process of mergers and acquisitions, creating huge transnational travel conglomerates specializing mainly in sending northerners to the Mediterranean. Interestingly, this expansion has primarily been horizontal in the sense that while some tour operators have established or acquired their own charter airline, they have predominantly concentrated on assembling the complex product and marketing it to potential customers in Northern Europe and have largely eschewed direct investment in hotel accommodation, thereby offloading risk to local SMEs and retaining the capacity to shift attention to other localities if they become more attractive in terms of cost structure or demand (Williams, 1995; Bieger and Wittmer, 2006). Secondly, innovations appear to have been market-driven in the sense that what Auliana Poon (1993) dubbed 'new tourism' with more diverse forms of demand that has resulted both in a wider variety of products being offered by mainstream tour operators, and the emergence of a fast growth of specialist tour operators catering for particular segments of, for example, cultural, nature or adventure tourism (Reimer, 1990; Fayos-Sola et al., 1994; Ioannides, 1998; Decelle, 2006).

9.3.3 Meetings Away: Knowledge Processes in Conference Tourism

While determining the size of the market for conference tourism in Europe – that is, meetings involving at least one overnight stay – is complicated by the slow growth of common standards of statistical reporting (Davidson and Cope, 2003: 20), the share of business tourism constituted by conferencing would still seem to be a sizeable one: for example in Denmark in 2004 organized meetings, incentives, conventions and exhibitions (MICE) activities accounted for more than half of business tourism turnover and hence more than 10 per cent of turnover for tourism as a whole (calculated on the basis of Mogensen and Therkelsen, 2007: 4–6). If this does indeed reflect more general patterns, the economic importance of conferencing will also be significant in especially Northern and Western parts of Europe where non-leisure tourism accounts for more than 20 per cent of international arrivals (World Tourism Organization, 2006: 44) and hence, because of the high levels of expenditure associated with business tourism, for an even larger share of tourism-related turnover (Mogensen and Therkelsen, 2007). Despite this, but by now perhaps unsurprisingly, relatively little research has been undertaken on conference tourism in general (Weber,

2001; Davidson and Cope, 2003; Therkelsen, 2003), but nonetheless it is possible to identify some basic features which clearly have implications for knowledge dynamics within this particular area of tourist activity.

This form of tourism is organized not mainly by the individual traveller but by some collective entity, for example a private firm, a public body, or an association of either individuals (for example academics) or collectivities (for example county councils). While the individual conference participant in the event therefore has to deal with a limited number of actors, as in package tours this simply reflects that many aspects of the event will have been assembled by the organizers. It should, however, be underlined that the reach of conference organizers varies a great deal along several dimensions:

- While some corporate organizers will organize everything from travel to on-site services to meeting programmes in minute detail to make the most of the valuable time of their employees, associations organizing for example academic conferences are likely to leave more of the organization to participants (for example travel, accommodation, catering) in order to keep down the headline price for the event (cf. Davidson and Cope, 2003) and because much of the content at academic conferences is driven by the participants through their submission of papers.
- Some conference organizers organize everything in-house, while others outsource particular parts of the event to specialists in the form of professional conference organizers and/or destination management bodies that offer their services for free or for a fee (Weber, 2001).
- Some conference organizers can use their authority to effectively order individual persons to attend their events – for example the employees of a particular firm – while others have to rely on promoting their events to a more or less well-defined group of professionals working in a particular area or sharing particular interests (cf. Swarbrooke and Horner, 2001).
- The locations of some conferences are more or less given in advance – firms are likely to choose venues in the vicinity and revisit them if satisfied with the quality of the services provided – while other conferences migrate within or between countries in a more or less predictable manner (cf. Davidson and Cope, 2003).
- Some organizers, especially corporate ones, often focus predominantly on business-related activities, while conferences organized by associations often include elements of leisure-related activities, either built into the programme by organizers or organized by the

participants themselves, who wander around the place hosting the
event when the programme is perceived to be boring (cf. Therkelsen,
2003).

This variety of conferencing as a form of tourism greatly complicates the
efforts of, for example, destination management bodies to attract events
to their part of the world, because while there is certainly a lot to play for,
how to play the game does seem much less obvious.

With regard to knowledge generation, the picture seems to be much
the same as in the forms of tourism already discussed: because of a large
number of shared features, the same knowledge types, synthetic and
symbolic, also dominate with regard to conference tourism, and again
it is interesting to note that existing research would seem to suggest that
despite the central role of large firms, organizations and associations as
buyers (and to some extent also customers) of conference services, still
relatively little market research is being undertaken except with regard to
customer satisfaction (Weber, 2001).

In terms of knowledge dynamics, this form of tourism would all in all
appear to be a relatively static activity. Although service providers may
suggest new conference formats and solutions to their customers, the level
of market research among professional conference organizers seems to be
very low and oriented towards fine-tuning products and providing a 'level
playing field' between locations competing for a share in the lucrative business of conferencing (Weber, 2001). Moreover, as conference venues are
more or less 'set in concrete' as physical infrastructure, and their buyers
appear to be focusing primarily on content rather than form – getting the
message across and/or providing networking opportunities – the main
source of product development in the traditional sense of the word would
seem to be more or less informal liaisoning between the conference organizers on the one hand, and their professional advisors and suppliers on the
other hand. It should, however, also be noted that competition between
destinations to attract conferences and between conference organizers to
attract the attention of potential delegates does instal a certain degree of
dynamics in the process, especially with regard to symbolic repositioning
of the image of particular localities and event.

9.4   CONCLUDING REMARKS: TOURISM AND KNOWLEDGE DYNAMICS BEYOND PAVITT

While Pavitt's (1984) notion of tourism as a 'supplier-dominated' personal service may hold true with regard to technology development,

the analysis above has strongly suggested that this is only a minor part of the overall picture in an area of economic activity that has gradually become a peculiar combination of 'high-tech' and 'high-touch' (Keller, 2006; Naisbitt et al., 1999). Despite the fact that tourism takes place for a variety of purposes and is being organized in many different ways, a common feature has been shown to be the preponderance of synthetic and symbolic forms of knowledge in combination with fairly low levels of systematic knowledge generation, especially with regard to attempts to explore what drives, for example, customers and hence demand for tourism services in new directions. This is in many ways a paradox. It is a general paradox because in a personal service industry like tourism, user-driven innovation would seem to be an important part of the knowledge process; and it is particularly paradoxical at the current historical juncture where market trends – and hence changing social motivations for leisure and other forms of travel – are changing rapidly, for example due to the increasing wealth in new and fast-growing potential markets (Central and Eastern Europe, Russia, China, India) and the growing availability of relatively cheap air travel, and thus competition between tourist destinations is becoming even more global and complex. Currently knowledge dynamics within the tourism sector do, however, seem to be dominated by two combinations of drivers and responses: on the one hand, the corporate dynamics associated with multinational corporations (MNCs) expanding their service brands to new destinations while occasionally adopting practices associated with SMEs operating in particular niches; and on the other hand, the policy-driven dynamics associated with public promotional bodies trying to fine-tune the tourist experience offers of SMEs within their destination through promotion and, to a lesser extent, innovation initiatives. If this diagnosis holds true, then it strongly suggests that changes beyond replication of what happens to be perceived as 'best practice' of successful destinations and firms would have to involve either particularly visionary entrepreneurs – on a large scale like, for instance, Michael O'Leary of Ryanair, or more modestly as niche producers of new types of tourism experiences – or extensive efforts on the part of destination management bodies, aided by the research and graduate output of knowledge institutions, to increase the learning capacity of SMEs through internal and external networking.

NOTES

1. While full responsibility for the chapter remains with the author, constructive comments from workshops in Savonlinna, Lisbon and Aalborg are gratefully acknowledged.

Special thanks to Anette Therkelsen for providing a running commentary on issues of
tourism conceptualization.

2. This chapter uses the two most commonly used international data sets with regard to
    European tourism, produced by Eurostat and the UN organization, World Tourism
    Organization, respectively.
3. The private sector interest organization the World Tourism and Travel Council claimed
    that while the 'direct industry impact' was '3.6 per cent of total GDP', 'the combined
    direct and indirect impact of the Travel & Tourism economy expected to total 10.3 per
    cent in 2006'. Eurostat more moderately claims 5.5 per cent as the tourism-related part
    of the European economy (Anastasiadou, 2006).
4. Calculated on the basis of World Tourism Organization (2006): 35, 45.
5. Given the low level of GDP in Bulgaria, this may not amount to much in real terms, but
    is nonetheless rather surprising and possibly the result of unreliable data.
6. Calculated on the basis of World Tourism Organization (2006).
7. For trips involving at least four nights away, the domestic share in France and Italy is
    83 and 75 per cent respectively, in sharp contrast to, for example, Germany and the UK
    which record 36 and 41 per cent.
8. The inspiration of Mario Vale is gratefully acknowledged.
9. Visiting relatives is, despite being more difficult to document fully, a major activity that
    is estimated to account for 30 per cent of all European tourism in 2004 (World Tourism
    Organization, 2006: 44), but comes close to leisure travel (with family duties installed
    as the main reason to go) both in terms of enabling factors (for example cheap and/or
    convenient transport) and activity profile at the destination, and has therefore not been
    considered separately.

10. Analysis and summaries from the seven sector chapters

Philip Cooke and Carla De Laurentis

10.1 INTRODUCTION

Theses sectoral studies reveal quite clearly the matrix nature of contemporary knowledge flows in industry. This phenomenon is still not widely understood, but it can be surmised to have evolved in a more pronounced way for the three following reasons. First, knowledge exploration, examination and exploitation for innovation grew as an imperative for European and other Western firms with the onset of Asian competition from the 1960s and 1970s onwards. Second, relatively few large non-Asian corporations, operating the 'silo model' of corporate organization that became especially de rigeur after the Second World War, really had the capabilities of flexibility, agility and interactivity necessary to meet the challenge. Finally, a relatively under-researched social phenomenon occurred simultaneously in most Western countries. University education grew from something mainly pursued by a wealthy elite to becoming more democratically available and affordable for families of modest income. This released a large supply of highly trained graduate and postgraduate labour on to the labour market. Although some firms, like Siemens and ICI for example, had always reserved quotas of the best young graduate engineers and chemists for their own recruitment, others did not always follow suit. Indeed in some countries it was more likely that senior corporate positions would be occupied by staff trained in military rather than university settings. As by the 1960s and subsequently university labour markets continued to expand with new, often technical, universities joining those of earlier provenance, so these were able to recruit the brightest and best of the new intakes. Gradually exploration and examination functions grew alongside more traditional teaching functions. Thereafter, by the 1980s the exploitation function was added as governments, industry and academe itself came to recognize the potential gold mine of academic entrepreneurship. Open science was proving highly successful in the first two knowledge capabilities, moderately so in the third, and all at much reduced cost compared to the research and development (R&D) 'armies' employed in corporate laboratories. Thus by the 1990s 'open innovation', pioneered in one of the most science-based industries of all – medical biosciences – began spreading in significant amounts from the corporate to the small and medium-sized enterprise (SME) and university sectors, as demonstrated by Chesbrough (2003).

In the brief synthesis that follows it is shown how distributed knowledge flows of the kind under discussion evolved and, moreover, the often unpredictable nature of the resulting knowledge interactions. The account presents the sectoral synthesis in a different order from that in which the sectoral accounts were presented. This is done for three reasons. First, by now it is evident that some sectors interact more with each other, such that a kind of sectoral platform shape emerges. In this, for example, knowledge-intensive business services (KIBS) are something of a fulcrum, with many interactions with the automotive, information and communication technology (ICT) and new media sectors, but also to a considerable extent with the tourism, agro-food, healthcare and energy biotechnology platform. A term like 'culinary tourism' (Long, 2005) captures this phenomenon to some extent. Here, travellers go to places with health infrastructure, landscape, quality food and, possibly, creative industry or cultural economy assets in preference to choosing the traditional mass-market package tour. This is highlighted in Halkier's Chapter 9 as the tourist move to what is more like a 'traveller' status pursuing dedicated, discretionary or self-customized tourism options. Something of this pattern may be observed in the account of the evolution of the Swiss watch region of Jura in Chapter 11.

Second, this captures two features of interest to the underlying 'transition' dimension of this book. Although theory initially suggested that 'related variety' can be anticipated because the probability of lateral absorptive capacity among subsectoral neighbour industries would be hypothetically high, this is not enough. Our research shows that *ex ante* suppositions do not always follow, and that unexpected, distant sector (that is, SIC or NACE industrial classification) interactions occur with considerable frequency. This *ex post* analytical dimension confirms the importance of primary, interview-based empirical research in relation to secondary data-set modelling of official statistics. Together, in this instance, they show how they are capable of creating hypotheses for each other against which to test scientific progress.

Thus, secondary analysis showed statistical related variety to be an extant phenomenon. Primary interviewing showed it not to be confined to neighbouring SIC/NACE categories. This has led to the creation of a concept of 'revealed related variety' which now poses an interesting challenge for secondary data-modelling. Some of the relevant data, which necessarily for this task measures change in outsourcing activity, exists embryonically at least in the US, where the National Science Foundation provides a valuable analysis of, for example, annual change in where and by which size category of firm industrial R&D is conducted. In Chesbrough (2003) it is shown how in-house R&D by large US corporations declined from 71 per cent in 1981 to 39 per cent in 2001. A concomitant rise of from less than 5 per cent of the US total industrial R&D being conducted by SMEs in 1981 to nearly 25 per cent in 2001 is indicative of this transition but much more research is needed, and not only in the field of R&D, to complete the structural, functional and geographical shifts here being addressed. Needless to say, the task is much harder in Europe, where no such data sets exist.

A comparable research requirement arising from these insights is to capture an aspect such as 'derived related variety' since much of the knowledge outsourcing in focus in this book concerns at least innovation if not only R&D. In innovation studies it is common to conceptualize innovation measures as capturing 'derived demand', since innovation for its own sake scarcely ever happens. Recall that 'innovation' differs from 'invention' in being intended for commercial exploitation in the market. Hence innovation occurs to meet other economic requirements such as competitiveness, market expansion and customer preference or satisfaction. Since much related variety of exploitation activity across sectoral and subsectoral boundaries occurs in pursuit of innovation, it can hypothetically be measured in terms of derived related variety. This, in turn, could be a useful policy tool rendering more efficient the evidently somewhat random, not to say shotgun, methods now deployed by even the most catalytical regional innovation agencies, some of which are described in Chapter 12.

Finally, conceptualizing major underlying processes in a revealed related variety way facilitates comparison in representational terms. Thus in section 10.2 below the manner in which particular industries co-occupy specific knowledge phases or categories in Table 10.1 underlines sectoral similarities and differences in new ways. Equally, in discussing cognate industries in relation to their 'worlds of production' it is rather telling to tackle two such revealed related variety industry structures together, possibly to reflect upon their derived related variety characteristics and possibly, in future, to measure these. To repeat, this is a ground-clearing rather than a garden-designing stage in the evolution of this social scientific endeavour, but that modern industry is suffused with platform-like interactions among a relatively randomly selected group of industries is hard not to accept in light of the relevant summary provided in Table 10.1.

Table 10.1   A stylized sector–region–firm typology

Knowledge Phase of Institution or Firm → Region ↓	Implicit (Explore)	Complicit (Explore–Examine)	Explicit (Examine–Exploit)
Knowledge Domain	(Invention/ Discovery) Bioscience (e.g. Molecule) ICT (e.g. Silicon Chip)	(Translator) Bioscience (e.g. Patent) ICT (e.g. VC)	(Appropriation> IPR) Bioscience (e.g. Drug) New Media (e.g. DC*) ICT (e.g. iPod)
Knowledge Capability	(Talent) New Media (e.g. Editing) KIBS (e.g. Chaos Theory) Automotive (e.g. GIS)	(Research) Food (e.g. Nutritionist) KIBS (e.g. Derivatives) Automotive (e.g. GPS)	(Technique) Food (e.g. Functional) KIBS (e.g. Hedge Fund) Automotive (e.g. SatNav)
Innovation System	(Institutions) Bioscience (e.g. Boston) Nutraceuticals (e.g. Skåne) ICT (e.g. Silicon Valley)	(Networks) Tourism (e.g. Wine) New Media (e.g. SoHo/ Soho)	(Digital, e.g. KMS**) Tourism (e.g. Wine Routes) New Media (e.g. Gaming)

Notes:
  *   DC is Digital Content.
 ** KMS is 'knowledge management system.' This may be a product of ICT, including
      New Media, firms or a process utilized by an industry or firm either by e.g. intranet,
      extranet, groupware or other KMS platform. Even some innovation agencies like
      VINNOVA (Sweden), SIVA (Norway) or Scottish Enterprise (UK) use KMS.

10.2   KNOWLEDGE DRIVERS AND RESPONSES IN THE EURODITE SECTORS

In Table 10.1, sectors in the Eurodite range of variety are selected for exemplification, and related to our preceding triple categorization of relevant knowledge types in regard to sectoral knowledge generation, testing and appropriation characteristics. According to OECD (1999) the Eurodite sectors can be differentiated as to whether or not they are strongly science-driven, moderately science-driven or hardly science-driven. For simplicity, each sector's main knowledge base is inserted in appropriate categories. This does not mean they may not be more or less occasionally science-utilizing, as in the case of food, which involves agro-bio 'functional foods' and also buys in testing and trialling examination knowledge for hygiene, packaging, bacterial analysis and so on. Given that these are thorough-going features of the agro-food industry, there is a case for questioning Organisation for Economic Co-operation and Development (OECD) cat-egorizations of agro-food as 'low-tech' and certainly 'low-science'-using, since with the onset of industrial agriculture in Europe in the 1950s, food chemistry, food technology, nutrition science and now bioscience have been at the heart of its production paradigm.

Most new media, especially based on Internet service provision, is com-moditized rather than science-driven, although technological innovation is very pronounced in new media, from digital content to computer gaming. Even KIBS (knowledge-intensive business services) are occasionally science (analytical knowledge)-driven in truth, as with applications of Black–Scholes chaos theorems to hedge fund algorithms and other derivatives and options products. To explain these allocations of sectors to categories, it is important to recognize the importance of science-driven exploration knowledge of an often implicit kind that characterizes bioscience and ICT in ways that it does not with such cognitive proximity in the other sectors. Also, as we have seen, such sectors rely strongly on innovation systems that mix public and private institutions and funding for research.

New media, KIBS and automotive sectors are less institutionally reliant and more 'entrepreneurial', through either large-firm vertical innovation chains or small-firm horizontal cooperation linkages mainly within market settings. In the complicit dimension, as we have seen with bioscience and ICT but also through outsourcing, most industries and firms that buy 'advice' nowadays rely on many intermediaries in the translation and, par-ticularly examination (testing and trialling) phases. Food, KIBS and auto-motive sectors frequently buy research and design capabilities in markets, while tourism and new media are rather connected to big institutions for innovation, like broadcasters, content customers and travel corporations for innovation demand.

Food, automotive, ICT and KIBS sectors patent less or in limited ways – software cannot be patented in the US although it can in the EU. Innovation in these industries relies mainly on technique. When it comes to exploitation, bioscience accounts for some 50 per cent of world patents; ICT is not such a pronounced patenting sector, even excluding software's regulatory anomalies; while new media is widely subject to copyright or trademark designations. Some automotive firms (for example Audi with more than 5000 patents for its 2007 model – many of which must be joint with suppliers) also patent exorbitantly. Meanwhile, to the extent that digital networks represent innovative processes available to the market to enhance competitiveness, tourism and new media are major users of such systems directly to the public, whereas for the other sectors such system usage is more private (see Sassen, 2007).

10.3   'WORLDS OF PRODUCTION' IN THE EURODITE SECTORS

10.3.1   Food

Moving on to the analysis of different knowledge drivers and responses that we summarized with the four tensions that arise from the 'worlds of production' paradigm, we start with the contemporary food landscape and the tourism industry. Although this approach is utilized in Morgan et al. (2006) in their study of 'worlds of food', it is more clearly utilized by Manniche (Chapter 3) in his review of tendencies in the European and global food industry. Manniche is constrained to using a threefold categorization of 'food cultures' because of the Eurodite methodological requirement to utilize three knowledge categories (analytical, synthetic and symbolic) to structure his discourse on functional foods (analytical, bioscience), conventional food (synthetic, standardized, mass production, intensive agriculture) and alternative food (organic, local, specialty, fair trade and so on). Fortunately, Morgan et al. (2006) note specialized processes for generic or comprehensive foods such as 'cook–chill' for prepared meals as capturing the fourth segment of the schema in Figure 10.1.

This indicates directions of the food industry as main innovation and renewal efforts are put in place to respond to new customer demands. Producers of industrial food are under increasing market pressure to develop more dedicated products and marketing strategies by emphasizing domestic, locally produced or organic qualities without losing the efficiency of standardized production and distribution technologies. In the organic food model innovation efforts are carried out to standardized products and technologies, and expand markets without losing the dedicated product qualities which differentiate them from mainstream products. There is an extra tension in the eco-food corner between a firm strategy of broadening the customer base by selling through the large-scale distribution channels of supermarket chains, or avoiding that route and utilizing low-energy consumption means of localized distribution. Those in the latter category hold that supermarket distribution compromises the dedicated product

Food/tourism

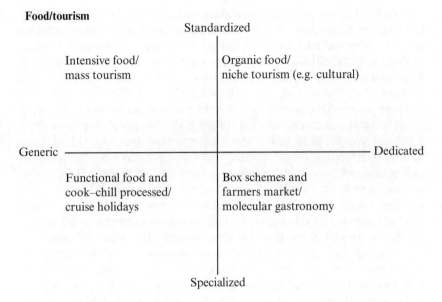

Figure 10.1   Regional 'worlds of production': agro-food industry and tourism

profile, changing it in the direction of conventional food products that their organic sensibility deems 'unhealthy'.

10.3.2   Tourism

Closely linked to this, and drawing fundamentally on the Eurodite tourism analysis produced by Halkier (Chapter 9) equivalent 'worlds of production' analysis is performed in Figure 10.1, taking account of developments in the 'experience economy' as elaborated with varieties of tourism experience in mind (Pine and Gilmore, 1999). Standardized tourism in the form of the package holiday has much in common with conventional, industrialized agriculture and intensive food production and distribution. Both are seriously destructive of environmental quality, whether through massive overuse of a few basic agro-chemicals that raise nitrogen levels dangerously, or vast increases in carbon dioxide emissions that influence climate, change, or simply by the destruction of marine landscapes through mass induced accommodation demand. Contrariwise, 'dedicated' tourism is distinctively niched and possibly specific to the individualized tourist requirement. Specialized tourism processes with a generic outcome would be captured by visiting beauty spots by cruise ship rather than by more conventional package holiday means. Finally, the tourism equivalent of a technologized 'functional food' experience might involve 'culinary tourism' to such 'molecular gastronomy' delights as Ferràn Adria's El Bulli restaurant in Gerona, Catalonia to compare his molecular gastronomy with that of Heston Blumenthal's Fat Duck near London and numerous imitators elsewhere (Long, 2005).

These categorizations help to locate the distinctive kinds of agro-food–cultural tourism region that might evolve in distinctive ways from a present condition in which some aspects may dominate. More commonly, overlapping categories may exist but profitability and rising or falling demand may point to new directions and requirements for policy assistance in institution building and targeted investment. Furthermore, recalling the four paradigms that Halkier (Chapter 9) identifies in tourism – namely leisure travel, package tours, accidental tourism and business tourism – we can argue that different 'worlds of production' coexist in tourism, involving distinct types of knowledge dynamics, distinct sets of associated actors and distinctive processes of interaction according to different formal or informal rules and incentives. Existing research noted in Halkier (Chapter 9) reveals innovation and renewal efforts being put in place to respond to new customer demands. Nevertheless, despite the central role in tourism of large corporates, still relatively little market research (knowledge generation) is being undertaken except in the form of formal monitoring of subcontractor performance and customer satisfaction (Reimer, 1990; Ioannides, 1998). However, compared to other parts of the tourism industry such as accommodation and catering, tour operators per se are relatively innovative in the quest for maintaining their market share and keeping up with consumer demands for more differentiated experiences.

Hence, two trends have been in evidence recently and would seem to be likely to continue in the foreseeable future. On the one hand, we observe the creation of larger national and international companies through mergers and acquisitions, leading to transnational travel corporations. On the other hand, market-driven innovation has led to the rapid emergence of specialist tour operators catering for particular segments of, for example, cultural, nature or adventure tourism markets. Interestingly, in large corporate 'standardized' and 'transnational' travel corporate expansion has primarily been horizontal. Thus although some tour operators have 'verticalized' by establishing or acquiring their own charter airline, they have predominantly concentrated on assembling the complex product and marketing it to potential customers in Northern Europe. Thus they have largely eschewed direct investment in hotel accommodation, thereby offloading risk to local SMEs and retaining the capacity to shift attention to other localities if they become more attractive in terms of cost structure or demand.

10.3.3 Knowledge-Intensive Business Services (KIBS)

Moving onto KIBS firms, as highlighted in the sector study of Strambach (Chapter 7), these firms are playing a more central role for economy-wide innovation as knowledge carriers, producers and mediators in national and regional economies. A fundamental characteristic of KIBS firms is the intense participation and involvement of clients in the production process. However, the sector study report highlights the composite nature of knowledge-based service products, responding increasingly to the need for interdisciplinary, application and problem-oriented knowledge of other sectors that form the client base. Thus, KIBS are confronted with a double tension (Figure 10.2): providing highly specialized knowledge-intensive expertise (for example in the case of hedge funds) and comprehensive problem solutions (for example supply chain management), adapting their knowledge products to client-specific business contexts; and at the same time achieving economies of scale and scope through product standardization (a typical example is provided by consumer banking). KIBS

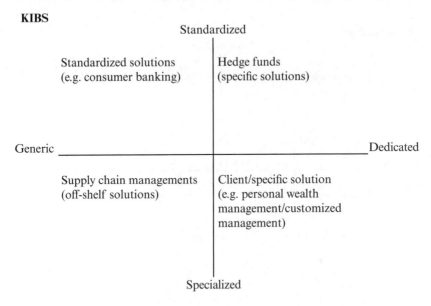

KIBS

Standardized

Standardized solutions
(e.g. consumer banking)

Hedge funds
(specific solutions)

Generic ———————————————————————— Dedicated

Supply chain managements
(off-shelf solutions)

Client/specific solution
(e.g. personal wealth
management/customized
management)

Specialized

Figure 10.2   Regional 'worlds of production': knowledge-intensive business services

increasingly show capabilities to access, combine and reconfigure implicit and explicit knowledge based in horizontal and vertical knowledge domains, and to contextualize this knowledge into 'products' in a customized way. The literature cited outlines that it is this category of services that plays a more central role in knowledge economies (see Strambach, Chapter 7). Within the KIBS sector, therefore, different driving institutions, network interactions and conventions can coexist.

10.3.4 Biotechnology

Turning to biotechnology, we have seen the implications for industry organization in pharmaceuticals of the rise of 'rational drug design' and the demise of the 'chance discovery' model of scientific research, and how recent developments in genomics have highlighted the importance of a genomics approach to drug development (Figure 10.3).

Genomics has allowed a means of constructing biological pathways by integrating genomic and proteomic expression information. Genomics is permeating many aspects of drug discovery processes as well as influencing the way diseases are managed. Inevitably, this will reshape healthcare markets in future, and the organization of firms is evolving to meet the needs of both their internal research departments and also their external

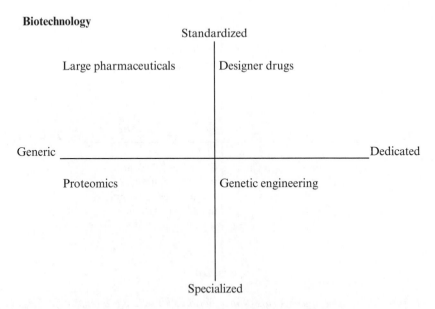

Figure 10.3   Regional 'worlds of production': biotechnology

clients. Hence, the fast-emerging multidisciplinary areas of bioinformatics, genomics and high-performance computing are moving toward safer drug design and designer drugs based on the patient's unique genetic makeup.[1]

Clearly, all of bioscience – even the traditional fermentation technology – is highly science-driven (analytic knowledge) but also has its established genetic engineering capability (synthetic knowledge). Biotechnology accounts for the majority of US and EU patents and the majority of start-up firms. In this study, the emphasis is upon healthcare-related knowledge exploration and exploitation (not forgetting the all-important examination dimension associated with patient trialling and testing of new or modified products). But biotechnology is well ensconced, as we have seen, in the heavy R&D-utilizing aspect of the agro-food industry related to 'functional foods' or 'nutraceuticals'. It is increasingly important in the agro-fuel industries associated with the production of non-fossil fuels like biodiesel, bioethanol and biomethane. Furthermore, it is important in bioremediation and bioenvironmental engineering of the soil, air and water contaminated by the excessive use of agro-chemicals and production of industrial pollutants in the environment, having a 'platform-like' relationship with the other main aspects of the bioeconomy. But biotechnology is also central nowadays to homeland security through DNA fingerprinting and suspect tracing, biomarkers for coding, and biometrics in security-related identification of persons. Other sectors like ICT are intimately connected with aspects of biotechnology, whether as suppliers of specialized equipment like gene sequencing equipment or bioinformatics, or as input technologies to ICT products. So biotechnology is becoming something of a broad-platform technology, rather as ICT became in the twentieth century.

10.3.5 Automotives

The automotive sector has been undergoing major changes since the mid-1990s – a 'third revolution' as argued in Jürgens, Blöcker and MacNeill (Chapter 8). The main driver of change is the cost pressure which, together with intense competition, has led car makers to seek economies of scale by increasing production volumes and led to the creation of the main production paradigms. This cost pressure has driven successive waves of mergers, the need to standardize components, the trend towards outsourcing to specialist suppliers, and the imperative for manufacturers to increase the high-value technology content of vehicles by the addition of 'luxury' items such as electrical, electronic and communications componentry (Figure 10.4).

In addition, increasing interest from both regulators and consumers

Automotive and ICT

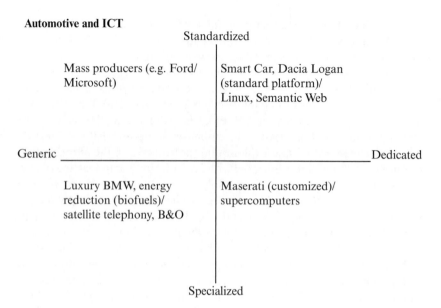

Figure 10.4   Regional 'worlds of production': automotive and ICT

has led to environmental pressures which, in turn, have created a drive for more efficient powertrains, reduced emissions and the development of new technologies for reduced weight, hybrid or electric vehicles and bio-fuels. Finally, manufacturers need to address consumer pressures which have led to the growth of new market segments, such as minivans or small 'city' cars (such as Smart car), and the need to offer increasing numbers of radical variations whilst still maintaining common 'under-skin' platforms. With increasing specialization, some companies have gained a clearly identifiable, specific science base (such as electronics experts, nanotechnology and paint experts, and so on.)

10.3.6   ICT

The current ICT sector has evolved by the ongoing merger of information technology and telecom technologies; consequently a range of new products, services, applications, markets, policy and regulatory domains have emerged. This, in turn, enables new business models that are changing the organization of the ICT industry at large in a fundamental way. Nevertheless, as Brossard and Vicente (2007: D3c) argue, the ICT sector is particularly concerned with the role played by knowledge networks in industrial organization. At the level of the sector, the questions of modularity, complementarity, compatibility and standardization are critical, and these specificities imply some consequences at the level of the innovative and market performance of the firm. Firms operate in a market in which their innovative capabilities are not guaranteed market success. Firms have to combine appropriation strategies in order to promote and exploit their knowledge in competitive markets with 'relational' strategies in order to find new opportunities and to enhance the integration of their knowledge in technical systems or platforms. Furthermore, in a complex and systemic view of knowledge dynamics, network relations in the ICT sector are becoming very important (Figure 10.4). End-users are offered a variety of ICT solutions with varying interoperability, convergence capabilities, and technical and operational security. Knowledge utilized and developed is primarily synthetic, but a considerable amount of resource investment is found in exploration, examination and exploitation activities, roughly equally according to subsector (for example software engineering is generally more synthetic than analytic; while telecom software is synthetic but more examination-focused than IT software).

Turning to the 'worlds of production' framework, the ICT sector can be mapped out on the basis of the applied technology and organization of production and the firms' market orientation; on the top left corner ICT is predominantly characterized by the existence of mass-manufactured personal computers and the use of an operating system and desktop applications predominance of the standardized technology; on the opposite side we have the semantic web, in which the focus is on encoding semantic resources (that is, machines 'understanding' the meaning of a question) in a machine-processable form, moving on to more advanced applications and functionality on the web that facilitates building online end-user applications that integrate, combine and deduce information needed to assist users in performing tasks. Supercomputers are clearly 'specialized' kinds of non-standard machine for heavy data analysis, while luxury, generic products like hi-fi systems embodying much ICT knowledge continue to find a market, as in the case of companies like Bang & Olufsen.

10.3.7 New Media

The sector report by Staines and Collinge (Chapter 6) highlights that there are several drivers of innovation and performance in new media, such as the increased penetration of broadband technologies; the disintermediation in the value chain as digitization opens new windows of opportunity for entrants; persistent advances in the quality, efficiency and number of media platforms; as well as changing consumer demand. Furthermore, frequent developments in intellectual property rights (IPR) regulations exert a strong influence on the development and availability of media content. These drivers of change shape the way knowledge is created, accessed and used in new media. It can be argued that new media represents a shift from one-way (asynchronous) mass communication to specialized and interactive communication between medium and user. The Internet has created a platform where the line between content creator and user is blurred. In the new economy, characterized by blogging, user-controlled websites such as YouTube, MySpace, Twitter and Wikipedia, the media audience is now vocal. Recipients are active participants on discussion boards, sharing information and shaping events. New media are not rigidly unidirectional, nor do they require the same level of capital investment as mass media. Audiences as users are increasingly to be understood as plural (that is, multiple, diverse, fragmented) and active (that is, selective, self-directed, producers as well as consumers of texts). Dedicated, specialized and generic process technologies are most active in fragmenting a standardized production world that the media in general was characterized by in earlier times. Symbolic knowledge predominates in the consumption of new media; symbolic and synthetic typify the production knowledges in this technology platform. A considerable amount of creative exploration knowledge is expended in the production and consumption of new media digital content.

For the providers of interactive software, advances in technological hardware and software are key drivers of growth. The convergent nature of new media technologies, comprising an interface of telecommunications, ICT and media, often means that these functions are integrated into a single device that can offer music, advanced computing services, regular mobile communication, video and sound recording and display, and a digital camera, as well as such diverse functions as global positioning system technology (Figure 10.5). The rise of online music attracts many new entrants and new intermediaries, creates new business models and generates new forms of product and process innovations. Although the creation of sound recording, to a large extent, still rests with artists and publishers, in the new digital music model, new forms of distribution and business functions have emerged. The creation of an online music store requires content creation and production; the digitization of content; the clearing of rights; the settling of technological issues, including digital rights management systems (DRMs); the creation of online music store-fronts; and secure billing systems and delivery networks.

In other segments such as the provision of educational content, standard technology is utilized even when the main objective is to provide creative content. Contrariwise, there is a symbiotic relationship between game developers and the technologies used for computer games, particularly the

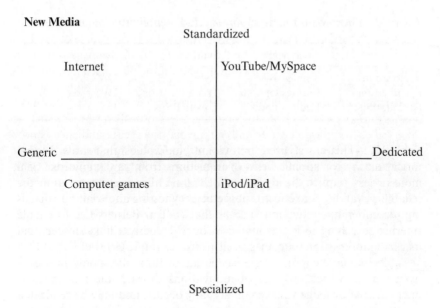

Figure 10.5   Regional 'worlds of production': new media

providers of game consoles. Developers incorporate cutting-edge synthetic knowledge advances in technology, such as three-dimensional (3D) animation, sound and graphics, from the upstream hardware and software suppliers in their game development process. Suppliers of game consoles rely on developers to engineer games that are compatible with their devices. This relationship is unique, as game developers have to negotiate to get their content onto particular platforms since console manufacturers have exclusive control over titles for their hardware. Therefore, it is critical that developers create more than one game per platform, particularly as the computer game development process is often long, very R&D-intensive and costly. Moreover, developers are often constrained in their ability to develop games for cross-platform use, given the significant difference in the technologies of each console. Thus, they spend considerable time and investment adapting games to new platforms.

Finally, we return to our knowledge framework (as in Chapter 1, Table 1.3) for consideration of distinct kinds of knowledge activity within firms in sectors, to analyse their simply illustrated knowledge value chains for products evolved through interactive innovation processes. Their distinctive character is defined in relation to their distinctive knowledge value-chain trajectory. Just three sectors are selected for exemplification but readers can easily fit examples from other sectors as appropriate

Table 10.2　Knowledge value chains in KIBS, automotive and new media

	Analytical	Synthetic	Symbolic
Exploration	Scholes–Black	Hybrid Fuel	DARPA
Examination	Futures/Options	Trialling/Testing	Hypertext
Exploitation	Hedge Funds	Toyota Prius	Internet

Table 10.2. This has stylized 'innovation biographies' that show the historical nature for specific firms of transitions from raw knowledge of a more-or-less implicit 'being articulated' kind through examination for reliability, validity and effectiveness/efficiency testing and trialling, including recombinant innovation such as that of Tim Berners-Lee to enable Internet searching to be facilitated through Hypertext links, to eventual marketed innovation outcomes by firms (for example Google).

Table 10.2 here captures the historic (innovation biography) processes by means of which progress of innovations through the iterative and interactive knowledge value chain actually occurs, and may be replicated for all innovations in any sector.[2] Thus a methodology has been presented for historical reconstruction of innovations as 'innovation biographies' linking all kinds of knowledge and innovation actors, whether 'fictions' like sectors or realities like firms, and their innovation practices as they move ideas from implicit through complicit to explicit commercial outcomes. The analysis allows for both spatial and temporal sensitivities to be emphasized at different stages of analysis.

10.4　GENDER DIMENSION IN THE EURODITE SECTORS

The gender dimension does not feature strongly in either the literature on regional economic development or that on the 'knowledge economy'; accordingly it deserves attention here even though two key points need to be understood. First, in these sector studies it is knowledge flows that are in focus. Knowledge in itself may be considered gender-neutral. Second, in society more generally, the responsibility for gender equality lies firstly with government. Governments may not discriminate among sectors, and as sectors, firms and regions are in focus here, inevitably the role of government in general is rather minimized analytically, except in respect of regulation regarding knowledge flows and innovation in product markets.

Nevertheless, gender segregation in science, engineering and technology is of particular relevance to the knowledge economy and, indeed, to many of the case study sectors in Eurodite. Although women constitute the majority of undergraduates in the vast majority of Western countries, patterns of gender segregation by subject remain particularly robust. Women are represented in medical and biological and life sciences but constitute a small minority in physics, mathematics and engineering, particularly across the EU. Vertical gender segregation is a rigid feature of European universities and research institutes where the majority of undergraduates are women but the majority of the professoriate are men. Women occupied 31 per cent of all academic positions in the EU-15 in 2000, but comprised only 13.2 per cent of women in senior posts (EC, 2003). This is coupled with dropout rates of women from scientific careers which are disproportionately higher at every stage in the career ladder, in both the private and the public sector (EC, 2003).

At present, women constitute about 15 per cent of 'industrial researchers.[3] However, there are significant national differences. Women make up between 18 per cent and 28 per cent of industrial researchers in eight out of the ten EU member states that provide gender-disaggregated statistics; however, in Germany and Austria, the figure remains below 10 per cent. More women are coming up through the system, and indeed, between 1995 and 2000, the employment of highly qualified women scientists and engineers in industry increased faster than that of men in the EU-15. These are usually under 34, therefore younger than their male counterparts, and are more likely to have temporary contracts and to be employed in small and medium-sized enterprises.

Two important aspects can be taken into consideration within the knowledge economy. Firstly, a considerable volume of research that focused on gender differences in labour market status and participation has indicated female entrepreneurship as a major force for innovation and growth (OECD, 1997). Although the literature has emphasized that the entrepreneurial motivations between women and men are often very similar, with independence and the need for self-achievement always being ranked first (Hisrich et al., 1996), some distinctions can be highlighted and only a small part of entrepreneurial motivations are acknowledged as gender-based. Gender-based differences often relate to factors such as: the need for a flexible schedule, which reflects the family caring role that is still expected from women; the problem of the 'glass ceiling', which encourages women to start their own business operations because of an inability to obtain proper recognition by their employers; and the need to accommodate work and child-rearing roles simultaneously (Cromie, 1987; Orhan and Scott, 2001; Brush, 1990; Buttner and Moore, 1997). Recent studies have also focused on gender-based differences in entrepreneurship and women's social orientations, arguing that women develop an interconnected system of relationships that include family, community and business (Brush, 1992).

Secondly, as argued in this book and in other contributions to the Eurodite project, the fostering of networks at the regional level by regional development agencies and local authorities is regarded as key to developing innovation. It has been argued that many of the venues used for networking either discriminate against women directly (for example some business and sports clubs) or exclude women indirectly through their ambience. The lack of women in senior positions in many of the player organizations makes it difficult for those who do participate to 'fit'. According to one recent report (Carter et al., 2001) the literature has also identified gender differences in the way networks are created and used, enabling improved access to finance and the development of strong relationships with financial backers. Differences emerged in both the establishment and management of networks (that is, the process of networking) and in the content of social networks (that is, what networks are used for), suggesting that women are more likely to have networks composed entirely of other women.

Nonetheless, while women may feel excluded from some networks, they have also created their own. Fisher's (2006) study shows that alternative women's networks began in Wall Street in the late 1950s. The growing fluidity of finance houses in the new economy has affected career trajectories: as a consequence, the '85 broads' is 'a cyber forum for former and current Goldman Sachs women to make contacts as they make career transitions in the new information-based business environment' (Fisher, 2006: 60). While some women's networks operate parallel to but outside the mainstream, others are more integrated, and it can be argued that the regional innovation system could play an important role in building bridges and establishing linkages between mainstream and professional women's networks as well as between the different women's associations.

10.5   CONCLUDING REMARKS

The Eurodite research has sought to provide a summary of the different sector studies conducted; to capture the historic processes by which progress of innovation through the iterative and interactive knowledge value chains actually occurs and may be replicated for all innovations in any sector; and to present a methodology for historical reconstruction of innovations as 'innovation biographies' linking many kinds of knowledge and innovation actors (research institutions, intermediaries, firms) and their innovation practices as they move ideas from implicit through complicit to explicit commercial outcomes. The framework identified allows

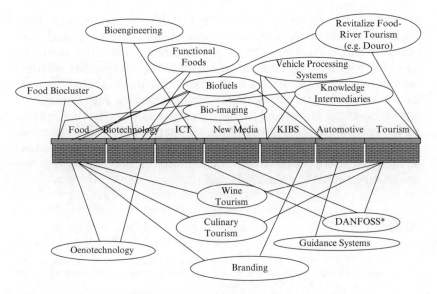

Note: * Danish 'green engineering' firm with Science and Technology theme park.

Figure 10.6 *Some cross-sector 'platform' candidate innovation biographies in firms and regions arising from the seven-sector knowledge flows analysis*

for both spatial and temporal sensitivities to be emphasized at different stages of industry or firm analysis.

A graphical exemplification of some cross-sector 'platform' candidate innovation biographies in firms and regions arising from Work Package 3 are shown in Figure 10.6. Using the methodology presented, many explanatory cases can be found, in both Eurodite-participating regions and others. Interesting examples are: the research carried out in Aquitaine (France), which integrates the wine industry and biotechnology to develop the new field of oenotechnology; the German automotive industry, which is actively engaged in innovative activity with a number of farms and agricultural research institutes in Brandenburg to develop biofuels; in Bornholm and North Jutland, Denmark the agro-food and tourism industries are collaborating on innovatory culinary tourism activities also involving the delineation of food cultures involving anthropological research; innovation research in Midi-Pyrenees, France focuses on specialized tourism-based vehicle guidance systems integrating knowledge from aerospace, automotives and ICT with that from tourism, agro-food and bioscience; in Jura, Switzerland the traditional watch-making industry is being transformed into a tourism asset by formation of agro-food, tourism, ICT, new media and traditional fine-mechanics 'experience economy' networks. Outside the Eurodite regions, we find research conducted in Emilia-Romagna (Italy) in which the food and ICT industries have collaborated to produce biosensors for testing the maturity of Parma ham; in Bavaria, bioscientific knowledge on milk-based lactiobacteria are the subject of research collaborations with the brewing and fermentation industries; and in Hordaland (Bergen), Norway tourism demand to experience aquaculture processes in organic fish farms has led to interactions between the agro-food industry, new media, ICT and knowledge-intensive services to realize a network facility. These results formed the basis for the work later reported in Chapters 11 and 12.

NOTES

1. This is another example of platform technologies as this has been made possible directly because of the advances in computing technology in the areas of grid computing, data mining and automated mapping and sequencing.
2. Because of current and anticipated high oil prices, hybrid fuel and fuel cells are currently topical innovations that have only recently, in the case of the Prius been marketed seriously in competition with standard models. Prius hybridization is of petrol (or diesel) and electrical power. An innovation biography of fuel cells, if they become a feasible alternative to either conventional internal combustion or current hybrid engines, would rest upon aerospace technology, especially rocketry, since that is where hydrogen fuel cells remain technologically supreme as they have since the days of Wernher Von Braun.
3. Defined as qualified people working in R&D in science, engineering and technology in the private sector.

11. Platforms of innovation: some examples

Philip Cooke and Carla De Laurentis

11.1 INTRODUCTION

We have seen from the preceding finely textured case material from key European industrial sectors that there are two main kinds of innovation-linked knowledge flows typically in operation. The first and more traditional of these is broadly intrasectoral, which we here term 'cumulative', while the second is newer and accordingly more interesting, which we here term 'combinatory'. Cumulative knowledge acquisition and application occurs within either lead-firms or their sectoral system. The term 'system' denotes repeated historic interactive relations with, for example, preferred suppliers. Thus even though it is well known that a complex sector such as automotives habitually procures from other sectors such as rubber or glass, such suppliers are likely to exist in a systemic relationship over time with their prime customer(s). Hence, knowledge flows are cumulative and systemic; we are obviously alluding to something akin to that described by Breschi and Malerba (1997) as a 'sectoral innovation system'. The more recently observed combinatory knowledge flows that are engaged in with respect to innovative interactions are extrasectoral, non-systemic and often involve combinations of distinctive, possibly unexpected interactions. These may, for reasons to be discussed, have elements of a more regional innovation system character.

For introductory purposes it is helpful to reflect upon the strong and necessary new knowledge flow networks occasioned in the automotive and agricultural industries by the rise of the twin forces of heightened oil prices on the one hand, and widespread intergovernmental concerns about the contribution that emissions from hydrocarbon-fuelled energy make to greenhouse gas (GHG) production. This is widely seen as a proximate cause of global warming and its correlate, climate change. As is well known, there are numerous candidate solutions to anthropogenic climate change, some of which would enable the continued utilization of hydrocarbon energy inputs provided that this resulted in zero GHG emissions. For the moment, it is easier to envisage this for large-scale energy produced in power stations than small-scale energy produced in petrol- or diesel-fuelled road vehicles. Thus 'clean coal' could be burnt in power stations and carbon emissions, notably CO_2, captured and stored (CCS – carbon capture and storage).

Currently, there are few non-experimental technologies being deployed to achieve full CCS. One that is deployed involves the Norwegian oil firm Statoil, which utilizes CCS in its operations in the North Sea. The process is extremely expensive, and whether or not there might be leakage problems as CO_2 percolates through undersea rock strata is a serious concern warranting constant monitoring. The reason that Statoil leads in this technology is regulatory, in that the Norwegian government threatened GHG emitters in the oil industry with a punitive climate change taxation regime. Statoil was thus incentivized to innovate its CCS application. That it might prove to be a profitable technology to market or license in future was a minor consideration.

CCS in cars is far off the innovation radar compared to other solutions that are essentially post-hydrocarbon in nature. Currently, biofuels are seen as a worthwhile technological response to the imperative to reduce GHG emissions substantially. This is, of course, why the research associations and specific producers of large-scale feedstocks for the production of bioethanol and biodiesel are engaging in detailed programmatic discussions regarding the implications for vehicle engines of greater usage of biofuels and, contrariwise, the implications for growers of the fact that conventional bioethanol is less calorific by measurement unit than conventional petrol. Thus, as noted, one negative by-product of bioethanol is that it erodes the sealants in modern engines more rapidly than hydrocarbon fuels. Second-generation biofuels, which would be converted to biogas, have other, more thoroughgoing engineering implications for combustion engines, which would have to be redesigned accordingly. The most likely solution, for the present, involves biofuels growing as a contributor to 'green energy' produced in large-scale power stations that supply electricity to power electric – or, more foreseeably – hybrid petrol and electrically powered vehicles. At this point, knowledge flows between vehicle producers and energy companies, especially energy storage companies, may be envisaged as rising up corporate innovation agendas. As, to a comparable extent and perhaps over a longer period, have risen the conversations among vehicle producers and designers of hydrogen fuel cells, as yet also a remote vehicular energy source but in time probably a viable one.

These extrasectoral conversations among hitherto rather unlikely industrial bedfellows signify a significant shift in production and consumption priorities. They further signify considerable uncertainty regarding what currently counts as valid and viable knowledge for innovation across a wide swathe of industries. Such uncertainties are consistent with a major shift in what sustainable development refers to nowadays. It is no longer adequate to focus only upon a narrow technological paradigm within an industrial landscape that has been hydrocarbon-dependent since the dawning of the Industrial Revolution more than 200 years ago. On the contrary, required now is a socio-technical perspective shift on the landscape itself: in this case co-evolution from a hydrocarbon to a post-hydrocarbon energy base across the socio-cultural, politico-economic and technological systems together. These new knowledge interactions exemplify the kind of experimentation to utilize evolved variety in production and consumption consistent with meta-regime change. Such platform interactions were foreshadowed in many accounts in the preceding chapters. They add up to one kind of transition – towards a knowledge economy – that overlaps with a greater one *in potentio* which is the transition from hydrocarbons dependence to a post-hydrocarbon landscape. The notion of 'platform' with its broader, more flexible, less determinedly sectoral system-focused character captures elements of this change in the 'framing' of innovative challenges and opportunities along with the knowledge flows and interactions such 'reframing' implies.

11.2   WHAT IS A PLATFORM AND HOW DOES IT DIFFER FROM A CLUSTER OR SECTOR?

A platform, in the sense utilized in this book, consists of a number of businesses and quite possibly knowledge or training and support services, agencies and firms that cross typical sectoral and even cluster boundaries. Comparable to clusters but not to the same extent sectors, there is spatial contiguity in the notion of platform. At this stage of the exposition it is convenient to say that, by and large, a cluster is a form of industry organization, usually composed of small and medium-sized enterprises (SMEs) and relevant private and non-private support agencies co-located in the geographic proximity of a locality. A locality might be a quarter of a city or a whole town. Traditionally, many Victorian industrial districts, of which clusters are the modern variant, were single-industry towns, like the spinning and weaving towns of Northern England, including a place like Macclesfield which was a single-industry silk manufacturing locality, or in the Midlands, Kidderminster which was, and retains aspects of its history as, a carpet manufacturing town. In Wales, Llanelli's nickname was 'Tinopolis' because it specialized in and dominated the UK tinplate market in cooking ware and food canning. Nearby, many small towns also specialized in tinplate production involving tinning, rolling and cutting, much of the workforce being female. This disappeared in the 1950s after nationalization which concentrated production in two large integrated tinplate works, only one of which survives in the area. As one thinks about this specialization phenomenon, it is recalled that Leicester was a hosiery town, Northampton a shoe manufacturing town, and Nottingham was known for its lace-making. Inside cities, Clerkenwell was once London's clock-making quarter, Birmingham sported a gun-making and a still-extant jewellery quarter while, elsewhere in Europe, Leipzig boasted a large *graphisches viertel*, literally a publishing quarter, that nowadays houses a media cluster (Bathelt, 2002).

Modern clusters have certain features in common with industrial districts but also many differences. Taking 'Tinopolis' as a case in point, there were not many 'technology transfer' or 'knowledge transfer' centres, there was no venture capital, there was no university (and still isn't). There were banks, ports, railways and by 1873 the Independent Tinplate Makers Association, a prefigurative trade union. By 1939 the Llanelli Associated Tinplate Companies represented the amalgamation of five remaining firms from a peak in the town of at least ten in 1872. Such was the town's and wider district's specialization in this product that it demonstrated acute vulnerability to economic downturns and institutional change. (Rees and Rees, 2004). Elsewhere it has been noted that the British industrial districts were unlike those still extant in, for example, Italy. The former were often conflictual, unionized to protect workers from steep wage cuts, and run indirectly as 'company towns' by the various owners, influential as these were through their agents in municipal government. They were not especially sociable and firms were throat-cuttingly competitive and relatively non-innovative as the districts matured. In Italy much of the literature points to a relatively high social capital, moderately benign industrial relations, and what Christensen (1997) terms a tradition of 'sustaining' innovation; that is, a practice of moving upmarket towards expensive, even luxury products, to escape cheaper imitators from abroad. This sustains the districts when many observers would predict their inevitable demise. Modern clusters have elements of Britain's Marshallian competitiveness but also of high 'associativeness', as in California, as described by Saxenian (1994) who stresses the networking advantage displayed in Silicon Valley, rooted also in a certain 'counter-culture' that eschewed prevailing corporate cultures practised by the likes of RCA and IBM (Sturgeon, 2000).

By referencing California and, specifically, its northern region in which Silicon Valley lies, we move closer to an exemplification of the 'platform' idea that illustrates the concept neatly. It is well known that the area of Central Valley land on which Silicon Valley's industrial complex now resides was once horticultural land, specifically plum orchards and other fruit production. This was an inheritance from the original opening-up of California with the coming of the rail system. Schumpeter (1975), the architect of innovation studies, called this process, rather cumbersomely, 'railroadization'. However, he also considered it one of the purest types of radical innovation known to mankind. This was because a kind of innovation chain-reaction occurred when what in historic times was itself a relatively recent innovation, namely an integrated railway system, penetrated new lands. It released cascades of other innovations.

Thus, as Guthman (2005) and many others make clear, California's Central Valley may have been the first place in the world to move from Native American semi-wilderness, large ranches and mission-subsistence agriculture to advanced industrialized agri-business without an intervening period of family farming. The Central San Joaquin and Sacramento river valleys were, in any case, exceedingly fertile and their scale and the level of agro-food industrialization then prevailing in the US meant that large producers could move into scale production that was easily shipped out to the eastern markets for the kind of horticulture that the climate, in association with irrigation, could support. In most guides to Californian agriculture, there are scarcely any cash crops that cannot be successfully grown there. Amongst the other Schumpeterian innovations spawned by 'railroadization' were the 'futures' markets that still, as the 2008 'credit crunch' demonstrated, continue to be regulated by the US Department of Agriculture even though their more sophisticated, and in many cases, toxic descendants in the form of collateralized debt obligations (CDOs) and related instruments brought the global financial markets too close to the abyss for comfort, mystifying their perpetrators, customers and regulators in the process (Tett, 2009). Flatpack farm buildings, furniture and equipment kits were ordered through the innovation of the sales catalogues such as Sears & Roebuck's and delivered by rail to persons new to farming in many cases, and for whom farming manuals had been produced by the railway firms. Cement grain silos were later perceived as the apotheosis of modernity and influenced modernist architecture emanating from centres such as Dessau, Germany's Bauhaus.

For industrial-scale agriculture of this kind to be sustained demanded increasing applications of chemical fertilizer that were associated with the rise of the hydrocarbon economy that also fuelled the railway trains connecting California to global markets. In parallel emerged the industrialized modes of pest, weed and fungal control known more familiarly by their Latinized names as pesticides, herbicides and fungicides. It is sometimes, in official statistics, asserted that agriculture is a 'low-tech' kind of economic activity. However, a moment's thought reveals it to continue to be an almost wholly science and technology-saturated business, from the aforementioned chemical concoctions applied to soil, plants and animals, to the monstrous and sophisticated agrarian sowing, nurturing and harvesting machinery that together locked in the agri-businesses to a high-debt regime. Organic farming, as it would now be called, was surpassed by the mechanized, chemicalized and financialized regime that outstripped it with vastly higher productivity everywhere that such agro-food platforms were established. When, to the production side, was added the similarly more productive consumption side in the form of the supermarket, and later, the out-of-town hypermarket reachable largely by private motor transport, fuelled also by hydrocarbons, what some refer to as the modern and prevailing hydrocarbon 'socio-technical landscape' (Kemp et al., 1998; Geels, 2006) had become socially and psychologically paradigmatic in the West.

11.3   THEORETICAL STEPS TOWARDS PLATFORM PROCESS AND POST-CUMULATIVE KNOWLEDGE FLOWS POLICY

The foregoing strongly suggests a flight of conceptual steps denoted by an imputed transition within recent capitalism from the industrial to the knowledge era. The main features of this (explored more deeply in Chapter 12) are the following. First and foremost, the contemporary corporation cannot simply function as a hierarchical command-and-control structure. Those that sought to remain that way became victims of their own short-sightedness, managerial panic reactions, and subsequent corporate folly. Good examples that come to mind here are the British trio, Imperial Chemical Industries (ICI), the General Electric Company (GEC) and the Rover car company. Each represents an almost exquisite variant on the three themes listed, which we here abbreviate to myopia, panic and folly (MPF).

One way of further characterizing the evolution of these three stages is in terms of the Kübler-Ross (1969) model of responding to grief. Although the latter is more suited to individuals confronted with loss, it offers certain insights into the first two stages of the more corporate MPF model of resignation to failure. This is because corporations, far more than individuals, should – in practice, but not always in reality – 'live in the future' (Drucker, 1999). Strategy, leadership and vision are each taken as shibboleths of the 'living strategy' of firms in a way that has yet to become embedded in the typical individual's psyche (de Geus, 1998). Individuals must perforce respond to the vagaries of existence and these, by definition, are ill-defined and unpredictable. Corporations have considerable leverage on the future, since it is they who largely make it, at least in terms of civilian consumption and production. They stake their existence on calculating risk from pre-learning that allows them the possibility of preprogramming their perceived need to embrace change. But, as the 2008–09 global financial crisis revealed to the horror of all but a few heretic academics and other observers, it is not always easy to walk the 'living strategy' talk.

11.3.1 Grief-Modelling: The Kübler-Ross Approach

Although created to envisage the individual confrontation with the death of a loved one, it is relevant to psychological responses to less serious traumas than death and bereavement, such as work redundancy, enforced relocation, crime and punishment, disability and injury, relationship break-up, serious financial indebtedness and bankruptcy. It is by now relatively well known that Kübler-Ross's (1969) five elements in the cycle of an individual's likely confrontation with a reason for grief are the following. First, and famously, denial, the conscious or unconscious refusal to accept facts, information, reality or presence of the grief-inducing event. 'Being in denial' is a term routinely used of, for example, politicians confronted with a significant and unpalatable truth, like major policy-failure and loss of an election; or investment bankers similarly afflicted with swathes of red on their share-price screens. Psychologically, it is understood as a natural though by no means universal first-up defence mechanism. Some deniers can become locked in to this first stage when dealing with a traumatic change that can be ignored, for example climate change.

After denial, the second emotional response to grief-inducing news is anger. This response can take a number of forms. Individuals can be angry with themselves, feeling with hindsight perhaps that they could have done more to prevent the upset. Or, more likely, anger may be directed both inwardly and outwardly or in extreme cases purely outwardly at others, especially those close to the individual. An instance of a concatenation of externalized denial and anger from three corporate colleagues is captured in the following report of the fate of Richard Fuld, former head of failed investment bank Lehman Bros, as reported by Swaine (2008). Mr Fuld was attacked on a Sunday, shortly after it was announced that the banking giant was bankrupt. A senior Lehman Bros source reported that:

> He went to the gym after . . . Lehman was announced as going under. He was on a treadmill with a heart monitor on. Someone was in the corner, pumping iron and he walked over and he knocked him out cold. And frankly after having watched Mr Fuld's testimony to the US House Oversight Committee, I'd have

done the same too. I thought he was shameless . . . I thought it was appalling.
He blamed everyone . . . He blamed everybody but himself.

Following anger, according to Kübler-Ross, comes bargaining. That
is, the sufferer of a break-up with a loved one may, following denial and
anger, inquire whether the parties might in future 'still remain friends'.
Or a terminated employee might seek re-employment at a lower grade;
while the grief-stricken losing politician asks his or her colleagues to 'just
give me one more chance'. This stratagem is generally understood not to
work in the long run, given the tougher but often preferred alternative of
partners, colleagues or employers ensuring 'a clean break with the past'.
Once again, the global financial crisis offered numerous examples of denial
followed by anger then bargaining as, for example, reported by Stewart
(2009): 'Sir Fred Goodwin, former head of newly part-nationalized British
bank RBS, told MPs that he should not be blamed for the banking crisis
that could cost millions of Brits their jobs.' The failed chief executive
angrily insisted: 'It's just too simple if you want to blame it all on me.' His
denial was the low point of a bizarre performance from four axed bank
chiefs carpeted by the House of Commons Treasury Committee. They all
delivered carefully scripted and rehearsed apologies over the credit crunch
disaster. But then, in nearly four hours of hostile exchanges, they insisted
that it was not really their fault. Furious MPs accused them of being 'in
denial' over the horrific consequences of their mistakes. UK Financial
Investments, a branch of the Treasury which manages taxpayers' stakes in
banks, said: 'UKFI have been vigorously pursuing with the new chairman
whether there is any scope for clawing back some or all of this pension'. In
June 2009 RBS announced that its former chief executive would volunteer
a 'substantial reduction' to his lucrative pension at age 50 to £342 500, a 38
per cent cut from an anticipated £555 000 per year.

The penultimate stage in the Kübler-Ross cycle is depression, when the
beginnings of acceptance of the reality of the negative event are registered.
For most, this will ultimately reach a point where the depression recedes
and something akin to normal life may be resumed. However, at the
extreme a different outcome may prevail. Hence, for at least seven senior
bankers or industrialists the recent credit freeze was associated with crisis-
induced depression that could not be withstood:

A multi-millionaire City banker shot himself in the head after leaving his job at
a bank which was at the centre of a disastrous takeover by the Royal Bank of
Scotland. The inquest was also told that in March Mr Boumeester went missing
for a number of hours after driving from his London home to woodland near
Ascot. A note found by police on his body said he could not 'go on any longer'
and blamed an 'immeasurable depth of depression'. He had been on the board

of the Dutch banking group ABN Amro and a number of other City firms. In 2007 the financier was said to have picked up a €1 million bonus. But his bank was the subject of the disastrous £50 billion takeover by the Royal Bank of Scotland that plunged RBS and its then chief executive Sir Fred Goodwin into crisis. (Smith, 2009)

Acceptance is the final stage in the Kübler-Ross cycle. It is widely perceived to be the point at which 'change management' of the kind discussed in business schools and texts actually occurs. We have seen that using a personalized model for institutional analysis is questionable. Nevertheless, in the Kübler-Ross model this is the point at which the victim moves back up the curve to acknowledgement and resolve recognizing that the old life is over and there is need to take steps towards beginning a new life. The opportunity to reflect and take stock of career and future options is taken. Finally, the acceptance of change and the evolution of a new life occurs. This may, with or without professional advice, lead to the setting of goals and integration of changes into the new trajectory. A good example of acceptance and 'moving on' is given in the following: 'New jobs for former executives of failed banks is a touchy subject. Andy Hornby, the former HBOS chief, became chief executive of Alliance Boots this summer without a fuss' (Osborne, 2009). However, the news that Adam Applegarth, former chief executive of Northern Rock had moved on was seen as 'outrageous' after it emerged that he has got a new job advising private equity firm Apollo on buying bad loans. The notion that Mr Applegarth could profit from his experience at the bank drew an angry response from Vince Cable, the Liberal Democrat Treasury spokesman. 'This is a guy who has destroyed his bank, left his shareholders without a penny, lost employees their jobs and left the taxpayer high and dry,' he said. 'Now he's popped up making money by advising someone else on the bad loans he helped create. It's quite outrageous. You couldn't make it up.' Mr Cable questioned the judgment of both Mr Applegarth and Apollo, but conceded: 'It's an ethical issue rather than a legal one.'

11.3.2 Corporate Change Modelling: Kotter

It is clear from the above that it is a simple matter to find telling case-material in support of the Kübler-Ross personalized change management model. However, it is also a simple matter to undermine its apparent certainties. This is without elaborating on variants that uncritically identify nine or more steps in the cycle (the Fisher transition curve) or, as with Kotter (1996), an eight-stage corporate change management recipe as follows. Said to translate the best of change management theories into practice, the steps involve the following:

1. Establish a sense of urgency.
2. Form a powerful guiding coalition.
3. Create a clear vision.
4. Communicate the vision.
5. Empower others to act on the vision.
6. Plan and create short-term wins.
7. Consolidate improvements and produce still more change.
8. Institutionalize new approaches.

These steps are said to be based on a solid foundation of communication, empowerment and focus. Once the change has been made, it is important to embed the new approaches, so that people do not slip into old habits. Monitoring, feedback and intervention are necessary for a sufficient period after the change has occurred. They clearly begin to move us away from the personalized to the institutionalized crisis management context, though by no means entirely. Hence, only steps 2, 5 and 8 unambiguously avoid pure personalization.

So what is the problem with Kübler-Ross, Kotter and others? First, despite the ease with which case-support can be mobilized, they are normative not empirical confections. Second, what is the problem with that? There is no way of knowing whether the cases are simply special cases, or representative of the population of change-facing events as a whole. Third, this lack of clear testing of the propositions embedded in the recipes undermines their value as guides to action. Fourth, it seems a priori unlikely that everyone would go through precisely such a five-step cycle of behaviour. For the Kübler-Ross framework, denial is, conceivably, rare and acceptance much more common. This is because many such grief-inducing events are, even if unwelcome, half-anticipated. In personal terms, hospitalization and poor prognosis may play a part in this: in the corporate world sliding share prices have historically been known to invoke actions in response even though many have undoubtedly failed. Instead of depression, it may be that relief is a psychologically more typical condition if there has been great struggle against negative outcomes. Imagine the demise of the cerebral palsy invalid, with effectively no normal interpersonal communication capabilities and the medical expectation of no positive change and a short life-expectancy. Numerous other situations can be imagined where 'a blessed relief' might equally be the response. Anger, too, might be psychologically misplaced at such a point.

What these recipes amount to is, in each case, a discourse giving labels to possible but by no means universal responses. Thus, grievers now are said to – frequently by themselves – 'seek closure', whereas such a notion was unheard of in that context until relatively recently. The etymology is slightly bewildering, the term having been first introduced by Wertheimer

(1923) in describing the perceptual trick by which humans fill in gaps to make a (*Gestalt*) whole image. Its progenitor was the anthropological idea of 'rite of passage' within 'ritual' (Van Gennep, 1909), later becoming 'retrospective completeness' (Grainger, 1974). In psychology it has the sense of 'debriefing' (Zinser, 1984). It then seems to have diffused into common language through the medium of 'counselling' and even 'social work' (Wilson et al., 2007), where it is seen as equivalent to saying 'goodbye'. This gives the hint that its rise coincides with the increased secularization of advanced societies and the perceived need to mark important events, even though religious institutions are seen to be less relevant in providing this than they once were. In the context of personal transition, even less than that of corporate change management, it is of course a largely meaningless notion in that sense that, on the one hand, the object of grief can never fully or even partly be erased from memory, while on the other hand, there is hardly likely to be a point in time when a 'tipping point' resulting in 'closure' can be safely identified, let alone measured.

So let us finally deconstruct the transliteration of Kübler-Ross into Kotter-type change management literature before returning to the undoubtedly simpler MPF perspective, non-normative and intended to be testable as it is. Let us look briefly at each step in turn. First, 'establish a sense of urgency', which is much like the onset of what elsewhere is called 'crisis management'. It is unclear who is responsible, self-selected or handed the hot potato in this injunction or how. This is underlined by the next step in which it is recommended to 'form a powerful guiding coalition' or crisis management team to create a vision of where to go and to tell others to follow ('communicate the vision'). What is wrong with this? The answer was articulated by former Shell planning chief Arie de Geus (1998) who showed decision-making under induced or real crisis conditions to be among the worst. Three reasons were advanced: time is too short for reflexivity; options for action are too constrained; and accordingly, the likelihood of non-imposed consensus is low. Hence all the other steps are vitiated by the earlier ones.

'Empower *others* to act on the vision' (emphasis added) that is, tell somebody else to get the dirty work done. 'Plan and create short-term wins' – somewhat late in the day, one might have thought; and once again who, in constrained circumstances and timeframes, can plan anything rationally? 'Consolidate improvements and produce still more change' means valuable thinking time has to be redirected to yet more re-engineering and associated uncertainty for an already harassed array of 'others'. Finally, it is advocated to 'institutionalize new approaches' – namely dismantle the pre-existing cognitive frames of all relevant actors, retrain or replace them, and learn, adapt or copy 'approaches' that are hypothetically or actually judged pervasively better frames. But on what basis can such judgements be based? It is unlikely that in the midst of this maelstrom a scientific study of a representative sample of good practice businesses will be performed. Hence 'new approaches' have to be invented in double-quick time. When required swiftly this makes it likely that 'sample of one' models are adapted or adopted. This is more likely if consultants have to be brought in. Given Kotter's predelictions for advising corporations, the likelihood is that the harassed and chastened management will opt for the latter. As O'Shea and Madigan (1997) demonstrate in vivid detail, this can have fatal effects for the corporate client of the consultant's wiles.

We may draw the interim conclusion from this important discussion about change management at the individual and corporate levels that both are largely exercises in 'the blind leading the blind'. From the perspective of this book, such approaches are weak because they do not recognize the importance of understanding change as evolutionary. Rather, it is presented as punctual, critical and urgent – a disturbance to the normal calm equilibrium in which economic relations are ideologized to persist normally. This is an inevitable element in the 'groupthink' that arises when even leading exponents of economic science come to believe the fundamental elements of their political perspective, rather than recognizing them as a possible but by no means demonstrable image of reality. Pushed to its extreme this became politically hegemonic in two recent periods of Western history. The first was the Reagan–Thatcher era in the US and UK (1980–90), when niche apologists for so-called 'efficient markets' began to gain purchase over governments and their electorates. The second was the period of the Bush administration in the US which can be characterized as 'neoliberal' and which pushed Reaganomics beyond their questionably rational limits in the 2000–2008 period. This culminated in globally massive destruction of value in the financial as well as the 'real' economy, bankruptcies of banks on a heroic scale, bankruptcies of small economies like Iceland, and the nationalization or part-nationalization – called after Galbraith (1955) 'socialism for the rich' – of major investing and lending banks in the US and worldwide.

11.3.3   Some Critical Comments

Clearly, Kotter's model buys into this perspective entirely. By contrast, an evolutionary approach allows for processes of learning, cooperation and innovation of an interactive, not purely competitive, style to be available as concepts for analysing reality. It starts with the presumption not that economic equilibrium is the norm but that various levels of disequilibrium are more accurately understood as punctuated by periods of relative economic stability. The evolutionary approach pays attention to articulation of discourse, the manner in which knowledge spillovers may assist company intelligence functions, and the importance of facilitating refinements in absorptive capacity. The 'change management' approach after Kotter looks entirely alien to this perspective, profoundly asocial and indeed militaristic in its hierarchical 'follow me' and 'tell others what to do' method of crisis management. Learning, another core concept in more evolutionary theories of the living corporation (de Geus, 1998) is clearly absent but replaced *in extremis* by calling in the consultants to do their duties. Trust seems at an absolute minimum, replaced by a kind of 'brute force' enforcement of norms, and particularly new norms, emanating from on high. Above all, the Kotter schema is closed-loop and closed-system in conception. Interaction is reduced to command and control, adjustment is largely through enforced ratiocination, 'not invented here' is a pronounced subtext, except for the resort to consult-ants who will be likely not to rock the boat and manipulate findings to suit the prejudices of the power-holders. The ideas of 'open innovation' (after Chesbrough, 2003) let alone user–producer learning interactions regarding organizational or process innovation (after Lundvall, 1988), or even 'open source' (after Raymond, 2001), are clearly remote from this particular discourse.

It is, in other words, the apotheosis of the kind of closed-mind, closed-system, closed-to-outsiders mentalities that accompanied the rise of the modern corporation as harbinger of the Industrial Age. As we show in many of the results of the research reported in preceding chapters, further updates of some of which are presented later in this chapter, this is a dying discourse, increasingly becoming internally and externally disarticulated and unappealing to those who practice or analyse business anthropology from a more evolutionary perspective. This is interested not so much in 'living strategy', a synonym for 'survival strategy', as we have seen, but the idea of economies as ecosystems in which niches are found that interact with and learn from actors in other niches on whom both types of actor may be in variable ways interdependent. This begins to open up a notion of 'platform' or 'articulated' business and non-business actors linked by willingness and interest to engage in collective learning. This is refined as lateral absorptive capacity (among industry branches), possibly co-located to some extent, to access the external economies, including knowledge spillovers, from geographical propinquity but open to distant network relations with other firms in other continents. Distributed knowledge flows, their identification and capture characterize this socio-technical learning system in which alert firms routinely thrive and survive even the biggest global shocks. Noticeable in the 2008–09 global financial crisis was the resilience of manufacturing and some service firms that had adopted the long-articulated academic injunction to structure their internal labour markets according to functional and numerical flexibility. Not cognate with the privileged 'core' and an 'exploited' peripheral labour market segments of yore, this compensated 'agency' workers for their relative vulnerability while allowing management to adjust to what in manufacturing turned out to be a shallower recession and a swifter recovery than expected, boosted in some instances by regulatory innovations such as automotive 'scrappage' schemes.

In Tett's (2009) account of the origins and catastrophic culmination of the 'credit crunch' she shows one of the leading innovator banks to have been J.P. Morgan. This company was responsible for introducing collateralized debt obligations (CDOs) to the market. Not only was J.P. Morgan relatively unaffected by the negative consequences of unregulated packaging and over-the-counter sale of CDOs, the financial vehicle largely responsible for the 2008–09 global financial crisis when applied to US sub-prime mortgages, but it also came through the resulting crisis significantly stronger. Tett shows this was not unconnected to the following managerial culture at the bank:

> [innovation head] Peter Hancock pushed his experimentation to unusual extremes. He hired a social anthropologist to study the corporate dynamics of the bank. He conducted firm-wide polls to ascertain which employees interacted most effectively with those from other departments, and he used the data as a benchmark for assessing employee compensation . . . He was convinced that departments needed to interact closely with each other . . . silos (or fragmented departments), he believed, were lethal. (Tett, 2009: 7–8)

Before winding up this part of the chapter's theoretical reflections upon 'paradigm erosion' in the normative frames of a passing generation of psychologists and business gurus, it behoves this author to say why the much simpler MPF is more realistic than either. The first contextual reason, it will be recalled, is that it is non-normative but rather observational. To be sure, the necessary detailed research of even a sample of large, failing or struggling firms cannot be essayed for chapter sections such as these, although in the research that is reported in this book there is plenty of evidence that combinative knowledge-utilizing firms are anticipators with good absorptive capacity and early adopters of external knowledge from elsewhere. A few of these cases are offered in the brief updates of some of the earlier sectoral chapters presented later in this chapter and in the next. Recall that the main chapters report research that yielded up evidence that sectors were eroding, even conceptually, although they had never meant as much to firms as policy-makers and, particularly, statisticians. The sketches below report cases where platform thinking about distributed knowledge has proceeded furthest and describes how this came about.

11.4 MYOPIA, PANIC AND FOLLY: SOME ILLUSTRATIONS

To return, first, to the observation that firms that get into trouble are myopic in the first place, we have to unpack the meaning of 'myopic' in this business and knowledge flows-relevant context. Myopia is, medically, an eyesight abnormality resulting in blurred distant vision. Short-sightedness is the non-medical term denoting the problem in both business leaders and other humans. Lack of focus is one characteristic of myopia, closure – from the Greek root of 'myopia' in the word *muein* – is, ironically, another; while in a non-medical sense it denotes lack of discernment or long-range perspective in thinking or planning. The last term, 'planning', became anathema to neoliberal ideology, welded as it is to the idea of efficient, if not perfect, markets. Similarly it also became virtually unsayable for post-Soviet policy-makers and firms in Central and Eastern Europe and, by extension, the West. What replaced it, even in governments? The new public management of contracting out to private consultants was one development. A consequence of this was loss of 'institutional memory' in organizations. Paraphrasing Marx, functionaries had to learn history as tragedy first time round and as farce the second.

Nowhere was this sentiment more articulated than in relation to banks in the midst of the global financial crisis. There is even a research hypothesis on this:

> The institutional memory hypothesis is driven by deterioration in the ability of loan officers over the bank's lending cycle that results in an easing of credit standards. This easing of standards may be compounded by simultaneous deterioration in the capacity of bank management to discipline its loan officers and reduction in the capacities of external stakeholders to discipline bank management. (Berger and Udell, 2003).

Contracted to the Bank for International Settlements, these authors were prophetic indeed of the worst global financial crisis to occur since the Great Depression. More particularly, they showed the absence of adequate buffers in the form of reserves held by banks against just such recessionary times to be one of the key syndromes of the times. Finding strong support for the institutional memory loss hypothesis, involving 2 202 000 transaction observations, their conclusion was that the prevailing state of affairs was unprecedented in modern times, and warranted countercyclicality initiatives by regulators, 'anti-herding' psychological training, and a broader knowledge base than that which prevailed on the part of junior officers. Accordingly, it is clear that Berger and Udell (2003) were themselves far from myopic – almost prescient – on economic analysis but, working for a bank, were effectively 'crying in the wilderness' of myopia in the wider community they sought to address.

A different kind of myopia that afflicts business involving heavily mathematically intensive activities, contributing further to the 'herd-like' context that Berger and Udell (2003) warned against, is captured in the analysis below by a leading economics commentator (O'Grady, 2009). Econometrics came in for a significant amount of criticism in explaining how the work of the so-called 'rocket scientists' (mathematical bankers) aided the detachment from reality of financial modelling and analysis, which tends to treat the real world as just a special case of many imaginable economic worlds. This is not the place to enter into a defence of mathematical economics any more than it is to defend mathematical engineering or biology. It is dangerous, or in the sense meant here, myopic usage of an unreflective kind that is to be guarded against, particularly outside the laboratory where savings and investments may be atomized, jobs may be decimated and those ultimately responsible may commit suicide. In yet another illustration taken from the world of knowledge-intensive business services (KIBS), of which investment banking is a progenitor, innocent but disastrous practice is highlighted:

> the mathematisation of economics fed through to finance and banking, and gave us the models that generated disastrous investment 'strategies' and misunderstood risk. Notoriously, the chief financial officer of Goldman Sachs, David Viniar, said during the financial crisis in the autumn of 2008 that 'we are seeing things that were 25 standard deviation moves several days in a row'. Or something that could happen once every 13.7 billion or so years – roughly the estimated age of the universe. In other words the market meltdown couldn't happen, though it evidently did. (O'Grady, 2009)

This is the kind of myopia classically associated with a lack of discernment or long-range perspective in thinking or planning combined with a blurring of model predictions and reality. Inevitably, among banking officers displaying closure to that extent, herding and groupthink require especially sensitive correction based on careful in-house training and a high degree of job rotation. The evolutionary virtues of search, selection, learning, interaction, valuation of variety and trust among others are scientific concepts just as 'rational economic man', 'consumer preference' and 'efficient markets' are meant to be treated. The ultimate problem is that neoliberal ideology rests upon neoclassical economics, which itself is designed to dehumanize its object – understanding economic behaviour – so that mechanical predictive models of the Newtonian kind can, in theory, be made to work. The absence of equivalent-status evolutionary modelling techniques merely reinforces this bias.

It is unclear whether Viniar's reaction constitutes panic in itself. But persons and businesses confronted with a failure of the cornerstone models that they relied upon synchronized with massive declines in the value of billions of dollars or euros in stock market valuations in the 'real world', were highly likely to experience panic. What is panic and how is it not catered for in the Kübler-Ross thesis or, for business, the Kotter recipe, which seems designed to cancel out panic with fairly mindless 'leadership' of the kind that amounts to inveigling others to do something? 'Panic on Wall Street' is a not uncommon newspaper headline in the recent and more distant past. So what is 'panic'?

In general, it is a sudden, overpowering terror, often affecting many people at once. From French *panique*, terrified, in turn from Greek *panikos*, 'of Pan' – it is a source of terror, as in flocks or herds. It is an emotion experienced in anticipation of some specific pain or danger, usually accompanied by a desire to flee or fight. In the financial sphere, it is widespread and significant fear that the market or economy is going to collapse. A panic leads to massive bank deposit withdrawals and possible banking collapses, as well as falling stock prices. Panics occurred at the height of the Great Depression in the US when bank depositors by the hundreds descended on their banks to withdraw their deposits for fear that the banks would fail and they would lose all of their money. A panic is usually a relatively short-lived phenomenon, in contrast to a recession or depression, which lasts six months to several years. It is in this sense characteristically a moment of 'punctual evolution', after Schumpeter (1975), and the precise expression of economic transition brought about by the Schumpeterian 'gales of creative destruction'. In other words, to an evolutionist, disasters, even species-death, are normal – more than 100 plant species alone became extinct globally in the twentieth century.

The question for economic policy concerns whether or not it will advise regulation that makes downturns or the malign effects of the business cycle significantly less socially disruptive, advise on the kinds of training bankers and other investors require to be professionally certified, and generate a learning propensity that encompasses a capability to learn responsibly to 'live in the future'. To do so would be to constrain 'efficient markets', outlaw reckless technical practices and undermine the neoliberal or 'Washington Consensus' (Capra, 2003).

This – more or less, and with varying success – has been done historically in many professions, notably medicine – arguably far more complex than banking or even manufacturing. Of fundamental importance to achieving this to the best standards found today is the Cinderella-like practice of testing. To repeat, this is the undervalued and seldom social-scientifically researched aspect of transforming raw scientific or techno-logical knowledge into products that mitigate extremely complex diseases, denoted by examination, testing and trialling of innovative new treat-ments or instrumentation. Not only is this mandatory in pharmaceutical medicine, but it has also gradually become more and more so in relatively mundane industries like automotive manufacturing. Often the instruments for the production of better, safer products and processes are improving standards imposed by national and, increasingly, international standard-setting organizations. Possibly testing and trialling was one of the most important, although unheralded, achievements of the Industrial Age. It may not offer protection from the complete folly that corporations can display where often they have proved myopic and panicky, but it offers some protection even there, though the consumer rather than the producer directly was traditionally meant to be the ultimate beneficiary. However, in KIBS, and especially the large part of it in banking and investment that have been much in focus here, there has been effectively no testing and trialling of anything prior to its release on the market. This is a problem of the non-manufacturing knowledge economy, notably in financial but also in other private services that do not have the manufacturing equivalents of even the ISO 9000 or ISO 14000 quality and environmental standards. This is an over arching folly of large parts of the contemporary knowledge economy. However, it is not true of much of modern manufacturing, from aerospace to the food industry to pharmaceuticals.

So folly follows panic and myopia with almost law-like determinacy. Mention was made earlier of the transformation of once giant UK busi-nesses like ICI, GEC and Rover into insignificance as barely extant subsid-iaries of the Dutch Akzo-Nobel, Swedish Ericsson and Chinese Shanghai Motor Company. How to characterize these failures? Each fits a different folly stereotype. First is ICI, which was formed in 1926 from the merger of four UK chemical companies. It coined the name 'plastic' and was behind the discovery of polythene and Perspex. Managerial incapabilities led to the divestiture of the key divisions except household paints. Then in the summer of 2007 the finishing touches were made to a deal that gave Akzo a 15 per cent share of the world paint market. That ICI Paints was the last vestige of one of the world's great chemicals firms is testimony to its rapid demise in the 1990s. Swedish partner firm Astra made a joint venture with ICI's pharma division, subsequently renamed Zeneca; Swiss firm Novartis also divested its agro-chemicals division to join ICI's as Syngenta; while the heavy chemicals and petrochemicals division was hived off to become

Avecia of Grangemouth, Scotland. A sister plant at Billingham, England became an animal protein plant making Pruteen in partnership with Rank Hovis MacDougall by late 2009. The 'folly' of divestiture is that ICI could probably have continued had management not been so myopic about the future shape of its global chemicals industry. Panic set in, and by the 1990s, the firm had been broken up. But at least something survives, albeit an experimental joint venture in animal food.

A more egregious case of myopia and panic followed by folly can hardly be imagined than the case of another former UK giant, the General Electric Company (GEC), now reduced to minor subsidiary status, which in effect means something close to obliteration. This firm grew following a merger between it and Radio & Allied Industries in 1963, becoming a 'national champion' in the 1960s era of state intervention through sector-based industrial policy. Its subsequent business model was based on that of Germany's Siemens, itself somewhat reminiscent of some features of Asian holding companies (*chaebol* in South Korea; *zaibatsu*, later *keiretsu*, in Japan). The central ideas were multiple divisions and an internal financing system. Thus GEC was involved in domestic electrical engineering, telecommunications, medical electronics, defence electronics and electronic devices. It was scarcely a leading innovator, and when it did innovate its products were outperformed by nimbler opponents, notably Ericsson of Sweden regarding the new, digital telecommunication exchange systems of which System X was GEC's offering. Merger and acquisition activity hid a stagnating business performance, keeping the stock price up. Eventually, the architect of this model, Baron Arnold Weinstock, retired having seen GEC turnover rise from £100 million in 1960 to £11 billion by 1996. Thereafter, the conservatism of the preceding 40 years, which had often been criticized in the financial press, caused the new management team, led by George Simpson (Baron Simpson of Dunkeld) and chief executive officer (CEO) John Mayo, to seek a corporate transformation. Simpson had previously been CEO of Rover and Lucas, automotive firms that were similarly carved up and sold off into present-day oblivion. GEC's cash pile was raided as it was transformed into a telecommunications firm, renamed Marconi. When he left the company in 2001 the share price had fallen from a peak of £13 to 2.2p.

'I am not bitter about the things that have been said about me, it goes with the patch', Lord Simpson said:

> Sure with hindsight we made mistakes but, tell me, did anyone else foresee what would happen to the world's telecom industry? It wasn't the Marconi management that propelled the share price to £13. At the time we did not hear too many complaints about the strategy from analysts, institutional investors or the financial press.

In the 2000–2001 telecoms recession Marconi's shares went into free-fall. Lord Simpson and Mr Mayo were blamed for frittering away the £2 billion cash pile they inherited from the old GEC and spending £4 billion on the overpriced acquisition of two US Internet equipment companies (Harrison, 2002). In 2005, Ericsson of Sweden bought Marconi, and renamed the remnants of the firm Telent, giving it a relatively insignificant focus on telecom services supply. 'Too much, too late' could summarize this exemplar of bad corporate practice. A firm with a cash-pile whose telecoms-challenged managers were looking to use it to create a so-called 'telco' paid massively over the odds, late in the day, as the telecoms boom was peaking, such that the money disappeared and with it, in effect, the firm. This is an exemplar of myopia, panic, folly – specifically, low absorptive capacity regarding the industry in question, crisis management and reduction of intrafirm related variety to a single electronics subsector with the management, accordingly, 'taken to the cleaners'.

As noted, Simpson was CEO of the Rover car company before being appointed chairman of GEC. After leading Leyland Daf, Simpson became head of the Rover Group when it was still owned by British Aerospace which bought it after the privatization of the parent company and Rover predecessor, British Leyland. With the assistance of a joint venture with Honda, Simpson turned Rover around, enough to persuade BMW to buy it for £800 million. It did not take long for BMW management to regret the decision. BMW sold the firm in 2000 to the Phoenix Group of local businessmen for a token £10. Moreover, the German firm agreed to hand over an extra £75 million to relieve it of warranty commitments. The UK government's official report into the case says that a number of schemes were considered which would have given the four personal options over that £75 million. Because ultimately only £10 million of this was handed to the four in the form of loan notes shortly after the takeover was completed, they sought to pay themselves bonuses of £65 million over five years to make up for the 'shortfall'. This target was later downgraded to £50 million. MG Rover, as the firm had been renamed collapsed in April 2005 with the loss of 6500 jobs, by which time the Phoenix Four and former MG Rover chief executive Kevin Howe had paid themselves a total of £42 million. From 2000 to 2004 MG Rover made losses of £611 million and began talks with the Chinese firm Shanghai Automotive Industry Corporation (SAIC). In 2005 SAIC withdrew from a deal to save the whole company and MG Rover went into administration. In 2006 MG Rover's assets were sold to Nanjing Automobile, also of China. The Mini was retained by BMW and it is now successfully produced at the former Rover plant in Oxford. The other relatively successful product,

Land Rover, is now owned by Tata of India although still produced near Birmingham, its traditional home.

Hence, we have discussed some negative features of a certain predominant kind of business decision-making. Many cases are set in the UK, though others might have been taken from France (for example computer 'national champion' Bull), Germany (for example, computer software firm Nixdorf) or Italy (Olivetti computers). Nor is the US immune as the travails of telcos like Lucent and car manufacturers like Chrysler and General Motors (GM) testify. Books are yet to be written on the 2008–09 nationalization and its aftermath upon the iconic US car manufacturer GM. However, much of its trouble arose from scarcely believable shortsightedness on economic or environmental grounds for a business model that, more and more, depended upon producing ever-larger, fuel-inefficient light trucks, vans and off-roaders (sports utility vehicles – SUVs) for increasingly urban populations that did not need them. Only the power of advertising, on the one hand, and industry lobbying to keep fuel efficiency and purchase taxes for light trucks low, on the other, kept this excessive and destructive vision of the 'American mobility dream' alive as long as it did. Once fuel prices started increasing, recession started biting and carbon concerns began rising up the political agenda, that business model faced up to its previous folly and began changing. Accordingly, fuel efficiency, renewable energy and a 'greener' vision of manufacturing, with subsidies from the Obama government in the US and other administrations elsewhere, have at last begun to impinge seriously upon that industry. Leading expertise in, for example 'green innovation' or 'green engineering' applied to the automotive or any other industry is as likely to lie outside as inside the industry. Hence the broken model discussed above is likely to have to change, and distributed knowledge flows will require aggregation. In what follows we identify early examples of precisely the beginnings of breakdowns in the vertical, hierarchical Industrial Age model, as what were once conceived as sectors transition into what are better described as 'platforms'.

11.5 FROM SECTOR (AND CLUSTER) TO PLATFORM

As reported in the first chapter of this book and reiterated through the seven empirical chapters on the selected industries studied in the first stages of the research, the target was to understand the extent to which knowledge flows in contemporary industry were changing, and whether these were becoming more or less sector-specific. Importantly, were the hypothesis that sectoral boundaries might be in question as never before to find support, or even if it were not, what if any role did the regional level of industry organization play in the contemporary period? That is, there was much discussion in the 1990s of the need to support key industries by enhancing clustering characteristics in geographical proximity to enhance the efficiency of the value chain, facilitating just-in-time supply and tailored industry support policy, possibly managed more regionally than hitherto. Regional universities were beginning to be perceived as possibly important partners for clustering industries as they had been in the emergence of wholly new industries like information and communication technologies (ICT) and biotechnology in very precise locations such as Silicon Valley and Greater Boston in the US. There it was evident that clustering gave considerable scope for flexible response as both of their regional economies had shown great resilience in recovering from recessions.

It will be recalled from the accounts in the empirical chapters that many industries appeared to be confronted with change imperatives of a relatively generic kind. That is, congruent with the possible passing of the Industrial Age model and the rise of a new Knowledge Age economy, sometimes abbreviated to just the 'knowledge economy' and sometimes the 'knowledge-based economy', firms were being faced with a decline in customer satisfaction with mass consumption, mass markets and mass production in favour of more discerning, knowledge-intensive, user-driven demand. Thus everywhere 'conventional' production was being challenged, albeit from a very low base in some industries by more dedicated or customized production, on the one hand, and more scientific, creative or traditional demand, on the other. Accordingly it seemed, on first inspection, that more combinative forms of knowledge were being brought to bear in many industries; that cumulative knowledge generation and exploitation continued to be strong, especially in industries in which production and even competition structures were distinctive (for example, aerospace, pharmaceuticals); but that knowledge from unexpected quarters was beginning to have to be absorbed.

In what follows, we report the lines of inquiry that were initially identified (Chapters 3–9) by research teams to explore this tendency towards horizontal knowledge flow as a complement, but also possibly a potentially powerful adjustment being made in industries or firms less characterized by myopic characteristics of the kind outlined above. The thesis was, it may be recalled, that the less myopic the firm, industry or, we would add, region is, the less the need for the accompanying traits of panic and folly. As an example of platform structure we begin (section 11.5.1) with biotechnology. Due to its pervasive applications the platform characteristic is widely found in, for example, food and energy as well as healthcare. This is an interesting case because it demonstrates a double movement from Industrial Age hierarchy and verticality of organization, notably when production was overwhelmingly controlled in knowledge-generation terms by large multinationals. But biotechnology began challenging that business model due to knowledge generation having migrated from pharmaceuticals firms labs to university research labs, so SMEs in clusters, sometimes joined by divisions (especially research and development – R&D) of large corporations, predominated by the end of the 1990s. Nowadays, biotechnology takes on certain pervasive qualities that mean its applications range far and wide, including energy, agro-food and environmental recycling, as well as healthcare, the major application. In sum, the accounts below are informed by an interest in the possibility of those two moves pertaining in fields other than biotechnology. The key elements in the transition, if it were to be found would be: (1) from sector to cluster; (2) from cluster to platform.

Hence core to the platform concept are two key categories of knowledge flow identified earlier in the book. These are related to combinatorial innovations, which means horizontal knowledge flows among sectors that lead to innovation possibilities; and cumulative, namely vertical knowledge flows, mainly intrasectoral for example intra-automotive or intra-tourism. Of particular interest in this quest is the extent to which any such change was necessitated and if not, why this continuation with past practice should prevail. Why, in other words, is change needed? Then the question is invoked concerning the extent to which industry may be increasingly perceived to begin to engage in knowledge search, selection and retention horizontally outside its industry home-base. To the extent that such behaviour is discernible, to what extent do any changes conform to the thesis that 'related variety' points to efficiency gains from horizontal absorptive capacity? And finally, something which is pursued in great detail in the second half of the next chapter, is there evidence that enterprise support policy has begun to develop 'platform' support mechanisms and even, for example, a role as innovation catalyst rather than simply a follower or handmaiden to meeting industry needs? The latter would be a significant sign of a sea-change in the modes of knowledge generation, examination and exploitation across the analytical, synthetic and symbolic knowledge categories of the industries of interest in this book. Recall that the accounts below constitute reasons for further investigation that were subsequently researched in detail, utilizing wherever possible the methodology of examining 'knowledge' and/or 'innovation biographies' to trace the etymologies of knowledge processing in industry (Chapter 12).

11.5.1   Agro-Food Biotechnology and its Possible Platform Connections

Here we begin with preliminary findings suggestive of noteworthy change in territorial knowledge dynamics in Aquitaine, France. The authors refer to this according to the French designation as 'pharma-foods', whereas in Northern Europe they are more commonly known as 'functional foods' that have health claims made for them because they promote the absorption by humans of, among others, healthy bacteria in varieties of dairy products processed from milk or acting as substitutes for it. Accordingly, the main dynamic of the account focuses on the development of collaborations between actors belonging to the pharmaceuticals, biotechnology, health and agro-food sectors. These industry and knowledge interactions occur in order to combine existing and heterogeneous sources of knowledge as well as to produce and use new transversal knowledge designed for the conception of new products belonging to a continuum of nutrition–health, such as 'pharma-foods' or nutritional complements.

Specific proximity and platform potentials in this complex depend intimately upon the following:

- The existence in the region of an important pool of public and academic research in the fields of biomedical applications, biotechnologies and nutrition–health interactions.
- The emergence of specialized industrial competencies in biotechnologies, especially in extraction and bioproduction processes, disseminated through SMEs rather than large companies.
- The historical importance of the agro-food industry in Aquitaine, first industry of the regional economy.
- The opportunity from market expansion to position activities towards the rapidly growing markets of pharma-foods and nutritional complements.
- The active role of regional public policies in promoting knowledge transfer and collaborations, at the regional level, and between firms and training and research institutions.

However, the expected convergence between agro-food industries and pharmaceuticals raises important issues:

- The two sectors are very heterogeneous in their knowledge bases and their historically grounded forms of collective action.
- The presence of an important regional public research capacity and the more established collaborations between pharmaceutical firms and public research institutions can bias knowledge flows toward

a science–industry collaboration focused on pharmaceutical and biopharmaceutical firms, at the expense of agro-food firms.

- The lack of regional industrial competencies in pharmaceuticals, notably due to the absence of R&D activities of large companies in the region, can prevent the development of industrially ambitious projects.

The main question under study is thus the identification of the different regional trajectories towards the conception of new products belonging to the nutrition–health continuum. The firms identified as potential case studies are thus all known to be engaged in embryonic or mature conception processes for products not belonging to the more traditional categories of agro-food or medicaments. Two main criteria are important for identifying possible firm case studies: the final market and the intra- and intersectoral orientation of knowledge interactions.

The final pharma-foods market can be approached either by pharmaceutical or agro-food firms, with critical differences in initial knowledge bases and access to external knowledge through collaborations with public research. The intra- and intersectoral orientation of knowledge interactions is also important. In this potential platform intrasectoral collaborations are expected to be easier for large firms to manage. This is due to more relational, not necessarily geographical, proximity in knowledge bases, existing collaborations and networks. However, in line with the above, geographical proximity in the form of regional biotechnology firms can be expected to become more prominent actors in managing intersectoral knowledge interactions. This is because these can be more complex than direct collaborations between pure agro-food and pharmaceutical companies. Crossing these two criteria, four possible case studies can be identified.

Sanofi-Aventis

Whereas Sanofi-Aventis owns only a single regional production unit, it is involved in an important R&D project supported by Prod'Innov and labelled 'Coginuts', the main purpose of which is to study the role of fatty acids in the prevention of disorders of cognition of old people. The project involves regional and extraregional research institutes, and another industrial partner, Lesieur, leader in the production of vegetable oils. The Prod'Innov association is an officially registered Innovative Cluster of the Aquitaine region. It specializes in agro-food, nutrition, health and medicine. Membership of the cluster is 110, including large French firms such as Air Liquide, Sanofi-Aventis, Total and so on; international firms such as Bristol-Myers Squibb, Syngenta, Monsanto and Kraft Foods, plus

50 SMEs. The whole is supported by 20 national public and university research centres.

Safisis
Safisis is a medium-sized biotechnology firm originally producing natural aromatic molecules (obtained by way of microbiologic or enzymatic techniques) for the agro-food industry. However, building on its technological learning and know-how, Safisis subsequently developed in two directions: fermentation subcontracting for the pharmaceutical industry; and development in the pharma-foods market through the conception and/or production of probiotics, that is, live microbial dietary supplements which beneficially affect the host human by improving its intestinal microbial balance. By 2006 Safisis was engaged in a collaborative project labelled 'Probisis', supported by Prod'Innov, aiming at the production of nutritional complements and new medications using probiotics.

Bionovation and Vitagermines
These two are small firms dedicated to the production of nutritional complements, obtained from biological agriculture. Due to the modification of public regulation on nutritional claims, they have to access new knowledge in order to attempt to prove the nutritional claims used as commercial arguments, including clinical tests.

As noted, these firms and their support institutions in research, policy and financing already constitute an intersectoral platform under the official Prod'Innov label. They are operating in a field which has been thought to offer great promise as 'healthy foods' ranging from bacteriological supplement dairy products to nutrition and even medically beneficial products. In 2009 a large-scale study commissioned by the European Union confirmed earlier studies in saying that for the moment there was no evidence of health effects from such products. However, the platform is embryonic in Aquitaine as elsewhere (for example Skåne in Sweden) and it is conceivable that research will identify promising new candidate treatments in future (EU, 2009).

11.5.2 Biofuels and the Automotive Industry

Biofuels became of clear interest to the automotive industry in 2007 when fuel prices rose and emergency legislation by the Bush administration in the US permitted greater use of agro-food products to fill the market gap for alternatives to gasoline. In the Berlin region are clustered numerous important research, business associations and corporations of the German automotive industry. Researchers based there noticed the emergent discourse of biofuels involving innovative conversations between agricultural research institutions and those of the automotive industry. Because of its geographical structure, these interactions were only partly held in the capital. Thus, when integrating new actors from biotechnology such as Choren Industries, one of the leading gasification technology companies for solid biomass and oil-based residue feedstock, into the traditional cooperation of car manufacturers (Volkswagen, Daimler) and oil groups (Shell), knowledge transfer (learning, patents, yield and so on) has typically been regulated by contract among vertically organised multinational corporate actors. The development of biofuels as conventional, already marketable fuels as well as new synthetic fuels made from synthesis gas using the Fischer–Tropsch and other methods has been significant for many years. This is particularly the case within the Volkswagen powertrain research field, where there is a special focus on synthetic fuels, the so called biomass-to-liquid-fuels (BTL).

However, as well as multinational corporate contracts, the development of biofuels is related to new cooperation partners as well as new forms of cooperation. These new partners and forms of cooperation combine sector-specific knowledge, new knowledge from different sectors (biotechnology, chemistry and agriculture) and firm-specific knowledge, at the same time as combining regional as well as supra-regional contexts. Several actors from different sectors, regions and policy fields are involved in the development and implementation of biofuels. The actors include Volkswagen as lead firm, and big international mineral oil companies. These range from the aforementioned firms like Choren Industries from Freiberg, Saxony to overseas specialists like Iogen in Canada. The line-up of actors in this field is complemented by regional manufacturers, and actors from agriculture and forestry. Their knowledge flows and dynamics can thus be seen as multi-actor dynamics across numerous industries. Related variety arises from traditionally unexpected intersectoral interactions. In this sense, revealed related variety can only be identified *ex post* rather than *ex ante*.

In future, synthetic biofuel produced by technical gasification can be used for diesel engines as well as for petrol engines. The particular influence the new fuels exert on how engines are going to be further developed is especially significant for original equipment manufacturers (OEMs). Here crucial developments for diesel combustion by the combined combustion system (CCS) are expected. CCS engines might combine the low fuel consumption of diesel engines with the high quality of other engines' exhaust emissions. New fuels like SunFuel, patent-registered by VW, are seen as key technologies for a new engine generation. The knowledge relevant for developing this new engine generation is widely spread. Powertrain engineers (at universities and research departments of OEMs) have the engine and combustion knowledge. The mineral oil industry shares its knowledge about fuels, and the actors from agriculture and forestry share their special knowledge about renewable primary products. Then technical chemistry specialists contribute their knowledge, seen to be crucial for the procedural transformation of the primary product into fuel.

In the special case of VW SunFuel the special know-how is distributed among four groups: VW powertrain research patented SunFuel; Shell contributes its fuel knowledge; Choren Industries technical engineering; the agriculture and forestry actors contribute their knowledge about wood and straw functioning as biomass. Significant technical knowledge of this particular example was patented in the Carbo-V method by Choren Industries. To demonstrate the functioning of this patent a 1 MW thermal pilot plant was set up and tested until 2003, and was expanded afterwards. Since 2003 the plant has been used to produce synthetic biofuels for commercial use (biodiesel). Besides this particular method others are also used for developing biofuels. Various actors, each with specific interests, interact within the social dimension. SMEs, including some from agriculture, have dominated the development and production of first-generation biofuels for a long time in Europe and especially in Germany. Automotive companies have supported these SME structures by the production for market of biodiesel vehicles since the 1990s. However, tax exemption for admixing biodiesel was not introduced until 2004. Mineral oil companies hardly engaged in these activities during the 1990s. Shell and BP focused on ethanol admixtures in the US and Brazil. Both countries have had promotional programmes for ethanol in place since the oil price crises of the 1970s and 1980s. With the emerging second-generation biofuels in recent years, mineral oil companies, in Europe Shell and BP, have changed their attitude toward biofuels.

Shell and BP approached the automotive industry to engage in common research projects. This led to new cooperation constellations between international corporations and SMEs. The above-mentioned cooperation in the case of VW SunFuel resulted from a EUCAR project initiated by a research department of the European Automobile Manufacturers' Association (Association des Constructeurs Européens d'Automobiles – ACEA). Involved in this were OEMs VW, Daimler, and Renault, and mineral oil companies Shell, Chevron and Total. From this project a subproject emerged, in which VW, Daimler and Shell cooperate. Daimler and Shell took on board Choren Industries in 1999, Choren Industries being the patent-holder for the thermal gasification of solid biomass according to the Fischer–Tropsch method, noted above. Shell has considerable expertise in the GtL (gas to liquid) field. Since 2003 Shell has also participated in the Choren group that produces fuels on the basis BtL (biomass to liquid) method. In 2003 Choren, Shell and VW (without then DaimlerChrysler) built an Alpha-pilot plant in Freiberg followed by the first, worldwide, BtL plant on an industrial scale with start of production implemented in 2009. According to the head of the VW powertrain research department, the central sources of knowledge in this field encompass MIT/Cambridge, University of California, RWTH (Rhenish-Westphalian University) at Aachen with its own special research field in biofuels, the Technical University Munich (BMW research), the Fraunhofer society and the Deutsche Luft- und Raumfahrtanstalt DLR (German Aerospace Institute) (for process engineering) (Pilot interview/ Summer 2007).

The territorial dimension of the VW SunFuel example shows differing geographical concentrations. First, only a few research centres concentrate on developing future engines and new fuels. The development of both is strongly dominated by the automotive and mineral oil industries. Second, contrariwise, process engineering (biotechnology and chemical engineering) is spatially widespread. Implementation of process engineering only exceptionally takes place in close proximity to automotive company R&D locations. All states in Germany except the city states have plants for producing first-generation biofuels. Locations for second-generation plants have yet to be found. More important for the choice of location than R&D proximity are the supply and infrastructure of primary products. With regard to territorial knowledge flow dynamics there are high expectations for employment creation in these respective regions. Considering the employment potential of biofuels, the IFO Institute estimated, based on an already existing total of 22 400 jobs, an increase of 27 500 up to 50 000 jobs in 2009 (IFO-Schnelldienst 17/2006, 28).

The question of political regulation stretches from political decisions in Europe, via regional regulations, to company politics. In early 2006 the European Commission agreed on a general EU strategy for biofuels (EU KOM 2006: 34 SEK 142) containing a detailed plan for implementation of this strategy. One point in the CARS21 programme for the European automobile industry is to develop biofuels further. VW is a leading member of the European Biofuels Technology Platform and thus directly contributing to the process of defining rules for developing and producing biofuels. The German government established a special agency for renewable primary products that operates nationwide as a coordinating platform. Within this platform all state and regional initiatives can participate in programmes for promoting biofuels. In Southeast Lower Saxony each of the initiatives mentioned above has established special biofuel projects to foster employment and economic growth in the region.

11.5.3   From Agro-Food Research to Biofuels Production and Use in Wales

In researching combinative as against cumulative knowledge flows in Wales, one of the case-study regions with a long history of producing – quite separately – high-quality food (meat, dairy, beverages) and energy from hydrocarbons (mainly coal), new cooperations were identified. Core to this is patented knowledge derived by the Institute of Grassland and Environmental Research (IGER) located in rural mid-Wales at Aberystwyth. In 2008 it became the IBERS (Institute of Biological, Environmental and Rural Sciences) of the nearby Aberystwyth University. Cumulative knowledge evolution had, for 70 years, rested on the cross-breeding of basic ryegrass commonly utilized for cattle and sheep fodder with varieties possessing enhanced sugar content. Eventually this also produced optimal results for utilizing grass as fuel as the centre realized that it had, in the form of these SugarGrasses, appropriate candidates. IGER than developed a renewables research division and this is been implemented in relation to biomass power generation in, amongst others, tourism applications. One of these is the establishment of a cooperative of 50 farmers that constituted an ESCO (Energy Supplier Company) that supplies heat and electricity to the Bluestone Holiday Village situated on the edge of the Pembrokeshire Coast National Park. This is being recognized as a first step to fulfilling the vision of a new kind of 'green tourism', becoming a showcase for renewable energy and sustainability. Thus, in this instance, not only is green energy used to fuel the development but also organic food is supplied from a further 30 regional farms to feed the tourists. Hence we see the emergence of a grassland–biofuels–tourism–food platform unified under the umbrella of 'green production' but also in relation to research, including biotechnological research (molecular or DNA markers for enhanced cross-breeding).

11.5.4   Brief Accounts of Other Candidate Platforms: The Emerging Laser Complex in Aquitaine

The laser industry in Aquitaine, France is recognized as an emerging and anticipatory cluster since the constitution of local collaborations, notably through the creation of public institutions designed for knowledge and technology transfer arising from greater openness to civilian application of important military technologies occurring 2009–11. Thus the complex under study can be defined as a territorially embedded and cumulative trajectory towards the production of new laser-based technologies and equipment. The knowledge interactions and technology transfer that take place within the platform occur at two distinctive levels. First, between public civil and military research and firms producing intermediary products such as optical equipment and/or laser-related instruments. Second, it occurs between intermediary product-producing firms and user firms in diversified sectors such as automotive, mechanics, ICT, the wood industry and aeronautics.

The use–generation issue thus appears to be crucial for the study of this combinative knowledge flows opportunity. It can be hypothesized, from preliminary analysis, that there is a dominant local generation trajectory contrasting with the use trajectories often associated with such transversal technologies. The preliminary analysis of the technical and social contexts of the emerging laser cluster indicates that the main knowledge dynamics take place between research institutions, public organizations and laser instruments producers, with the production of innovative and high-level laser instruments and technologies as main output. The main markets for these equipments and technologies appear to be mainly non-local, or even national: Northern European countries, and specifically Germany, actually constitute the main markets for local firms. The knowledge flows may be expected to be tied essentially to interactions between fundamental regional research and specialized producing firms, rather than to user–producer interactions at the regional level.

There is a potentially somewhat problematic integration of use and generation dynamics: although there appears to be no critical role of local user needs in the emergence of the laser cluster, some key regional sectors and/or firms are currently using laser applications in their production processes:

- the aeronautic, space and defence sector, with major subcontractors such as Thales using laser technologies in very specific applications;
- the wood industry, using laser applications for cutting out;
- the textile industry with a world leader producing cutting-out machines for textiles (Lectra).

Active firms include the following.

Eolite Systems
Founded in 2004, Eolite Systems is a small firm (eight employees) dedicated to short-pulse high-power fibre laser technologies (optics). The applications concern some rising industrial sectors like microelectronics and flat screens. It works in close cooperation with the research team of the University of Bordeaux 1 and CELIA, which was founded by one of the

two Eolite Systems managers. This firm is also well recognized as innovative, winning OSEO (an innovation funding agency) funds for its development projects three times (two loans and a prize for winning the 'National Competition of Innovative Firms' set up by the Research Ministry) as well as Regional Council subsidies for launching the Femscan laser. Further, Eolite Systems also mobilises a national industrial network: since 2006, it has initiated a cooperation agreement with Quantel, a French leader of laser technologies for medical instrumentation.

Amplitude Systems
Founded in 2001, Amplitude Systems is a small-size firm (seven employees) dedicated to industrial femtosecond lasers (optics). The main applications of its technology lie in medical biology, for neuroscience and embryology. It received a prestigious ANVAR (French national innovation agency) label in 2002 for start-up creations.

Novalase
Founded in 2001, Novalase has its core competence in laser micro-machining with expertise in producing equipment for both high-value-added production and standardized processes. Though the firm is not a direct maker of lasers, it optimizes the potential of this technology for industrial clients. Novalase has a huge local network, involving Universities Bordeaux 1 and 2 and actively participating to the construction of the cluster.

Ciris
Ciris is a medium-sized firm (45 employees) in the wood sector. It is a typical user of laser technology. It proposes techniques designed for wood cutting. Its subsidiary, Edit Process Control, offers expertise for laser applications (spectrometry, cutting and so on) Ciris can then be active over the whole range of cutting in the wood industry. It is one of the most actively participating firms (as a user) in the emergence of the cluster.

Thales Avionics
Thales Avionics (Sagem group) is a French leader in the aerospace and defence industries. It is especially active in advancing measuring equipment using laser technologies for piloting (metrology). As a key actor of Aquitaine industry, Thales Avionics is highly implicated in the elaboration of the laser and optics cluster in Aquitaine. It will be of central interest to examine whether this firm seizes the opportunity of such a concentration of competences for laser R&D.

11.5.5 New Media in Skåne: Film Tourism – Place Marketing and Responding to New Demand

There are a number of different aspects of the connections between film production and tourism in Skåne, Sweden. An important reason for Film i Skåne but particularly for Region Skåne, Ystad district council and the Sparbanken Syd savings bank to invest in film production is the impact on the local and regional economy generated through film production. Partly this is to do with visitor numbers when the film is shot, but increasing focus is placed on the place marketing generated when the films showing Ystad and other parts of the region are seen in the cinema and on television in many countries across the world. The Wallander films have generated an increase in visitors that demand more attractions than traditionally those visiting due to their interest in the Wallander books. The difference between 'literary tourists' and 'film tourists' is important to understand, to cater for the different types of visitors. In response to demand, particularly from German tourists, the attraction Cineteket was established by Ystad district council in 2006. This film attraction has developed further and also started collaboration with two other film attractions in the region to develop the film tourism offer further.

11.5.6 Watch Making: Jura Region, Switzerland

Swiss watch making knowledge dynamics has become a complex system. Technical knowledge is not the only component of a watch. Watches have become fashion and luxury products. Many other activities are tightly connected to the watch making sector (press, tourism, design, fashion, events organization, new media and automotive). Those activities have their own knowledge flows and these are complementary to more general watch making interactions. For example, the research reported here discovered intimate interconnections with the UK car platform, the residual of a much larger former car producing district in the Birmingham region, whose luxury products such as Morgan, Aston Martin and, further north, Bentley were joint-branded by Swiss firms like Hublot, Jaeger-Le Coulture and Breitling. In two cases the watch took the car brand, as in the Morgan Hublot and Breitling Bentley, using shared traditions in fine mechanics and precision engineering as the strapline. Here we see an emergent horizontality in interactions aimed at market building through shared imagery or symbolic knowledge flows.

In the watch making industry can be identified several actors such as firms, schools or different institutions. Swiss watch making firms have traditionally had a strategy of cumulative knowledge development because they aim to sell a product based on a continual traditional know-how (for example Longines). Some foreign multinational firms specializing in fashion such as Cartier or Gucci have developed more combinatorial knowledge because they adapt their traditional design knowledge to watch making technical competences. We see new variants of that in the above-mentioned case of cross-branding between luxury automotive and Swiss watch products. Fewer than ten companies employ more than 500 people. Most Swiss firms are small enterprises (less than 100 employees). Small firms cooperate with subcontractors for composite (combinatory) knowledge such as documentation or design.

To service these developments, knowledge-intensive business services firms have evolved dealing with industrial branding and luxury design, or to create related Internet services. Media companies have created special newspapers or magazines for luxury watches and jewellery. In addition to the traditional watch techniques or micro-mechanics schools, some education and R&D entities have developed complementary knowledge. For instance schools for industrial design or art schools were created or developed, indicating that combinatorial knowledge has become an important issue for education. Different institutions are involved on various levels in the watch making system. Some traditional sectoral associations such as the Federation of Swiss Watch Industry or the Fondation de la Haute Horlogerie are mainly focused on cumulative knowledge dynamics. Furthermore, other institutions such as watch making museums or tourism promotion institutions have been created to combine the regional industrial culture with the knowledge of tourism promotion. Thus watch making has evolved tourist potential rather as it is suspected of so doing in relation to the Skåne film industry. La Chaux-de-Fonds and Le Locle, two historic centres of watch production, have an application to become UNESCO (United Nations Educational, Scientific and Cultural Organization) World Heritage sites. This is underlined by activity in the Jura area, which is the traditional part of the cumulative industrial and technical knowledge dynamics for watch making as well as the 'Watch Valley' tourism knowledge dynamic.

Public policies have been important in the revival of the Swiss watch making region following the devastation wrought by Japanese quartz technology that massively cheapened the key energy input of the low-end watch product market. First, European research projects in the field of micro-techniques, for example, can have an impact on the watch making cumulative knowledge dynamics. Second, the Swiss participation in the European InterReg Programme has an impact on multi-local and combinatorial knowledge dynamics. But the impacts of such policies are weak. At the national scale, three policies have influence. First, the Agglomeration

Policy influences the way knowledge dynamics articulate and concentrate in metropolitan areas, notably Geneva and Basel. Second, knowledge and technology transfer between universities and firms are in Switzerland still weak, and particularly in the sectors of services. Accordingly, the Policy for Education, Research and Innovation encourages universities to specialize in specific fields and execute technological transfers which have a bigger influence on the territorial generation and use of knowledge. Third, the New Regional Policy does not support special fields of activity (not sector-driven) but innovative projects. This encourages projects with combinatorial knowledge dynamics. Finally, at the regional scale, policies are very different from one canton to another. Some policies are sectorally driven and support cumulative knowledge dynamics and others offer platform support to more combinatorial knowledge dynamics (for instance micro-technical knowledge with biotechnologies or tourism with the watch industry).

11.5.7 Automotive Safety: Region Västra Götaland

The candidate territorial knowledge dynamics case here is within the field of automotive crash safety, traditionally a stronghold for the Swedish car industry. This subfield of the automotive industry is, in Sweden, currently in a process where product and technology logic is changing from a cumulative product-centred one towards an integrated network-based and, to a larger degree, knowledge-driven system. The manifestation of this and the point of departure for the identification of this kind of interaction is the publicly funded SAFER project where actors from academia and industry have formed a national centre of excellence with its location in the region.

Volvo, the regional mainstay, has traditionally used safety as one of its main competitive advantages, introducing safety-belts as standard as early as 1959. In subsequent decades knowledge was primarily related to the technological development of specific products such as safety-belts and body-parts, followed by air bag technology. This was largely cumulative sector-specific synthetic knowledge (engineering) aiming at minimizing the impact of the crash. Since 2007 this field has changed towards the use of much more composite knowledge involving the combination of analytical and synthetic knowledge. Today crash safety still involves traditional engineering knowledge around the car, but to a much greater extent combined with new fields such as crash testing, biometrics, driver behaviour, traffic planning, traffic safety policy and so on. In order to stay competitive in this new knowledge environment, the industry, the policy sphere and the academic sector, inspired by an earlier collaborative project on whiplash injuries, work together in order to establish the new knowledge-base crash safety platform as a long-term competitive advantage.

Traditionally, the car manufacturers and to some extent suppliers have been the nexus of knowledge relations. Volvo Car and Volvo Truck have been major factors in the knowledge development process. But there is also a long history of research on traffic safety at the Chalmers University of Technology located in Göteborg. These two actors, later joined by the supplier Autoliv, were probably the main players during the cumulative knowledge era. Today the scope is much wider and in terms of knowledge much more combinatorial. Below are listed key partners in the SAFER project as an example of the diversity of knowledges and actors. Important interactions can be identified between, for example, Chalmers University of Technology, Volvo, Autoliv and Folksam. Besides traditional research projects, knowledge within the field of crash safety has been part of Chalmers education since 1987, including 15 PhD theses.

11.5.8 Baden-Württemberg, Technical Engineering Services and Software Engineering (KIBS)

The knowledge products of technical engineering services are very relevant to the industrial demand side, especially for the automotive industry. Firms of this subsector have been active on the market for quite a long time and a large proportion of them have already made important steps in internationalization by following their customers. Technical engineering services in the region are members not only of regional but also of international knowledge networks. They cooperate with OEMs and first-tier suppliers in national and international terms. As our first case study with an engineering firm has shown, these firms combine and integrate heterogeneous knowledge stocks. This firm is a leading technical engineering service firm and one of the largest in Germany. It has developed routines for using distance relationships and local relationships in its project-based work for clients. The project base environment implies a great challenge for such firms, because rapidly changing knowledge inputs are required in developing engineering services for clients. Since the mid-1990s the investigated firm has started its internationalization process in close connection with its clients and is an ongoing process. This process is combined with necessary internal organizational innovations to coordinate in an efficient way the increasing spatial distribution of internal knowledge with external knowledge in client-specific projects.

Nevertheless, links to the region are strongly dependent on interactions with customers (OEMs and suppliers) in the automotive cluster. Links to regional institutions are mainly based on universities and other educational institutions. The availability of potential human resources in the Stuttgart region is high. But the demand seems to be even higher, hence international recruiting gains importance.

Territorial knowledge flows and dynamics influence and are influenced by the OEM firms, mainly by their network and the implicit knowledge of human resources. With their knowledge-intensive products, they support the existing specialization of the region towards the automotive industry. Here the researched company is a first-tier supplier to international companies like Daimler, Bosch and so on. As multi-local companies these are not circumscribed only by the Stuttgart region. To gain geographical proximity to its clients for facilitating communication transfer, only four years after founding the company its first subsidiary in Sindelfingen was opened. This was quite near the home base but in the following years more and more subsidiaries were opened in Germany: Cologne, Munich, Ingolstadt and Wolfsburg for example. Today this service firm has subsidiaries in five European countries and is represented in the USA, too. The new subsidiaries were built near large car manufacturers like BMW (Munich), Audi (Ingolstadt), VW (Wolfsburg) and Ford (Cologne).

Following its customers is a clue for the interest in geographical proximity and the importance of knowledge exchange that is possible because of this kind of proximity. One example is the cooperation with BMW. In this case the technical engineering company is using a testing facility of BMW while there is an intensive knowledge exchange between those two partners. On the other hand, they open up new (vertical and horizontal) knowledge domains through their knowledge flows stemming from other regions. The corporation has built up a joint venture with firms in Hamburg and Bremen to combine knowledge related to aviation. The firm contributes to building up aviation competence in the Stuttgart region. Recently the firm has been engaged with local actors anchoring such knowledge in the Stuttgart region.

This suggests not only ways in which Baden-Württemberg's economy was able to introduce incremental changes, but also how firms like the proposed case study may ensure their economic success by working like this. In this case, a clear opening for new knowledge domains can be recognized. This opening and the new combination of different knowledge fields underlines the importance of cross-sectoral technologies where KIBS dealing with different knowledge categories have a composite knowledge base. If this is true for technical KIBS in the Stuttgart region, learning processes will not be concentrated locally but opened for distant learning and for this reason opened for other knowledge flows. This would mean a step from cumulative knowledge or learning processes of the traditional automotive and engineering cluster in Baden-Württemberg to a kind of composite or combinatory knowledge, or learning processes. While there is a bundling of resources and a concentration on specific knowledge domains, governmental and private organizations want to build inter-section platforms to bring together different knowledge domains, and develop policy in support of this.

11.5.9 Veneto Region: Examples from Nanotechnology and Design Industries – Nanotechnology Developments in Mature Industries

The Italian National Plan for Research 2002–04 aimed at contributing to Italy's competitiveness through innovative policies based on technology clusters in high-tech industries that could potentially benefit and contrib-ute to the upgrading of traditional industries. The Ministry for Universities and Research co-financed, together with the regional administration, the development of a nanotechnology cluster in the region.

The technical dimension
Activities related to nanotechnology R&D mainly involve knowledge of nanoscale materials and processes targeted towards local industries. Specific knowledge identified during the preliminary investigation relates to nanostructured materials (nanoparticles, polymers) and treatments. Traditional industries that are benefiting from nanotech knowledge are eyewear, construction, car manufacturing, sporting goods, clothing and apparel.

The social dimension
Based on the preliminary observations, the research team identified the following key actors in the cluster: SMEs in traditional industries; inno-vative start-ups in the field of nano-fabrication and R&D; universities and research centres. Specifically, three universities are active players in this field (the University of Padua, Ca' Foscari and Verona), and one nanofabrication facility (Nanofab) which is supported financially by the Veneto Region, the three mentioned universities and seven privately held companies. Governing bodies and companies are actively organizing the matching between SMEs and research centres and universities. Veneto Nanotech in particular is active in the governance of relationships between the actors in the cluster.

The territorial dimension
Actors considered in the analysis of this specific case are geographically spread in the region. As far as traditional SMEs are concerned, they are located typically in traditional industrial districts within the Veneto

Region. In particular, manufacturers of eyewear are mainly located in the province of Belluno, sporting equipment manufacturers are located in the province of Treviso, and plastics and construction companies are spread between the provinces of Treviso, Padua and Venice. As far as the institutions and public and private research centres are concerned, they are mainly located in the provinces of Venice and Padua.

The policy dimension
The relevant policy-making levels to be taken into account for the analysis of this example are the national and regional levels. R&D activities and academic developments in high-tech fields are objects of policy-lines of the Ministry for Universities and Research, while the Veneto Region has co-financed the development of the cluster and is actively investing in educa-tion initiatives and in providing companies with funds for specific research and experimentation projects in the field of nanotechnology.

The technical dimension
The technical knowledge related to these knowledge dynamics is related to the specific field of design on the one hand, and to the field of com-munication and marketing on the other. As far as the design knowledge is concerned, it can be represented as the field of knowledge related to the conception, development and industrialization of consumer products. Detailed fields of knowledge within design knowledge are related to aes-thetics, ergonomics and innovative materials. As far as communication and marketing knowledge is concerned, we refer to it as the field of knowl-edge related to branding, communicating and constructing rich experi-ences around the consumption of consumer products such as clothes, sporting equipment, eyeglasses, shoes and other products typical of the so-called 'Made in Italy' brand.

11.6 CONCLUSIONS

We have now had a good opportunity to consider the lineaments of a probable new industrial form typical of the knowledge economy era. In this, large firms are clearly not, if they ever were, relatively self-sufficient islands of capability and competitiveness. The model was shown in the section that considered weaknesses in the mindsets imputed to humans and other corporate leaders. The ideology of vertical, hierarchical, command-and-control structuring of business decision-making was shown to be questionable even in its heyday. Now, the rise of competing knowledge centres, the knowledge flows among them, and their peculiarly distributed localizations has contributed to a model of competition in markets that is rooted in cooperation of firms not only in similar albeit complementary, knowledge segments, but also in wholly unrelated ones. The exigencies of new regulatory pressures on the free-riding character of Industrial Age business models regarding emissions and other environmental pollution brings together strange bedfellows. Also, the rise of the highly knowledge-based 'creative industries' emanating from the cultural economy points to new opportunities for profit-taking from unusual cross-fertilizations in fashion, watch making, and culinary or cinematic tourism. In the chapter that follows, these hints will be explored in even greater depth and with strong empirical support in more detailed case analysis, preceded by theoretical exegesis of the key theoretical components of the analyses conducted.

12. The matrix: evolving policies for platform knowledge flows

Philip Cooke and Carla De Laurentis

12.1 INTRODUCTION

Today, advanced societies become more and more based upon 'knowledge economies' as routine manufacturing and many lower-order services migrate to Asia and other emerging markets. Much of this discussion is based in consensus about social and economic 'megatrends'. The discussion stresses how important it is that firms engage with these realities. But it is equally important to recognize that enterprise support agencies, many of which are regional or, if not, specialized in innovation, need to overhaul or introduce the knowledge absorbing, analysing and adapting capabilities and functions that enable rapid anticipation and response to megatrend shifts as they affect their jurisdictions. One of the important policy and practice innovations of the 1990s – which we argue below was associated with the accelerated demise of the Industrial Age in advanced economies – concerned clusters. These fundamentally regional phenomena portended the rise of networked forms of knowledge distribution and flow, clusters forming nodes in such global networks. Accordingly, new challenges impact upon cluster firms and cluster governance. Much of the following explores these two spotlit phenomena, set within a distributed knowledge flows model of regional dynamics. Hence, in line with the aspirations of the research being reported on, most of the analysis focuses on the regional level, involving global knowledge flow dynamics among firms, industries and regions per se. However, the cluster and economic governance models outlined and explored are also relevant to specialist national agencies (for example TEKES in Finland, Innovation Norway or VINNOVA in Sweden) that are tasked to be supportive of innovation.

Since 1990, when the early experiments with industry networks and cluster building began, it has frequently been the case that cluster policy has been managed by either regional bodies or specialist national agencies such as those listed above. However, interestingly, the smaller geographical focus of the typical cluster means that many have evolved their own day-to-day management practices. These have often been part of the cluster strategy handed down from above, and possession of a working or feasible cluster policy implementation body has sometimes been an important criterion for competitive policy selection of some cluster candidates over others (for example VinnVäxt by VINNOVA). Nevertheless, the decision to pursue a definite cluster programme and to manage that strategically is usually operated at regional or national level. It could be said that, with the intervention of the EU Directorate General (DG) Enterprise cluster support programme, some element of strategy for clustering also operates at the supranational level, something explored in section 12.2 below. It is also the case that cluster policies have been strongly advocated and supported by multilateral bodies such as the United Nations Industrial Development Organization (UNIDO) and the World Bank for developing countries. Clearly, the market alone is not the only or surest guide for policy regarding cluster programmes. Markets have produced clusters throughout industrial history, often with spectacular results – as in Silicon Valley – but with remarkable inequities in spatial and social terms. Cluster programmes seek to ensure a fairer distribution of perceived benefits of clusters. Therefore, the task of cluster policy-makers is difficult, especially as they are operating at one remove from day-to-day market signals regarding entrepreneurial opportunities. Nevertheless, one of the main themes of this chapter is that closing the knowledge gap regarding the megatrends, as well as local microtrends, that affect clusters is one of the grand challenges facing territorial, including cluster programmes, today.

In the following account, section 12.2 devotes attention to territorial knowledge dynamics. These form the new mode by which innovation, no longer bound mainly by the in-house research and development (R&D) laboratories of large firms, is conducted. Interactive learning has overturned the linear model of innovation to a very large extent. Knowledge nowadays comes across boundaries of many kinds: intellectual, industrial and international.

Section 12.3 of this chapter is devoted to the exploration of policy levels and the division of labour, but also interactions between the key elements of multilevel governance in Europe. This shows clearly that such hierarchies are crucial constraints and facilitators of action, but that for such key activities as clustering and innovation, the regional level has a definitive and distinctive role to play. Clearly, this applies best for reasonably maturely governed regions with democratic assemblies, ministries and so on (for example *Länder*, Belgian regions, Spanish Autonomous Communities, French and Italian regions, and UK smaller countries). Resource allocations and moderate administrative authority allow for significant potential interdepartmental cooperation. Of course, this does not always happen, but it can. In section 12.3 we begin discussing the regional level of the multilevel governance structure in a manner relevant to considering present and future challenges for cluster policy and programmes. Three such models suggested themselves from the outset: issue-focused governance, problem-focused governance and platform governance (Kaiser, 2009). A variant that further distinguishes platform governance according to a reactive or a proactive disposition is introduced.

Section 12.4 brings together the emergent analyses of the preceding two main sections by discussing the 'knowledge economy' implications for regional governance of clusters and particular the innovation dimension of cluster firms, which has been a frequently occurring theme in the rationale for designing or promoting clusters. Using the 'innovation biography' approach it is shown how 'clusterization' is perceived at the frontier to be an input to construction of regional advantage through platforms of related variety industry. These local and global networks operating to cross-pollinate innovation opportunities are becoming a pronounced feature of advanced industrial innovation.

12.2   TERRITORIAL KNOWLEDGE DYNAMICS

Delineation of some of the key general integrating aspects of contemporary innovation makes discussion of schematized theoretical reflection and findings organized as an integrating framework deserving of discussion (Table 12.1). This portrayal is more focused specifically upon the transition from a traditional to a territorial knowledge dynamics (TKD) type of new paradigm. First, in Table 12.1, are contrasted in the first row a sector or cluster-type of practice focused upon innovation. This then transitions into more of a platform-type interaction involving less specialized and vertical knowledge dynamics. Knowledge exploration, examination and exploitation are more pervasive in the new paradigm than the old. In the latter they had to await R&D lab outcomes in most cases.

Through theory and its iteration with representative empirical materials, transition modelling can thus be used as a lens to capture meta-changes on a global scale as hitherto dominant paradigms begin to be challenged and gradually replaced by elements of a new socio-technical landscape, something we are seeing as the advanced economies experienced the decline of industry and the rise of a knowledge economy. Key elements of this contrast are captured in Box 12.1.

They clearly involve a shift away from practices of planning industry trajectories as was once done in countries that sought to support 'national champion' businesses. Temporarily, of course, Western governments have

*Table 12.1   Transition to territorial knowledge dynamics (TKDs)
              paradigm*

	Traditional paradigm: Innovation and Proximity	New paradigm: Territorial Knowledge Dynamics
Unit of change	Innovation	Knowledge dynamics
Mobilization of new knowledge	Punctual (technological trajectory)	Permanent
Knowledge articulation	Cumulative trajectory	Combinative dynamic
Territory	Spatial division of activities/labour	Multi-local knowledge networks
Regional governance	Regional coherence between use and generation of knowledge (cluster policy)	Capacity to take part in multi-local dynamics and anchor mobile knowledge

Source: Crevoisier and Jeanneret (2009).

BOX 12.1   INSTANCES OF TRANSITION FROM INDUSTRIAL PARADIGM TO KNOWLEDGE PARADIGM

An Integrated Regional Knowledge Flows & Transition Policy Model

Industrial & Fossil Fuel Paradigm	Knowledge and 'Green' Paradigm
Fossil Fuels	Renewable Energy/Green Knowledge
Industry policy – sectors, clusters	Knowledge policy – networks, platforms
Closed innovation (General Electric)	Open innovation (Procter & Gamble)
Closed source (Microsoft)	Open source (Linux)
Disciplinary science (e.g. chemistry, Mode 1)	Interdisciplinary (e.g. biochemistry, Mode 2)
Silo government	Joined-up governance
Regime/paradigm governance	Transition governance
State deregulating (e.g. utilities)	State re-regulating (e.g. banks)

been assailed by requests from failing industries like financial services, automotive production and electrical goods for 'bailouts' and other forms of subsidy. Some have been successful, but their fundamental problem is adherence for too long to the old-fashioned Fordist consumption paradigm based on private cars, houses and domestic appliances produced without thought for either changing consumer demand or the state of the planet. In the knowledge paradigm, policy support is evidently more forthcoming if firms, including banks, adhere to more intelligent loan and investment practices.

Associated with shifts towards less excessive loan terms for consumption are demands from policy-makers for a 'green turn' in production of goods and services. This echoes the further move away from corporate reliance upon internal 'groupthink' norms and towards a more 'open-minded' recognition of networked knowledge from science, software and in innovation. The relative power of public labs over corporate labs is a striking feature of this change in direction and source of key knowledge flows, and regions may become 'living labs' for some such 'bundled innovations' as we have seen. Notice that the model is suitable precisely to the context of transition from industrial to knowledge economy paradigms, also that of hydrocarbon to renewable energy regimes, and conceivably 'old KIBS' to 'new KIBS' paradigms (less financial innovation of the 'toxic' kind; fewer 'generous' mortgages and no subprime mortgages; separation of 'merchant' from 'plain vanilla' banks, and so on).

12.2.1 Cumulative and Combinative Knowledge

This is particularly relevant for the discovery of cumulative knowledge and innovation which has been traditional for sectors and even clusters (although clusters may be precisely 'transitional' forms), and combinative knowledge and innovation dynamics typical of the emergent and evolving 'platform' knowledge flows model. This, it will be recalled, is based on 'related variety' of interindustry knowledge spillovers and lateral absorptive capacity among firms. Whereas intracorporate spatial divisions of labour placed routine assembly industry at geographical peripheries and management headquarters in core regions, knowledge dynamics under knowledge economy conditions are multilocational, distributed and innovation is more 'open' because it is cognate to norms associated with public 'open science' than in the older, 'closed innovation' model. Accordingly, regional governance moves away from the localized 'container' model of knowledge geography even associated with clustering towards distributed knowledge platforms with pronounced 'global antennae'.

In Table 12.1 these characteristics are outlined largely at the firm level while in Box 12.1 important aspects of economic governance and the relationship with other important transition dynamics, notably environmental, and the position of for example university research in the transition are highlighted. The impetus for change in governance modes away from stable policy management to transition policy management is recognized. Together, these two schemas capture a flavour of the overarching perspective deployed in thinking about knowledge dynamics in the Eurodite project. They are inevitably incomplete, but express the inclination of the research with its emphasis upon industry knowledge flow dynamics and their relationship with economic and environmental governance issues in a context of global financial crisis.

Recognition of these transitional shift impulses poses enormous difficulties for a policy process still largely rooted in Industrial Age and Fossil Fuels exploiting approaches. As shown in section 12.3 below on governance, relatively few of our sample of governance regimes practise what can be called 'platform policy'. Recall that this looks for connections across boundaries far more than the easier, traditional model of looking for impact within vertical structures (Kaiser, 2009). Cumulative knowledge built on existing path-dependences will continue to be created, and much innovation is known to be incremental and therefore inclined to be cumulative. But future knowledge and that most associated nowadays with less incremental, more disruptive innovation cross-pollinates among industries in the form of general-purpose knowledge like information and communication technology (ICT), biotechnology and nanotechnology. Policy must catch up with this also at levels besides the regional pioneers (and there are small signs that this evolves both at EU (European Commission, 2006b)) and, for example, the UK's Technology Strategy Board levels (TSB, 2009).

12.3 GOVERNMENT, GOVERNANCE AND TOWARDS POLICY

The long-mooted evolution of vertically structured, closed, stand-alone, disciplinary knowledge production, otherwise known as Mode 1 knowledge, into the more laterally connected, open, interdisciplinary and interactive Mode 2 knowledge production typifies the manner in which this industry-to-knowledge paradigm shift has occurred. Ultimately, though perhaps not yet fully approached, such shifts become expressed in modes of administration, notably regarding government. Citizens and politicians have long bemoaned the vertical nature of decision-making and information on action practised by government departments still wedded

Table 12.2   *Multilevel governance responsibilities and priorities in the current transition*

Multilevel governance systems: policy emphases (current transition)		
European Union	Member state	Region
1. Monetary €/ECB & Coordination	1. Financial Intervention	1. Energy
2. Agro-food	2. Business Support	2. Economic Development
3. Infrastructure/Regions	3. Training & Skills	3. Agro-food
4. Competition Policy	4. Environment/ Energy	4. Education/Skills
5. Innovation/S&T	5. Home/Interior	5. Environmental Planning
6. Energy Regulation & Coordination		

to a closed 'silo' model of authoritative action (compare Tett's, 2009 quote on bank management style in Chapter 11). The call for 'joined-up-governance' has yet to be fully approached, let alone met. However, change in this dimension will have to accompany change in the knowledge and economic dimensions of society and a move from the relative certainties of the deregulated, liberal market model that has been hegemonic in Western countries since 1985. This highly linear, new public management plus audit approach (see Power, 1997) is being faced with huge needs consequent upon the failure of the 'neoliberal experiment' in so many advanced countries. The reluctance of governments to 'nationalize' banks, insurance companies and auto-firms in the financial crisis was significant in this respect because it revealed recognition that in the past such 'patient care' seldom worked well. But it also represented a failure of imagination to evolve policy forms that can deal adequately with transition and the necessary transition management methods implied by the shift to a new, more knowledge-based paradigm involving wholly different forms of more efficient, healthier and sustainable production and consumption.

This can also be seen in the varying degrees of integration but, nevertheless, elements of accommodation among different strata of the multilevel governance systems are currently struggling with transition without adequate tools to do so (Table 12.2). The EU showed staggering incapacity to mobilize policy and its core financial strategy (exchange rate mechanism – ERM rules) was left in ruins in the 2008–09 financial and economic emergency. Virtually all responsibility for responding to the emergency had to be taken by national governments, which resorted to 'learning by doing' (that is, making mistakes). At regional level, by contrast, where such fiscal authority is seldom found, there were nevertheless emerging efforts to develop integrated policies on such aspects as environment, planning and economic development. These are the spheres for which they frequently do have some authority and which are important to nurturing niche businesses, and promoting insofar as they can 'regime' change at regional level. From the results of the Eurodite research, which was future-oriented in prospecting for new, more horizontal modes of business practice and policy formation attuned to 'platforms of innovation', it emerged that the regional governance level was where such innovation governance had progressed furthest in terms of implementation strategies. Results that illustrate this finding are presented in section 12.4 of this chapter below.

Despite emergent divisions of labour in multilevel governance roles, there is also alignment, mostly among states and supranational bodies that, at the margin, also involves some regions as the following account demonstrates. An indication of the lumbering, even dated nature of purported policy-renewal in widely perceived 'master institutions' of modern governance is signified by a recent major development in industry policy whereby some member states and the EU DG Enterprise and Innovation have, possibly belatedly, made clusters and cluster support their main business support policy. In October 2008 the European Commission (DG Enterprise and Innovation) established the European Cluster Policy Group. Its mandate is to advise the Commission and member states on how better to support the development of more world-class clusters in the EU. The objectives of the European Cluster Policy Group are as follows:

- to make recommendations on how better to design cluster policies in the Community;
- to assess international trends in cluster development;
- to identify future challenges for cluster policies in response to globalization;
- to explore tools for the removal of existing barriers to transnational cluster cooperation;
- to analyse complementarities between the main Community-level policies and the financial instruments that support clusters.

This has led to the formation of the the European Cluster Alliance which is an open platform for permanent policy dialogue at EU level. It unites those regions responsible for developing cluster policies and managing cluster programmes. In turn, this has led to the formation of the European Cluster Academy, a self-organized cluster knowledge transfer and partnership group. Both of these initiatives aim to raise excellence and efficiency in European clusters and policies. This aim is officially confirmed and approved by the Commission Communication on Clusters.

Interestingly, these moves have in turn given rise to member state, but mostly regional, initiatives in, for example, Denmark to establish a professional training programme for cluster and regional innovation system managers, licensed as part of DG Enterprise and Innovation's professional certification policy for improving intermediary skills in knowledge transfer, regional innovation and cluster building.

This new intermediary is known as REG X, a commercial strapline for the Danish Cluster Academy. It opened in late 2009 with a global focus on clusters. As such it addresses primarily Danish needs contingent upon economic governance reform. New regional administrations were formed in Denmark in 2007 with new economic governance tasks for the Danish regions. These included for the first time the preparation of regional development strategies. The justification for such capabilities development and training was perceived as the limited amount of existing knowledge sharing between Danish regions and the paucity of examples of cross-regional cluster collaboration. Moreover, it was noted that the image of Danish clusters was not visible at the European level despite exemplary cluster formation practice, mainly industry-led. Accordingly, there was a perceived need for learning international good practice on cluster development. This episode gives an insight into the manner in which multilevel economic governance works in the vertical dimension in the EU although, as noted above, such efficiency can only be hoped to be reflected in swift understanding that contemporary knowledge flows and learning among firms and with enterprise support agencies is increasingly horizontal.

In conclusion, different levels of the policy system tend to have distinctive responsibilities. These rise and fall on the policy agenda over time. Member state focus is, in these 'birth pang/death throe' times, as cited from Gramsci by the UK Prime Minister Gordon Brown, intensively on 'saving financial system' and 'business support' more than 'green transition' or 'creative industries'. Regions may still be quite wedded to 'green issues' also for 'economic development' as they have policy influence there. The appropriate directorates of the EU stress coordination and 'concern' for the condition of member state and bank finances, but the European Central Bank is responsible for euro management. In the crisis, competition policy was widely ignored, and key member states suffered as euro management of a high currency exchange rate prevailed. In early 2010 fears were expressed that some member states like Greece might have to leave the euro and its associated economic governance strictures (Oborne, 2010). Various large-scale funds like the Common Agricultural Policy (CAP), Structural and Framework funds also became 'neoliberal' and less Keynesian (for example regional policy) in inspiration as the EU aped the Bush administration's reification of 'free and efficient markets'.

Accordingly, in different ways, at all multilevels, knowledge economy issues (finance, energy, education and skills) challenged industrial era priorities (industry and sector policies, 'national champions', agricultural subsidies and so on).

12.3.1 Implications of the New Knowledge Dynamics Paradigm for Policy

We see from the foregoing that the biggest 'Grand Challenge' for cluster programmes in future will be to enable their member firms and organizations to manage territorial knowledge flows. No longer will it be sufficient to advocate closer links to the regional university, as so many cluster route-maps habitually did in the past. It may be that neighbouring industry and a range of distant universities or independent laboratories are called for as cluster partners. In fortuitous circumstances, a well-developed cluster may have numerous specialist research centres, laboratories and training facilities in the same region as user-firms. These firms may have been responsible for the evolution of such a territorial knowledge system by sponsoring needed innovations in the institutional knowledge base. A case in point here is the celebrated automotive parts cluster in Ontario, Canada (Box 12.2). Notice the immense reliance in this very large and relatively medium-to-high-tech cluster upon a massive range of specialist science and engineering knowledge institutes and materials research laboratories within and beyond the university sector. It is in large part through the networks of globally leading researchers and trainers elsewhere that this cluster keeps its leading-edge knowledge capability, which is in turn relayed back into the pedagogy of students and the knowledge content of companies in the cluster. Of course, they have their own company-based in-house knowledge capabilities, including accessing corporate knowledge from within what, in many cases, are multinational firms. Hence, a top cluster is both locally and globally knowledge-integrated to the intellectual, industry and international flows of ideas, practice and solutions available from its relevant 'knowledge communities' – sometimes also referred to as 'epistemic communities'.

So what, in the face of demands of the kind indicated here, is the new role of administrations responsible for facilitating economic governance exemplified by the aforementioned cluster policies and the clustering process? We may begin to understand the kinds of skill-sets needed by the competent regional jurisdiction prevailing in recent times of turbulence and transition with which all are faced in evolving appropriate cluster programmes (Figure 12.1). First let us look at some key governance dependencies in the platform paradigm (Figure 12.1). Then we can consider how in the three basic models – issue-based government, problem-focused

---

BOX 12.2 THE TORONTO–WEST ONTARIO AUTOMOTIVE PARTS CLUSTER

Ontario, Canada: The #2 automotive cluster in North America with large supplier plants:

- Location of a strong supplier base of more than 280 companies, including: ABC Group, ArclelorMittal Dofasco, Bridgestone/Firestone, Burlington, Denso Manufacturing Canada, Linamar Corporation, Magna International, Mahle, Martinrea International, Meritor Suspension Systems, Mobiletron Electronics, NTN Bearing Mfg., OMRON Dualtec Automotive Electronics, Showa Canada, TS Tech Canada, Tsubaki of Canada, Westcast Industries, Woco, Woodbridge Group, and Yazaki North America
- Home to 89 science and engineering university programmes
- 30 steel and materials science research institutes
- Producing a highly educated and highly skilled workforce – over 4300 engineering graduates per year
- A leading research location; for example, the region is ranked #4 in North America for renewable fuels

---

governance and platform governance – policy is dealt with in each. For simplicity we take the relevant conceptualized case of a regional governance model where the focus is upon innovation support for industries that have, or can be envisaged to have, the character of a regional economic development platform. The key government and governance capabilities are the following:

- Visionary capability – influenced by foresight, networks, antennae.
- Innovative capability – influenced by dissatisfaction with the status quo.
- Networking capability – especially bringing in networked governance.
- Learning capability – influenced by openness of internal and external networks.
- Leadership capability – influenced by confidence, consensus and capabilities in general.
- Resource configurations – related to envisioned policy prioritizations.

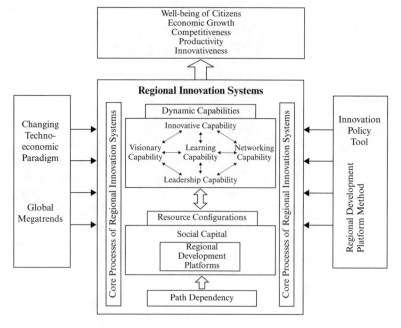

Source: After Harmaakorpi (2009).

Figure 12.1   Governance model for transitional conditions

- Social capital – of government, platforms, community and policy performance.

In Figure 12.1 the first five of these key governance attributes are represented as an interactive matrix of 'dynamic capabilities'. These capabilities are at the disposal of the fundamental responsibilities of modern, democratic economic governance (growth, competitiveness, and so on). In 'good governance' terms these capabilities draw upon embedded networks and regional social capital. This constitutes a regional innovation system base for policy. It is informed on the input side by contextual, anticipatory 'megatrend' knowledge, and produces innovative platform policies on the output side. In what follows we exemplify a variety of approaches to this.

12.3.2   Issue-Based Government Model

Here, in an issue-based governmental setting, there will be, by definition, relatively low governance in the modern understanding of external advice, lobbying and pressure of various networked kinds. Hence, two of the seven elements above (networking and learning capabilities) are immediately removed. This may be a benefit in that various layers of participation are taken out but ability to leverage consensus and social capital are also weakened. Such a model looks rather like the real case presented graphically in Figure 12.2. It is important to notice that this is fundamentally a government rather than a governance model. The task of achieving 'joined-up government' is one of the great challenges of contemporary administrations that have ballooned in scale and responsibilities.

Even in apparently accomplished settings such as the Israeli armed forces, new challenges, such as the Hezbollah incursions from Lebanon, displayed communication barriers. This occasioned an interactive and integrated response across the army and air force, in particular, with the navy also involved, unlike previous military campaigns that were more vertically structured and linear in the relationships among the armed services. Each service discovered it had its own vocabulary, even for standard features like 'road' or 'hillside' that could not be immediately understood outside the specific 'community of practice'. At a far lower level of intensity, many cluster programme officers may have felt the experience of such 'Chinese whispers' in their efforts at cross-disciplinary and cross-jurisdictional interaction and communication, even within their single region or country.

Hence this model depends for functionality upon vision, innovation, leadership and resources. Here a relatively constrained regional government, not especially desirous of much 'governance', gets a 'vision' that climate change requires policy action, prioritizes sustainability and does what it can to promote renewable energy and green jobs, making strong internal consensus linkage to education and skills, economic development, environmental, energy and spatial planning ministers and ministries to facilitate its leadership on this issue but with resources accessed in such a way that other stakeholders may benefit from replenishing their programmes in line with the evolving and emergent green policy trajectory. Hence innovation along with much else has been embedded in the same green policy trajectory. However, there may be external hostility, failure of understanding and significant opposition to and weakening of what is quite a strong policy formation process. The four core strengths may eventually ensure that it triumphs.

12.3.3   Problem-Focused Governance

This can be exemplified by the scenario, based in numerous distinctive cases from many regionalized administrations in numerous countries, where a

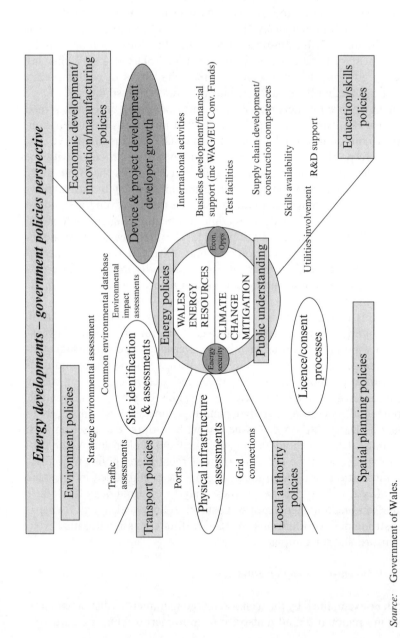

Energy developments – government policies perspective

Economic development/ innovation/manufacturing policies

Environment policies

Education/skills policies

Device & project development developer growth

Strategic environmental assessment

Common environmental database

International activities

Business development/financial support (inc WAG/EU Conv. Funds)

Environmental impact assessments

Test facilities

Supply chain development/ construction competences

Traffic assessments

Skills availability

Energy policies

R&D support

Site identification & assessments

WALES' ENERGY RESOURCES

Econ. Opps

CLIMATE CHANGE MITIGATION

Public understanding

Utilities involvement

Transport policies

Energy security

Ports

Physical infrastructure assessments

Licence/consent processes

Grid connections

Local authority policies

Spatial planning policies

Source: Government of Wales.

Figure 12.2   Green policy joined-up governance model

324

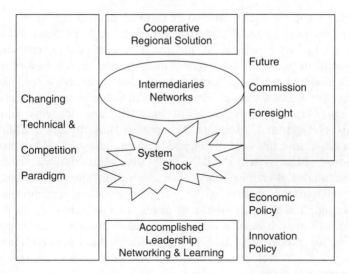

Figure 12.3   Reactive problem-focused regional governance

core regional industry competence is threatened or actually harmed by globalization processes, notably cheaper production of the core product portfolio at equivalent or better quality, undermining key markets. Let us assume, once again, a 'platform' of such industries with varying degrees of relatedness as found in, for example, engineering regions.

By definition, it is likely that although as a competent government this one regularly commissions or conducts research into its future possible and desirable strategies, these have tended to remain conservatively path-dependent on 'more of the same'. Since we have privileged innovation in the examples developed so far, we underline that 'more of the same' has meant increasing budgets for research (to the extent that the governance system can influence these), perhaps promoting a Regional Science Foundation or Research Council with modest but not insignificant resources. This has been a mainstay to help support regional innovation of the kind Figure 12.3 expresses, involving regional coherence between use and generation of knowledge in cluster policy. Now, that path-dependence has been exposed as misguided. Both vision and innovation as defined are thus absent or largely so, since they 'didn't see it coming' and they were 'satisfied with the status quo'.

However, and by contrast, it is a regional governance system inter-twined with a regional innovation system. Hence networking, learning (ideally innovative, and in implementation terms, inevitably rapid) and social capital would be strong. Leadership may not necessarily be especially strong in such a context because of 'open governance' and flat hierarchies. Bear in mind that the fate of the region's main industries may not be a highly prioritized function over which the government has any specific or particular competence or authority, yet it is looked to and interlocuted by industry to help by 'doing something'. So it easily brings together key stakeholders of consequence to the problem for emergency meetings – leading firms, suppliers, industrial and academic research organizations from the region. The region thus rapidly facilitates a conversation and bilateral dialogues. Understanding (rapid learning) of the nature of the 'system shock' is facilitated. Industrial organization is deemed in need of change; more 'open innovation' and outsourcing generally are required; related to, for example, prevailing 'lean production' norms. Suppliers complain that they never did innovation before. A consortium of research associations is proposed as trainer to the suppliers. Funding for 'model projects' is found by the lead ministry co-funded by industry and research labs. Problem solved, engineering industry saved . . . for the time being.

12.3.4 Reactive and Proactive Platform Governance

Finally, the model that confronts the propositions of 'platform leadership' most closely as these have evolved over the course of the research is – from the point of view of policy – that concerning platform governance. We take innovation as continuing to be the focus, and a crisis of the regional economy worse than the previous case, whereby foreign competition has virtually wiped out the indigenous industry, an established one with a strong vertical supply chain from raw materials to final design-intensive products – something of an industrial monoculture. To repeat, this scenario envisages not simply an adjustment but a transition imperative.

In this case, all the matrix capabilities listed are in force and it should prove a more resilient administration and policy system than either of the preceding models. Notice the vertical sidebars on 'changing techno-economic paradigm' and 'global megatrends' which are under regular if not constant surveillance by the leadership team. Hence they have some inkling that transition is 'in the air' and are ready to move in some direction but they cannot fully anticipate which way until it happens. Innovation capability is accordingly high because they are dissatisfied with the status quo. Networking and learning capabilities are good because it is an open governance, not closed governmental system. Knowledge is distributed but accessible, including, as needed, technical knowledge from beyond the region to at least national level, possibly beyond even that. Social capital is historically strong, not least because of the monoculture, and leadership is at the very least adequate though not overbearing in such a highly networked context.

The task, once the industrial base has been devastated, is to discover whether or not the regional economy has 'related variety' that can aid construction of a platform of activities, path-dependent on the old but capable of mutating into something new. To do this, the leadership sets in train a reactive 'regional development platform methodology' to identify regional development platforms and policies that may assist the fulfilment of this vision.

In this the anticipatory knowledge of the changing techno-economic paradigm and global megatrends work assists because many stakeholders are more or less accultured to them. Expert panels of entrepreneurs and others are called to explore how innovatory industry may form, utilizing skills and technologies from the defunct one in the context of such paradigm and megatrends changes. They meet on numerous occasions, reporting back to the regional governance system leadership. Extra expertise from outside the region in subjects like nanotechnology is called in from national centres of expertise to advise.

A consensus is reached that two megatrend platforms evolving from the skills and techniques of the old 'cluster' can fit, suitably modernized by innovative knowledge and judicious application of development resources. These are clean technologies, and healthcare. The regional platform policy is designed accordingly and a new regional economy is designed, drawing upon regionally and globally distributed knowledge bases, interactivity and a coherent methodology for building consensus for taking resource-dependent actions. These inform resource allocation for enterprise and innovation support for regional businesses.

Multilevel governance programmes are identified and targeted to assist in the progress towards building the new regional platforms. These arrive from both national and EU levels and are packaged in ways that seek to maximize their complementarities to what has been designed at regional level. Hence platform policy is a bottom-up approach par excellence.

However, better still is such a model that shows capabilities in the proactive dimension. Such a model is found in Bayern (Bavaria) Germany as summarized below and focused upon the platform-building activities of Bayern Innovativ, a governance agency for regional development (Figure 12.4). Here the agency identified key industries that were beneficiaries of cluster policy paid for by Bavaria's resource windfall when it sold its share in the regional energy supplier. These were cross-tabulated against key technologies to find the interdisciplinary and interindustry innovation potentials of 'related variety' in the regional economy. Many innovations have ensued from the more than 1000 per year 'conversations' facilitated

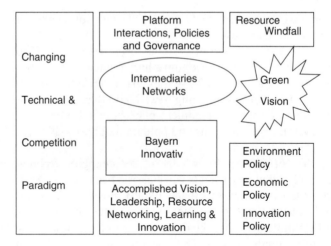

Figure 12.4   Proactive platform governance of innovation

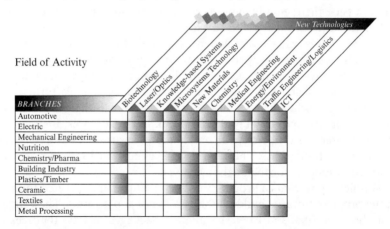

Note: The marked fields symbolize combinations of technologies and branches and change according to new tasks.

Source: Bayern Innovativ, 2009, http://www.bayern-innovativ.de/.

Figure 12.5   Bayern Innovativ: technology platforms

between neighbouring sectors concerning technological applications and resulting innovations. Part of the new platform thinking involved recognition of the importance of enhancing sustainable development as part of a new green vision concerning renewable energy and clean technologies.

How does Bayern Innovativ's proactive regional innovation policy work? Figure 12.5 gives an indication, whereby matrix management of potential innovation opportunities at intersections between industries, some having been beneficiaries of earlier cluster programme investments, and technologies occur. These are points where conversations among distinct and by no means obviously neighbouring business sectors are facilitated. Accordingly, where these facilitate personal discussion between experts and customers, sustainable cooperation networks are developed.

More than 1000 new cooperations are initiated annually – examples include:

- Laser technology adapted to beam nanoscale droplets onto microarrays for rapid bioanalysis.
- Mechatronic systems for car engine management that have been transferred to bus steering systems.
- Portable fuel cells that have been applied in automotive electronics.
- Plastic injection moulding processes from button manufacturing which have been implemented in automotive plastic components.
- A logistics and transport company that has secured a contract with one of the world's largest Internet suppliers.
- A technical textile producer that won a contract in medical engineering.

Hence, Bayern Innovativ (BI) initiates business-driven project cooperations across disciplines and branches, taking into account the latest results from the scientific community. Since 1997 the agency has forged new pathways and created a portfolio of cooperation platforms and networks that have generated an extended, sustainable network structure. Both the platforms and the networks are in demand at regional, national and international levels.

Lower Austria

It is worth noting that this approach may have been pioneered in the 1990s in Upper Austria where a Technology Policy Matrix cluster programme was first implemented. Unlike the BI approach, that in Lower Austria is thematically formed into a matrix policy structure by infusing each member cluster with the common goal of enhancing 'sustainability'. There are nowadays five key clusters evolving and receiving support around the theme of eco-innovation. These are, respectively:

- Green building – the economic hub of a network of appropriate firms in the region's green construction industry. The cluster team includes architects, energy experts, building and interior design

professionals. The cluster is coalescing towards energy and environmental technology fields.
- Automotives – companies are supported in; internationalization,
  qualification and cooperation with research facilities.
- Food cluster – supporting the regional food industry, from farm to
  fork. Food quality, safety, organic and regional products are supported and promoted.
- Logistics – this involves shippers, transporters and logistics services
  to enhance transport bundling, reduction of empty journeys, and
  more efficient transport and shipping.
- Plastics – an interregional cluster also involving the Salzburg
  region. Development of bioplastics and fibre composites (biofibres).
  Expansion into medical technology and recycling is planned.

12.4   SOME KEY RESEARCH FINDINGS ON PRIVATE PLATFORM INNOVATION WITH REGIONAL PLATFORM GOVERNANCE

Finally, it is worth noting that governance of regional innovation policy
does not always have to be guided by the public sector, as occurred in all
the governance styles described above. Particularly with regard to scientific
and technological innovation it is not unusual in, for example, the USA or
Canada to see private associations managing innovation. Silicon Valley is the
most obvious case but in the rising technology complex at Ottawa, Canada,
where Research In Motion produces the BlackBerry mobile communications device, much of the steering of interactions, subsidies and facilities is
conducted by the Ottawa Centre for Research and Innovation (OCRI) which
is a member-based economic development corporation for fostering the
advancement of the region's knowledge-based institutions and industries.
OCRI delivers its economic development services through a unique partnership with the City of Ottawa, where the City and OCRI, through its members,
set the strategy and manage the programmes that move Ottawa's economy
forward. OCRI is a non-profit, partnership organization that operates on
an annual budget that comes from a variety of sources including: municipal,
federal and provincial government; membership fees; professional development programmes; and private sector contributions (Wolfe, 2002).

In what follows, insights into some of the more interesting cases
researched from the viewpoint of the study's interest in different types and
categories of knowledge flow in the contemporary European economy are
explored. Space limits mean that just a few are given lengthy treatments
while a further group of cases are outlined. In some cases the study-

contender status of the initial proposal was not followed through into the final empirical knowledge flows research. This was the case, for example, with the German automotive biofuels lead. In other cases, the empirics took a more specific turn as might be expected, and as follows below in the account of the Aquitaine aerospace case. Further information and exegesis are found on the Eurodite website, http://www.eurodite.bham.ac.uk/.

12.4.1 Skåne New Media Platform

Arising from the comparative research project, one of Europe's most successful innovation platforms is to be found centred in the Skåne region in Sweden. This is one of the Eurodite study regions, as are Bavaria, Wales and North Jutland – to which reference was made in Chapter 11, with some updating continuation in the present chapter, below. Here, as is indicated below, the regional development agency has had an intensive 'Future Vision' analysis conducted by a number of different external peer groups. One recommendation arising from such peer group analysis, enthusiastically seized upon by the regional government, is to engage in more 'transversal' regional innovation policy. This is partly because of a major problem of fragmentation in knowledge sharing in the region (it has 51 innovation and enterprise support agencies, many very small) and, although a somewhat fragmented and uneven cluster strategy has been embarked upon since (in the case of agro-food) 1994, there is little cross-fertilization although there is potential to stimulate this.

Some Skåne clusters, such as the two mentioned briefly below, are new and rather embryonic. One, which is discussed elsewhere, is Mobile Heights, which focuses on innovation in mobile telephony; while the second, studied in depth here and in the Eurodite project (Dahlstrom et al., 2009) is Moving Media.

Moving media
New media are different from traditional media mainly in the three following ways: (1) the diversification of media forms, contents and channels; (2) the personalization of media content; and (3) a shift from consumption to production. It may be argued that it is misleading to call new media a sector since it is a diverse and complex set of activities that is linking up with other industrial sectors in terms of both technology and content. Furthermore, new media activities are constantly changing and developing. It may therefore be more accurate to see new media as a platform of activities requiring platform policy support. Despite the diversity, there are common characteristics of new media, for example that it integrates still and moving images, text, graphics, pictures, sound and data electronically,

Table 12.3   Components in the supply chain for moving media

Production process		Market channels	
Production	Infrastructure	Distribution	Consumption
● TV production	● Production techniques	● Distributors	● Dealers
● Film production	● Graphic design and animation	● Publishers	● Online sales
● Game development	● Software development	● Operators and suppliers within Internet, TV, mobile telephony	● Interactive consumption
	● Moving Media-related advertising agencies	● Events	● Cinema
	● Studios		● Film and game rental
	● Management		

and even animation and interactivity. The difficulties with identifying new media as a sector also become clear regarding defining it in terms of statistical classifications. The classification used in this study was made for the purpose of the development of a strategic programme for moving media in Skåne and Blekinge (Table 12.3). Here, we focus on moving media rather than 'new media', since 'moving media' is the terminology used for the strategic work in Skåne.

Moving Media itself is scarcely a subsector, but rather a specific group of firms and individuals focusing on 'symbolic knowledge work'. Looking at employment figures it is a very limited subsector. It employs around 5100 individuals in Skåne, or 1 per cent of the employment. However, despite its small size, the subsector is interesting because moving media companies and individuals interact with companies and institutions belonging to other sectors, for example ICT and tourism. This platform interaction, where moving media firms are involved, contributes to innovation and value added in several sectors. Furthermore, new media is a growth sector in Skåne, particularly moving media. The growth builds on existing institutions, for example the regional film production centre Film i Skåne in Ystad, and a growing and thriving sector of companies in mobile user interface and computer games.

Here, in Moving Media, we focus on the production side, but with links into distribution and consumption particularly in relation to film tourism. On the production side, game development and film production are important, but TV production is also important in Skåne. Players in the production phase include firms as well as freelancers. Firms and freelancers in the 'infrastructure' phase of the production process provide various types of technical or specialized and strategic services. These can include sound specialists that are hired by a game development company, or graphic designers hired by film tourism companies. In terms of the market channels in the model, these can include suppliers within TV who play an important role in film tourism. Film tourism also takes its point of departure from the new media sector and the subsector of moving media, more specifically in film production in Skåne. The basis for film tourism in Skåne lies in film production activities and hence moving media is the primary sector. Tourism is seen as secondary but necessary and related.

Film production in Skåne has from a limited basis experienced a major increase since 2000. There are deep roots of film making in Skåne, dating back to the very first studio films being made in Sweden in 1909. The tourism sector also has a long tradition in Skåne and it is a strong and important part of the economy. Skånska Filmproducentföreningen represents 16 film production companies based in the region. These companies span over the entire spectrum of film productions: short, documentaries, features, animated films. Some are also involved in producing advertisements, and music videos.

Computer gaming
Moving media and game development have a development path from within the south-western part of Skåne. The historical roots of game development can be found in information and communication technologies, later integrated with software providers of applications and creators of media content. Malmö has a tradition within 'old media' in the shape of the newspapers, publishers, and also publishing of comics and games for children and youth. Lund, on the other hand, is both a university and an industrial city where particularly the strong ICT sector, including education, research and major firms such as Sony Ericsson and Ericsson Mobile Platforms, contributes an important element of continuity with regard to the moving media and game development activities. Fourteen of the 91 firms in Sweden that state that their main activity is computer game development are located to Malmö or Lund.

Key actors in the area of moving media and game development are higher education institutions such as the University of Malmö and Faculty of Engineering at Lund University (LTH), public actors such as the City of

Malmö and Region Skåne, and a number of companies. In the region there are both providers of software and hardware producers. Another important key actor within moving media is SVT, the national Swedish public service broadcaster. Their Malmö office is moving into the Västra Hamnen (harbour) area where a new complex called Moving Media City is being developed. An important stimulant here is SVT's new production policy to buy a greater share of products from other producers. This opens up the market for content producers within moving media. The Department of Art, Culture and Communication (K3) Malmö University offers education in the field. Students at K3 have work placements, for example at game development companies. Several members of staff at K3 are also entrepreneurs running their own firms. There is also a Game Academy in Malmö. It is an Advanced Vocational Education and Training course of 2.5 years run by the education company Hermods. The MINC incubator helps to commercialize ideas from the University of Malmö as well as from entrepreneurs with other backgrounds. New media firms are a priority for the incubator. For instance a recently established game development firm here is Ozma game development, run by two women. Furthermore, VINNOVA has co-funded Living Lab New Media in Malmö University, which is hoped will result in new competitive information technology (IT)-based game development services. Since 2004 Malmö University has also had a knowledge partnership with Massachusetts Institute of Technology (MIT). The project 'Agent O' is a game built upon a platform developed by the MIT Teacher Education Programme as a so-called 'Augmented Reality Outdoor GPS based Game'. The game is intended to be used for classes for sustainable development, chemistry and technology. Awnic, the firm that now owns 'Agent O' is a spin-off from the university, and is a small company working with game development.

There is also education concerning game development in neighbouring regions. For instance in Blekinge there are several education institutes, including the Blekinge Institute of Technology and Hyper Island, that offer education programmes of relevance for game development.

Media interaction in Skåne includes several game development companies and also national, regional and local policy initiatives related to moving media. There are for instance related initiatives from the Regional Structural Funds Programme 2007–13, in which moving media is one focus area. The cluster development platform Moving Media Southern Sweden (MMSS) initiated by Skåne regional council and the neighbouring region Blekinge also aims at stimulating innovation and creating companies in the moving media sector in the two regions. The Media Mötesplats Malmö (MMM) funded by the national actor Knowledge Foundation, Region Skåne and the City of Malmö also provides an arena for developing media by providing, for instance, competence and business development. Here it is important that actors from other parts of Sweden and from overseas are included in the projects.

The project Nordic Game Programme financed by the Nordic Council of Ministers is an important actor that among other things enables participation of game development companies at international conferences and fairs, and also provides financial development support to game development companies. The project also organizes the annual Nordic Game Conference, located in Malmö, an important meeting place for individuals and actors within game development from many countries.

The relocation of a number of companies or institutions of relevance for game development to the Western harbour area (Västra Hamnen), such as Swedish television, the incubator MINC, Malmö University, the MMM and the Nordic Game Programme, implies that the cluster distance between those actors is short.

Film tourism

Film tourism in Skåne is an interesting growth area that is developing through the interaction between different actors and activities. There are a number of key agents, institutions, organizations and firms within the film sector in Skåne. In film production, the regional production centre Film i Skåne is important and is active within the production of feature films and TV drama series, shorts and documentaries in addition to media pedagogic film activities. Public funding from the national, regional and local level is supporting production activities in addition to private money. The public money is of importance for ensuring that film teams shoot in the region and employ staff. This may be seen as a way to anchor knowledge in the region. The international co-production of films that is increasingly the norm, and the pattern in the case of the major film projects in Ystad, generate film production teams that are built up by people from many different places. Film teams consist of people from many different places and countries, and in Skåne, the closeness to the capital region of Denmark is particularly noticeable in the film teams. The Oresund Film Commission promotes Skåne and greater Copenhagen as a location for shooting films. The non-profit organization provides services free of charge for film teams that wish to shoot in the region. The Commission is part funded by the European Regional Development Fund (ERDF) through Interreg, and through public authorities on both sides of the border.

Skånska Filmproducentföreningen represents film production companies based in the region. These companies span the spectrum of film productions, including shorts, documentaries, features and animated films. Some are also involved in producing adverts and music videos. There are also other film companies in the region that are not part of this association. Of these, Yellow Bird, founded in 2002 and from 2007 owned by Zodiac Television, is the production company that has had the largest effect on the film sector in Skåne. The company was established in Ystad with a plan to focus on projects larger than one individual film, to be able to collaborate and co-produce with international broadcasters. The success of Yellow Bird started with the project of producing 13 films based on Henning Mankell's books about Inspector Wallander of the Ystad police.

The three key actors for developing the marketing collaboration known as Film Track are Cineteket, Hasse & Tage Museum and the Regional Museum. Cineteket is located in Ystad. This public–private partnership runs a film-related experience centre. The base for the activities was the fact that the Wallander films were shot in the studios next to the centre. The municipality of Ystad actively supported the shooting of the first Wallander films in 2003 and aims to develop Ystad into a film-friendly place by offering training programmes. A film coordinator has been hired by the municipality. The municipality also started Cineteket as a project that has now developed into a public–private partnership. The involvement of private actors, such as the local savings bank Sparbanken Syd, shows that film production is perceived as having economic and symbolic value for both local and regional development.

Regarding education and training, the two-year film worker programme exists at Skurup Folkhögskola and the two new Masters programmes based in Ystad are run by the University of Lund and Malmö Academy of Music. These programmes are in film production and in composition of film music. The basis for film tourism in Skåne is the fact that films are shot in locations across the region and in Ystad studios. Within the framework of the national policy to support film productions in Sweden, a regionalization of film production has taken place. This process started in 1997 and has developed in various ways over the years. From a national point of view, regionalization is driven by the cultural policy aim to facilitate story-telling from all over the country by many different actors to be performed in film media. Film Track is a leading film tourism production initiative, which represents collaboration between three different attractions – two publicly owned museums and one publicly owned visitor attraction – that has developed in to a public–private partnership. The collaboration is related to marketing and the exchange of ideas and has deepened into a product development collaboration. It is also an example of interpersonal and interorganizational relations.

Moving Media has some embryonic cluster characteristics, especially in cooperation among multiple actors. However computer games and film tourism are separate, small subsystems rather than a significantly overlapping set of skills. They are differently located and of distinct character: the former more in the market, the latter more publicly dependent. Both nevertheless are selling the region innovatively and with interesting external relationships such as MIT and Öresund with Copenhagen. The key interpretations of knowledge flow policies to be drawn here are the following. First, it may be seen that Skåne is an interesting but by no means exceptional regional administration which contains embryonic clusters such as those described, large-scale industry in the shape of the agro-food sector, tourism, life sciences – which the region supports through an international regional innovation system at Öresund, which connects Skåne to the greater Copenhagen region in Denmark – and an aspirational cleanness cluster. Second, many of these could have innovation-inducing cross-pollination of ideas if the necessary mechanisms were established. However, it is by means of having external assessments on the changing economic paradigm and the implications for innovation of adoption of platform policy to support regional innovation that the region has come to see the importance of furthering it. As such, Skåne is a beacon for other 'ordinary' regional enterprise support agencies. Finally, Skåne is a good example of a regional economic governance agency being proactive by utilizing mainly its own existing economic assets. Few of the elements in the regional economic structure from which enhanced innovation is anticipated have been brought in from outside. Rather, knowledge of modern industry organization has been imported and applied to indigenous industry.

12.4.2   Midi-Pyrenees Global Navigation Satellite Systems (GNSS)

A combinative knowledge platform
GNSS is a standard term for the systems that provide positioning and navigation solutions from signals transmitted by orbiting satellites. In the past decades these technologies were mainly developed by the defence industry (missile guidance) and the aircraft industry (air fleet management). The knowledge dynamics were cumulative, based on incremental innovations dedicated to the narrow aerospace industry market. Nowadays, these technological dynamics present the characteristics of a combinative knowledge platform (CKP). Indeed, in the technological and symbolic paradigm of mobility, GNSS represents technologies which find complementarities and integration opportunities in many other technological and socio-economic contexts.

The GNSS field is a worldwide technological field which combines clusters and pipelines. Indeed, considering the European level, seven main GNSS clusters have been identified in the regions of Midi-Pyrenees (MP), Upper Bavaria, Ile de France, Inner London, Community of

Madrid, Tuscany, and Lazio. In this study we only focus on the knowledge relations starting from (and inside) the MP so as to explain how CKPs combine local and non-local relations. The choice of the MP is not random. Indeed, the MP has a concentration of more than 12 000 jobs dedicated to spatial activities and was recently identified by the French government as being the worldwide 'competitiveness cluster' in aerospace and on-board systems (Dupuy and Gilly, 1999; Zuliani, 2008). The MP is a historical leader in Europe for the design and creation of space systems and home to the main actors working on the two major GNSS European programmes, EGNOS and Galileo, such as the CNES (National Centre of Space Studies), EADS Astrium and Thales Alenia Space (TAS). In particular, the coexistence within the same place of the two major competing companies EADS Astrium and TAS is a remarkable point. It should be interesting to study how organizations that display a weak level of cognitive distance coexist in the same place, and how each one manages the intended and unintended knowledge spillovers through its position in the relational structure of the cluster.

An intensive amount of deskwork enabled us to list all the main regional organizations involved in the GNSS technological field, from space and ground infrastructures to applications and related services, and from large firms to small and medium-sized (SMEs) and research units. In doing so we constructed a database of 30 collaborative projects in which these organizations are involved, ensuring a 'snowball effect' by bringing together other firms that consequently add complementary pieces of knowledge to the CKP, inside and outside the region, through these collaborative R&D projects. The data aggregation decision tree starts with two main sets of sources: regional sources[1] (through the review of websites dedicated to GNSS), and European sources,[2] focusing only on projects that include 'navigation' or 'positioning' and Galileo or EGNOS. Once the collaborative projects were identified in a nested system of publicly funded collaborative projects, all the websites of the projects were visited in order to have a look at their work package organization and hence remove non-relevant knowledge relations (see below).

Innovation biography analysis by projects
A relational database brings together projects which differ in size. These depend greatly on the geographical scale of the funding, bearing in mind that regional and national projects bring together fewer units than European Projects (3–14 partners in regional and national projects, 18–57 partners in four of the European projects). Selecting the ties consists of cleaning up the relational database by removing pairwise relations between partners who are not involved in the same work packages for

the whole of the project, and maintaining pairwise relations between the project leader and all the partners. Moreover, when the leader of the project is outside the region, we only consider the work packages in which MP organizations are involved.

Such a methodology implies comments relating to both its advantages and its limitations. Firstly, starting from publicly funded projects is certainly a non-exhaustive way of capturing all the relations between firms, but the advantage is that our analysis thereby resides on a clear definition of what a knowledge relation is and avoids the vagueness of the nature of the relations we can perceive when we understand relations uniquely through interviews. In particular, the density of relations can be approximated objectively by using an index referring to the number of projects in which organizations are involved pairwise. Nevertheless, our data can be perceived as being representative of the knowledge process of GNSS in (and from) the Midi-Pyrenees for the period 2005–08:[3]

1. GNSSs are emerging technologies which concern applications dedicated to public utilities such as transport security, environment observation, telecommunications and so on. In this way, GNSSs are among the priorities for policy-makers, whatever their geographical scale.
2. Considering that public funding is conditional on 'requests for tender', the organizations in our database are those which have succeeded in obtaining the funding due to their legitimacy in this technological field. This legitimacy results from their experience in past relations, so our relational database is strongly representative of the knowledge trends in the technological field.

Secondly, using projects as a starting point is dependent on the geographical scale of the public funding, which can be regional, national or European. Nevertheless, this limitation can be transformed into a convenient advantage since these three scales of funding are distinguished. The aggregation of these projects and their transformation into a unified network structure thus ensures a representative view of the embeddedness of regional organizations into the European GNSS field. Consequently, our protocol follows the multilevel governance system that typifies research funding in Europe and constitutes the current 'circuitry of network policy' (Cooke, 2002a). As a perfect exhaustiveness is difficult to reach, it is possible that marginal data are missing. Data concerning knowledge relations, in which local organizations are involved and are supported or funded at the regional level, but by another region, could be missing. Nevertheless, a test conducted from the public information available on the organizations' websites confirmed that these missing data are marginal. Moreover, the results of one of the major Midi-Pyrenean requests for tender in Navigation Satellite Systems (VANS), which includes five collaborative R&D projects from within our database, show that the MP organizations represent 80 per cent of the selected partners. Similarly, ULISS, the French requests for tender on EGNOS and Galileo applications, restricts the eligibility to organizations located in France.

In the early stages of technological dynamics such as GNSS the problem is one of regularizing a standard and finding applications that will ensure its diffusion. This might generate an intense competition between incumbent firms seeking to impose their standards, and geographical proximity might be a problem in this case because of the risk of unintended knowledge spillovers between rival firms. In the Midi-Pyrenees GNSS network we have two strong competitors in the infrastructure segment – Thales Alenia Space (TAS) and EADS Astrium – and in addition there is the French National Centre of Space Studies (CNES) which is also a key player in the domain of satellite building. The way they position themselves in this context of intense competition is an important issue in the efficiency and stability of the GNSS cluster. Do they frequently interact or do they, on the contrary, try to avoid any contact by differentiating their neighborhood as much as possible? To answer this question it is necessary to analyse the cliques or quasi-cliques present in the network. The more organizations belong to the same clique, the more they will display a structural equivalence and the more the flows of knowledge between them will be dense. Obviously, the MP+ Network involving outsiders will display as many cliques as collaborative projects, since naturally each project is a clique. This problem can be circumvented if we use the bipartite network in order to reconstruct the simplified MP+ Network. Note that a clique is defined as the biggest group of nodes having all possible ties present within the group.

The biggest clique is composed of a set of local SMEs that interact frequently. It is worth noticing that TAS appears frequently in cliques composed of local organizations (CNES, TESA, Rockwell Collins, M3 System and Skylab) while EADS Astrium has in preference chosen to interact with non-local actors (Infoterra, Nottingham sc. Ltd). Here we obtain an answer to our question about the networking strategies chosen by these two rivals; in spite of their geographical proximity they have chosen not to interact with the same pools of actors. TAS has preferred a local interaction strategy while EADS Astrium has chosen an outward-oriented strategy. Nevertheless, it is worth noticing that TAS and EADS Astrium belong to the same clique along with the CNES, the French National centre of space studies, which is central in the standardization process of GNSS. This situation is typical of the 'co-opetition process' observed in many network industries: while companies try to avoid competition and unintended knowledge spillovers by limiting knowledge flows between them as much as possible, they need to cooperate on standardization since the extent of the potential market depends strongly on users' and consumers' preferences for standards. This 'battle of standards' is resolved by research units and public agencies which take on the role of intermediaries in the standard-setting process.

Global networks of a nodal cluster
In both geographical and relational dimensions an efficient location is a critical parameter of the modern innovative firm because it is the best way to gain access to new pieces of knowledge and to ensure, at the same time, a good level of knowledge appropriation. Since the GNSS technological field is a composite one, the choice of relational and geographical localizations is determined by a twofold challenge: there is a need to understand that organizations endowed with different knowledge bases must interact but, at the same time, they need to design their innovations around a common technological standard. This implies that some central organizations will develop a special kind of absorptive capacity allowing them to detect complementary blocks of knowledge and to integrate them. It also means that a GNSS network should be structured in such a way that ensures: (1) a good circulation of knowledge between the MP and other places; (2) a good circulation of knowledge between the different knowledge segments; and (3) a central role for some organizations endowed with a knowledge integration capacity.

Some actors (TAS and the CNES) seek to access external knowledge by shortening the distance to other actors, by multiplying the opportunities of contacts and by positioning themselves as intermediaries. Others (EADS, Actia, France Telecom R&D) have more specific networking strategies focused on the search for betweenness centrality. Moreover, it is worth noting that, whatever the centrality measure is, 20–25 per cent of the top 20 most central organizations is made up of non-local nodes, which means that some external organizations are well positioned in the network. By supposing 'embedded clusters' rather than clusters per se, it becomes possible to show the pathways of knowledge and the organizations that play a central role in these pathways, even if some of them can be located outside the cluster.

In our particular case, this result is interesting, because by construction of the relational database, local organizations are more likely to be central than external ones. It shows clearly that the Midi-Pyrenees GNSS cluster is strongly embedded in a wider European network. It is mainly explained by the geography of the space industry, which has for a long time developed research collaborations in Europe. It is especially true for the GNSS industry, because research collaborations between organizations coming from different countries are a strategic issue for the European Union, in order to develop its own global navigation satellite system (Galileo) and become independent from the American global positioning system (GPS). Thus it is not surprising that outside organizations display a certain degree of influence in the MP network, due to the European pipelines that support the development of the European infrastructure. These results show that it would be irrelevant nowadays to analyse clusters independently of the technological field: firstly, firms embedded in local networks are also involved in larger ones; and secondly, non-local firms bring knowledge from outside and capture knowledge from inside through gatekeeping strategies. Consequently, even if we have identified a GNSS cluster in the Midi-Pyrenees region, the aggregate efficiency of this local structure depends not only on the internal relations, but also on the way the cluster connects itself to larger pipelines through a subset of nodes.

12.4.3   Renewable Energy from Food Research in Wales

Bioenergy innovation
The renewable energy industry is quite diverse and dynamic, showing rapid growth. It covers long-established industries such as energy and agriculture and encompasses newer industries at the leading edge of technological innovation, such as ad hoc renewable energy companies, clean technologies and biotechnology firms. As stressed in Chapter 11, this research focused on bioenergy, which refers to energy produced from the direct and indirect combustion of biomass material such as energy crops, wood and waste, and biogas. Most current bioenergy activities are integrated with other industries such as biomass or biofuels obtained from organic matter either directly from plants or indirectly from industrial, commercial, domestic or agricultural products. The research presented on this subject in Chapter 11 showed how agro-food research and development (R&D) focused on high-energy grassland animal fodder also resulted in the discovery of excellent candidate feedstock for renewable energy. The production of energy from biomass involves a range of technologies that include solid combustion, gasification and fermentations. These technologies produce liquid and gas fuels from a diverse set of biological resources: traditional crops (sugarcane, maize and oilseed – called first-generation biofuels), as well as crop residues and waste (maize stover, wheat straw, rice hulls, cotton waste), energy-dedicated crops (grasses and trees – second-generation), dung, and the organic component of urban waste.

The results are bioenergy products that provide multiple energy services: cooking fuels, heat, electricity and transportation fuels.

Energy crops are grown specifically for use as fuel. The types of energy crops currently grown in the UK for the generation of electricity and heat include: fast-growing tree species which can be continually harvested every three to four years (so-called short-rotation coppice) or, depending on the tree species, coppiced over longer periods; grasses such as Miscanthus which can be harvested annually; and agricultural residues such as straw.

Bioenergy innovations (combined heat and power plants – CHP) as well as first-generation biofuels are considered incremental innovations in the sense that they substitute sustainable for fossil fuel feedstock, but not necessarily at greater cost, and they utilize existing agricultural products for energy; but second-generation biofuels transform the nature of the input through gasification, which with increasing returns to scale will be cost competitive, hence disruptive in the foreseeable. The core knowledge within the industry is technical but also encompasses project management, marketing, financial, legal and developmental knowledge.

The type of technical knowledge can range from feedstock management to industrial enzymes, equipment, infrastructure, other production factors or project development. The skills required are also varied as they combine existing skills and new skills. Knowledge sources are both internal and external, combining knowledge deriving from different sectors but also intersectoral knowledge, requiring high absorptive capacity. The knowledge links investigated involve many UK-wide, large firms and some international as well as intraregional novel agricultural products business linkages. Knowledge is also path-dependent and entrepreneurial history shows the extent of sectoral migration and related variety.

The bioenergy-related knowledge is often linked closely to universities and private research centres and in recent years there has been an explosion in bioenergy research, especially for second-generation biofuels. BP in 2007 pledged $500 million for an Energy Biosciences Institute and, in January 2008, the Biotechnology and Biological Sciences Research Council (BBSRC) funded the biggest ever single UK public investment in bioenergy research (£27 million) to provide the science to underpin and develop the important and emerging UK sustainable bioenergy sector. The BBSRC Sustainable Bioenergy Centre is focused on six research hubs of academic and industrial partners, based at each of the universities of Cambridge, Dundee and York ,and Rothamstead Research and two at the University of Nottingham. Another seven universities (among these, the Aberystwyth University Institute of Biological, Environmental and Rural Sciences – IBERS) and institutes are involved, and 15 industrial partners across the hubs are contributing around £7 million of the funding.

Research activities have often involved many different stages of bioenergy production, from widening the range of materials that can be the starting point for bioenergy, to improving the crops used by making them grow more efficiently, to changing plant cell walls. Key research challenges are to improve the productivity and yield of bioenergy crops, to enhance the conversion processes and streamline the efficiency with which solid biomass and liquid biofuels can be utilized. These challenges are not independent of each other and a 'whole systems approach' is required. Crops can be 'designed' with subsequent enzymic conversion and/or combustion processes in mind. There is also a major challenge in joining up activity along the complex bioenergy supply chain. Systems-level research on linkages to energy policy, land use patterns, agricultural activity and environmental impacts is essential. Furthermore research is also focusing on the concept of 'biorefineries' where crops are processed into multiple product streams.

Biomass energy applications

There have been several studies into the barriers to increased supply of biomass for bioenergy production, the most comprehensive of which was that of the Biomass Task Force (2005). This found that the development of a 'biomass industry' was constrained by a lack of market confidence brought about by three main factors: (1) the lack of a mature, robust fuel supply chain; (2) lack of knowledge, interest or awareness of the potential of bioenergy; and (3) lack of strong market signals and the appreciation of the true costs and long-term benefits of bioenergy, due either to regulatory or structural issues, particularly in the heat market.

Wales is an established energy-producing economy that has also shown interesting capabilities in bioenergy. This represents a move from coal and oil refining industries towards a more integrated 'green economy' where green innovation by mostly indigenous actors is arising, supported and promoted by a strong science base and an active policy environment. Wales accounts for a number of internationally recognized university research groups at Glamorgan (hydrogen, combustion, controls), Cardiff (power engineering, renewables, sustainable architecture), Swansea (materials, marine energy), IBERS (biocrops) and Bangor (marine, photovoltaics, alternative crops).

These capabilities have attracted £400 million investment from Prenergy Power, a group of power and energy professionals with experience of the biomass sector (as developers and operators of biomass power plants, and as suppliers and traders of the biomass feedstock), to develop the world's largest biomass (wood chip)-burning power station at Port Talbot. The large-scale biomass power station, a 350MW wood chip-fuelled plant, will be located in Port Talbot, a deepwater port, to take advantage of the efficiencies of large-scale sea transport. The Port Talbot site is an established area for industrial use, close to electricity connection, with well-developed local infrastructure and the availability of local workforce, suppliers and service contractors. The operation of the plant will result in the import of an additional 2.5–3 million tonnes of cargo annually in the form of wood chip fuel. The project is expected to contribute approximately 70 per cent of the Welsh Assembly's 2010 renewable electricity target.

A further development is represented by the Western Wood Energy project, the first commercial-scale biomass plant in Margam, Port Talbot. This project was initiated by a Cardiff-based renewable energy company, Eco2, which specializes in initiating, developing, financing and operating renewable energy projects throughout the UK. Eco2 and Western Log Group, a leading UK supplier in the timber industry, set up a joint venture to develop the power plant that will generate 13.8 MW of electricity by burning untreated wood from sawmills and sustainable forestry sources. The plant, which is under construction, has been built with £9.3 million of grant aid from the European Union's Objective One programme, delivered through the Welsh Government, and £4.65 million of aid from the UK Business Ministry under the Bioenergy Capital Grant Scheme. The project was originally envisaged by the Western Log Group. Partnering in the Western Wood Energy project was also the consultancy company Sustainable Energy Ltd, of Cardiff. It also developed and project-managed the installation of the first commercial biodiesel production facility in Wales.

A third major development concerns Welsh Power, owner of a conventional power station at Uskmouth, Newport, proposing development of Nevis Power, a 49.9 MW green power plant, to Newport City Council. The company plans to build the plant on a 10-acre brownfield site at Newport Docks, a designated area for industrial works, with an investment of more than £140 million. Nevis Power, which will be built and maintained by CEC Generation (Welsh Power's power engineering group) will use biomass fuels comprising a mix of primarily wood chip and energy crops.

The main current applications of biomass energy in Wales are in local biomass boilers and the co-firing of biomass in coal-fuelled stations. Wales now has 15 biomass power stations (as of 2009) and two co-firing arrangements with large coal-burning power stations in Uskmouth and Aberthaw (both in South Wales). Co-firing is considered an efficient way of producing renewable energy, and unlike some renewable energy sources benefits from predictable output. The UK Environment Agency, which regulates all industrial plant, granted permission for Uskmouth to co-fire renewable energy in 2005. Uskmouth is currently using shea pellets, which are a waste product from the production of shea butter, widely used in cosmetics; whereas Aberthaw is using wood products. Aberthaw already burns sawdust to produce 4 per cent of its output through biomass, but it is also able to burn other fuels such as willow or miscanthus. This represents a long-term commitment by RWE npower as it increases the proportion of its energy produced from renewable sources. This is in line with UK government requirements that 10 per cent of electricity should be generated from renewable sources by 2010. Aberthaw power station has made a commitment to burn 200000 tonnes of biomass crops annually, thus creating a demand for some 10000 ha of energy crops; however, although co-firing is an important market for energy crops, most of the biomass material co-fired is imported.

A further biomass boiler has been fitted by UPM (UPM of Finland is one of the world's leading forest industry groups and the leading producer of printing papers) in its Shotton paper mill in North Wales, that replaced an existing boiler built in the 1980s. The new boiler, operational in late 2006, has a sludge-burning capacity to combust all sludge produced from UPM's recovered paper recycling process. To support the combustion of the mill sludge, biomass fuels will be co-combusted. The total investment cost was €75 million (£51.7 million at prevailing rates in the late 2000s) and was partly funded with €15 million (£10.6 million) from the UK Government's Waste and Resources Action Programme.

Green tourism

The Bluestone Holiday Village in environmentally highest category Pembrokeshire has already become a showcase for renewable energy and sustainability. All heat is generated from the Biomass Energy Centre, fitted with two 26 tonne Talbott biomass boilers capable of generating up to 1.6 MW of heat, which is purchased per unit by Bluestone. The Biomass Energy Centre is owned by a local co-operative set up in response to Bluestone's needs, Pembrokeshire BioEnergy. The centre runs on wood chip, miscanthus and willow coppices, which are sourced from 50 farms within a 5-mile radius of the site.

Alongside these nationally significant projects, there are a number of smaller-scale projects and installations used by smaller domestic, industry and local community users. The Welsh Government has invested in biomass technology for its own buildings, installing a biomass boiler fuelled by locally sourced wood chip for its Senedd at Cardiff Bay. The numerous green credentials of the building led to it being awarded the prestigious Sustainability Award by the Royal Institution of Chartered Surveyors in May 2006. Other developments are listed in Table 12.4.

Table 12.4   Smaller-scale projects or installations

Company name	Example case studies
Dulas (private firm)	• Dol Llys Hall 60 kW wood chip/pellet boiler
	• Nant yr Arian 35kW boiler
Welsh Biofuels	• Llandysul, Ceredigion 260 kW boiler
Forestry Commission	• Environment Building Cardiff 49 kW boiler
Wood Energy Business	• Penpont Estate 149 kW wood chipboiler
Scheme (WEBS)	• Penmorfa, Aberaeron 550 kW boiler
	• Bespoke Kitchen Systems 100 kW boiler

Wales also has a pronounced green innovation production platform, with many newly formed and more established firms. The Business Ministry report suggested that as of the late 2000s there are in total 769 firms in Wales in Renewable Energy, employing 13 700. Among these are: Pembrokeshire BioEnergy, the aforementioned energy supply company (ESCO), set up originally as a farmers' cooperative, that supplies the Bluestone green tourism facility; BSL, which is a bioethanol-producing company utilizing an ethanol biorefinery; BioWales at Swansea; and, among others, ECO2, which is a well-established and award-winning Cardiff-based 30-company group designing biomass burners connected to landfill sites.[4] Dulas Ltd, a small company established in 1982 that brings together expertise, skills and knowledge in a wide range of renewable energy systems including solar, wind, biomass and hydro was awarded the Queens Award for Enterprise in 2004 and Welsh Small Business of the Year 2006. Biotech Oils and Sundance Renewbales are two small firms that specialize in biodiesel production from the recycling of cooking oils. Welsh Biofuels established the UK's first large-scale wood pelletizing processing plant; and Inetec Ltd is a company formed in 1997 to address the problem relating to food and non-recyclable packaging waste, and to convert it into energy. Wales also shows strong capabilities in enzymes production, such as Biotal, one of the UK's leading companies specializing in the development of enzyme technology; and Neem BioTech, which specializes in the extraction of high-purity compounds from botanical sources (marine and plant extracts) on a commercial scale, also working in the field of climate change producing an extract with standardized allicin content (from garlic) useful in methane reduction in cattle.

Alongside these companies, the supply chain of renewable energy in Wales is populated with a number of consultancies and networks that provide advices, technical services, technology transfer and commercialization services to public and private sector organizations; among these:

Sustainable Energy Ltd, Madryn, Future Farmers of Wales, the Centre for Alternative Technology and the Centre for Alternative Land Use.

Wales has strengthened its research capabilities, creating the Wales Low Carbon Energy Research Institute in 2008 and the Welsh Energy Research Centre. The latter is an independent all-Wales collaborative body formed by research groups from the Universities of Cardiff, Swansea, Glamorgan and Bangor, and from the Institute of Grassland and Environmental Research. These groups, which have leading-edge expertise in energy-related matters, have decided to collaborate on research activities as the Welsh Energy Research Centre. To strengthen further the sector within Wales and to facilitate the more rapid commercialization of developments, the academic groups, supported by the Welsh Assembly Government, have combined to create the Welsh Energy Research Centre (WERC). WERC is a virtual centre, based at the Engineering Centre for Manufacturing and Materials (ECM2) at Port Talbot. WERC will enable much closer collaboration between the groups, which will lead to the development of integrated energy projects. An industrial membership scheme will enable early commercial involvement in projects.

The Low Carbon Energy Research Institute, on the other hand, builds on the Cardiff University research capabilities in the field of sustainable architecture and aims at creating a virtual organization that will change the landscape of the academic discipline of energy research in Wales. Its objectives are to develop capacity and facilities around the existing areas of low carbon and energy expertise in Wales and to coordinate research, technology development and demonstration and transfer, to enable the Welsh government to deliver its energy policy. Partners of this research institute are Cardiff School of Architecture (Cardiff University), the Cardiff School of Engineering (Cardiff University), the School of Chemistry (Bangor University), the Sustainable Environment Research Centre (University of Glamorgan) and the School of Engineering (Swansea University).

All these developments are coupled with research traditions of the Institute of Biological, Environmental and Rural Science (IBERS) (formerly the Institute of Grassland and Environmental Research, IGER). The work around the IBERS research centre has been of particular importance in the development of bioenergy innovation which has strengthened the region capabilities in the field. Having been for 70 years the UK's main specialist grassland research institute, IBERS is regarded as a world leader in the development of energy grasses, and has since 2004 opened up a biofuels division further to exploit biofuels research and commercialization utilizing evolving expertise in understanding and improving the calorific content of feedstock plants, by experimenting with ryegrass, short-rotation willow and miscanthus (Asian elephant grass).

Accompanying this research line are projects to improve and maximize yields of miscanthus and willow coppicing as biomass fuels. The research centre's expertise in the field of perennial bioenergy crops warranted IBERS a place in the newly established Biotechnology and Biological Sciences Research Council (BBSRC) Sustainable Bioenergy Centre.

12.5   KIBS IN BADEN-WÜRTTEMBERG'S AUTOMOTIVE INDUSTRY

12.5.1   DTS

The first firm chosen for the analysis of firm knowledge dynamics is DTS, an engineering service provider mainly working for the automotive sector in Baden-Württemberg. In order to examine an innovation and its specific knowledge biography, the development of the interior for the Mercedes Vaneo was selected. Therefore, Daimler assigned its Austrian supplier Magna to design and produce the whole interior for the planned vehicle. Magna redistributed parts of this assignment to subcontractors such as DTS which was involved in the designing and prototyping process. DTS was chosen for the project because of its special competence in the field of engineering and its knowledge about the vertical knowledge domain of the automotive industry. Consequently, this assignment represents an essential project that tied up a large part of DTS's capacities for approximately three years. As a special aspect of this constellation, Daimler was not aware of the fact that DTS Engineering acted as an independent firm. The project had four main phases.

Phase I
The project began with Daimler's order to develop the interior for the upcoming Vaneo in 1998. Fulfillment of this assignment meant that involved firms executed the interior design, including aspects such as ergonomics and functionality, in the first three months. This phase ended with the creation of a three-dimensional model to function as a basis for the prototype construction which follows in phase II.

From the knowledge perspective it could be observed that the design phase was rich in exchanging synthetic and symbolic knowledge. Moreover the project partners involved in this phase deployed their cumulative and composite knowledge bases to a different extent. Daimler's design department brought in its cumulative symbolic knowledge about interior design by creating templates which were used as the foundation for further developments. Additionally, their cumulative synthetic knowledge about internal processes, technological requirements and production parameters was important in order to meet the technological specifications for the design.

As a long-term supplier to Daimler, the Karmann Corp. had to contribute cumulative synthetic knowledge, especially about body shell construction and metal processing. Due to the fact that Karmann was situated at the interface between interior and exterior, its main task was to match the interior design with the specifications of the body shell construction. Therefore, the insertion of cumulative symbolic knowledge can also be assumed. In phase I it was up to DTS Engineering to absorb the mainly external knowledge stemming from Daimler's and Karmann's knowledge bases. In a second step DTS had to combine this with its cumulative synthetic knowledge about vehicle engineering. Taking into account that DTS previously worked on engineering solutions in the field of design, its knowledge base can also be considered to represent parts of composite or combinatory knowledge. Concerning the spatial dimension of phase I, DTS and Daimler are both located in the Stuttgart region. Only Karmann's location can be found outside of the Baden-Württemberg, namely in Osnabrück in the north-west of Germany. This aspect shows that the design phase is a good example in how far firms combine knowledge from intra-and extra-regional sources even in the process of knowledge exploration.

Phase II

The second phase of the interior development was about how to construct a prototype based upon the design worked out in the previous phase. In contrast to Daimler and DTS, Karmann was no longer directly involved in the project as the technical interfaces of the interior module were clearly specified at this time. A new project partner, Magna Steyr, represents the supplier who was finally responsible for the production of the interior module. The Austrian firm is a system supplier that holds specialized cumulative knowledge in the field of plastic materials and thus was integrated in phase II in order to gain access to information about production specifics and standards which necessarily had to be fulfilled by the prototype. On the other hand, Magna chose DTS as a subcontractor because DTS's engineering knowledge is complementary to its material specialization. Furthermore, the intensive learning processes involved in the Vaneo project required physical proximity and face-to-face contacts. DTS as a regional firm fulfilled this task and hence has taken over a boundary-spanning role.

From the research perspective this knowledge can be regarded as cumulated synthetic knowledge. On the other hand, the knowledge contributed by Daimler's design department seems to be more focused on design per se and therefore has to be regarded as symbolic knowledge. The main task of DTS in this phase was to create a digital computer image of the Vaneo's interior. In addition, this digital model was used by DTS Prototyping, a majority-owned DTS subsidiary, to construct first real-size prototype parts. The reason for DTS Engineering to choose a majority-owned subsidiary was, according to the respondent's explanations, that no additional trust had to be generated and that the process of searching for companies with corresponding competences could be avoided. At this point phase II shows that DTS once again had to contribute both synthetic knowledge and symbolic knowledge.

As a very critical aspect of phase II, DTS had to meet the temporal guidelines of Daimler (12 months) which exceeded the firm's personnel capacities. Since in Germany skill shortage has been a pressing issue since the mid-2000s, DTS had to recruit engineers from other sources outside of Germany. In order to solve this problem the firm's chief executive officer (CEO) used its personal contacts to employees of the Czech car manufacturer Skoda. Due to a high degree of social proximity, the firm was able to recruit 20 Skoda engineers who had initially been trained at the Volkswagen Corp. Interestingly, Volkswagen uses the same software as Daimler, the computer-aided design (CAD) software CATIA V, so that the newly hired engineers were directly able to enter the Vaneo project.

Accordingly, this aspect led to the fact that the Czech engineers' external cumulative synthetic knowledge was anchored in DTS. Consequently, the enlargement of the DTS synthetic knowledge base can be regarded as being mainly achieved by integrating human resources from abroad. Furthermore, it can be expected that symbolic knowledge was also brought in, but apparently to a lower degree. Against that background DTS Engineering created composite or combinative knowledge out of the different types of internal cumulative knowledge and the external knowledge that was provided by the project partners. In the prototyping phase, knowledge sharing and implicit knowledge still appear to be very important, a fact which is documented by the weekly meetings and by the on-site work of DTS employees at Daimler. At this stage spatial proximity and face-to-face contacts were essential for the creation of composite knowledge.

Phase III

Phase III mainly dealt with the process of converting the prototype into a serial model and therefore can be regarded as an examination knowledge phase. With the beginning of the third phase symbolic knowledge became less important. Furthermore a change from the creation of knowledge to knowledge application could be observed. This becomes clear regarding the fact that the design did not change significantly in phase III while fine-tuning procedures and final optimizations gained in importance. In this context Daimler played a decisive role by carrying out all the car and components tests and thereby giving feedback about its functionality and reliability. The phase ended with the completion of a Vaneo model ready for the upcoming production after 18 months. The external knowledge contributed by Magna Steyr changed successively to explicit knowledge. This aspect is mirrored by the fact that the physically distant project leader of Magna in Austria did not attend each of the weekly meetings any longer. Instead many of the specifications could be clarified via phone or e-mail. On the other hand, weekly meetings involving DTS Engineering and Daimler were still in use, including the aspect that the DTS engineers still worked on-site at Daimler. This point underpins that implicit knowledge and face-to-face communication still remained important in phase III, especially with regard to the knowledge exchange between Daimler and DTS.

Phase IV
Phase IV had the purpose of providing three months of support to Daimler and Magna after production had already started. In this context it was the task of DTS to carry out minor adjustments to improve the interior parts as far as details were concerned. Since this process involved fewer efforts than the previous phases, only two to three DTS employees were permanently engaged. In this phase synthetic (or engineering) knowledge was still dominating, whereas symbolic knowledge nearly dropped out. External knowledge was brought in once again by Magna and by Daimler's design department. Additionally, Daimler's production department in Ludwigsfelde (north-east Germany) provided the project partners with information concerning problems which occurred during the production process.

In this last phase the optimization of details first of all represented a process of knowledge application. Therefore weekly meetings were not necessary any more. The partners now met monthly at the production site in Ludwigsfelde. Another reason for the small number of meetings is that only few minor production errors were found, due to the precise work completed in the serial phase. The relatively infrequent meetings, in combination with the fact that the DTS engineers did not work on-site at Daimler's headquarters in Stuttgart any longer, could also be taken as a hint that implicit knowledge was less important than in the previous phases. At this time the creation of knowledge appeared almost to be replaced by knowledge application. In 2001 the development of the Vaneo's interior finally came to an end.

12.5.2   Mackevision

The second case we chose for the development of the knowledge biography is Mackevision. Mackevision is a service provider specialized in 3D-visualization. Even though the firm's main customers still can be found within the automotive industry, other sectors such as architecture or pharmaceutics have recently been gaining importance. Despite this strong focus on a few manufacturing industries, Mackevision's products and services are mostly related to marketing activities and therefore the firm employs approximately 60 professionals located in Stuttgart, Munich and Detroit.

The development of the automated content management tool F-Box was chosen as an innovation that will be discussed in the following. The tool represents a software program which automates standard visualization procedures and thus facilitates the management of large projects. Additionally, the tool offers new technological opportunities as far as 3D computing is concerned. According to Mackevision's CEO one of the main features is that the F-Box makes it possible to add digital computer models to any kind of photographic or cinematic environment. The novelty about this tool is that the added objects, such as cars, look like actual objects so that the manipulated pictures and films cannot be distinguished from 'real' ones.

In 1994 the firm was founded in Sindelfingen (Baden-Württemberg) and operated in various fields such as graphic animation and digital postproduction. After a period of serious crises at the beginning of the twenty-first century the firm specialized in 3D visualization for the automotive industry. It took some months until Mackevision had recovered in such a successful way in 2005 that the acquisition of new customers was not to be accomplished without a fundamental organizational change. This situation was the starting point for the development of the F-Box. Since this innovation is closely interwoven with the firm's general restructuring processes, both will be described and discussed in parallel.

Phase I
Starting in 2006, the first phase mainly mirrors a nine-month process of finding ideas in order to advance the required restructuring process. A large-scale assignment from Daimler offered the appropriate occasion to tackle the organizational obstacles. While usual projects include an output of about five pictures, for instance, the Daimler project involved the production of 350 000 high-quality photos and thus required fundamental changes in the generation of outputs. Against that background the respondent explained that it was necessary to change from a 'manufactory'

to a 'factory'. Previous projects had been organized almost without any division of labour; in fact the employed '3D artists' passed through the whole production process. As mentioned above, in 2005 a point was reached when the outlined organization hampered further growth and led to a permanent capacity overload among the employees. In view of this problem the CEO decided to change the situation. However, due to his vocational background in the field of design, he had no exact strategy to improve the situation.

To solve the problem Mackevision hired an external management consultant who analysed the firm's routines and procedures. This complex cooperation can be understood as an interaction process wherein ideas and goals for a new business are discussed and developed. In the course of the cooperation process the consultant contributed his experiences in organizational change, resulting in a plan about the strategic goals to be pursued by the firm in the future. In dealing with these questions the idea to develop an automated content management tool, the F-Box, first came into play. While the outlines of the new business model gained clarity it became apparent that the other shareholders would not join this vision. Due to this refusing attitude the respondent considered the shareholders' drawback from business as a decisive milestone in phase I.

This example shows how knowledge-intensive business services (KIBS) indirectly contribute to a firm's competitiveness. In particular, their boundary-spanning position at the interface of different knowledge environments enables KIBS to function as a driver of knowledge dynamics.

On the other hand the technological aspects of the F-Box idea are mainly based upon the cumulative knowledge provided by Mackevision. Moreover the implementation of cumulative symbolic knowledge can be assumed as well. Since the F-Box in the first place represents a tool for marketing purposes, the firm's knowledge about the effects of images on potential target groups was of great importance. In this context the respondent explained that due to his experiences in the visualization business he had felt that the market would respond positively to software which automates many steps of the visualization process. Additionally, this estimation about the market potential was underpinned by his specialized and experience-based knowledge about the needs of customers in the automotive industry. Consequently, the firm's long-time competence in the field of 3D computing appears to be critical for both the ability suggest an idea like the F-Box, and the reduction of innovation-related uncertainties so that the idea could finally be realized.

Like Mackevision, the external management consultant is located in Baden-Württemberg. The link between both firms was established using personal contacts of Mackevision's CEO. This aspect corroborates the conclusion that social proximity is important to initiate contacts to new partners and complementary service providers. Moreover it becomes clear that as far as the spatial dimension is concerned, the whole knowledge involved in phase I was obtained from actors located in Baden-Württemberg.

Phase II

One central goal formulated in phase I was to organize the firm's various processes with a much higher degree of division of labour. Consequently, specialized knowledge about how to achieve this change played a significant role, especially regarding the production process of the firm's products and services. In order to gain access to this important knowledge the CEO hired a business associate he knew from past projects, in a first step. Meanwhile this 'old' business partner had gained experience in the game industry and hence embodied lots of know-how in the field of software production. Because of the cumulative synthetic knowledge he was able to introduce into the firm, he was assigned to develop the new organizational framework for the upcoming 3D visualization projects, including the development of the F-Box.

Characteristically, this new process structure allocated the employees highly standardized production steps and thus was given the name 'production pipeline'. The main advantage of this change can be seen in the increased output. Since the employees, especially the '3D artists', now had to work within a small part of the entire project, a high degree of efficiency was achieved by specialization.

Remarkably, this process of smaller production steps also included an interregional and international dimension. Before the reorganization process was initiated, the subsidiaries' structure in Detroit and Munich hardly differed from the headquarters structure. The CEO explained that all employees had been involved in all production steps and had similar competences as the staff in Stuttgart. The situation changed in phase II when the tasks of the different locations were reorganized. From that time on, Detroit was mainly involved in data preparation. In contrast, Munich was given the task to specialize in project finalization, whereas the core activities, the 3D visualization and sales, remained in Stuttgart.

At the beginning of phase II Mackevision employed only 12 professionals. With the focus on meeting the challenge of the large-scale project commissioned by Daimler, the recruiting of further visualization specialists was necessary to complement the hitherto existing staff. Therefore the position of a personnel manager was newly established in the firm and finally a person was hired who had been well known to the CEO for approximately eight years. In terms of the restructuring process, this professional was able to contribute with his experience-based knowledge about personnel matters to the firm's human resources development. Taking into account that personnel recruitment to a high degree involves an understanding of the judgement of peoples' appearance and behaviour, cumulative symbolic knowledge has probably played an important role. Besides this aspect, the recruiter imparted his personal connections to the media sector. Consequently these new network links could enhance the firm's capability to find appropriate professionals on the regional labour market. Furthermore the recruiter fulfilled a lectureship at a nearby university, and thus established a valuable access point to talented graduates in the field of visualization.

Another important aspect to be mentioned is that the recruiter's work indirectly facilitated the development of the F-Box, since from now on the CEO had more capacities to advance the firm's projects and other strategic goals. Even though we can identify a whole group of advantages here, the creation of the personnel management position initially represented a significant risk to the firm. In this context the respondent mentioned the problem that positions which do not directly contribute to increase the firm's turnover are hard to justify paying, especially in small firms. Linking this problem to a more general perspective, this example shows a typical aspect concerning small KIBS firms and their disposition towards economic risks. Even though the exploration of new fields of knowledge appears to be very important for the long-run competitiveness of firms, for KIBS in many cases it seems to be difficult to employ professionals whose knowledge is not directly exploitable in terms of the market. Because of this situation the integration of staff only contributing to knowledge exploration often represents a serious venture, so that economic chances sometimes remain unexploited. In the case of Mackevision the firm was able to take the risk, and thus extended its capacities within a year from 12 to 60 employees at the time of writing. With regard to the firm's further development, this growth represents a central driver especially concerning the capability to push forward the F-Box development.

In addition to the employee with the game software background and the personnel manager, two further key positions were staffed with external human resources. First, a Canadian professional with experience in project management was hired once again using the CEO's social networks. Second, a system administrator was integrated in the firm. Both positions, the project manager and the system administrator, have presumably brought in their cumulative synthetic knowledge of the fields they are specialized in.

Phase III

The last phase of this knowledge biography deals with the process of programming and prototyping. As mentioned above, in phase II the technological base of the automated content creation system was developed. On the other hand, final adjustments were still necessary to ensure important aspects like IT compatibility. Furthermore Mackevision followed the plan that the F-Box should also include a project management system. As a special feature the respondent outlined that the F-Box, for instance, supports Internet-based communication and data exchange. These functions are intended to facilitate the coordination of 3D visualization projects, but still had to be implemented. Therefore phase III mainly represented the process of further programming activities and ended with the completion of the prototype in April 2008. With regard to the knowledge flows of phase III, apart from Mackevision no other actors were involved at this time. Even the external management consultant dropped out here, since the parallel running restructuring process from this point on could be pushed forward without the consultant's guidance. Here we can assume that the human resources integration of phase II has led to a situation in which the firm's competence could be raised to a degree such that the organizational change no longer depends on external knowledge.

12.6   CONCLUSIONS

This reflection upon the meaning for future economic evolution of setting our research findings in the context of territorial knowledge flows, transition and the 'knowledge economy', and the need to propose policy models to facilitate transition governance, has resulted in at least framework outlines at macro- and meso-levels that are in broad consensus.

Transitions thinking is not that widely understood in governance minds, except those few that deal with policy responses to the transitions brought about by climate change. To our knowledge, this is the first time that it has been used to accommodate transitions outside the 'sustainability' sphere. Our key transition is that from a mostly vertically structured industrial paradigm to a more horizontally networked knowledge paradigm. The latter is as complementary to the 'green' turn in global perspectives on consumption and production as the former is to the 'fossil fuel' perspective in which it has, since the first Industrial Revolution, been rooted. Whether a transition of equivalent relative performance is occurring in global financial management is as yet unclear.

There are a series of transition governance categories that are rooted in concrete reality rather than conjectured or conjured up. The main ones are

Table 12.5   Regional governance models

	Issue-based governance	Problem-focused governance	Platform governance	Proactive platform governance
Key Actors	Governments	Governments, intermediaries	Intermediaries (regional expert panels)	Intermediaries (related variety aggregators)
Rationality	Issue-specific transition	Transition after system shock	Adaptation to socio-technical transition	Early adaptation to S-T transition
Instruments	Coordination of public policies and agencies, issue-specific horizontal policy coordination	Networking, stakeholder Activation, limited horizontal policy coordination	Megatrend analysis, platform support policies, limited horizontal policy coordination	Megatrend anticipation, cluster interaction, horizontal policy coordination

Source: Kaiser (2009).

categorized in Table 12.5. It may well be worth considering Lower Austria as a refinement of the Bayern Innovativ model, however. It has been commented that it is a rather exclusive model in which funding support and the main focus is upon Bavarian firms. This is questionable in terms of EU state aid principles, but also perhaps unduly narrow. It should be considered whether a matrix model of proactive platform governance operated in support of cluster programmes should be inclusive towards overseas firms that are members of innovation networks. We see precisely this in the methodology and aspiration for integrating disparate but complementary clusters into a more fully fledged regional innovation system in Skåne. There, being open to the world for understanding, but applying transferred knowledge to indigenous economic assets, is exemplary. This is a paradigm Eurodite case of aspiring and strategizing to combine industrial and governance knowledge flows in a specific territory with international innovation system proximities (it is involved intimately in the EU DG Enterprise & Innovation initiative to network the whole Baltic Sea Region, as well as Medicon Valley, which is a kind of prototype). Whether these findings are a useful guide to the future of economic governance remains an open question.

NOTES

1. http://www.navigation-satellites-toulouse.com/?lang=en,   http://www.aerospace-valley. com/en/.
2. http://www.galileoju.com/, http://www.gsa.europa.eu/.
3. All the collaborative projects are included in this period, even if some of them started before and others finished after this base period.
4. As already noted, the focus here is the bioenergy platform. However, it is worth noting that broader 'green innovation' capabilities are found in photovoltaics, hydrogen fuel cells and marine energy. Lomox is a leading low-energy lighting firm utilizing thin-film technology; G24i is the worldwide leader in the manufacture of flexible photovoltaic films. The photovoltaics cluster in North Wales has world-leading technologies such as solar paint from Corus Colours, and leading thin-film surface technology photovoltaics from Sharp Solar. Eco2 is a leading marine energy systems integrator while Connaught Engineering and NaroCar are active in hydrogen fuel cells technologies.

References

ACEA (2006), 'Industry Report 2006', Brussels, http://www.acea.be/index.php/news/news_detail/statistics.

Acha, V., D. Gann and A. Salter (2005), 'Episodic innovation: R&D strategies for project-based environments', *Industry and Innovation*, **12**, 255–81.

ACNielsen (2005), 'Functional food and organics: a global ACNielsen online survey on consumer behaviour and attitudes', November, New York: ACNielsen.

Amabile, T., H. Conti, J. Coon and H. Lazenby (1996), 'Assessing the work environment for creativity', *Academy of Management Journal*, **39**, 1154–84.

Anastasiadou, C. (2006), '*Tourism and the European Union*', in D. Hall, M. Smith and B. Marciszewska (eds), *Tourism in the New Europe: The Challenges and Opportunities of EU Enlargement*, London: CABI publishing, pp. 20–31.

Antonelli, C. (2005), 'Models of knowledge and systems of governance', *Journal of Institutional Economics*, **1**, 51–73.

Antonelli, C. (2006), 'The business governance of localized knowledge: an information economics approach for the economics of knowledge', *Industry and Innovation*, **13**, 227–61.

Antonelli, C. and M. Calderini (2006), 'The governance of knowledge compositeness and technological performance: the case of the automotive industry in Europe', EURODITE Working Paper, http://www.eurodite.bham.ac.uk/.

Aoki, M. and H. Takizawa (2002), 'Information, incentives and option value: the Silicon Valley model', *Journal of Comparative Economics*, **30**, 759–86.

Arora, A. and S. Athreye (2001), *The Software Industry and India's Economic Development*, World Institute for Development, Economics Research, Oxford: Oxford University Press.

Arrow, K. (1962), 'Economic welfare and the allocation of resources for invention', in R. Nelson (ed.), *The Rate and Direction of Inventive Activity: Economic and Social Factors*, Princeton, NJ: Princeton University Press, pp. 609–26.

Asheim, B. and M.S. Gertler (2005), 'The geography of innovation:

regional innovation systems', in J. Fagerberg, D. Mowery and R. Nelson (eds), *The Oxford Handbook of Innovation*, New York: Oxford University Press, pp. 291–317.

Asheim, B., L. Coenen and J. Vang-Lauridsen (2006), 'Face-to-face, buzz and knowledge bases: socio-spatial implications for learning, innovation and innovation policy', Working Paper, Lund University, Department of Social and Economic Geography.

ATV (2003), *Fødevareforskningen i Danmark – fundamentet for udvikling og værdiskabelse*, Denmark: Akademiet for de Tekniske Videnskaber.

Audretsch D. and M. Feldman (1996), 'R&D spillovers and the geography of innovation and production', *American Economic Review*, **86**, 630–40.

Backlund, A.-K. and A. Sandberg (2002), 'New media industry development: regions, networks and hierarchies – some policy implications', *Regional Studies*, **36**, 87–91.

Baden-Württemberg Government (2006), *Baden-Württemberg Biotechnology Guide*, Stuttgart: Gwz.

Bærenholdt, J., M. Haldrup, J. Larsen and J. Urry (2004), *Performing Tourist Places*, Abingdon: Ashgate.

Baldwin, C. and K. Clark (2000), *Design Rules: The Power of Modularity*, Cambridge, MA, USA and London, UK: MIT Press.

Banks, M., D. Calvey, J. Owen and D. Russell (2002), 'Where the art is: defining and managing creativity in new media SMEs', *Creativity and Innovation Management*, **11**, 255–64.

Bargigli, L. (2005), The limits of modularity in innovation and production', CESPRI WP no. 176, University of Milan.

Bastakis, C., D. Buhalis and R. Butler (2004), 'The perception of small and medium sized tourism accommodation providers on the impacts of the tour operators' power in the eastern Mediterranean', *Tourism Management*, **25**: 151–70.

Bathelt, H. (2002), 'The re-emergence of a media industry cluster in Leipzig', *European Planning Studies*, **10**, 583–611.

Batt, R. and S. Christopherson, (2001), 'Net working: new media workers in Silicon Alley', Working Paper, Institute for Workplace Studies, Cornell University.

Benner, M. and U. Sandström (2000), 'Internationalising the triple helix: research funding and norms in the academic system', *Research Policy*, **29**, 291–301 .

Berger, A. and G. Udell (2003), 'The institutional memory hypothesis and the procyclicality of bank lending behaviour', Bank for International Settlements Working Paper 125, Basel, Switzerland.

Berger, R. (2004), *Automotive Engineering 2010*, Detroit, MI: Roland Berger.

Bessant, J. and H. Rush (2000), 'Innovation agents and technology transfer', in M. Boden and I. Miles (eds), *Services and the Knowledge-Based Economy: European Evidence*, London: Continuum, pp. 155–69.

Best, M. (2001), *The New Competitive Advantage*, Oxford: Oxford University Press.

Bettencourt, L., A. Ostrom, S. Brown and R. Roundtree (2002), 'Client co-production in knowledge-intensive business services', *California Management Review*, **44**, 100–128.

Bieger, T. and A. Wittmer (2006), 'Air transport and tourism: perspectives and challenges for destinations, airlines and governments', *Journal of Air Transport Management*, **12**, 40–46.

Biomass Task Force (2005), 'Report to government' London: BTF.

Boden, M. and I. Miles (eds) (2000), *Services and the Knowledge-Based Economy: European Evidence*, London: Continuum.

Bolter, J. (2001), *Writing Space: Computers, Hypertext, and the Remediation of Print*, 2nd edn, Mahwah NJ: Lawrence Erlbaum Associates.

Boschma, R. (2005), 'Proximity and innovation: a critical assessment', *Regional Studies*, **39**, 61–74.

Boschma, R. and K. Frenken (2003), 'Evolutionary economics and industry location', *Review of Regional Research*, **23**, 183–94.

Bouba, O. and M. Grossetti (2006), 'Une (re)définition des notions de proximité', unpublished research note.

Bourassa, F. (2006), 'ICT sector classification standards proposals based on ISIC Revision 4', OECD, EAS Division, ITU – World Telecommunication/ICT Indicators Meeting, Geneva, 11–13 October.

Bovagnet, F. (2006), *How Europeans Go on Holiday: Statistics in Focus: Industry, Trade and Services*, New York: Springer.

Boyer, R. and M. Freyssinet (2003), Produktionsmodelle. Eine Typologie am Beispiel der Automobilindustrie. Berlin.

Braczyk, H., P. Cooke and M. Heidenreich (eds) (1998), *Regional Innovation Systems*, London: Routledge.

Bramwell, B. and A. Sharman (1999), 'Collaboration in local tourism policy making', *Annals of Tourism Research*, **26**, 292–415.

Breschi, S. and F. Lissoni (2001), 'Knowledge spillovers and local innovation systems: a critical survey', *Industrial and Corporate Change*, **10**, 975–1005.

Breschi, S. and F. Malerba (1997), 'Sectoral innovation systems: technological regimes, Schumpeterian dynamics, and spatial boundaries', in C. Edquist (ed.), *Systems of Innovation*, London: Palmer, pp. 130–56.

Brossard, O. and J. Vincente (2007), 'Cognitive and relational distance in alliance networks: evidence on the knowledge value chain in the European ICT sector', *Cahiers du GRES* 2007-18.

Brown, J. and P. Duguid (2001), 'Knowledge and organization: a social-practice perspective', *Organization Science*, **12**, 198–213.

Brush, C. (1990), 'Women and enterprise creation: barriers and opportunities', in S.Gould and J. Parzen (eds), *Enterprising Women: Local Initiatives for Job Creation*, Paris: OECD pp. 37–58.

Brush, C. (1992), 'Research on women business owners: past trends, a new perspective and future directions', *Entrepreneurship: Theory and Practice*, Summer, 5–30.

Buhalis, D. and C. Cooper (1998), 'Competition or co-operation? Small and medium sized tourism enterprises at the destination', in E. Laws, W. Faulkner and G. Moscardo (eds), *Embracing and Managing Change in Tourism: International Case Studies*, London: Routledge, pp. 324–46.

Burton-Jones, A. (1999), *Knowledge Capitalism*, Oxford: Oxford University Press.

Buttner, H. and D. Moore (1997), 'Women's organizational exodus to entrepreneurship: self reported motivations and correlates with success', *Journal of Small Business Management*, **35**, 34–46.

Calvert, J. and P. Patel (2002), *University–Industry Collaborations in the UK*, Brighton: SPRU.

Cantwell, J. and G. Santangelo (2002), 'The new geography of corporate research in information and communications technology', *Journal of Evolutionary Economics*, **12**, 163–97.

Capra, F. (2003), *The Hidden Connections*, London: Flamingo.

Carter, S., S. Anderson and E. Shaw (2001), 'Women's business ownership: a review of the academic, popular and Internet literature', Report to the UK Small Business Service.

Casper, S. and A. Karamanos (2003), 'Commercialising science in Europe: the Cambridge biotechnology cluster', *European Planning Studies*, **11**, 805–22.

Castells, M. (1996), *The Rise of the Network Society*, Oxford: Blackwell.

Caves, R. (2000), *Creative Industries: Contracts Between Art and Commerce* Cambridge, MA: Harvard University Press.

Cawley, A. and P. Preston (2007), 'Broadband and digital "content" in the EU-25: recent trends and challenges', *Telematics and Informatics*, **24**, 246–58.

Chanaron, J. (2004), 'Relationships between the core and the periphery of the European automotive system', *International Journal of Automotive Technology and Management*, **4**, 198–222.

Chesbrough, H. (2003), *Open Innovation*, Boston, MA: Harvard Business School Press.

Chesbrough, H. and S. Socolof (2000), 'Creating new ventures from Bell Labs', *Research Technology Management*, **43**, 13–17.

Christensen, C. (1997), *The Innovator's Dilemma*, Boston, MA: Harvard Business School Books.

Christensen, K. (2006), 'How tourism net-works', Department of History, International and Social Studies, Aalborg University, Master of Tourism Studies thesis.

CIAA (2004), 'Data and trends of the EU food and drink industry 2004', December, Brussels, Confederation of Food and Drink Industries of the EU.

CIAA (2006), 'Data and trends of the European food and drink industry 2006', Brussels, Confederation of Food and Drink Industries of the EU.

Clark, K. and T. Fujimoto (1991), *Product Development Performance,* Boston, MA: Harvard Business School Press.

Cohendet, P. and F. Meyer-Krahmer (2001), 'The theoretical and policy implications of knowledge codification', *Research Policy*, **30**, 1563–91.

Coles, T. and C. Hall (2008), *International Business and Tourism*, London: Routledge.

Commission of the European Communities (2004), *European Action Plan for Organic Food and Farming*. Brussels, 10 June, SEC (2004) 739.

Commission of the European Communities (2006), 'A renewed EU tourism policy: towards a stronger partnership for European tourism', DG Enterprise, Commission of the European Communities.

Cooke, P. (2002a), 'Biotechnology clusters as regional, sectoral innovation systems', *International Regional Science Review*, **25**, 8–37.

Cooke, P. (2002b), 'New media and new economy cluster dynamics', in L. Lievrouw and S. Livingstone (eds) *The Handbook of New Media: Social Shaping and Consequences of ICTs*, London: Sage, pp. 266–86.

Cooke, P. (2004), 'Regional innovation systems: an evolutionary approach', in P. Cooke, M. Heidenreich and H. Braczyk (eds), *Regional Innovation Systems*, 2nd edn, London: Routledge, pp. 1–20.

Cooke, P. (2005a), 'Rational drug design, the knowledge value chain and bioscience megacentres', *Cambridge Journal of Economics*, **29**, 325–42.

Cooke, P. (2005b), 'Regionally asymmetric knowledge capabilities and open innovation: exploring "Globalisation 2" – a new model of industry organisation', *Research Policy*, **34**, 1128–49.

Cooke P. (2006a), 'Markets and networks in the knowledge value chain', Working Paper prepared for EU-FP6 Eurodite.

Cooke, P. (2006b), 'Proximities, knowledge and innovation biographies', Eurodite Working Paper, Cardiff, Centre for Advanced Studies, http://www.eurodite.bham.ac.uk/.

Cooke, P. (2006c), 'Introduction: regional asymmetries, knowledge categories and innovation intermediation', in P. Cooke and A. Piccaluga (eds), *Regional Development in the Knowledge Economy*, London: Routledge, pp. 1–21.

Cooke, P. (2007a), *Growth Cultures: the Global Bioeconomy and Its Bioregions*, London: Routledge.

Cooke, P. (2007b), 'Environmental, energy and agro-food bioregions', in *Growth Cultures: The Global Bioeconomy and its Bioregions*, London: Routledge, pp. 192–213.

Cooke, P. (2009), 'The economic geography of knowledge flow hierarchies among internationally networked bioclusters: a scientometric analysis', *Tijdschrift voor Economische en Sociale Geografie*, **100**, 236–49.

Cooke, P., C. De Laurentis, F. Tödtling and M. Trippl (eds) (2004), *Regional Innovation Systems: The Role of Governance in a Globalized World*, 2nd edn, London, Routledge.

Cooke, P. et al. (2006), *Constructing Regional Advantage*, Brussels: European Commission, DG Research, http://www.dime-eu.org/files/active/0/regional_advantage_FINAL.pdf.

Cooke, P., C. De Laurentis, F. Tödtling and M. Trippl (2007), *Regional Knowledge Economies*, Cheltenham, UK and Northampton, MA, USA: Edward Elgar.

Crevoisier, O. and H. Jeannerat (2009), 'Territorial knowledge dynamics: from the proximity paradigm to multi-locational milieux', *European Planning Studies*, **17**, 1223–42.

Cromie, S. (1987), 'Motivations of aspiring male and female entrepreneurs', *Journal of Occupational Behaviour*, **8**, 251–61.

Crozier, M. and E. Friedberg (1993), 'Die Zwänge kollektiven Handelns', Über Macht und Organisationen, Königstein.

Dahlstrom, M. et al. (2009), 'Knowledge dynamics in the Skåne film tourism industry', Eurodite Project, input paper to Work Package 8, http://www.eurodite.bham.ac.uk/.

David, P. (1985), 'Clio and the economics of QWERTY', *American Economic Review*, **75**, 332–7.

David, P. and G. Wright (1999), 'General purpose technologies and surges in productivity: historical reflections on the future of the ICT revolution', Stanford Economics Working Papers, University of Stanford, CA.

Davidson, R. and B. Cope (2003), *Business Travel: Conferences, Incentive Travel, Exhibitions, Corporate Hospitality and Corporate Travel*, Harlow: FT Prentice Hall.

de Aquino, R., J. Bierhoff, T. Orchard and M. Stone (2002), 'The European multimedia news landscape, multimedia content in the digital age', Heerlen, MUDIA, EU-IST Research Project.

Debbage, K. and P. Daniels (1998), 'The tourist industry and economic geography: missed opportunities', in D. Ioannides and K. Debbage (eds), *The Economic Geography of the Tourist Industry*, London: Routledge, pp. 17–30.

Decelle, X. (2006), 'A dynamic conceptual approach to innovation in tourism', in OECD (ed.), *Innovation and Growth in Tourism*, Paris: OECD, pp. 85–106.

DEFRA (2006), 'Economic Note on UK grocery retailing', London, HM Government: Department for Development, Food and Rural Affairs.

de Geus, A. (1998), *The Living Company*, London: Nicholas Brealey Publishing.

den Hertog, P. and R. Bilderbeek (2000), 'The new knowledge infrastructure: the role of technology-based knowledge-intensive business services in national innovation systems', in M. Boden and I. Miles (eds) *Services and the Knowledge-Based Economy*, London and New York: Continuum, pp. 247–65.

Dicken, P. (2003), *Global Shift: Reshaping the Global Economic Map in the 21st Century*, London, UK and Thousand Oaks, CA, USA: Sage.

Djellal, F., D. Francoz, C. Gallouj, F. Gallouj and Y. Jacquin (2003), 'Revising the definition of research and development in the light of the specificities of services', *Science and Public Policy*, **30**, 415–29.

Dolfsma, W. (2004), 'Some economics of digital content', ERIM Report Series, Research in Management, Nijmegen, Erasmus Research Institute of Management.

Dorey, E. (2003), 'Emerging market Medicon Valley: a hotspot for biotech affairs', *BioResource*, March, www.investintech.com.

Dredge, D. (2006), 'Policy networks and the local organisation of tourism', *Tourism Management*, **27**, 269–80.

Drucker, P. (1999), *Management Challenges for the 21st Century*, New York: HarperBusiness.

Dunning, J. (ed.) (2000), *Regions, Globalisation and the Knowledge-Based Economy*, Oxford: Oxford University Press.

Dupuy, C. and J.-P. Gilly (1999), 'Industrial groups and territories: the case of Matra Marconi Space in Toulouse', *Cambridge Journal of Economics*, **23**, 207–23.

EC (European Commission) (2003), *Women in Industrial Research: Analysis of Statistical Data and Good Practices of Companies*, Luxembourg: Office for Official Publications of the European Communities.

EC (European Commission) (2004a), 'Report on Competition in Professional Services', Brussels.

EC (European Commission) (2004b), 'Proposal for a Directive of the European Parliament and of the Council on services in the internal market', Brussels.

EC (European Commission) (2006a), 'Employment in Europe', Luxembourg.

EC (European Commission) (2006b), 'Constructing regional advantage', www.dime-eu.org/files/active/0/regional_advantage_FINAL.pdf

EC (European Commission) (2006c), 'DG Enterprise and Industry: Cars 21: a Competitive Automotive Regulatory System for the 21st century', Luxembourg: European Commission.

Economides, N. (1996), 'The economics of networks', *International Journal of Industrial Organization*, **16**, 673–99.

Egan, E. and A. Saxenian (1999), 'Becoming digital: sources of localisation in the Bay Area multimedia cluster', in H. Braczyk, G. Fuchs and H. Wolf (eds), *Multimedia and Regional Economic Restructuring*, London: Routledge, pp. 11–29.

EMCC (European Monitoring Centre on Change) (2005), 'Sector futures: the knowledge-intensive business services sector', Dublin, European Foundation for the Improvement of Living and Working Conditions.

EMCC (European Monitoring Centre on Change) (2006a), 'Trends and drivers of change in the food and beverage industry in Europe: mapping report', Dublin, European Foundation for the Improvement of Living and Working Conditions.

EMCC (European Monitoring Centre on Change) (2006b), 'Trends and drivers of change in the European knowledge-intensive business services sector: mapping report', Dublin, European Foundation for the Improvement of Living and Working Conditions.

EPA (2004), 'Compelling content interactive software: extending the digital entertainment revolution to broadband users', Washington, DC: EPA.

Ernst & Young (2005a), *Global Biotechnology Report*, London: Ernst & Young.

Ernst & Young (2005b), *The Power of Evolution: German Biotechnology Report*, London: Ernst & Young.

Ernst & Young (2005c), *Swiss Biotech Report*, Zurich: Ernst & Young.

European Council (2002), *Contribution to the Spring European Council in Barcelona: The Lisbon Strategy – Making Change Happen*, COM (2002) 14 final.

EU (European Union) (2008), 'Challenging Europe's research: rationales for the ERA', Brussels: DG Research.

EU (European Union) (2009), *European Nutrition and Health Report*, Brussels: European Food Safety Administration.

Eurostat (2004a), 'European business facts and figures 1998–2002', Luxembourg: European Commission.

Eurostat (2004b), 'Business services: an analysis of foreign affiliates and business demography statistics – Data 2001', Luxembourg: European Commission.

Eurostat (2007), 'Jährliche Beschäftigungsdaten im Technologiebereich und in Sektoren mit umfassenden Kenntnissen auf regionaler Ebene', http://epp.eurostat.ec.europa.eu/portal/.

Eurostat (2008), 'Main economic variables by employment, size, class', http://epp.eurostat.ec.europa.eu/portal/.

Fayos-Sola, E. (1996), 'Tourism policy: A Midsummer Night's Dream?' *Tourism Management,* **17**, 405–12.

Fayos-Sola, E., A. Marin and C. Meffert (1994), 'The strategic role of tourism trade fairs in the new age of tourism', *Tourism Management*, **15**, 9–16.

FIAM (2003), 'The multimedia and interactive digital content industry', International Federation of Multimedia Associations, Montreal: FIAM.

FIDIC (International Federation of Consulting Engineers) (2006), International Consulting Engineering Conference 2006: Where the Roads Meet, Workshop Reports.

Fisher, M. (2006), 'Enterprising women: remaking gendered networks on Wall Street in the new economy', in D. Perrons, C. Fagan, L. McDowell, K. Ray and K. Ward (eds) *Gender Divisions and Working Time in the New Economy*, Cheltenham, UK and Northampton, MA, USA: Edward Elgar, pp. 58–74.

Florida, R. and T. Sturgeon (2000), 'Globalization and jobs in the auto industry', Cambridge, MA and Pittsburgh, PA, Report to the International Labour office.

Flynn, A., T. Marsden, and E. Smith (2003), 'Food regulation and retailing in a new institutional context', *Political Quarterly*, **74**, 38–46.

Folkerts, H. and H. Koehorst (1998), 'Challenges in international food supply chains: vertical co-ordination in the European agribusiness and food industries', *British Food Journal*, **100**, 385–8.

Foray, D. and C. Freeman (1993), *Technology and the Wealth of Nations: The Dynamics of Constructed Advantage*, London: Pinter.

Fuchs, G. (2000), 'The role of geography in the information economy: the case of multimedia', *Vierteljahrshefte zur Wirtschaftsforschung*, **69**, 559–73.

Galbraith, J.K. (1955), *The Great Crash 1929*, London: Penguin.

Gallouj, F. (2002), 'Knowledge-intensive business services: processing knowledge and producing innovation', in J. Gadrey and F. Gallouj (eds), *Productivity, Innovation and Knowledge in Services*, Cheltenham, UK and Northampton, MA, USA: Edward Elgar, pp. 256–84.

Geels, F. (2006), 'Co-evolutionary and multi-level dynamics in transitions:

the transformation of aviation systems and the shift from propeller to turbojet (1930–1970)', *Technovation*, **26**, 999–1016.

Gehlhar, M. and A. Regmi (2005), 'Factors shaping global food markets', in A. Regmi and M. Gehlhar (eds), *New Directions in Global Food Markets,* Washington, DC: US Department of Agriculture, Economic Research Service.

Gerybadze, A. (2004), *Technologie- und Innovationsmanagement. Strategie, Organisation und Implementierung*, München: Verlag Vahlen.

Getz, D. and P.Å. Nilsson (2004). 'Responses of family businesses to extreme seasonality in demand: the case of Bornholm, Denmark', *Tourism Management*, **25**, 17–30.

Gibbons, M., C. Limoges, H. Nowotny, S. Schwartzman, P. Scott and M. Trow (1994), *The New Production of Knowledge*, London: Sage.

Gilsing, V. and B. Nooteboom (2006), 'Exploration and exploitation in innovation systems: the case of pharmaceutical biotechnology', *Research Policy*, **35**, 1–23.

Girard, M. and D. Stark (2002), 'Distributing intelligence and organizing diversity in new-media projects', *Environment and Planning A*, **34**, 1927–49.

Glaeser, E., H. Kallall, J. Scheinkman and A. Shleifer (1992), 'Growth in cities', *Journal of Political Economy*, **100**, 1126–52.

Glückler, J. and T. Armbruster (2003), 'Bridging uncertainty in management consulting: the mechanisms of trust and networked reputation', *Organizational Studies*, **24**, 269–97.

Gold, B. (1986), 'Technological change and vertical integration', *Managerial and Decision Economics*, **7**, 169–76.

Goméz, M. and F. Rebollo (1995), 'Coastal areas: processes, typologies and prospects', in A. Montanari and A. Williams (eds), *European Tourism: Regions, Spaces and Restructuring*, Chichester: John Wiley, pp. 111–26.

Goodman, D. (2002), 'Rethinking food production–consumption: integrative perspectives', *Sociologia Ruralis*, **42**, 271–77.

Goodman, David (2004), 'Rural Europe redux? Reflections on alternative agro-food networks and paradigm change', *Sociologia Ruralis*, **44**, (1), 3–16.

Grabher, G. (2004), 'Learning in projects, remembering in networks? Communality, sociality, and connectivity in project ecologies', *European Urban and Regional Studies*, **11** (2), 103–23.

Grabher, G. and D. Stark (1997), 'Organising diversity: evolutionary theory, network analysis and post-socialism', in G. Grabher and D. Stark (eds), *Restructuring Networks in Post-Socialism: Legacies, Linkages and Localities*, Oxford: Oxford University Press, pp. 1–32.

Grainger, R. (1974), *The Language of the Rite*, London: Longmans.

Green, K. and C. Foster (2005), 'Give peas a chance: transformations in food consumption and production systems', *Technological Forecasting and Social Change*, **72**, 663–79.

Gulati, R. and H. Singh (1998), 'The architecture of cooperation: managing coordination costs and appropriation concerns in strategic alliances', *Administrative Science Quarterly*, **43**, 781–814.

Gunn, C. and T. Var (2002), *Tourism Planning: Basics, Concepts, Cases*, 4th edn, London: Routledge.

Guthman, J. (2005), *Agrarian Dreams*, Berkeley, CA: Berkeley University Press.

Hack, L. and I. Hack (2005), 'Wissen, Macht und Organisation. Internationalisierung industrieller Forschung und Entwicklung – ein Fallvergleich', Berlin: Edition Sigma.

Hagedoorn J., A. Link and N.S. Vonortas (2000), 'Research partnerships', *Research Policy*, **29**, 567–86.

Halkier, H. (2002), 'Regional turismeudvikling mellem udbud og efterspørgsel. Nordjylland og den store verden – hvem lærer af hvem?' in H. Halkier, S. Jensen and P. Kvistgaard (eds), *Regional turisme mellem udbud og efterspørgsel*, Aalborg: Aalborg Universitetsforlag, pp. 119–28.

Halkier, H. (2006), *Institutions, Discourse and Regional Development: The Scottish Development Agency and the Politics of Regional Policy*, Brussels: PIE; New York: Peter Lang.

Hall, C. (2000), *Tourism Planning: Policies, Processes and Relationships*, Harlow: Prentice Hall.

Hall, P. and D. Soskice (eds) (2001), *Varieties of Capitalism: The Institutional Foundations of Comparative Advantage*, Oxford: Oxford University Press.

Harmaakorpi, V. (2009), 'Platforms to develop regional capabilities', presentation to VINNOVA seminar series on Post-cluster Innovation Policy, 24 February, Stockholm, VINNOVA.

Harrison, B. (1994), *Lean and Mean: the Changing Face of Corporate Power in the Age of Flexibility*, New York: Basic Books.

Harrison, M. (2002), 'The rise and fall of Marconi: Simpson breaks his silence', *The Independent*, 28 November, p. 25.

Harvey, M., A. McMeekin and A. Warde (2004), 'Introduction', in M. Harvey, A. McMeekin and A. Warde (eds) *Qualities of Food*, Manchester: Manchester University Press, pp. 1–18.

Hauknes, J. (2000), 'Dynamic innovation systems: what is the role of services?', in M. Boden and I. Miles (eds), *Services and the Knowledge-based Economy*, London and New York: Continuum, pp. 38–63.

Hein, J., B. Ilbery and M. Kneafsey (2006), 'Distribution of local food activity in England and Wales: an index of food relocalisation', *Regional Studies*, **40**, 289–302.

Helpman, E. (ed.) (1998), *General Purpose Technologies and Economic Growth*, Cambridge, MA: MIT Press.

Herslund, L. and L. Nyberg (2001), 'Bornholm og turisterhvervet i Øresundsregionen. Samarbejde og integration?' Nordregio Working Paper (2001:11).

Heydebrand, W. and A. Miron (2002), 'Constructing innovativeness in new-media start-up firms', *Environment and Planning A*, **34**, 1951–84.

Hill C.W.L. (1997), 'Establishing a standard: competitive strategy and technological standards in winner-take-all industries', *Academy of Management Executive*, **11** (2), 7–25.

Hinoul, M. (2005), *Knowledge Economy Europe, a Risky Jump*, Leuven: KU Press.

Hinrichs, C. (2000), 'Embeddedness and local food systems: notes on two types of direct agricultural market', *Journal of Rural Studies*, **16**, 295–303.

Hipp, C. and H. Grupp (2005), 'Innovation in the service sector: the demand for service-specific innovation measurement concepts and typologies', *Research Policy*, **34**, 517–35.

Hisrich, R., C. Brush, D. Good and G. De Souza (1996), 'Some preliminary findings on performance in entrepreneurial ventures: does gender matter?' Frontiers of Entrepreneurship Research, April, Babson College, Wellesley, MA.

Hjalager, A.-M. (2000a), 'Organisational ecology in the Danish restaurant sector', *Tourism Management*, **21**, 271–80.

Hjalager, A.-M. (2000b), 'Tourism destinations and the concept of industrial districts', *Tourism and Hospitality Research*, **2**, 199–213.

Hjalager, A.-M. (2001), 'Den teoretiske referenceramme – en kort gennemgang', Nordregio Working Paper (2001:11).

Hjalager, A.-M. (2002), 'Repairing innovation defectiveness in tourism', *Tourism Management*, **23**, 465–74.

Hjalager, A.-M. and S. Jensen (2001), 'Nordjylland – en turismeregion i Danmark', Nordregio Working Paper (2001:11).

Hodgson, G. (1993), *Economics and Evolution: Bringing Life Back Into Economics*, Cambridge: Polity.

Hornibrook, S. and A. Fearne (2005), 'Demand driven supply chains: contractual relationships and the management of perceived risks', Paper submitted to 2nd European Forum on Market-Driven Supply Chains, The European Institute for Advanced Studies in Management, Milan, Italy, April.

Howells, J. (2001), 'The nature of innovation in services', in OECD (ed.), *Innovation and Productivity in Services*, Paris, pp. 57–82.

Howells, J. (2006), 'Outsourcing for innovation: systems of innovation and the role of knowledge intermediaries', in: M. Miozzo and D. Grimshaw (eds), *Knowledge Intensive Business Services: Organizational Forms and National Institutions*, Cheltenham, UK and Northampton, MA, USA: Edward Elgar, pp. 61–81.

Humphrey, J. and O. Memedovic (2003), 'The global automotive industry value chain: what prospects for upgrading by developing countries?' Vienna: UNIDO.

Humphrey, J. and H. Schmitz (2004), 'Chain governance and upgrading: taking stock', in H. Schmitz (ed.), *Local Enterprises in the Global Economy: Issues of Governance and Upgrading*, Cheltenham, UK and Northampton, MA, USA: Edward Elgar, pp. 349–81.

IFO-Schnelldienst (2006), 'Jobs increase from biofuels', 17/2006.

Ilbery, B. and M. Kneafsey (2000), 'Producer constructions of quality in regional speciality food production: a case study from south west England', *Journal of Rural Studies*, 16, 217–30.

Ilbery, B. and D. Maye (2006), 'Retailing local food in the Scottish–English borders: a supply chain perspective', *Geoforum*, 37, 352–67.

Ilbery, B., C. Morris, H. Buller, D. Maye and M. Kneafsey (2005), 'Product, process and place: an examination of food marketing and labelling schemes in Europe and North America', *European Urban and Regional Studies*, 12, 116–32.

Interbrand (2006), 'Best Global Brands Report: 2006', http://www.ourfish-bowl.com/images/surveys/BGB06Report_072706.pdf.

Ioannides, D. (1998), 'Tour operators: the gatekeepers of tourism', in D. Ioannides and K. Debbage (eds), *The Economic Geography of the Tourist Industry*, London: Routledge, pp. 139–58.

Ioannides, D. and K. Debbage (1998), 'Neo-Fordism and flexible specialisation in the travel industry: dissecting the polyglot', in D. Ioannides and K. Debbage (eds), *The Economic Geography of the Tourist Industry*, London: Routledge, pp. 99–122.

Jacobs, J. (1969), *The Economy of Cities*, New York: Random House.

Jaffe, A.B. (1996), 'Economic analysis of research spillovers: implications for the advanced Technology Program', GCR 97-708, US Department of Commerce, National Institute of Standards and Technology Program, Gaithersburg, MD.

Jamal, T. and D. Getz (1995), 'Collaboration theory and community tourism planning', *Annals of Tourism Research*, 22,186–204.

Jensen, C.F., J. Mattsson and J. Sundbo (2002), 'Succesfuld turistudvikling. Nøglen til innovation i turisme', Forskningsrapport, Center for Servicestudier, RUC 02(1), University of Roskilde.

Jürgens, U. (2000), 'Toward new product and process development networks: the case of the German car industry', in Ulrich Jürgens (ed.), *New Product Development and Production Networks: Global Industrial Experience*, Heidelberg: Springer pp. 259–87.

Jürgens, U. (2003), 'Characteristics of the European automotive system: is there a distinctive European approach?' WZB discussion paper SP III 2003-301, Berlin.

Jürgens, U. (2004), 'Gibt es einen europaspezifischen Entwicklungsweg in der Automobilindustrie?' WZB dicsussion paper, Berlin.

Jürgens, U. and H. Meißner (2005), 'Arbeiten am Auto der Zukunft', Berlin.

Kaiser, R. (2003), 'Multi-level science policy and regional innovation: the case of the Munich cluster for pharmaceutical biotechnology', *European Planning Studies*, **11**, 841–58.

Kaiser, R. (2009), 'Governance cloud intermediate report', Eurodite Project, input paper to Work Package 8, http://www.eurodite.bham.ac.uk/.

Kaiser, R. and M. Liecke (2006), 'Recent developments in the four leading German biotechnology clusters', Munich: Ludwig Maximilians University.

Kastis, N. (2006), 'The corporate e-learning market: state of play. Benchmarking e-learning in Europe', Brussels.

Kay, J. (2003), *The Truth About Markets*, London: Allen Lane.

Keeble, D. and L. Nachum (2002), 'Why do business service firms cluster? Small consultancies, clustering and decentralization in London and Southern England', *Transactions of the Institute of British Geographers*, **27**, 67–90.

Keller, P. (2006), *Innovation and Tourism Policy: Innovation and Growth in Tourism*, Paris: OECD.

Kemp, R., J. Schot and R. Hoogma (1998), 'Regime shifts to sustainability through processes of niche formation: the approach of strategic niche management', *Technology Analysis and Strategic Management*, **10**, 175–96.

Kennedy Information (2005), 'The global consulting marketplace 2005–2007: key data, trends and forecasts', Peterborough, NH.

Key Note (2004), *Market Assessment 2004*, 4th edn, January, Key Note Ltd, http://public.cranfield.ac.uk/glm/mirc02/Marketass.pdf.

Klein, A. (2003), *Stealing Time: the Collapse of AOL Time Warner*, London: Simon & Schuster.

Klein, L. (1998), 'Evaluating the potential of interactive media through a new lens: search versus experience goods', *Journal of Business Research*, **41**, 195–203.

Kotter, J. (1996), *Leading Change: Eight Steps to Transform Your Organisation*, MA: Boston, Harvard Business School Press.

KPMG Corporate Finance (2000), 'Europe's recipe for success: innovate and consolidate', KPMG Corporate Finance, http://www.kpmg.de/library/pdf/food_survey_fas.pdf.

Krugman, P. (1991), *Geography and Trade*, Cambridge, MA, USA and London, UK: MIT Press.

Krugman, P. (1995), *Development, Geography and Economic Theory*, Cambridge, MA, USA and London, UK: MIT Press.

Kübler-Ross, F. (1969), *On Death and Dying*, New York: Simon & Schuster/Touchstone.

Kuusisto, J. and M. Meyer (2003), 'Insights into services and innovation in the knowledge intensive economy', *Technology Review*, **134**, 1–68.

Kvistgaard, P. (2006), *Problemer og magt i regional turismepolicy*, Aalborg: Aalborg University Press.

Kvistgaard, P. and K. Smed (2005), 'Oplevelsesprofil for feriedestination Møn. En undersøgelse i tre dimensioner af ferieoplevelser på feriedestination Møn i sommeren og efteråret 2004', Tourism Research Unit, Aalborg University.

Laestedius, S. (1998), 'The relevance of science and technology indicators: the case of pulp and paper', *Research Policy*, **27**, 385–95.

Lash, S. and A. Wittel (2002), 'Shifting new media: from content to consultancy, from heterarchy to hierarchy', *Environment and Planning A*, **34**, 1985–2001.

Lawton Smith, H. (2004), 'The biotechnology industry in Oxfordshire: enterprise and innovation', *European Planning Studies*, **12**, 985–1002.

Leadbeater, C. (1999), *Living On Thin Air*, London: Viking.

Leisink, P. (2000). 'Multimedia industry networks and regional economic development policies: the case of the Netherlands', *Vierteljahrshefte zur Wirtschaftsforschung*, **69**, 574–86.

Lemarié, S., V. Mangematin and A. Torre (2001), 'Is the creation and development of biotech SMEs localised? Conclusions drawn from the French case', *Small Business Economics*, **17**, 61–76.

Lewis, A. (2000), *The New New Thing*, New York: Norton.

Lindkvist, K.and J. Sánchez (2008), 'Conventions and innovation: a comparison of two localised natural resource-based industries', *Regional Studies*, **42**, 343–54.

Livingstone, S. (1999), 'New media, new audiences', *New Media and Society*, **1**, 59–66.

Long, L. (ed.) (2005), *Culinary Tourism*, Lexington, KY: University of Kentucky Press.

Lowe, Janet (1997), *Warren Buffett Speaks: Wit and Wisdom from the World's Greatest Investor*, New York and Chichester, John Wiley & Sons.

Lundtorp, S. (1997), 'Turisme – Struktur, økonomi og problemer', Nexø, Bornholms Forskningscenter.

Lundvall, B. (1988), 'Innovation as an interactive process', in G. Dosi, C. Freeman, R. Nelson, G. Silverberg and L. Soete (eds), *Technical change and Economic Theory*, London: Pinter.

Lury, C. (2004), *Brands: The Logos of the Global Economy*, Routledge: London.

Macher, J. and D. Mowery (2004), 'Vertical specialisation and industry structure in high technology industries', *Advances in Strategic Management*, **21**, 317–56.

MacNeill, S. and J-J. Chanaron (2005), 'Trends and drivers of change in the European automotive industry: mapping the current situation', *International Journal of Automotive Technology and Management*, **5**, 83–106.

Malerba, F. (2004), 'Sectoral systems of innovation: basic concepts', in F. Malerba (ed.), *Sectoral Systems of Innovation: Concepts, Issues and Analyses of Six Major Sectors in Europe*, Cambridge: Cambridge University Press, pp. 9–41.

Malerba, F. (2005), 'Sectoral systems of innovation: how and why innovation differs across sectors', in J. Fagerberg, D. Mowery, and R. Nelson (eds), *Handbook of Innovation*, New York: Oxford University Press, pp. 380–406.

Malerba, F. and I. Orsenigo (2000), 'Knowledge, innovation activities and industrial evolution', *Industrial Corporate Change*, **9** (2), 289–314.

Malik, A., G. Pinkus & S. Sheffer (2002), 'Biopharma's capacity crunch', *McKinsey Quarterly*, www.mckinsey.co.uk.

March, J. (1991), 'Exploration and exploitation in organisational learning', *Organization Science*, **2**, 71–87

Mariussen, A. and B. Asheim (2003), 'Innovation systems, institutions and space', in B. Asheim and A. Mariussen (eds), *Innovation, Regions and Projects: Studies in New Forms Of Knowledge Governance*, Stockholm: Nordegio, pp. 13–40.

Marklund, G. (2000), 'Indicators of innovation activities in services', in M. Boden and I. Miles (eds), *Services and the Knowledge-based Economy*, London and New York: Continuum, pp. 86–108.

Marsden, T. (1998), 'New rural territories: regulating the differentiated rural spaces', *Journal of Rural Studies*, **14**, 107–17.

Marsden, T., J. Banks and G. Bristow (2000), 'Food supply chain approaches: exploring their role in rural development', *Sociologia Ruralis*, **40**, 424–38.

Massey, D. (1984), *Spatial Divisions of Labour*, London: Macmillan.

Massey, J. (2004), 'The eLearning industry and market in Europe', Danish Technological Institute, Competence and IT/Analyses.

McKelvey, M. H. Alm and M. Riccaboni (2003), 'Does co-location matter for formal knowledge collaboration in the Swedish biotechnology–pharmaceuticals sector?', *Research Policy*, **32**, 485–501.

McKinsey/PTW (2003), 'HAWK 2015 – Wissensbasierte Veränderung der automobilen Wertschöpfungskette', VDA-Materialien zur Automobilindustrie, Bd 30, Frankfurt and Main.

Medina-Munoz, R., D. Medina-Munoz and M. Garcia-Falcon (2003), 'Understanding European tour operators' control on accommodation companies: an empirical evidence', *Tourism Management*, **24**: 135–47.

Menrad, K. (2003), 'Market and marketing of functional food in Europe', *Journal of Food Engineering*, **56**, 181–8.

Menrad, K. (2004), 'Innovation in the food industry in Germany', *Research Policy*, **33**, 845–78.

Mercer/FhG (2004), 'Future automotive structure 2015', München.

Miles, I. (2001), 'Knowledge-intensive business services revisited', Nijmegen Lectures on Innovation Management, Antwerp.

Miles, I. (2005), 'Innovation in services', in J. Fagerberg, D. Mowery and R. Nelson (eds), *Oxford Handbook of Innovation*, Oxford and New York: Oxford University Press, pp. 433–58.

Miles, I., N. Kastrinos and K. Flanagan (1996), 'Knowledge-intensive business services: users, carriers and sources of innovation', European Innovation Monitoring System (EIMS) Publication, 15, Luxembourg, European Commission.

Millstone, E. and T. Lang (2003), *The Atlas of Food: Who Eats What, Where and Why*, London: Earthscan Publications.

Miozzo, M. and D. Grimshaw (2006), 'Modularity and innovation in knowledge intensive business services: IT-outsourcing in Germany and the UK', in M. Miozzo and D. Grimshaw (eds), *Knowledge Intensive Business Services. Organizational Forms and National Institutions*, Cheltenham, UK and Northampton, MA, USA: Edward Elgar, pp. 82–120.

Mogensen, A. and A. Therkelsen (2007), 'Nordjysk Erhvervsturisme 2006 – Status Over Den Mødebaserede Erhvervsturisme', Tourism Research Unit, Aalborg University.

Morgan, K., T. Marsden and J. Murdoch (2006), *Worlds of Food: Place, Power and Provenance in the Food Chain*, Oxford: Oxford University Press.

Morgan, K. and J. Murdoch (2000), 'Organic vs. conventional agriculture: knowledge, power and innovation in the food chain', *Geoforum*, **31**, 159–73.

Mossberg, L. and E. Johansen (2006), *Story-telling: Marknadsföring i opplevelsesindustrin*, Lund: Studentlitteratur.

Moulaert, F. and F. Tödtling (eds) (1995), 'Geography of advanced producer services', *Progress in Planning*, **43**, 89–274.

Mowery, D., J. Oxley and B. Silverman (1996), 'Strategic alliances and interfirm knowledge transfer', *Strategic Management Journal*, **17**, 77–91.

Mowery, D., J. Oxley and B. Silverman (1998), 'Technological overlap and interfirm cooperation: implications for the resource-based view of the firm', *Research Policy*, **27**, 507–23.

MUDIA (2003), 'Multimedia Content in the Digital Age – final project report, Heerlen: MUDIA.

Muller, E. and D. Doloreux, (2007), 'The key dimensions of knowledge-intensive business services (KIBS) analysis: a decade of evolution (Discussion Paper)', Fraunhofer Institute for Systems and Innovation Research, Karlsruhe.

Murdoch, J., T. Marsden and J. Banks (2000), 'Quality, nature, and embeddedness: some theoretical considerations in the context of the food sector', *Economic Geography*, **76**, 107–25.

Murdoch, J. and M. Miele (2004), 'Culinary networks and cultural connections: a conventions perspective', in A. Hughes and S. Reimer (eds), *Geographies of Commodity Chains*, London: Routledge, pp. 102–19.

Naisbitt, J., N. Naisbitt and D. Philips (1999), *High Tech High Touch: Technology and Our Search for Meaning*, New York: Broadway Books.

Nelund, R. and J. Norus (2003), 'Competences and opportunities: building an island of innovation apart from Europe's innovative centre', in U. Hilpert (ed.), *Regionalisation of Globalised Innovation*, London: Routledge, pp. 193–210.

Nonaka, I. and H. Takeuchi (1997), *Die Organisation des Wissens. Wie japanische Unternehmen eine brachliegende Ressource nutzbar machen.* Frankfurt/Main: Campus Verlag.

Nooteboom, B. (2000), 'Learning by interaction: absorptive capacity, cognitive distance and governance', *Journal of Management and Governance*, **4**, 69–92.

Noyelle, T. (1996), 'The economic importance of professional services', in OECD (ed.), *International Trade in Professional Services: Assessing Barriers and Encouraging Reforms*, Paris: OECD, pp. 19–28.

Nyberg, L. (1995), 'Scandinavia: Tourism in Europe's Northern Periphery', in A. Montanari and A.M. Williams (eds), *European Tourism: Regions, Spaces and Restructuring*, Chichester: John Wiley, pp. 87–107.

Oborne, P. (2010), 'Eurozone in trouble', *Independent*, 2 January, p. 16.

O'Dell, T. (2005), 'Experiencescapes: blurring borders and testing connections', in T. O'Dell and M. Billing (eds), *Experiencescapes: Tourism, Culture and Economy*, Copenhagen: Copenhagen Business School Press, pp. 1–33.

OECD (1997), Women Entrepreneurs in Small and Medium Enterprises: A Major Force for Innovation and Job Creation, OECD Conference, Paris, 16–18 April.

OECD (1999a), *S&T Indicators: Benchmarking the Knowledge-Based Economy*, Paris: Organisation for Economic Co-operation and Development.

OECD (ed.) (2001), *Innovation and Productivity in Services*, Paris.

OECD (ed.) (2005a), 'Enhancing the performance of the services sector', Paris.

OECD (2005b), 'Digital broadband content: music', Directorate for Science, Technology and Industry.

OECD (2006a), 'The future digital economy: digital content creation, distribution and access'.

OECD (ed.) (2006b), 'Innovation and knowledge-intensive service activities', Paris.

O'Grady, S. (2009), 'The master of the dismal science – with equations', *Independent*, 15 December, p. 35.

Omland, N. and H. Ernst (2004), 'Vitalisation of industry through the regional promotion of knowledge-intensive new firms – the case of German biotechnology', paper to Japanese Institute for Labour Policy and Training conference on Globalisation and Revitalisation of Regional Employment: Comparison of Germany and Japan, 26 March, Tokyo.

Ooi, C. (2005), 'A theory of tourism experiences: the management of attention. Experiencescapes', in T. O'Dell and P. Billing (eds), *Tourism, Culture and Economy*, Copenhagen: Copenhagen Business School Press, pp. 51–68.

Orfila-Sintes, F., R. Crespi-Cladera and E. Martinez-Ros (2005), 'Innovation activity in the hotel industry: evidence from Balearic Islands', *Tourism Management* **26**, 851–65.

Orhan, M. and D. Scott (2001), 'Why women enter into entrepreneurship: an explanatory model', *Women in Management Review*, **16**, 232–43.

Osborne, A. (2009), 'Anger as Northern Rock's Adam Applegarth lands advisory job', *Daily Telegraph*, 1 October, p. 23.

O'Shea, J. and C. Madigan (1997), *Dangerous Company: The Consulting Powerhouses and the Businesses they Save and Ruin*, London: Nicholas Brealey.

Owen-Smith, J. and W. Powell (2004), 'Knowledge networks as channels and conduits: the effects of spillovers in the Boston biotechnology community', *Organization Science*, **15**, 5–21.

Parrott, N., N. Wilson and J. Murdoch (2002), 'Spatialising quality: regional protection and the alternative geography of food', *European Urban and Regional Studies*, **9**, 241–61.

Patel, P. and K. Pavitt (1997), 'The technological competencies of the world's largest firms: complex and path-dependent, but not much variety', *Research Policy*, **26**, 141–56.

Pavitt, K. (1984), 'Sectoral patterns of technical change: towards a taxonomy and a theory', *Research Policy*, **13**, 343–73.

Pavlik, J. and A. Clayton Powell (2003), 'New media', in D. Johnston (ed.), *Encyclopedia of International Media and Communications, Volume 3*, pp. 225–33.

Pine, J. and J. Gilmore (1999), *The Experience Economy*, Boston, MA: Harvard Business School Press.

Poon, A. (1993), *Tourism, Technology and Competitive Strategies*, Oxford: Cabi.

Potter, J. (2009), 'Evaluating regional competitiveness policies: insights from the new economic geography', *Regional Studies*, **43**, 1225–36.

Powell, W. (1996), 'Interorganisational collaboration in the biotechnology industry', *Journal of Institutional and Theoretical Economics*, **120**, 197–215.

Powell W. and S. Grodal (2005), 'Networks of innovators', in J. Fagerberg, D. Mowery and R. Nelson (eds) *The Oxford Handbook of Innovation*, New York: Oxford University Press, pp. 56–85.

Power, M. (1997), *The Audit Society*, Oxford: Oxford University Press.

Pratt, A.C. (2000), 'New media, the new economy and new spaces', *Geoforum,* **31**, 425–36.

Preissl, B. and L. Solimene (2003), *The Dynamics of Clusters and Innovation*, Heidelberg: Physica Verlag.

Preston, P. (2002), 'Paradigm shift? Knowledge, R&D and innovation in media services', unpublished mimeo.

Preston, P. and A. Kerr (2001), 'Digital media, nation-states and local cultures: the case of multimedia "Content" production', *Media, Culture and Society*, **23**, 109–31.

Raymond, F. (2001), *The Cathedral and the Bazaar: Musings on Linux and Open Source by an Accidental Revolutionary*, Sebastopol, CA: O'Reilly.

Rees, W. and B. Rees (2004), *Llanelli: Birth of a Town,* ART Designs, CD-ROM.

Reimer, G.D. (1990), 'Packaging dreams: Canadian tour operators at work', *Annals of Tourism Research*, **17**, 501–12.

Renting, H., T. Marsden and J. Banks (2003), 'Understanding alternative food networks: exploring the role of short food supply chains in rural development', *Environment and Planning A*, **35**, 393–411.

Rentmeister, B. (2002), 'Einbindung und standörtliche Organisation von Ingenieurdienstleistern in der Automobilentwicklung', IWSG Working Papers 12-202, Frankfurt/Main.

Roberts, J. (1998), *Multinational Business Service Firms: The Development of Multinational Organisational Structures in the UK Business Services Sector*, Aldershot: Ashgate.

Robertson, M., H. Scarbrough and J. Swan (2003), 'Knowledge creation in professional service firms: institutional effects', *Organizational Studies*, **24**, (6), 831–57.

Romer, P. (1990), 'Endogenous technical change', *Journal of Political Economy*, **98**, 338–54.

Roth, S. (2006), 'Zukunftsperspektiven für die europäische Automobilindustrie', in L. Pries and C. Bosowski (eds), *Europäische Automobilindustrie am Scheideweg,* München and Mering: IAQ, pp. 29–45.

Rubalcaba-Bermejo, L. (1999), *Business Services in European Industry: Growth, Employment And Competitiveness*, Luxembourg: European Commission.

Russell, R. and B. Faulkner (2004), 'Entrepreneurship, chaos and the tourism area lifecycle', *Annals of Tourism Research*, **31** (3), 556–79.

Sassen, S. (2007), 'Electronic networks, power, and democracy', in R. Mansell, C. Avgerou, D. Quah and R. Silverstone (eds), *The Oxford Handbook of Information and Communication Technologies*, Oxford: Oxford University Press, pp. 339–61.

Saxenian, A. (1994), *Regional Advantage*, Cambridge, MA: Harvard University Press.

Schamp, E., B. Rentmeister and V. Lo (2003), 'Dimensionen der Nähe in wissensbasierten Netzwerken. Investment-Banking und Automobil-Entwicklung in der Metropolregion, Frankfurt/Rhein-Main', IWSG Working Papers 11-2003, Frankfurt/Main.

Schmitz, H. and S. Strambach (2008), 'The organisational decomposition of the innovation process: what does it mean for the global distribution of innovation activities?' IDS Working Paper 304, Brighton.

Schumann, M., M. Kuhlmann, F. Sanders and H.J. Sperling (eds) (2006), 'Auto 5000: ein neues Produktionskonzept? Die deutsche Antwort auf den Toyota-Weg?' Hamburg: VSA.

Schumpeter, J. (1975), *Capitalism, Socialism and Democracy*, New York: Harper.

Schweitzer, L. and M. Rajes (2006), 'Erfolgshonorare für Beratungsleistungen', *Zeitschrift für Führung und Organisation*, **6**, 320–24.

Scott, A. (1988), *New Industrial Spaces*, London: Pion.

Scottish Enterprise (2000 and 2006), *Biotechnology Sourcebook*, Glasgow: Scottish Enterprise.

Shaw, G. and A. Williams (1998), 'Entrepreneurship, small business culture and tourism development', in D. Ioannides and K. Debbage (eds), *The Economic Geography of the Tourist Industry*, London: Routledge, pp. 235–55.

Shaw, G. and A.M. Williams (2004), *Tourism and Tourism Spaces*, London: Sage.

Smith, A. (1776), *Wealth of Nations*, New York: Modern Library.

Smith, A. (1984), 'The new media as contexts for creativity', *Leonardo*, **17** (1), 46–8.

Smith, J. (2009), 'Multi-millionaire City banker committed suicide after disastrous RBS takeover', *Independent*, 10 November, p. 24.

Sonnino, R. and T. Marsden (2006), 'Beyond the divide: rethinking relationships between alternative and conventional food networks in Europe', *Journal of Economic Geography*, **6**, 181–99.

Sorenson O., J.W. Rivkin and L. Fleming (2006), 'Complexity, networks and knowledge flow', *Research Policy*, **35**, 994–1017.

Spörel, U. (2006), *Regional Tourism in the European Union: Statistics in Focus: Industry, Trade and Services*, Brussels: Eurostat.

Stamboulis, Y. and P. Skyannis (2003), 'Innovation strategies and technology for experience-based tourism', *Tourism Management*, **24**, 35–43.

Stewart, S. (2009), 'Shamed banker Fred Goodwin draws £650k pension at just 50', *Daily Record*, 26 February, p. 29.

Storper, M. (1997), *The Regional World: Territorial Development in a Global Economy*, London: Guildford.

Storper, M. and R. Salais (1997), *Worlds of Production: the Action Frameworks of the Economy*, Cambridge, MA: Harvard University Press.

Strambach, S. (2001), 'Innovation processes and the role of knowledge-intensive business services (KIBS)', in K. Koschatzky M. Kulicke and A. Zenker (eds), *Innovation Networks: Concepts and Challenges in the European Perspective*, Technology, Innovation and Policy 12, Heidelberg: Physica Verlag, pp. 53–68.

Strambach, S. (2004), 'Wissensintensive unternehmensorientierte Dienstleistungen in Deutschland', in Leibnitz-Institut für Länderkunde (eds), *Nationalatlas Bundesrepublik Deutschland*, Unternehmen und Märkte, Bd 12, Heidelberg: Elsevier Spektrum Akademischer Verlag, pp. 50–53.

Strambach, S. (2008), 'Knowledge-intensive business services (KIBS) as drivers of multilevel knowledge dynamics', *International Journal of Services and Technology Management*, **10**, Special Issue on KIBS, guest editors D. Doloreux and E. Mueller, 152–74.

Sturgeon, T. (2000), 'How Silicon Valley came to be', in M. Kenney (ed.),

Understanding Silicon Valley, Stanford, CA: Stanford University Press, pp. 15–47.

Sundbo, J. (2000), 'Organization and innovation strategy in services', in M. Boden and I. Miles (eds), *Services and the Knowledge-Based Economy*, London and New York: Continuum, pp. 109–28.

Susaria, A., M. Parameswaran and A.B. Whinston (2000), 'Emerging market structures in the digital supply chain', *IT Pro*, September–October, 33–9.

Swarbrooke, J. and S. Horner (2001), *Business Travel and Tourism*, Oxford: Butterworth-Heinemann.

Swaine, J. (2008), 'Richard Fuld punched in face in Lehman Brothers gym', *Daily Telegraph*, 10 July, 26.

Tesla, S. and S. Massa (2008), '"Localness" is good for business? An intellectual capital-based perspective in the Italian food industry', *International Journal of Innovation and Regional Development*, **1**, 192–209.

Tesla, S., S. Massa, and P.P. Puliafito (2008), 'It's no use crying over spilt milk! Innovation paths in the dairy sector', *International Journal of Management Practice*, **3**, 3–13

Tett, G. (2009), *Fool's Gold: How Unrestrained Greed Corrupted a dream, Shattered Global Markets and Unleashed a Catastrophe*, London: Little, Brown.

Therkelsen, A. (2002), 'Konferencedeltagere som turister i Nordjylland – Hvad er de ude på nor konferencen er slut?', in H. Halkier, S. Jensen and P. Kvistgaard (eds) *Regional turisme mellem udbud og efterspørgsel*, Aalborg: Aalborg Universitetsforlag, pp. 67–76.

Therkelsen, A. (2003), 'All work and no play? Tourism-related demand patterns of conference participants', Tourism Research Unit, University of Aalborg.

Therkelsen, A. and H. Halkier (2004), 'Umbrella place branding: a study of friendly exoticism and exotic friendliness in coordinated national tourism and business promotion', Spirit Discussion Papers (26), Aalborg: University of Aalborg.

Thevenot, L., M. Moody and C. Lafaye (2000), 'Forms of valuing nature: arguments and modes of justification in French and American environmental disputes', in M. Lamont and M. Thevenot (eds), *Rethinking Comparative Cultural Sociology. Repertoires of evaluation in France and the United States*. Cambridge: Cambridge University Press.

Tidd, J., J. Bessant and K. Pavitt (2005), *Managing Innovation Integrating Technological, Market and Organizational Change*, Hoboken: Wiley.

Toivonen, M. (2002), 'Internationalisation of knowledge-intensive business services in a small European Country: experiences from Finland', in M. Miozzo and I. Miles (eds), *Internationalization, Technology and*

Services, Cheltenham, UK and Northampton, MA, USA: Edward Elgar, pp. 206–26.

Toivonen, M. (2004), 'Expertise as business: long-term development and future prospects of knowledge-intensive business services', unpublished PhD dissertation, Helsinki.

Tremblay, P. (1998), 'The economic organisation of tourism', *Annals of Tourism Research*, **25**, 837–59.

Trippe, B. and D. Guenette (2007), 'The agile business and its digital media supply chains', Content Management Technology White Paper, Gibane Group.

TSB (Technology Strategy Board) (2009), 'Innovation platforms and technology development', http://www.innovateuk.org/ourstrategy/innovationplatforms.ashx.

Uglow, J. (2003), *The Lunar Men: The Friends Who Made the Future*, London: Faber & Faber.

UNCTAD (2004), *World Investment Report: The Shift Towards Services*, New York and Geneva: UNCTAD.

Valcke, P. and D. Stevens (2007), 'Graduated regulation of "Regulatable" content and the European Audiovisual Media Services Directive: one small step for the industry and one giant step for the legislator?' *Telematics and Informatics*, **24**, 272–84.

Van Gennep, A. (1909), *Rites of Passage*, Chicago, IL: University of Chicago Press.

Vicente, J. and R. Suire (2007), 'Informational cascades vs. network externalities in locational choice: evidences of "ICT clusters" formation and stability', *Regional Studies,* **41**, 173–84.

VINNOVA (2003), *Swedish Biotechnology–Scientific Publications, Patenting & Industrial Development*, Stockholm: VINNOVA (Swedish Agency for Innovation Systems).

Watts, D., B. Ilbery and D. Maye (2005), 'Making reconnections in agro-food geography: alternative systems of food provision', *Progress in Human Geography*, **29**, 22–40.

Watts, M. and D. Goodman (1997), 'Agrarian questions – global appetite, local metabolism: nature, culture and industry in *fin-de-siècle* agro-food systems', in D. Goodman and M. J. Watts (eds), *Globalising Food: Agrarian Questions and Global Restructuring*, London: Routledge, pp. 1–32.

Weaver, D. and L. Lawton (2002), *Tourism Management*, 2nd edn, Milton: Wiley.

Weber, K. (2001), 'Meeting planners' use and evaluation of convention and visitor bureaus', *Tourism Management*, **22**, 599–606.

Weiermair, K. (2006), 'Product improvement or innovation: what is the key to success in tourism?', in OECD (ed.), *Innovation and Growth in Tourism*, Paris: OECD, pp. 53–69.

Wenger, E. (1999), *Communities of Practice: Learning, Meaning and Identity*, Cambridge: Cambridge University Press.

Westkämper, E. (2006), *Manufuture. RTD Roadmaps. From Vision to Implementation*, Munich and Trondheim: Manufuture Norge.

Williams, A. (1995), 'Capital and the transnationalisation of tourism', in A. Montanari and A. Williams (eds) *European Tourism: Regions, Spaces and Restructuring*, Chichester: John Wiley, pp. 163–76.

Wilson, E. R. Elkan and K. Cox (2007), 'Closure for patients at the end of a cancer clinical trial: a literature review', *Journal of Advanced Nursing*, **59**, 445–53.

Winter, J. (2006), ‚Kompetenzaufteilung in konzerninternen Netzwerken der Automobil-industrie' *Berliner Debatte Initial*, **17**, 186–98.

Winter, M. (2003), 'Geographies of food: agro-food geographies – making reconnections', *Progress in Human Geography*, **27**, 505–13.

Wirtz, B.W. (2001), 'Reconfiguration of value chains in converging media and communications markets', *Long Range Planning*, **34**, 489–506.

Wolfe, D. (2002), 'Knowledge, learning and social capital in Ontario's ICT clusters', presentation to Annual Meeting of the Canadian Political Science Association, University of Toronto, 29–31 May (see also Gertler and Wolfe in Cooke et al., 2004)

Womack, J., D. Jones and D. Roos (1990), *The Machine that Changed the World*, London: Macmillan.

Wood, P. (ed.) (2002), *Consultancy and Innovation: The Business Service Revolution in Europe*. London: Routledge.

Woodman, R., J. Sawyer and R. Griffin (1993), 'Toward a theory of organisational creativity', *Academy of Management Review*, **18**, 293–321.

World Tourism Organization (2006), *Tourism Market Trends: Europe, 2005*, Madrid: World Tourism Organization.

Wuyts, S., M. Colombo, S. Dutta and B. Nooteboom (2005), 'Empirical tests of optimal cognitive distance', *Journal of Economic Behaviour and Organization*, **58**, 277–302.

Zegveld, W. (2005), 'Critical factors in innovation', ECORYS 75th Anniversary Conference Enhancing Competitiveness, Rotterdam, January.

Zinser, O. (1984), *Basic Principles of Experimental Psychology*, New York: McGraw-Hill.

Zuliani, J.M. (2008), 'The Toulouse cluster of on-board systems: a process of collective innovation and learning', *European Planning Studies*, **16** (5), 711–26.

Index